Microsoft® Official Academic Course

Windows Server® 2008 Network Infrastructure Configuration (70-642)

WILEY

Credits

EXECUTIVE EDITOR	John Kane
DIRECTOR OF MARKETING AND SALES	Mitchell Beaton
MICROSOFT STRATEGIC RELATIONSHIPS MANAGER	Merrick Van Dongen of Microsoft Learning
DEVELOPMENT AND PRODUCTION	Custom Editorial Productions, Inc.
EDITORIAL ASSISTANT	Jennifer Lartz
PRODUCTION MANAGER	Micheline Frederick
PRODUCTION EDITOR	Kerry Weinstein
CREATIVE DIRECTOR	Harry Nolan
COVER DESIGNER	Jim O'Shea
TECHNOLOGY AND MEDIA	Lauren Sapira/Elena Santa Maria

This book was set in Garamond by Aptara, Inc. and printed and bound by Bind Rite Graphics.
The covers were printed by Phoenix Color.

Foreword from the Publisher

Wiley's publishing vision for the Microsoft Official Academic Course series is to provide students and instructors with the skills and knowledge they need to use Microsoft technology effectively in all aspects of their personal and professional lives. Quality instruction is required to help both educators and students get the most from Microsoft's software tools and to become more productive. Thus our mission is to make our instructional programs trusted educational companions for life.

To accomplish this mission, Wiley and Microsoft have partnered to develop the highest quality educational programs for Information Workers, IT Professionals, and Developers. Materials created by this partnership carry the brand name "Microsoft Official Academic Course," assuring instructors and students alike that the content of these textbooks is fully endorsed by Microsoft, and that they provide the highest quality information and instruction on Microsoft products. The Microsoft Official Academic Course textbooks are "Official" in still one more way—they are the officially sanctioned courseware for Microsoft IT Academy members.

The Microsoft Official Academic Course series focuses on *workforce development*. These programs are aimed at those students seeking to enter the workforce, change jobs, or embark on new careers as information workers, IT professionals, and developers. Microsoft Official Academic Course programs address their needs by emphasizing authentic workplace scenarios with an abundance of projects, exercises, cases, and assessments.

The Microsoft Official Academic Courses are mapped to Microsoft's extensive research and job-task analysis, the same research and analysis used to create the Microsoft Certified Technology Specialist (MCTS) exam. The textbooks focus on real skills for real jobs. As students work through the projects and exercises in the textbooks they enhance their level of knowledge and their ability to apply the latest Microsoft technology to everyday tasks. These students also gain resume-building credentials that can assist them in finding a job, keeping their current job, or in furthering their education.

The concept of life-long learning is today an utmost necessity. Job roles, and even whole job categories, are changing so quickly that none of us can stay competitive and productive without continuously updating our skills and capabilities. The Microsoft Official Academic Course offerings, and their focus on Microsoft certification exam preparation, provide a means for people to acquire and effectively update their skills and knowledge. Wiley supports students in this endeavor through the development and distribution of these courses as Microsoft's official academic publisher.

Today educational publishing requires attention to providing quality print and robust electronic content. By integrating Microsoft Official Academic Course products, *WileyPLUS*, and Microsoft certifications, we are better able to deliver efficient learning solutions for students and teachers alike.

Bonnie Lieberman

General Manager and Senior Vice President

Preface

Welcome to the Microsoft Official Academic Course (MOAC) program for Microsoft Windows Server 2008. MOAC represents the collaboration between Microsoft Learning and John Wiley & Sons, Inc. publishing company. Microsoft and Wiley teamed up to produce a series of textbooks that deliver compelling and innovative teaching solutions to instructors and superior learning experiences for students. Infused and informed by in-depth knowledge from the creators of Windows Server 2008, and crafted by a publisher known worldwide for the pedagogical quality of its products, these textbooks maximize skills transfer in minimum time. Students are challenged to reach their potential by using their new technical skills as highly productive members of the workforce.

Because this knowledgebase comes directly from Microsoft, architect of the Windows Server operating system and creator of the Microsoft Certified Technology Specialist and Microsoft Certified Professional exams (www.microsoft.com/learning/mcp/mcts), you are sure to receive the topical coverage that is most relevant to students' personal and professional success. Microsoft's direct participation not only assures you that MOAC textbook content is accurate and current; it also means that students will receive the best instruction possible to enable their success on certification exams and in the workplace.

■ The Microsoft Official Academic Course Program

The *Microsoft Official Academic Course* series is a complete program for instructors and institutions to prepare and deliver great courses on Microsoft software technologies. With MOAC, we recognize that, because of the rapid pace of change in the technology and curriculum developed by Microsoft, there is an ongoing set of needs beyond classroom instruction tools for an instructor to be ready to teach the course. The MOAC program endeavors to provide solutions for all these needs in a systematic manner in order to ensure a successful and rewarding course experience for both instructor and student—technical and curriculum training for instructor readiness with new software releases; the software itself for student use at home for building hands-on skills, assessment, and validation of skill development; and a great set of tools for delivering instruction in the classroom and lab. All are important to the smooth delivery of an interesting course on Microsoft software, and all are provided with the MOAC program. We think about the model below as a gauge for ensuring that we completely support you in your goal of teaching a great course. As you evaluate your instructional materials options, you may wish to use the model for comparison purposes with available products.

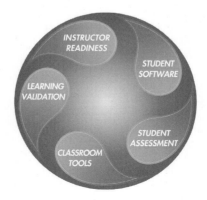

■ Pedagogical Features

The MOAC textbook for Windows Server 2008 Network Infrastructure Configuration is designed to cover all the learning objectives for that MCTS exam, which is referred to as its "objective domain." The Microsoft Certified Technology Specialist (MCTS) exam objectives are highlighted throughout the textbook. Many pedagogical features have been developed specifically for *Microsoft Official Academic Course* programs.

Presenting the extensive procedural information and technical concepts woven throughout the textbook raises challenges for the student and instructor alike. The Illustrated Book Tour that follows provides a guide to the rich features contributing to *Microsoft Official Academic Course* program's pedagogical plan. Following is a list of key features in each lesson designed to prepare students for success on the certification exams and in the workplace:

- Each lesson begins with an **Objective Domain Matrix.** More than a standard list of learning objectives, the Domain Matrix correlates each software skill covered in the lesson to the specific MCTS "objective domain."

- Concise and frequent **Step-by-Step** instructions teach students new features and provide an opportunity for hands-on practice. Numbered steps give detailed, step-by-step instructions to help students learn software skills. The steps also show results and screen images to match what students should see on their computer screens.

- **Illustrations:** Screen images provide visual feedback as students work through the exercises. The images reinforce key concepts, provide visual clues about the steps, and allow students to check their progress.

- **Key Terms:** Important technical vocabulary is listed at the beginning of the lesson. When these terms are used later in the lesson, they appear in bold italic type and are defined. The Glossary contains all of the key terms and their definitions.

- Engaging point-of-use **Reader aids,** located throughout the lessons, tell students why this topic is relevant (*The Bottom Line*), provide students with helpful hints (*Take Note*), or show alternate ways to accomplish tasks (*Another Way*). Reader aids also provide additional relevant or background information that adds value to the lesson.

- **Certification Ready?** features throughout the text signal students where a specific certification objective is covered. They provide students with a chance to check their understanding of that particular MCTS objective and, if necessary, review the section of the lesson where it is covered. MOAC offers complete preparation for MCTS certification.

- **Knowledge Assessments** provide three progressively more challenging lesson-ending activities.

■ Lesson Features

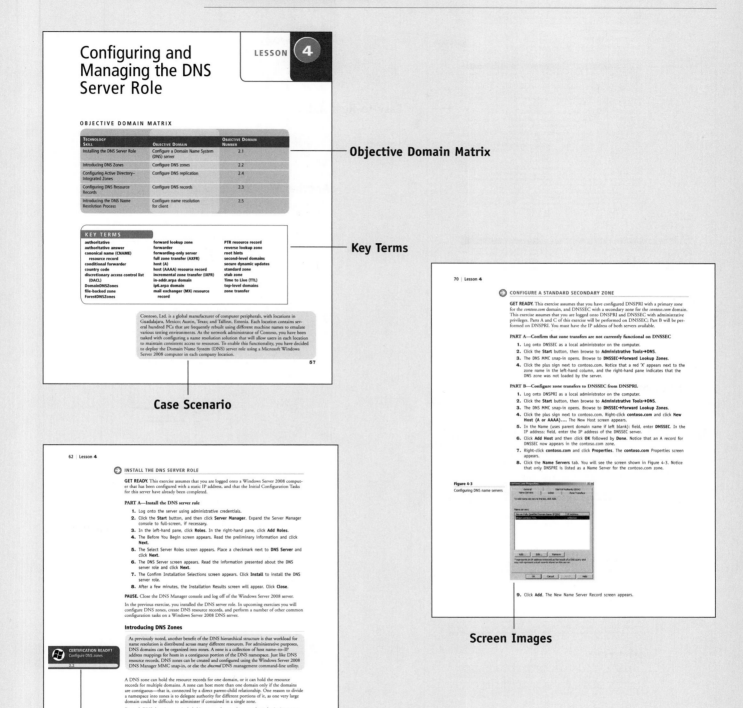

Objective Domain Matrix

Key Terms

Case Scenario

Screen Images

MCTS Certification Objective Alert

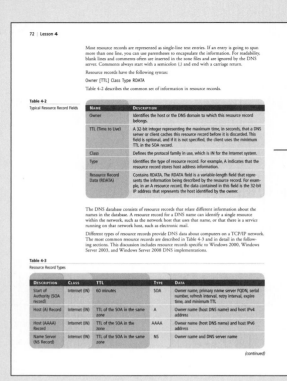

Easy-to-Read Tables

Another Way Reader Aid

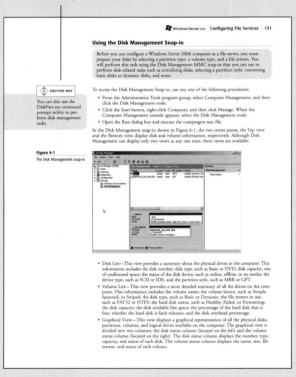

The Bottom Line Reader Aid

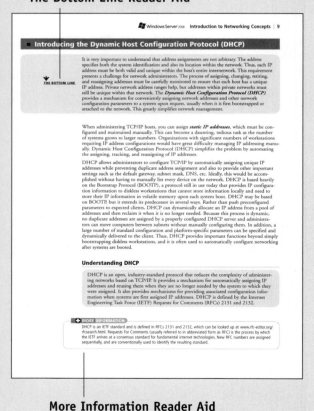

More Information Reader Aid

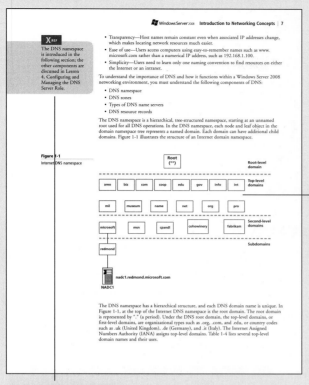

X Ref Reader Aid

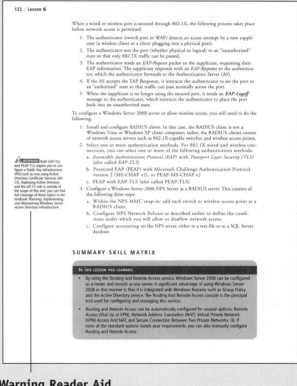

Informative Diagrams

Warning Reader Aid

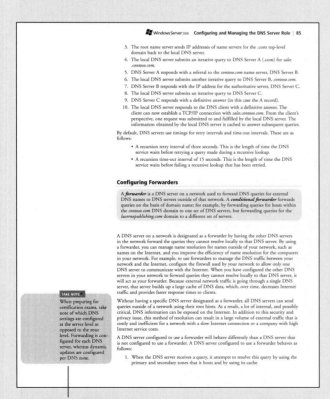

Take Note Reader Aid

14 | Lesson 1

XREF

The Routing and Remote Access server role is discussed further in Lesson 5.

• Remote Access—A Windows Server 2008 computer can act as a remote access server, which can allow remote network clients to access resources on a network as though they were physically connected to the LAN. The Windows Server 2008 remote access server can provide remote access using either dial-up connections via a modem, or else through a Virtual Private Network (VPN) connection over the Internet or another public network.

Introducing Network Access Protection (NAP)

THE BOTTOM LINE

One of the principal challenges in corporate networks is the ability to secure networks against unwarranted access. In addition to configuring perimeter firewalls, network administrators also need to protect the network against "inside threats," laptop computers that are physically brought inside the corporate network or that gain access to the company network through remote access technologies such as Virtual Private Networks (VPNs.) For network administrators, this creates a challenge of enforcing corporate security standards such as up-to-date anti-virus protection definitions and a consistent firewall configuration. To assist with this endeavor, Windows Server 2008 provides the Network Access Protection platform, which provides a policy enforcement mechanism to control access to a 2008 network.

Network Access Protection is a new feature in Windows Server 2008 that allows network administrators to specify one or more policies that define the conditions under which network access will or will not be permitted. For example, consider a user who brings his home laptop into the office, and this laptop does not have anti-virus software installed. By connecting this laptop to the corporate network, this user runs the risk of propagating a network virus or worm throughout the corporate network, because the perimeter firewall does not offer any protection against a computer that is located inside of the perimeter. If Network Access Protection is in place, this laptop can be placed into a "quarantine" area where it cannot cause harm to the remainder of the computers on the network.

XREF

Network Access Protection is discussed at length in Lesson 10.

SUMMARY SKILL MATRIX

IN THIS LESSON YOU LEARNED:

• Network protocols create a logical language that allows computers to communicate.

• The most commonly used network protocol on modern networks is the Transmission Control Protocol/Internet Protocol (TCP/IP) protocol suite.

• There are currently two implementations of TCP/IP: TCP/IP version 4, or IPv4, and TCP/IP version 6, or IPv6.

• Each host on a TCP/IP network needs to be configured with a unique IP address.

• TCP/IP networks use the Domain Name System (DNS) to map human-readable machine names to IP addresses and vice versa, such as mapping the *www.cpandl.com* host name to the 10.10.1.104 IP address.

• Network administrators can use the Dynamic Host Configuration Protocol (DHCP) to automatically assign IP addresses to multiple client computers.

• The Routing and Remote Access service provides the ability to use a Windows Server 2008 computer as a router, which passes network traffic from one TCP/IP network to another, as well as remote access capabilities using either dial-up or VPN technology.

• To allow administrators to enforce network security policies such as mandatory anti-virus or firewall configurations, Windows Server 2008 has introduced the Network Access Protection (NAP) enforcement platform.

• Network addressing is fundamental to successful communication between systems.

Summary Skill Matrix

Case Scenarios

100 | Lesson 4

10. The following feature is available only on Active Directory-integrated DNS zones:
   a. Dynamic updates
   b. Incremental zone transfers
   c. Reverse lookup zones
   d. Secure dynamic updates

Case Scenarios

Case Scenario 4-1: Enabling Network Users to Connect to Internet Host Names

You are the network administrator for Contoso, Ltd. The Contoso network consists of a single domain, *contoso.com*, which is protected from the Internet by a firewall. The firewall runs on a computer named NS1 that is directly connected to the Internet. NS1 also runs the DNS Server service, and its firewall allows DNS traffic to pass between the Internet and the DNS Server service on NS1 but not between the Internet and the internal network. The DNS Server service on NS1 is configured to use round robin. Behind the firewall, two computers are running Windows Server 2003—NS2 and NS3, which host a primary and secondary DNS server, respectively, for the *contoso.com* zone.

Users on the company network report that, although they use host names to connect to computers on the local private network, they cannot use host names to connect to Internet destinations, such as *www.microsoft.com*.

Which of the following actions requires the least amount of administrative effort to enable network users to connect to Internet host names?

a. Disable recursion on NS2 and NS3.
b. Enable netmask ordering on NS1.
c. Configure NS2 and NS3 to use NS1 as a forwarder.
d. Disable round robin on NS1.

Case Scenario 4-2: Implementing DNS Updates

You are the system administrator for Contoso, Ltd. The company has grown rapidly over the past year, and currently Contoso is using only a single DNS zone. Recently, the Marketing department has made several requests for DNS changes that were delayed. Users would like the ability to make their own DNS updates.

What should you do to try to address this problem?

a. Create a secondary server in the Marketing department so that users can manage their own zone.
b. Delegate the marketing domain to a DNS server in the Marketing department.
c. Place a domain controller running DNS in the Marketing department so that people in the department can make changes.
d. Upgrade the network infrastructure to improve network performance.

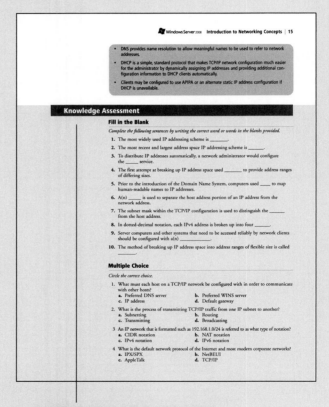

Windows Server 2008 Introduction to Networking Concepts | 15

• DNS provides name resolution to allow meaningful names to be used to refer to network addresses.

• DHCP is a simple, standard protocol that makes TCP/IP network configuration much easier for the administrator by dynamically assigning IP addresses and providing additional configuration information to DHCP clients automatically.

• Clients may be configured to use APIPA or an alternate static IP address configuration if DHCP is unavailable.

Knowledge Assessment

Fill in the Blank

Complete the following sentences by writing the correct word or words in the blanks provided.

1. The most widely used IP addressing scheme is _____.

2. The most recent and largest address space IP addressing scheme is _____.

3. To distribute IP addresses automatically, a network administrator would configure the _____ service.

4. The first attempt at breaking up IP address space used _____ to provide address ranges of differing sizes.

5. Prior to the introduction of the Domain Name System, computers used _____ to map human-readable names to IP addresses.

6. A(n) _____ is used to separate the host address portion of an IP address from the network address.

7. The subnet mask within the TCP/IP configuration is used to distinguish the _____ from the host address.

8. In dotted-decimal notation, each IPv4 address is broken up into four _____.

9. Server computers and other systems that need to be accessed reliably by network clients should be configured with a(n) _____.

10. The method of breaking up IP address space into address ranges of flexible size is called _____.

Multiple Choice

Circle the correct choice.

1. What must each host on a TCP/IP network be configured with in order to communicate with other hosts?
   a. Preferred DNS server   b. Preferred WINS server
   c. IP address   d. Default gateway

2. What is the process of transmitting TCP/IP traffic from one IP subnet to another?
   a. Subnetting   b. Routing
   c. Transmitting   d. Broadcasting

3. An IP network that is formatted such as 192.168.1.0/24 is referred to as what type of notation?
   a. CIDR notation   b. NAT notation
   c. IPv4 notation   d. IPv6 notation

4. What is the default network protocol of the Internet and most modern corporate networks?
   a. IPX/SPX   b. NetBEUI
   c. AppleTalk   d. TCP/IP

Knowledge Assessment Questions

---

www.wiley.com/college/microsoft *or*
call the MOAC Toll-Free Number: 1+(888) 764-7001 (U.S. & Canada only)

Conventions and Features
Used in This Book

This book uses particular fonts, symbols, and heading conventions to highlight important information or to call your attention to special steps. For more information about the features in each lesson, refer to the Illustrated Book Tour section.

CONVENTION	MEANING
NEW FEATURE	This icon indicates a new or greatly improved Windows feature in this version of the software.
THE BOTTOM LINE	This feature provides a brief summary of the material to be covered in the section that follows.
CLOSE	Words in all capital letters and in a different font color than the rest of the text indicate instructions for opening, saving, or closing files or programs. They also point out items you should check or actions you should take.
CERTIFICATION READY?	This feature signals the point in the text where a specific certification objective is covered. It provides you with a chance to check your understanding of that particular MCTS objective and, if necessary, review the section of the lesson where it is covered.
TAKE NOTE	Reader aids appear in shaded boxes found in your text. *Take Note* provides helpful hints related to particular tasks or topics.
ANOTHER WAY	*Another Way* provides an alternative procedure for accomplishing a particular task.
X REF	These notes provide pointers to information discussed elsewhere in the textbook or describe interesting features of Windows Server 2008 that are not directly addressed in the current topic or exercise.
Alt + Tab	A plus sign (+) between two key names means that you must press both keys at the same time. Keys that you are instructed to press in an exercise will appear in the font shown here.
A *shared printer* can be used by many individuals on a network.	Key terms appear in bold italic.
Key **My Name is**.	Any text you are asked to key appears in color.
Click **OK**.	Any button on the screen you are supposed to click on or select will also appear in color.

Instructor Support Program

The *Microsoft Official Academic Course* programs are accompanied by a rich array of resources that incorporate the extensive textbook visuals to form a pedagogically cohesive package. These resources provide all the materials instructors need to deploy and deliver their courses. Resources available online for download include:

- The **MSDN Academic Alliance** is designed to provide the easiest and most inexpensive developer tools, products, and technologies available to faculty and students in labs, classrooms, and on student PCs. A free 3-year membership is available to qualified MOAC adopters.

  Note: Microsoft Windows Server 2008 can be downloaded from MSDN AA for use by students in this course.

- **Windows Server 2008 Evaluation Software.** DVDs containing an evaluation version of Windows Server 2008 are bundled inside the front cover of this text.

- The **Instructor's Guide** contains Solutions to all the textbook exercises as well as chapter summaries and lecture notes. The Instructor's Guide and Syllabi for various term lengths are available from the Book Companion site (www.wiley.com/college/microsoft) and from *WileyPLUS*.

- The **Test Bank** contains hundreds of questions in multiple-choice, true-false, short answer, and essay formats and is available to download from the Instructor's Book Companion site (www.wiley.com/college/microsoft) and from *WileyPLUS*. A complete answer key is provided.

- **PowerPoint Presentations and Images.** A complete set of PowerPoint presentations is available on the Instructor's Book Companion site (www.wiley.com/college/microsoft) and in *WileyPLUS* to enhance classroom presentations. Tailored to the text's topical coverage and Skills Matrix, these presentations are designed to convey key Windows Server concepts addressed in the text.

  All figures from the text are on the Instructor's Book Companion site (www.wiley.com/college/microsoft) and in *WileyPLUS*. You can incorporate them into your PowerPoint presentations, or create your own overhead transparencies and handouts.

  By using these visuals in class discussions, you can help focus students' attention on key elements of Windows Server and help them understand how to use it effectively in the workplace.

- When it comes to improving the classroom experience, there is no better source of ideas and inspiration than your fellow colleagues. The Wiley Faculty Network connects teachers with technology, facilitates the exchange of best practices, and helps to enhance instructional efficiency and effectiveness. Faculty Network activities include technology training and tutorials, virtual seminars, peer-to-peer exchanges of experiences and ideas, personal consulting, and sharing of resources. For details visit www.WhereFacultyConnect.com.

WileyPLUS

Broad developments in education over the past decade have influenced the instructional approach taken in the Microsoft Official Academic Course program. The way that students learn, especially about new technologies, has changed dramatically in the Internet era. Electronic learning materials and Internet-based instruction is now as much a part of classroom instruction as printed textbooks. *WileyPLUS* provides the technology to create an environment where students reach their full potential and experience academic success that will last them a lifetime!

WileyPLUS is a powerful and highly-integrated suite of teaching and learning resources designed to bridge the gap between what happens in the classroom and what happens at home and on the job. *WileyPLUS* provides instructors with the resources to teach their students new technologies and guide them to reach their goals of getting ahead in the job market by having the skills to become certified and advance in the workforce. For students, *WileyPLUS* provides the tools for study and practice that are available to them 24/7, wherever and whenever they want to study. *WileyPLUS* includes a complete online version of the student textbook, PowerPoint presentations, homework and practice assignments and quizzes, image galleries, test bank questions, gradebook, and all the instructor resources in one easy-to-use Web site.

Organized around the everyday activities you and your students perform in the class, *WileyPLUS* helps you:

- **Prepare & Present** outstanding class presentations using relevant PowerPoint slides and other *WileyPLUS* materials—and you can easily upload and add your own.
- **Create Assignments** by choosing from questions organized by lesson, level of difficulty, and source—and add your own questions. Students' homework and quizzes are automatically graded, and the results are recorded in your gradebook.
- **Offer context-sensitive help to students, 24/7.** When you assign homework or quizzes, you decide if and when students get access to hints, solutions, or answers where appropriate—or they can be linked to relevant sections of their complete, online text for additional help whenever—and wherever they need it most.
- **Track Student Progress.** Analyze students' results and assess their level of understanding on an individual and class level using the *WileyPLUS* gradebook, or export data to your own personal gradebook.
- **Administer Your Course.** *WileyPLUS* can easily be integrated with another course management system, gradebook, or other resources you are using in your class, providing you with the flexibility to build your course, your way.

Please view our online demo at **www.wiley.com/college/wileyplus**. Here you will find additional information about the features and benefits of *WileyPLUS*, how to request a "test drive" of *WileyPLUS* for this title, and how to adopt it for class use.

MSDN ACADEMIC ALLIANCE—FREE 3-YEAR MEMBERSHIP AVAILABLE TO QUALIFIED ADOPTERS!

The Microsoft Developer Network Academic Alliance (MSDN AA) is designed to provide the easiest and most inexpensive way for universities to make the latest Microsoft developer tools, products, and technologies available in labs, classrooms, and on student PCs. MSDN AA is an annual membership program for departments teaching Science, Technology, Engineering, and Mathematics (STEM) courses. The membership provides a complete solution to keep academic labs, faculty, and students on the leading edge of technology.

Software available in the MSDN AA program is provided at no charge to adopting departments through the Wiley and Microsoft publishing partnership.

As a bonus to this free offer, faculty will be introduced to Microsoft's Faculty Connection and Academic Resource Center. It takes time and preparation to keep students engaged while giving them a fundamental understanding of theory, and the Microsoft Faculty Connection is designed to help STEM professors with this preparation by providing articles, curriculum, and tools that professors can use to engage and inspire today's technology students.

* Contact your Wiley rep for details.

For more information about the MSDN Academic Alliance program, go to:

msdn.microsoft.com/academic/

Note: Microsoft Windows Server 2008 can be downloaded from MSDN AA for use by students in this course.

Important Web Addresses and Phone Numbers

To locate the Wiley Higher Education Rep in your area, go to the following Web address and click on the "*Who's My Rep?*" link at the top of the page.

www.wiley.com/college

Or Call the MOAC Toll Free Number: 1 + (888) 764-7001 (U.S. & Canada only).

To learn more about becoming a Microsoft Certified Professional and exam availability, visit www.microsoft.com/learning/mcp.

Student Support Program

Book Companion Web Site (www.wiley.com/college/microsoft)

The students' book companion site for the MOAC series includes any resources, exercise files, and Web links that will be used in conjunction with this course.

WileyPLUS

WileyPLUS is a powerful and highly-integrated suite of teaching and learning resources designed to bridge the gap between what happens in the classroom and what happens at home and on the job. For students, *WileyPLUS* provides the tools for study and practice that are available 24/7, wherever and whenever they want to study. *WileyPLUS* includes a complete online version of the student textbook, PowerPoint presentations, homework and practice assignments and quizzes, image galleries, test bank questions, gradebook, and all the instructor resources in one easy-to-use Web site.

WileyPLUS provides immediate feedback on student assignments and a wealth of support materials. This powerful study tool will help your students develop their conceptual understanding of the class material and increase their ability to answer questions.

- A **Study and Practice** area links directly to text content, allowing students to review the text while they study and answer.
- An **Assignment** area keeps all the work you want your students to complete in one location, making it easy for them to stay on task. Students have access to a variety of interactive self-assessment tools, as well as other resources for building their confidence and understanding. In addition, all of the assignments and quizzes contain a link to the relevant section of the multimedia book, providing students with context-sensitive help that allows them to conquer obstacles as they arise.
- A **Personal Gradebook** for each student allows students to view their results from past assignments at any time.

Please view our online demo at www.wiley.com/college/wileyplus. Here you will find additional information about the features and benefits of *WileyPLUS*, how to request a "test drive" of *WileyPLUS* for this title, and how to adopt it for class use.

Wiley Desktop Editions

Wiley MOAC Desktop Editions are innovative, electronic versions of printed textbooks. Students buy the desktop version for 50% off the U.S. price of the printed text, and get the added value of permanence and portability. Wiley Desktop Editions provide students with numerous additional benefits that are not available with other e-text solutions.

Wiley Desktop Editions are NOT subscriptions; students download the Wiley Desktop Edition to their computer desktops. Students own the content they buy to keep for as long as they want. Once a Wiley Desktop Edition is downloaded to the computer desktop, students have instant access to all of the content without being online. Students can also print out the sections they prefer to read in hard copy. Students also have access to fully integrated resources within their Wiley Desktop Edition. From highlighting their e-text to taking and sharing notes, students can easily personalize their Wiley Desktop Edition as they are reading or following along in class.

Windows Server 2008 Evaluation Edition

All MOAC Windows Server 2008 textbooks are packaged with an evaluation edition of Windows Server 2008 on the companion DVDs. Installing the Windows Server Evaluation Edition provides students with the state-of-the-art system software, enabling them to use a full version of Windows Server 2008 for the course exercises. This also promotes the practice of learning by doing, which can be the most effective way to acquire and remember new computing skills.

Evaluating Windows Server 2008 software does not require product activation or entering a product key. The Windows Server 2008 Evaluation Edition provided with this textbook may be installed without activation and evaluated for an initial 60 days. If you need more time to evaluate Windows Server 2008, the 60-day evaluation period may be reset (or re-armed) three times, extending the original 60-day evaluation period by up to 180 days for a total possible evaluation time of 240 days. After this time, you will need to uninstall the software or upgrade to a fully licensed version of Windows Server 2008.

System Requirements

The following are estimated system requirements for Windows Server 2008. If your computer has less than the minimum requirements, you will not be able to install this product correctly. Actual requirements will vary based on your system configuration and the applications and features you install.

PROCESSOR

TAKE NOTE*

An Intel Itanium 2 processor is required for Windows Server 2008 for Itanium-Based Systems.

Processor performance depends not only on the clock frequency of the processor, but also on the number of processor cores and the size of the processor cache. The following are the processor requirements for this product:

- Minimum: 1 GHz (for x86 processors) or 1.4 GHz (for x64 processors)
- Recommended: 2 GHz or faster

RAM

The following are the RAM requirements for this product:

- Minimum: 512 MB
- Recommended: 2 GB or more
- Maximum (32-bit systems): 4 GB (for Windows Server 2008 Standard) or 64 GB (for Windows Server 2008 Enterprise or Windows Server 2008 Datacenter)
- Maximum (64-bit systems): 32 GB (for Windows Server 2008 Standard) or 2 TB (for Windows Server 2008 Enterprise, Windows Server 2008 Datacenter, or Windows Server 2008 for Itanium-Based Systems)

Disk space requirements

The following are the approximate disk space requirements for the system partition. Itanium-based and x64-based operating systems will vary from these estimates. Additional disk space may be required if you install the system over a network. For more information, see www.microsoft.com/windowsserver2008.

- Minimum: 10 GB
- Recommended: 40 GB or more
- DVD-ROM drive
- Super VGA (800 x 600) or higher-resolution monitor
- Keyboard and Microsoft mouse (or other compatible pointing device)

Important Considerations for Active Directory Domain Controllers

The upgrade process from Windows Server 2003 to Windows Server 2008 requires free disk space for the new operating system image, for the Setup process, and for any installed server roles.

For the domain controller role, the volume or volumes hosting the following resources also have specific free disk space requirements:

- Application data (%AppData%)
- Program files (%ProgramFiles%)
- Users' data (%SystemDrive%\Documents and Settings)
- Windows directory (%WinDir%)

The free space on the %WinDir% volume must be equal or greater than the current size of the resources listed above and their subordinate folders when they are located on the %WinDir% volume. By default, dcpromo places the Active Directory database and log files under %Windir%—in this case, their size would be included in the free disk space requirements for the %Windir% folder.

However, if the Active Directory database is hosted outside of any of the folders above, then the hosting volume or volumes must only contain additional free space equal to at least 10% of the current database size or 250 MB, whichever is greater. Finally, the free space on the volume that hosts the log files must be at least 50 MB.

A default installation of the Active Directory directory service in Windows Server 2003 has the Active Directory database and log files under %WinDir%\NTDS. With this configuration, the NTDS .DIT database file and all the log files are temporarily copied over to the quarantine location and then copied back to their original location. This is why additional free space is required for those resources. However, the SYSVOL directory, which is also under %WinDir% (%WinDir%\SYSVOL), is moved and not copied. Therefore, it does not require any additional free space.

After the upgrade, the space that was reserved for the copied resources will be returned to the file system.

Installing and Re-Arming Windows Server 2008

Evaluating Windows Server 2008 software does not require product activation. The Windows Server 2008 Evaluation Edition may be installed without activation, and it may be evaluated for 60 days. Additionally, the 60-day evaluation period may be reset (re-armed) three times. This action extends the original 60-day evaluation period by up to 180 days for a total possible evaluation time of 240 days.

How To Install Windows Server 2008 Without Activating It

TAKE NOTE *

After Windows Server 2008 is installed, the edition cannot be changed without reinstalling it.

1. Run the Windows Server 2008 Setup program.
2. When you are prompted to enter a product key for activation, do not enter a key. Click No when Setup asks you to confirm your selection.
3. You may be prompted to select the edition of Windows Server 2008 that you want to evaluate. Select the edition that you want to install.
4. When you are prompted, read the evaluation terms in the Microsoft Software License Terms, and then accept the terms.
5. When the Windows Server 2008 Setup program is finished, your initial 60-day evaluation period starts. To check the time that is left on your current evaluation period, run the Slmgr.vbs script that is in the System32 folder. Use the **-dli** switch to run this script. The **slmgr.vbs -dli** command displays the number of days that are left in the current 60-day evaluation period.

How To Re-Arm the Evaluation Period

This section describes how to extend, or re-arm, the Windows Server 2008 evaluation period. The evaluation period is also known as the "activation grace" period.

When the initial 60-day evaluation period nears its end, you can run the Slmgr.vbs script to reset the evaluation period. To do this, follow these steps:

1. Click **Start**, and then click **Command Prompt**.
2. Type **slmgr.vbs -dli**, and then press **ENTER** to check the current status of your evaluation period.
3. To reset the evaluation period, type **slmgr.vbs –rearm**, and then press **ENTER**.
4. Restart the computer.

This resets the evaluation period to 60 days.

How To Automate the Extension of the Evaluation Period

You may want to set up a process that automatically resets the evaluation period every 60 days. One way to automate this process is by using the Task Scheduler. You can configure the Task Scheduler to run the Slmgr.vbs script and to restart the server at a particular time. To do this, follow these steps:

1. Click **Start**, point to **Administrative Tools**, and then click **Task Scheduler**.
2. Copy the following sample task to the server, and then save it as an .xml file. For example, you can save the file as **Extend.xml**.

```xml
<?xml version="1.0" encoding="UTF-16"?> <Task version="1.2"
xmlns="http://schemas.microsoft.com/windows/2004/02/mit/task">
<RegistrationInfo> <Date>2007-09-17T14:26:04.433</Date>
<Author>Microsoft Corporation</Author> </RegistrationInfo>
<Triggers> <TimeTrigger id="18c4a453-d7aa-4647-916b-
af0c3ea16a6b"> <Repetition> <Interval>P59D</Interval>
<StopAtDurationEnd>false</StopAtDurationEnd> </Repetition>
<StartBoundary>2007-10-05T02:23:24</StartBoundary>
<EndBoundary>2008-09-17T14:23:24.777</EndBoundary>
<Enabled>true</Enabled> </TimeTrigger> </Triggers>
<Principals> <Principal id="Author">
<UserId>domain\alias</UserId>
```

```
<LogonType>Password</LogonType>
<RunLevel>HighestAvailable</RunLevel> </Principal>
</Principals> <Settings> <IdleSettings>
<Duration>PT10M</Duration> <WaitTimeout>PT1H</WaitTimeout>
<StopOnIdleEnd>true</StopOnIdleEnd>
<RestartOnIdle>false</RestartOnIdle> </IdleSettings>
<MultipleInstancesPolicy>IgnoreNew</MultipleInstancesPolicy>
<DisallowStartIfOnBatteries>true</DisallowStartIfOnBatteries>
<StopIfGoingOnBatteries>true</StopIfGoingOnBatteries>
<AllowHardTerminate>true</AllowHardTerminate>
<StartWhenAvailable>false</StartWhenAvailable>
<RunOnlyIfNetworkAvailable>false</RunOnlyIfNetworkAvailable>
<AllowStartOnDemand>true</AllowStartOnDemand>
<Enabled>true</Enabled> <Hidden>false</Hidden>
<RunOnlyIfIdle>false</RunOnlyIfIdle>
<WakeToRun>true</WakeToRun>
<ExecutionTimeLimit>P3D</ExecutionTimeLimit>
<DeleteExpiredTaskAfter>PT0S</DeleteExpiredTaskAfter>
<Priority>7</Priority> <RestartOnFailure>
<Interval>PT1M</Interval> <Count>3</Count>
</RestartOnFailure> </Settings> <Actions Context="Author">
<Exec> <Command>C:\Windows\System32\slmgr.vbs</Command>
<Arguments>-rearm</Arguments> </Exec> <Exec>
<Command>C:\Windows\System32\shutdown.exe</Command>
<Arguments>/r</Arguments> </Exec> </Actions> </Task>
```

3. In the sample task, change the value of the following "UserID" tag to contain your domain and your alias:

   <UserId>domain\alias</UserId>

4. In the Task Scheduler, click **Import Task** on the **Action** menu.

5. Click the sample task .xml file. For example, click **Extend.xml**.

6. Click **Import**.

7. Click the **Triggers** tab.

8. Click the **One Time** trigger, and then click **Edit**.

9. Change the start date of the task to a date just before the end of your current evaluation period.

10. Click **OK**, and then exit the Task Scheduler.

The Task Scheduler will now run the evaluation reset operation on the date that you specified.

Preparing to Take the Microsoft Certified Technology Specialist (MCTS) Exam

The Microsoft Certified Technology Specialist (MCTS) certifications enable professionals to target specific technologies and to distinguish themselves by demonstrating in-depth knowledge and expertise in their specialized technologies. Microsoft Certified Technology Specialists are consistently capable of implementing, building, troubleshooting, and debugging a particular Microsoft Technology.

For organizations, the new generation of Microsoft certifications provides better skills verification tools that help with assessing not only in-demand skills on Windows Server, but also the ability to quickly complete on-the-job tasks. Individuals will find it easier to identify and work towards the certification credential that meets their personal and professional goals.

To learn more about becoming a Microsoft Certified Professional and exam availability, visit www.microsoft.com/learning/mcp.

Microsoft Certifications for IT Professionals

The new Microsoft Certified Technology Specialist (MCTS) and Microsoft Certified IT Professional (MCITP) credentials provide IT professionals with a simpler and more targeted framework to showcase their technical skills in addition to the skills that are required for specific developer job roles.

The Microsoft Certified Database Administrator (MCDBA), Microsoft Certified Desktop Support Technician (MCDST), Microsoft Certified System Administrator (MCSA), and Microsoft Certified Systems Engineer (MCSE) credentials continue to provide IT professionals who use Microsoft SQL Server 2000, Windows XP, and Windows Server 2003 with industry recognition and validation of their IT skills and experience.

Microsoft Certified Technology Specialist

The new Microsoft Certified Tehnology Specialist (MCTS) credential highlights your skills using a specific Microsoft technology. You can demonstrate your abilities as an IT professional or developer with in-depth knowledge of the Microsoft technology that you use today or are planning to deploy.

The MCTS certifications enable professionals to target specific technologies and to distinguish themselves by demonstrating in-depth knowledge and expertise in their specialized technologies. Microsoft Certified Technology Specialists are consistently capable of implementing, building, troubleshooting, and debugging a particular Microsoft technology.

You can learn more about the MCTS program at www.microsoft.com/learning/mcp/mcts.

Microsoft Certified IT Professional

The new Microsoft Certified IT Professional (MCITP) credential lets you highlight your specific area of expertise. Now, you can easily distinguish yourself as an expert in database administration, database development, business intelligence, or support.

By becoming certified, you demonstrate to employers that you have achieved a predictable level of skill not only in the use of the Windows Server operating system, but with a comprehensive set of Microsoft technologies. Employers often require certification either as a condition of employment or as a condition of advancement within the company or other organization.

You can learn more about the MCITP program at www.microsoft.com/learning/mcp/mcitp.

The certification examinations are sponsored by Microsoft but administered through Microsoft's exam delivery partner Prometric.

Preparing to Take an Exam

Unless you are a very experienced user, you will need to use a test preparation course to prepare to complete the test correctly and within the time allowed. The *Microsoft Official Academic Course* series is designed to prepare you with a strong knowledge of all exam topics, and with some additional review and practice on your own, you should feel confident in your ability to pass the appropriate exam.

After you decide which exam to take, review the list of objectives for the exam. You can easily identify tasks that are included in the objective list by locating the Objective Domain Matrix at the start of each lesson and the Certification Ready sidebars in the margin of the lessons in this book.

To take the MCTS test, visit www.microsoft.com/learning/mcp/mcts to locate your nearest testing center. Then call the testing center directly to schedule your test. The amount of advance notice you should provide will vary for different testing centers, and it typically depends on the number of computers available at the testing center, the number of other testers who have already been scheduled for the day on which you want to take the test, and the number of times per week that the testing center offers MCTS testing. In general, you should call to schedule your test at least two weeks prior to the date on which you want to take the test.

When you arrive at the testing center, you might be asked for proof of identity. A driver's license or passport is an acceptable form of identification. If you do not have either of these items of documentation, call your testing center and ask what alternative forms of identification will be accepted. If you are retaking a test, bring your MCTS identification number, which will have been given to you when you previously took the test. If you have not prepaid or if your organization has not already arranged to make payment for you, you will need to pay the test-taking fee when you arrive.

Student CD

The CD-ROM included with this book contains five practice exams that will help you hone your knowledge before you take the MCTS Windows Server 2008 Network Infrastructure, Configuring (Exam 70-642) certification examination. Each exam has between 40 and 50 questions and is timed for 90 minutes. The exams are meant to provide practice for your certification exam and are also good reinforcement of the material covered in the course.

The enclosed Student CD will run automatically. Upon accepting the license agreement, you will proceed directly to the exams. The exams also can be accessed through the Assets folder located within the CD files.

Acknowledgments

MOAC Instructor Advisory Board

We would like to thank our Instructor Advisory Board, an elite group of educators who has assisted us every step of the way in building these products. Advisory Board members have acted as our sounding board on key pedagogical and design decisions leading to the development of these compelling and innovative textbooks for future Information Workers. Their dedication to technology education is truly appreciated.

Charles DeSassure, Tarrant County College

Charles DeSassure is Department Chair and Instructor of Computer Science & Information Technology at Tarrant County College Southeast Campus, Arlington, Texas. He has had experience as a MIS Manager, system analyst, field technology analyst, LAN Administrator, microcomputer specialist, and public school teacher in South Carolina. DeSassure has worked in higher education for more than ten years and received the Excellence Award in Teaching from the National Institute for Staff and Organizational Development (NISOD). He currently serves on the Educational Testing Service (ETS) iSkills National Advisory Committee and chaired the Tarrant County College District Student Assessment Committee. He has written proposals and makes presentations at major educational conferences nationwide. DeSassure has served as a textbook reviewer for John Wiley & Sons and Prentice Hall. He teaches courses in information security, networking, distance learning, and computer literacy. DeSassure holds a master's degree in Computer Resources & Information Management from Webster University.

Kim Ehlert, Waukesha County Technical College

Kim Ehlert is the Microsoft Program Coordinator and a Network Specialist instructor at Waukesha County Technical College, teaching the full range of MCSE and networking courses for the past nine years. Prior to joining WCTC, Kim was a professor at the Milwaukee School of Engineering for five years where she oversaw the Novell Academic Education and the Microsoft IT Academy programs. She has a wide variety of industry experience including network design and management for Johnson Controls, local city fire departments, police departments, large church congregations, health departments, and accounting firms. Kim holds many industry certifications including MCDST, MCSE, Security+, Network+, Server+, MCT, and CNE.

Kim has a bachelor's degree in Information Systems and a master's degree in Business Administration from the University of Wisconsin Milwaukee. When she is not busy teaching, she enjoys spending time with her husband Gregg and their two children—Alex, 14, and Courtney, 17.

Penny Gudgeon, Corinthian Colleges, Inc.

Penny Gudgeon is the Program Manager for IT curriculum at Corinthian Colleges, Inc. Previously, she was responsible for computer programming and web curriculum for twenty-seven campuses in Corinthian's Canadian division, CDI College of Business, Technology and Health Care. Penny joined CDI College in 1997 as a computer programming instructor at one of the campuses outside of Toronto. Prior to joining CDI College, Penny taught productivity software at another Canadian college, the Academy of Learning, for four years. Penny has experience in helping students achieve their goals through various learning models from instructor-led to self-directed to online.

Before embarking on a career in education, Penny worked in the fields of advertising, marketing/sales, mechanical and electronic engineering technology, and computer programming. When not working from her home office or indulging her passion for lifelong learning, Penny likes to read mysteries, garden, and relax at home in Hamilton, Ontario, with her Shih-Tzu, Gracie.

Margaret Leary, Northern Virginia Community College

Margaret Leary is Professor of IST at Northern Virginia Community College, teaching Networking and Network Security Courses for the past ten years. She is the co-Principal Investigator on the CyberWATCH initiative, an NSF-funded regional consortium of higher education institutions and businesses working together to increase the number of network security personnel in the workforce. She also serves as a Senior Security Policy Manager and Research Analyst at Nortel Government Solutions and holds a CISSP certification.

Margaret holds a B.S.B.A. and MBA/Technology Management from the University of Phoenix, and is pursuing her Ph.D. in Organization and Management with an IT Specialization at Capella University. Her dissertation is titled "Quantifying the Discoverability of Identity Attributes in Internet-Based Public Records: Impact on Identity Theft and Knowledge-based Authentication." She has several other published articles in various government and industry magazines, notably on identity management and network security.

Wen Liu, ITT Educational Services, Inc.

Wen Liu is Director of Corporate Curriculum Development at ITT Educational Services, Inc. He joined the ITT corporate headquarters in 1998 as a Senior Network Analyst to plan and deploy the corporate WAN infrastructure. A year later he assumed the position of Corporate Curriculum Manager supervising the curriculum development of all IT programs. After he was promoted to the current position three years ago, he continued to manage the curriculum research and development for all the programs offered in the School of Information Technology in addition to supervising the curriculum development in other areas (such as Schools of Drafting and Design and Schools of Electronics Technology). Prior to his employment with ITT Educational Services, Liu was a Telecommunications Analyst at the state government of Indiana working on the state backbone project that provided Internet and telecommunications services to the public users such as K-12 and higher education institutions, government agencies, libraries, and healthcare facilities.

Wen Liu has an M.A. in Student Personnel Administration in Higher Education and an M.S. in Information and Communications Sciences from Ball State University, Indiana. He used to be the director of special projects on the board of directors of the Indiana Telecommunications User Association, and used to serve on Course Technology's IT Advisory Board. He is currently a member of the IEEE and its Computer Society.

Jared Spencer, Westwood College Online

Jared Spencer has been the Lead Faculty for Networking at Westwood College Online since 2006. He began teaching in 2001 and has taught both on-ground and online for a variety of institutions, including Robert Morris University and Point Park University. In addition to his academic background, he has more than fifteen years of industry experience working for companies including the Thomson Corporation and IBM.

Jared has a master's degree in Internet Information Systems and is currently ABD and pursuing his doctorate in Information Systems at Nova Southeastern University. He has authored several papers that have been presented at conferences and appeared in publications such as the Journal of Internet Commerce and the Journal of Information Privacy and Security (JIPC). He holds a number of industry certifications, including AIX (UNIX), A+, Network+, Security+, MCSA on Windows 2000, and MCSA on Windows 2003 Server.

MOAC Windows Server Reviewers

We also thank the many reviewers who pored over the manuscript, providing invaluable feedback in the service of quality instructional materials.

Windows Server® 2008 Network Infrastructure Configuration Exam 70-642

Fidelis Ngang, Houston Community College

John Crowley, Bucks County Community College

Brian Bridson, Baker College of Flint

Focus Group and Survey Participants

Finally, we thank the hundreds of instructors who participated in our focus groups and surveys to ensure that the Microsoft Official Academic Courses best met the needs of our customers.

Jean Aguilar, Mt. Hood Community College

Konrad Akens, Zane State College

Michael Albers, University of Memphis

Diana Anderson, Big Sandy Community & Technical College

Phyllis Anderson, Delaware County Community College

Judith Andrews, Feather River College

Damon Antos, American River College

Bridget Archer, Oakton Community College

Linda Arnold, Harrisburg Area Community College–Lebanon Campus

Neha Arya, Fullerton College

Mohammad Bajwa, Katharine Gibbs School–New York

Virginia Baker, University of Alaska Fairbanks

Carla Bannick, Pima Community College

Rita Barkley, Northeast Alabama Community College

Elsa Barr, Central Community College–Hastings

Ronald W. Barry, Ventura County Community College District

Elizabeth Bastedo, Central Carolina Technical College

Karen Baston, Waubonsee Community College

Karen Bean, Blinn College

Scott Beckstrand, Community College of Southern Nevada

Paulette Bell, Santa Rosa Junior College

Liz Bennett, Southeast Technical Institute

Nancy Bermea, Olympic College

Lucy Betz, Milwaukee Area Technical College

Meral Binbasioglu, Hofstra University

Catherine Binder, Strayer University & Katharine Gibbs School–Philadelphia

Terrel Blair, El Centro College

Ruth Blalock, Alamance Community College

Beverly Bohner, Reading Area Community College

Henry Bojack, Farmingdale State University

Matthew Bowie, Luna Community College

Julie Boyles, Portland Community College

Karen Brandt, College of the Albemarle

Stephen Brown, College of San Mateo

Jared Bruckner, Southern Adventist University

Pam Brune, Chattanooga State Technical Community College

Sue Buchholz, Georgia Perimeter College

Roberta Buczyna, Edison College

Angela Butler, Mississippi Gulf Coast Community College

Rebecca Byrd, Augusta Technical College

Kristen Callahan, Mercer County Community College

Judy Cameron, Spokane Community College

Dianne Campbell, Athens Technical College

Gena Casas, Florida Community College at Jacksonville

Jesus Castrejon, Latin Technologies

Gail Chambers, Southwest Tennessee Community College

Jacques Chansavang, Indiana University–Purdue University Fort Wayne

Nancy Chapko, Milwaukee Area Technical College

Rebecca Chavez, Yavapai College

Sanjiv Chopra, Thomas Nelson Community College

Greg Clements, Midland Lutheran College

Dayna Coker, Southwestern Oklahoma State University–Sayre Campus

Tamra Collins, Otero Junior College

Janet Conrey, Gavilan Community College

Carol Cornforth, West Virginia Northern Community College

Gary Cotton, American River College

Edie Cox, Chattahoochee Technical College

Rollie Cox, Madison Area Technical College

David Crawford, Northwestern Michigan College

J.K. Crowley, Victor Valley College

Rosalyn Culver, Washtenaw Community College

Sharon Custer, Huntington University

Sandra Daniels, New River Community College

Anila Das, Cedar Valley College

Brad Davis, Santa Rosa Junior College

Susan Davis, Green River Community College

Mark Dawdy, Lincoln Land Community College

Jennifer Day, Sinclair Community College

Carol Deane, Eastern Idaho Technical College

Julie DeBuhr, Lewis-Clark State College

Janis DeHaven, Central Community College

Drew Dekreon, University of Alaska–Anchorage

Joy DePover, Central Lakes College

Salli DiBartolo, Brevard Community College

Melissa Diegnau, Riverland Community College

Al Dillard, Lansdale School of Business

Marjorie Duffy, Cosumnes River College

Sarah Dunn, Southwest Tennessee Community College

Shahla Durany, Tarrant County College–South Campus

Kay Durden, University of Tennessee at Martin

Dineen Ebert, St. Louis Community College–Meramec

Donna Ehrhart, State University of New York–Brockport

Larry Elias, Montgomery County Community College

Glenda Elser, New Mexico State University at Alamogordo

Angela Evangelinos, Monroe County Community College

Angie Evans, Ivy Tech Community College of Indiana

Linda Farrington, Indian Hills Community College

Dana Fladhammer, Phoenix College

Richard Flores, Citrus College

Connie Fox, Community and Technical College at Institute of Technology West Virginia University

Wanda Freeman, Okefenokee Technical College

Brenda Freeman, Augusta Technical College

Susan Fry, Boise State University

Roger Fulk, Wright State University–Lake Campus

Sue Furnas, Collin County Community College District

Sandy Gabel, Vernon College

Laura Galvan, Fayetteville Technical Community College

Candace Garrod, Red Rocks Community College

Sherrie Geitgey, Northwest State Community College

Chris Gerig, Chattahoochee Technical College

Barb Gillespie, Cuyamaca College

Jessica Gilmore, Highline Community College

Pamela Gilmore, Reedley College

Debbie Glinert, Queensborough Community College

Steven Goldman, Polk Community College

Bettie Goodman, C.S. Mott Community College

Mike Grabill, Katharine Gibbs School–Philadelphia

Francis Green, Penn State University

Walter Griffin, Blinn College

Fillmore Guinn, Odessa College

Helen Haasch, Milwaukee Area Technical College

John Habal, Ventura College

Joy Haerens, Chaffey College

Norman Hahn, Thomas Nelson Community College

Kathy Hall, Alamance Community College

Teri Harbacheck, Boise State University

Linda Harper, Richland Community College

Maureen Harper, Indian Hills Community College

Steve Harris, Katharine Gibbs School–New York

Robyn Hart, Fresno City College

Darien Hartman, Boise State University

Gina Hatcher, Tacoma Community College

Winona T. Hatcher, Aiken Technical College

BJ Hathaway, Northeast Wisconsin Tech College

Cynthia Hauki, West Hills College – Coalinga

Mary L. Haynes, Wayne County Community College

Marcie Hawkins, Zane State College

Steve Hebrock, Ohio State University Agricultural Technical Institute

Sue Heistand, Iowa Central Community College

Heith Hennel, Valencia Community College

Donna Hendricks, South Arkansas Community College

Judy Hendrix, Dyersburg State Community College

Gloria Hensel, Matanuska-Susitna College University of Alaska Anchorage

Gwendolyn Hester, Richland College

Tammarra Holmes, Laramie County Community College

Dee Hobson, Richland College

Keith Hoell, Katharine Gibbs School–New York

Pashia Hogan, Northeast State Technical Community College

Susan Hoggard, Tulsa Community College

Kathleen Holliman, Wallace Community College Selma

Chastity Honchul, Brown Mackie College/ Wright State University

Christie Hovey, Lincoln Land Community College

Peggy Hughes, Allegany College of Maryland

Sandra Hume, Chippewa Valley Technical College

John Hutson, Aims Community College

Celia Ing, Sacramento City College

Joan Ivey, Lanier Technical College

Barbara Jaffari, College of the Redwoods

Penny Jakes, University of Montana College of Technology

Eduardo Jaramillo, Peninsula College

Barbara Jauken, Southeast Community College

Susan Jennings, Stephen F. Austin State University

Leslie Jernberg, Eastern Idaho Technical College

Linda Johns, Georgia Perimeter College

Brent Johnson, Okefenokee Technical College

Mary Johnson, Mt. San Antonio College

Shirley Johnson, Trinidad State Junior College–Valley Campus

Sandra M. Jolley, Tarrant County College

Teresa Jolly, South Georgia Technical College

Dr. Deborah Jones, South Georgia Technical College

Margie Jones, Central Virginia Community College

Randall Jones, Marshall Community and Technical College

Diane Karlsbraaten, Lake Region State College

Teresa Keller, Ivy Tech Community College of Indiana

Charles Kemnitz, Pennsylvania College of Technology

Sandra Kinghorn, Ventura College

Bill Klein, Katharine Gibbs School–Philadelphia

Bea Knaapen, Fresno City College

Kit Kofoed, Western Wyoming Community College

Maria Kolatis, County College of Morris

Barry Kolb, Ocean County College

Karen Kuralt, University of Arkansas at Little Rock

Belva-Carole Lamb, Rogue Community College

Betty Lambert, Des Moines Area Community College

Anita Lande, Cabrillo College

Junnae Landry, Pratt Community College

Karen Lankisch, UC Clermont

David Lanzilla, Central Florida Community College

Nora Laredo, Cerritos Community College

Jennifer Larrabee, Chippewa Valley Technical College

Debra Larson, Idaho State University

Barb Lave, Portland Community College

Audrey Lawrence, Tidewater Community College

Deborah Layton, Eastern Oklahoma State College

Larry LeBlanc, Owen Graduate School– Vanderbilt University

Philip Lee, Nashville State Community College

Michael Lehrfeld, Brevard Community College

Vasant Limaye, Southwest Collegiate Institute for the Deaf – Howard College

Anne C. Lewis, Edgecombe Community College

Stephen Linkin, Houston Community College

Peggy Linston, Athens Technical College

Hugh Lofton, Moultrie Technical College

Donna Lohn, Lakeland Community College

Jackie Lou, Lake Tahoe Community College

Donna Love, Gaston College

Curt Lynch, Ozarks Technical Community College

Sheilah Lynn, Florida Community College– Jacksonville

Pat R. Lyon, Tomball College

Bill Madden, Bergen Community College

Heather Madden, Delaware Technical & Community College

Donna Madsen, Kirkwood Community College

Jane Maringer-Cantu, Gavilan College

Suzanne Marks, Bellevue Community College

Carol Martin, Louisiana State University– Alexandria

Cheryl Martucci, Diablo Valley College

Roberta Marvel, Eastern Wyoming College

Tom Mason, Brookdale Community College

Mindy Mass, Santa Barbara City College

Dixie Massaro, Irvine Valley College

Rebekah May, Ashland Community & Technical College

Emma Mays-Reynolds, Dyersburg State Community College

Timothy Mayes, Metropolitan State College of Denver

Reggie McCarthy, Central Lakes College

Matt McCaskill, Brevard Community College

Kevin McFarlane, Front Range Community College

Donna McGill, Yuba Community College

Terri McKeever, Ozarks Technical Community College

Patricia McMahon, South Suburban College

Sally McMillin, Katharine Gibbs School–Philadelphia

Charles McNerney, Bergen Community College

Lisa Mears, Palm Beach Community College

Imran Mehmood, ITT Technical Institute–King of Prussia Campus

Virginia Melvin, Southwest Tennessee Community College

Jeanne Mercer, Texas State Technical College

Denise Merrell, Jefferson Community & Technical College

Catherine Merrikin, Pearl River Community College

Diane D. Mickey, Northern Virginia Community College

Darrelyn Miller, Grays Harbor College

Sue Mitchell, Calhoun Community College

Jacquie Moldenhauer, Front Range Community College

Linda Motonaga, Los Angeles City College

Sam Mryyan, Allen County Community College

Cindy Murphy, Southeastern Community College

Ryan Murphy, Sinclair Community College

Sharon E. Nastav, Johnson County Community College

Christine Naylor, Kent State University Ashtabula

Haji Nazarian, Seattle Central Community College

Nancy Noe, Linn-Benton Community College

Jennie Noriega, San Joaquin Delta College

Linda Nutter, Peninsula College

Thomas Omerza, Middle Bucks Institute of Technology

Edith Orozco, St. Philip's College

Dona Orr, Boise State University

Joanne Osgood, Chaffey College

Janice Owens, Kishwaukee College

Tatyana Pashnyak, Bainbridge College

John Partacz, College of DuPage

Tim Paul, Montana State University–Great Falls

Joseph Perez, South Texas College

Mike Peterson, Chemeketa Community College

Dr. Karen R. Petitto, West Virginia Wesleyan College

Terry Pierce, Onandaga Community College

Ashlee Pieris, Raritan Valley Community College

Jamie Pinchot, Thiel College

Michelle Poertner, Northwestern Michigan College

Betty Posta, University of Toledo

Deborah Powell, West Central Technical College

Mark Pranger, Rogers State University

Carolyn Rainey, Southeast Missouri State University

Linda Raskovich, Hibbing Community College

Leslie Ratliff, Griffin Technical College

Mar-Sue Ratzke, Rio Hondo Community College

Roxy Reissen, Southeastern Community College

Silvio Reyes, Technical Career Institutes

Patricia Rishavy, Anoka Technical College

Jean Robbins, Southeast Technical Institute

Carol Roberts, Eastern Maine Community College and University of Maine

Teresa Roberts, Wilson Technical Community College

Vicki Robertson, Southwest Tennessee Community College

Betty Rogge, Ohio State Agricultural Technical Institute

Lynne Rusley, Missouri Southern State University

Claude Russo, Brevard Community College

Ginger Sabine, Northwestern Technical College

Steven Sachs, Los Angeles Valley College

Joanne Salas, Olympic College

Lloyd Sandmann, Pima Community College–Desert Vista Campus

Beverly Santillo, Georgia Perimeter College

Theresa Savarese, San Diego City College

Sharolyn Sayers, Milwaukee Area Technical College

Judith Scheeren, Westmoreland County Community College

Adolph Scheiwe, Joliet Junior College

Marilyn Schmid, Asheville-Buncombe Technical Community College

Janet Sebesy, Cuyahoga Community College

Phyllis T. Shafer, Brookdale Community College

Ralph Shafer, Truckee Meadows Community College

Anne Marie Shanley, County College of Morris

Shelia Shelton, Surry Community College

Merilyn Shepherd, Danville Area Community College

Susan Sinele, Aims Community College

Beth Sindt, Hawkeye Community College

Andrew Smith, Marian College

Brenda Smith, Southwest Tennessee Community College

Lynne Smith, State University of New York–Delhi

Rob Smith, Katharine Gibbs School–Philadelphia

Tonya Smith, Arkansas State University–Mountain Home

Del Spencer – Trinity Valley Community College

Jeri Spinner, Idaho State University

Eric Stadnik, Santa Rosa Junior College

Karen Stanton, Los Medanos College

Meg Stoner, Santa Rosa Junior College

Beverly Stowers, Ivy Tech Community College of Indiana

Marcia Stranix, Yuba College

Kim Styles, Tri-County Technical College

Sylvia Summers, Tacoma Community College

Beverly Swann, Delaware Technical & Community College

Ann Taff, Tulsa Community College

Mike Theiss, University of Wisconsin–Marathon Campus

Romy Thiele, Cañada College

Sharron Thompson, Portland Community College

Ingrid Thompson-Sellers, Georgia Perimeter College

Barbara Tietsort, University of Cincinnati–Raymond Walters College

Janine Tiffany, Reading Area Community College

Denise Tillery, University of Nevada Las Vegas

Susan Trebelhorn, Normandale Community College

Noel Trout, Santiago Canyon College

Cheryl Turgeon, Asnuntuck Community College

Steve Turner, Ventura College

Sylvia Unwin, Bellevue Community College

Lilly Vigil, Colorado Mountain College

Sabrina Vincent, College of the Mainland

Mary Vitrano, Palm Beach Community College

Brad Vogt, Northeast Community College

Cozell Wagner, Southeastern Community College

Carolyn Walker, Tri-County Technical College

Sherry Walker, Tulsa Community College

Qi Wang, Tacoma Community College

Betty Wanielista, Valencia Community College

Marge Warber, Lanier Technical College–Forsyth Campus

Marjorie Webster, Bergen Community College

Linda Wenn, Central Community College

Mark Westlund, Olympic College

Carolyn Whited, Roane State Community College

Winona Whited, Richland College

Jerry Wilkerson, Scott Community College

Joel Willenbring, Fullerton College

Barbara Williams, WITC Superior

Charlotte Williams, Jones County Junior College

Bonnie Willy, Ivy Tech Community College of Indiana

Diane Wilson, J. Sargeant Reynolds Community College

James Wolfe, Metropolitan Community College

Marjory Wooten, Lanier Technical College

Mark Yanko, Hocking College

Alexis Yusov, Pace University

Naeem Zaman, San Joaquin Delta College

Kathleen Zimmerman, Des Moines Area Community College

We also thank Lutz Ziob, Jim DiIanni, Merrick Van Dongen, Jim LeValley, Bruce Curling, Joe Wilson, Rob Linsky, Jim Clark, Jim Palmeri, and Scott Serna at Microsoft for their encouragement and support in making the Microsoft Official Academic Course programs the finest instructional materials for mastering the newest Microsoft technologies for both students and instructors.

Brief Contents

Contents

Introduction to Networking Concepts

OBJECTIVE DOMAIN MATRIX

TECHNOLOGY SKILL	OBJECTIVE DOMAIN	OBJECTIVE DOMAIN NUMBER
Configuring IPv4 and IPv6 addressing	Configure IPv4 and IPv6 addressing	1.1

KEY TERMS

Automatic Private IP Addressing (APIPA)
CIDR notation
classful addressing
Classless Inter-Domain Routing (CIDR)
default gateway
DHCP relay agent above
dotted-decimal notation
Dynamic Host Configuration Protocol (DHCP)
fully qualified domain name (FQDN)

host
host address
HOSTS files
Internet Service Providers (ISPs)
IP address
IP version 4 (IPv4)
IP version 6 (IPv6)
name resolution
network address
network address translation (NAT)
network protocols

octets
routing
static IP address
subnet mask
subnets
subnetting
Transmission Control Protocol/Internet Protocol (TCP/IP)

Engulf & Devour (E&D) is a fast-growing, venture-funded new media company, specializing in acquiring smaller, technology-based media companies and integrating their operations to benefit from economies of scale. As a network-based, consumer market–driven enterprise, E&D must manage the assimilation of technical environments from acquired companies without disrupting network operations and still provide the efficiencies promised to the venture capitalists backing the corporation. Network accessibility must be maintained to provide service levels expected by consumers, while adding new systems, retiring obsolete systems, and redeploying existing systems. Network address management and name resolution tools are fundamental requirements for this situation. In this lesson you will learn the basic concepts of network address management and name resolution.

In this lesson we will begin our discussion of Windows Server 2008 with an overview of general TCP/IP networking concepts. The lesson begins with a discussion of the TCP/IP protocol, focusing on how IPv4 and IPv6 IP addresses are managed and configured. Once we have concluded our overview of TCP/IP addressing, we will take an introductory look at a number of networking services offered by Windows Server 2008, including the Domain Name System (DNS), the Dynamic Host Configuration Protocol (DHCP), the Routing & Remote Access (RRAS) service, and the Network Access Protection (NAP) service. This lesson is meant to provide an introduction only to DNS, DHCP, RRAS, and NAP; each of these will be discussed at length in later lessons in this text.

■ Understanding TCP/IP Addressing

↓
THE BOTTOM LINE

From as early as the 1950s, one of the main challenges in the field of computer science has been finding ways to allow different computers to communicate with one another. Before networking technologies became prevalent, files would be transferred manually from one computer to another using portable media such as a floppy disk. Over time, this process was replaced by various networking technologies that allowed computers to communicate using different types of network cables, which are the physical means of communicating, as well as *network protocols*, which provide the logical "language" for communication. Just like two human beings must speak the same language in order to communicate, two computers must be configured with the same network protocols in order to communicate and transfer information. Numerous networking protocols have gained varying levels of prevalence over the years, but the most common networking protocol in use today is ***Transmission Control Protocol/Internet Protocol (TCP/IP)***. Rather than a single network protocol, TCP/IP consists of a suite of different protocols that work in concert to allow computers to communicate on a TCP/IP network. TCP/IP networks are arranged in a hierarchical fashion that allows for a great deal of flexibility and scalability; by subdividing TCP/IP networks into smaller groupings called *subnets*, the administration of a TCP/IP network can be as centralized or as decentralized as the needs of a particular organization might dictate. (You can see this in action in the largest TCP/IP network in the world, which is "owned" and administered by hundreds and thousands of separate entities. The name of this TCP/IP network? The Internet.) This lesson introduces fundamental concepts related to TCP/IP networking, including the fundamentals of IP network addressing, and the distinction between IPv4 and IPv6. The lesson also introduces the basic concepts of various TCP/IP network services such as DHCP, DNS, and *routing*, the process of transferring data across a network from one LAN to another.

In order for any computer or *host*, a computer, printer, or other device configured with a network interface, to communicate on a TCP/IP network, it must be configured with a valid ***IP address***. This IP address, analogous to the postal address of a house or an office building, provides a way to identify a device that is connected to a TCP/IP network and provides a means for one computer to contact another in order to transmit information. Each IP address consists of two components:

- *network address*—This portion of the IP address is shared by all TCP/IP hosts on a particular network or subnet.
- *host address*—This comprises the portion of the IP address that is unique to a particular computer or host. The combination of the network address plus the host address creates the IP address as a whole, each of which must be unique across an entire TCP/IP network.

In addition to the IP address, each TCP/IP host must be configured with the following:

- *subnet mask*—Used to identify which network the TCP/IP host resides on by defining where the network address stops and the host address begins.
- *default gateway*—Allows a host to communicate with devices that reside on a remote network or location. (On the extremely rare occasion when you are configuring hosts that never need to communicate outside of their own subnet, a default gateway is not required; however, with the prevalence of Internet connectivity, you will almost always find a default gateway configured on TCP/IP-enabled devices.)

Introducing TCP/IP Addressing

The TCP/IP protocol suite has undergone several revisions since it was first developed in the 1960s. The version of TCP/IP that is most commonly used on modern networks is *IP version 4(IPv4)*. *IP version 6 (IPv6)* is a new TCP/IP implementation that is increasing in prevalence, as it addresses a number of shortcomings that have appeared in IPv4 over time. IPv4 was the first implementation of the Internet Protocol (IP) to be widely deployed, predating the public Internet. It uses 32 bits (four bytes, or *octets*) for addressing, thus providing a mathematical limit of 2^{32} possible addresses. Some of the possible addresses are reserved (for example, for private networks or multicast addresses), so that the maximum number of possible network addresses is somewhat less than the theoretical maximum. IPv4 addresses are commonly represented using what is called *dotted-decimal notation*, in which the decimal value of each byte is shown, using periods to separate the bytes; for example, 192.1.120.84 or 192.5.18.102 would be IPv4 addresses in dotted-decimal notation.

When IPv4 was first introduced, only the first octet was used for the network number and the remaining three octets were used for the host number. This limited the number of possible networks to a maximum of 254, which was quickly seen to be inadequate. The next revision defined what is termed *classful addressing*, in which the field for the network number was a different length for different classes of network, and the remaining bits were used for the host number, so each network class had a different maximum number of nodes. As shown in Table 1-1, the first one to four bits identified the network class, and the remaining bits comprised the network and host address fields. Class A networks had the most significant bit as "0" and used the remainder of the first octet for the network number. Thus there were 126 Class A networks, with a maximum of 16,777,214 hosts in each. Note that the number of valid networks and hosts available is always $2^N - 2$ (where N is the number of bits used, and the 2 adjusts for the special function of the first and last address in each network). Class B networks had the two most significant bits as "10," with the remainder of the first two octets, or fourteen bits, representing the network number. Thus there were 16,384 Class B networks, with a maximum of 65,534 hosts in each. Class C networks had the three most significant bits as "110," with the remainder of the first three octets as the network number and the last octet as the host number. Thus there were 2,097,152 Class C networks, each with a maximum of 254 host addresses. Network addresses with the four most significant bits "1110" (Class D, multicast) and "1111" (Class E, reserved) were also defined.

Table 1-1

IP Network Classes

Network Class	Leading Bits	Bits for Network Number	Number of Networks	Bits for Host Number	Maximum Hosts
Class A	0	7	126	24	16,777,214
Class B	10	14	16,384	16	65,534
Class C	110	21	2,097,152	8	254
Class D (multicast)	1110				
Class E (reserved)	1111				

Using this classful addressing scheme created a few large networks with many possible host addresses, and a much larger number of small networks with fewer possible host addresses, so it was considerably more flexible. However, there were still problems and limitations in this design. Some networks required more host addresses than their network class allowed, and other networks had many more host addresses than they used.

To overcome these issues and to improve flexibility for public **Internet Service Providers (ISPs)** to allocate many small networks to their customers, **Classless Inter-Domain Routing (CIDR)** evolved. CIDR creates a hierarchical addressing structure by breaking the network address space into CIDR blocks, which are identified by the leading bit string, similar to the classful addressing just described. However, the length of the bit string identifying a CIDR block is specified as part of the block name, using **CIDR notation**. CIDR notation describes a network by specifying the base address and the number of bits used for the network portion; i.e., 10.0.0.0/8 would describe a network using 24 bits for host numbering and thus having a maximum of $2^{24} - 2$ possible host addresses. The CIDR notation can be viewed as representing a bitmask dividing the routing (network) information and a block of local addresses. The classful networking address structure can also be described using CIDR notation, as shown in Table 1-2.

Table 1-2

CIDR Representation of Classful Addresses

NETWORK CLASS	STARTING ADDRESS	ENDING ADDRESS	CIDR BLOCK	BITMASK
Class A	0.0.0.0	127.255.255.255	/8	255.0.0.0
Class B	128.0.0.0	191.255.255.255	/16	255.255.0.0
Class C	192.0.0.0	223.255.255.255	/24	255.255.255.0
Class D (multicast)	224.0.0.0	239.255.255.255	/4	
Class E (reserved)	240.0.0.0	255.255.255.255	/4	

This hierarchical structure can be even further divided by **subnetting**. Subnetting refers to the logical partitioning of an organization's network address range into smaller blocks, by using a subnet mask to further distinguish the contents of the network address as a subnet number and a subnet address block. CIDR can be viewed as a method of subnetting the entire public IP address space, essentially carving it up into blocks that can be managed by service providers. A subnet mask is analogous to defining CIDR blocks within internal networks, allowing ISPs to delegate address management within the blocks assigned to their customers. Thus the CIDR block number contains information required for external routing, and the subnet mask distinguishes information required for routing internally from the host numbers (or hierarchical subnet addresses) contained within the subnet.

A big advantage of subnetting is that systems within a subnet need not be burdened with information about external network addressing. Systems within the same subnet share the same network address, so they can communicate directly without additional information about the external network. A default gateway is then used to route traffic for addresses outside the local subnet. Only the gateway requires any information about external network addressing.

For convenience, several network address blocks were reserved for private networks, and they were defined to be non-routable outside of the private network. Hosts using private network addresses can communicate with public networks only by using **network address translation (NAT)**, which enables routing by mapping their private network address to a different, routable network address. The private IPv4 network address ranges are shown in Table 1-3.

Table 1-3

Private Network Address Ranges

ADDRESS RANGE	DESCRIPTION	MAXIMUM ADDRESSES	CLASSFUL DESCRIPTION	CIDR DESCRIPTION
10.0.0.0 – 10.255.255.255	24-bit block	16,777,216	Single Class A network	10.0.0.0/8
172.16.0.0 – 172.31.255.255	20-bit block	1,048,576	16 contiguous Class B networks	172.16.0.0/12
169.254.0.0 – 169.254.255.255	16-bit block	65,536	256 contiguous Class C networks	169.254.0.0/16
192.168.0.0 – 192.168.255.255	16-bit block	65,536	256 contiguous Class C networks	192.168.0.0/16

Introducing IP version 6 (IPv6)

With the popularization of the public Internet, the limitations of the address space, that is, the list of usable TCP/IP addresses, provided by IPv4 became a concern. When IPv4 reached prevalence in the 1960s, no one foresaw the Internet explosion of the 1990s that would threaten to exhaust even the 4-billion-plus IP addresses available through IPv4. While the use of private IP networks and NAT have alleviated the problem somewhat, a long-term solution is still required. To this end, *IPv6*, the next generation of the TCP/IP protocol, was developed to provide a significantly larger address space for current and future implementations of TCP/IP networks.

X REF

IPSec is a suite of protocols for establishing cryptographic keys and using them to secure IP communications, which we will discuss at length later in this text.

IPv6 uses 128 bits, or 16 bytes, for addressing, thus providing 2^{128} (about 340 billion) unique addresses. To put this in perspective, the IPv6 address space would allow each human being on the planet Earth to possess multiple IPv6 IP addresses that were assigned only to them, without ever being re-used.

IPv6 address notation is noticeably different from the dotted-decimal of IPv4, using eight groups of four hexadecimal digits, separated by colons. IPv6 includes a few other enhancements for performance and security. Notably, IP security through the use of IPSec is an integral part of IPv6, whereas it was an optional feature under IPv4.

Unlike IPv4 addresses, which are 32 bits in length and expressed in dotted-decimal notation, IPv6 addresses are 128 bits in length and expressed in hexadecimal notation. For example, `192.168.1.101` is an example of an IPv4 IP address, while `2001:0db8:85a3:08d3:13 19:8a2e:0370:7334` is an example of an IPv6 IP address. If an IPv6 address contains a series of sequential zeroes, the address can be shortened to use a single zero in each group, or else the entire grouping can be represented using a double colon (`::`). So the following three strings all represent the same IPv6 address:

TAKE NOTE*

The loopback address in IPv4 is written as `127.0.0.1`; in IPv6 it is written as `::1`.

- `2001:0000:0000:0000:0000:0000:0000:7334`
- `2001:0:0:0:0:0:0:7334`
- `2001::7334`

IPv6 addresses have retained from IPv4 the delineation between host address and network address, and IPv6 networks can be expressed using CIDR notation such as `2001:0db8:1234::/48` to represent the `2001:0db8:1234` network configured with a 48-bit subnet mask.

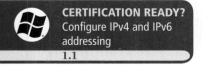

CERTIFICATION READY?
Configure IPv4 and IPv6 addressing
1.1

IPv6 has been supported in the Windows operating systems since Windows Server 2003; however, Windows Vista and Windows Server 2008 are the first Microsoft operating systems to have IPv6 support turned on right out of the box. IPv6 can be managed using the Network and Sharing Center graphical user interface, or using the netsh command-line utility.

■ Introducing the Domain Name System (DNS)

THE BOTTOM LINE

For network devices, such as computers and printers, to communicate on the Internet or within your organization's TCP/IP network, they must be able to locate one another. This ability is provided by the IP address, as we discussed in the previous section. But it is cumbersome to use IP addresses as the only means of identifying systems. A more common practice is to use human-readable names as a more convenient way for humans to refer to systems. Thus, in order for Computer A to communicate with Computer B using TCP/IP, Computer A must obtain the IP address of Computer B. It is also convenient to be able to refer to a network, or part of a network, by its name instead of its address range.

The Domain Name System (DNS) provides the mechanism for associating meaningful host names with network addresses. Because DNS plays such a key role in Microsoft Windows Server 2008 and the public Internet, it is critical that you have a strong grasp of its concepts, processes, and methods of configuration. Without DNS, your network will most likely not function—clients won't be able to resolve names to Internet Protocol (IP) addresses. In addition, Active Directory clients use DNS to locate domain controllers; therefore, it is important that you understand key DNS concepts and how to properly configure DNS for your network.

The process of obtaining an IP address for a computer name (for example, "ComputerA") is called **name resolution**. Originally, before the evolution of what we now know as the Internet, name resolution was handled by text files called **HOSTS files**. The text file listed each name of the host and its corresponding IP address within the HOSTS file. Whenever a new host was added to the network, the HOSTS file was updated with the host name and IP address. Periodically, all systems would download and then use the updated HOSTS file. Because the HOSTS file was flat, rather than hierarchical, every host name using this system had to be unique. There was no method for creating namespaces such as DNS domains like *www.adatum.com*.

Another problem with HOSTS files was an inability to distribute the workload that resulted from parsing this file across multiple computers. Every HOSTS file listed every available host, which meant that every computer that parsed the HOSTS file did all of the work to resolve client names into IP addresses. Clearly, this was inefficient, and a better name resolution system had to be devised.

Using DNS for Name Resolution

DNS was developed to provide a method of associating such names with network addresses. DNS provides mechanisms for communicating names and network addresses publicly, so that system names can be resolved to network addresses from anywhere that the address would be reachable. Because DNS is designed as a distributed database with a hierarchical structure, it can serve as the foundation for host name resolution in a TCP/IP network of any size, including the Internet. The distributed nature of DNS enables the name resolution workload to be shared among many computers. Today, most internetworking software, such as e-mail programs and Web browsers, use DNS for name resolution. Also, because of the hierarchical design of DNS, it provides a means of naming networks as well as end devices.

In a Windows Server 2008 network, the primary means of identifying network devices and network services is through the use of DNS. Although DNS is most commonly associated with the Internet, private networks also use DNS because of the following benefits:

• Scalability—Because DNS is capable of distributing workload across several databases or computers, it can scale to handle any level of name resolution required.

The DNS namespace is introduced in the following section; the other components are discussed in Lesson 4, Configuring and Managing the DNS Server Role.

- Transparency—Host names remain constant even when associated IP addresses change, which makes locating network resources much easier.
- Ease of use—Users access computers using easy-to-remember names such as www. microsoft.com rather than a numerical IP address, such as 192.168.1.100.
- Simplicity—Users need to learn only one naming convention to find resources on either the Internet or an intranet.

To understand the importance of DNS and how it functions within a Windows Server 2008 networking environment, you must understand the following components of DNS:

- DNS namespace
- DNS zones
- Types of DNS name servers
- DNS resource records

The DNS namespace is a hierarchical, tree-structured namespace, starting at an unnamed root used for all DNS operations. In the DNS namespace, each node and leaf object in the domain namespace tree represents a named domain. Each domain can have additional child domains. Figure 1-1 illustrates the structure of an Internet domain namespace.

Figure 1-1

Internet DNS namespace

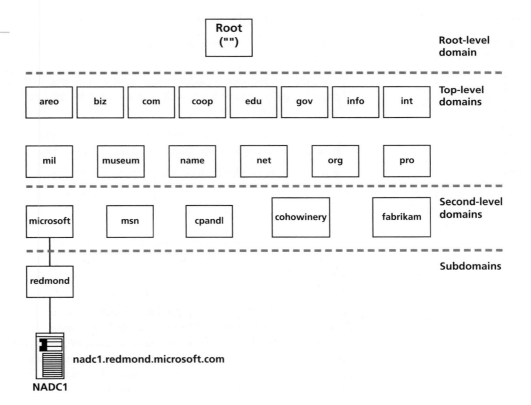

The DNS namespace has a hierarchical structure, and each DNS domain name is unique. In Figure 1-1, at the top of the Internet DNS namespace is the root domain. The root domain is represented by "." (a period). Under the DNS root domain, the top-level domains, or first-level domains, are organizational types such as .org, .com, and .edu, or country codes such as .uk (United Kingdom), .de (Germany), and .it (Italy). The Internet Assigned Numbers Authority (IANA) assigns top-level domains. Table 1-4 lists several top-level domain names and their uses.

Table 1-4

Generic Top-Level Domain Names

Domain Name	Use
.aero	Exclusively reserved for the aviation community
.biz	A top-level domain that is aimed at large and small companies around the world
.com	Commercial organizations, such as microsoft.com for the Microsoft Corporation
.coop	A top-level domain for cooperatives
.edu	Educational institutions, now mainly four-year colleges and universities, such as wustl.edu for Washington University in St. Louis
.gov	Agencies of the U.S. federal government, such as fbi.gov for the U.S. Federal Bureau of Investigation
.info	An unrestricted domain aimed at providing information for worldwide consumption
.int	Organizations established by international treaties, such as nato.int for NATO
.mil	U.S. military, such as af.mil for the U.S. Air Force
.museum	A domain restricted to museums and related organizations and individuals
.name	A global domain for use by individuals that possibly develops into a global digital identity for users
.net	Computers of network providers, organizations dedicated to the Internet, Internet service providers (ISPs), and so forth, such as internic.net for the Internet Network Information Center (InterNIC)
.org	A top-level domain for groups that do not fit anywhere else, such as nongovernmental or nonprofit organizations (for example, w3.org, which is the World Wide Web Consortium)
.pro	A top-level domain for professionals, such as doctors, lawyers, and accountants

DNS uses a ***fully qualified domain name (FQDN)*** to map a host name to an IP address. The FQDN describes the exact relationship between a host and its DNS domain. For example, *computer1.sales.adatum.com* represents a host name, *computer1*, in the *sales* domain, in the *adatum* second-level domain, and in the *.com* top-level domain, which is under the "." root domain.

Second-level DNS domains are registered to individuals or organizations, such as *microsoft.com*, the Microsoft Corporation in the corporate (.com) domain; or *wustl.edu*, which is Washington University of St. Louis in the education (.edu) domain; or *gov.au*, the domain for the Australian government. Second-level DNS domains can have many subdomains, and any domain can have hosts. A host is a specific computer or other network device within a domain, such as *computer1* in the *sales* subdomain of the *microsoft.com* domain.

One benefit of the hierarchical structure of DNS is that it is possible to have two hosts with the same host names that are in different locations in the hierarchy. For example, two hosts named computer1—*computer1.sales.adatum.com* and *computer1.cpandl.microsoft.com*—can both exist without conflict because they are in different locations in the namespace hierarchy.

As previously noted, another benefit of the DNS hierarchical structure is that workload for name resolution is distributed across many different resources, through the use of DNS caching, DNS zones, and delegation of authority through the use of appropriate resource records. DNS zones, name servers, and resource records are discussed in more detail later in this book. For now, it is sufficient to understand that DNS is the way that IP addresses can be given a unique name.

■ Introducing the Dynamic Host Configuration Protocol (DHCP)

THE BOTTOM LINE

It is very important to understand that address assignments are not arbitrary. The address specifies both the system identification and also its location within the network. Thus, each IP address must be both valid and unique within the host's entire internetwork. This requirement presents a challenge for network administrators. The process of assigning, changing, retiring, and reassigning addresses must be carefully monitored to ensure that each host has a unique IP address. Private network address ranges help, but addresses within private networks must still be unique within that network. The ***Dynamic Host Configuration Protocol (DHCP)*** provides a mechanism for conveniently assigning network addresses and other network configuration parameters to a system upon request, usually when it is first bootstrapped or attached to the network. This greatly simplifies network management.

When administering TCP/IP hosts, you can assign **static IP addresses**, which must be configured and maintained manually. This can become a daunting, tedious task as the number of systems grows to larger numbers. Organizations with significant numbers of workstations requiring IP address configurations would have great difficulty managing IP addressing manually. Dynamic Host Configuration Protocol (DHCP) simplifies the problem by automating the assigning, tracking, and reassigning of IP addresses.

DHCP allows administrators to configure TCP/IP by automatically assigning unique IP addresses while preventing duplicate address assignment and also to provide other important settings such as the default gateway, subnet mask, DNS, etc. Ideally, this would be accomplished without having to manually list every device on the network. DHCP is based heavily on the Bootstrap Protocol (BOOTP), a protocol still in use today that provides IP configuration information to diskless workstations that cannot store information locally and need to store their IP information in volatile memory upon each system boot. DHCP may be based on BOOTP, but it extends its predecessor in several ways. Rather than push preconfigured parameters to expected clients, DHCP can dynamically allocate an IP address from a pool of addresses and then reclaim it when it is no longer needed. Because this process is dynamic, no duplicate addresses are assigned by a properly configured DHCP server and administrators can move computers between subnets without manually configuring them. In addition, a large number of standard configuration and platform-specific parameters can be specified and dynamically delivered to the client. Thus, DHCP provides important functions beyond simply bootstrapping diskless workstations, and it is often used to automatically configure networking after systems are booted.

Understanding DHCP

DHCP is an open, industry-standard protocol that reduces the complexity of administering networks based on TCP/IP. It provides a mechanism for automatically assigning IP addresses and reusing them when they are no longer needed by the system to which they were assigned. It also provides mechanisms for providing associated configuration information when systems are first assigned IP addresses. DHCP is defined by the Internet Engineering Task Force (IETF) Requests for Comments (RFCs) 2131 and 2132.

➕ MORE INFORMATION

DHCP is an IETF standard and is defined in RFCs 2131 and 2132, which can be looked up at www.rfc-editor.org/rfcsearch.html. Requests For Comments (usually referred to in abbreviated form as RFC) is the process by which the IETF arrives at a consensus standard for fundamental internet technologies. New RFC numbers are assigned sequentially, and are conventionally used to identify the resulting standard.

IP addressing is complex, in part because each host connected to a TCP/IP network must be assigned at least one unique IP address and subnet mask in order to communicate on the network. Additionally, most hosts will require additional information, such as the IP addresses of the default gateway and the DNS servers. DHCP frees system administrators from manually configuring each host on the network. The larger the network, the greater the benefit of using DHCP. Without dynamic address assignment, each host has to be configured manually and IP addresses must be carefully managed to avoid duplication or misconfiguration.

Managing IP addresses and host options is much easier when configuration information can be managed from a single location rather than coordinating information across many locations. DHCP can automatically configure a host while it is booting on a TCP/IP network, as well as change settings while the host is connected to the network. All of this is accomplished using settings and information from a central DHCP database. Because settings and information are stored centrally, you can quickly and easily add or change a client setting (for example, the IP address of an alternate DNS server) for all clients on your network from a single location. Without a centralized database of configuration information, it is difficult to maintain a current view of the host settings or to change them.

All Microsoft Windows clients automatically install the DHCP Client service as part of TCP/IP, including Microsoft Windows Vista, Microsoft Windows XP, Microsoft Windows 2000, Microsoft Windows NT 4, Microsoft Windows Millennium Edition (Windows Me), and Microsoft Windows 98.

In brief, DHCP provides five key benefits to those managing and maintaining a TCP/IP network:

- Centralized administration of IP configuration—DHCP IP configuration information can be stored in one location, enabling the administrator to centrally manage it. A DHCP server tracks all leased and reserved IP addresses and lists them in the DHCP console. You can use the DHCP console to determine the IP addresses of all DHCP-enabled devices on your network. Without DHCP, not only would you need to manually assign addresses, but you would also be required to devise a method of tracking and updating them.

- Dynamic host configuration—DHCP automates the host configuration process for key configuration parameters. This eliminates the need to manually configure individual hosts when TCP/IP is first deployed or when IP infrastructure changes are required.

- Seamless IP host configuration—The use of DHCP ensures that DHCP clients get accurate and timely IP configuration parameters, such as the IP address, subnet mask, default gateway, IP address of the DNS server, and so on, without user intervention. Because the configuration is automatic, troubleshooting of misconfigurations, such as mistyped numbers, is largely eliminated.

- Scalability—DHCP scales from small to large networks. DHCP can service networks with ten clients as well as networks with thousands of clients. For very small, isolated networks, Automatic Private IP Addressing (APIPA) can be used, which is a component of Windows networking that automatically determines the client IP configuration without access to an external DHCP server.

- Flexibility—Using DHCP gives the administrator increased flexibility, allowing the administrator to more easily change IP configurations when the infrastructure changes.

X REF

APIPA is defined and discussed in more detail later in this lesson.

USING THE DHCP RELAY AGENT

DHCP relies heavily on broadcast messages. Broadcast messages are generally limited to the subnet in which they originate and are not forwarded to other subnets. This poses a problem if a client is located on a different subnet from the DHCP server. A DHCP relay agent can solve this problem.

A ***DHCP relay agent*** is either a host or an IP router that listens for DHCP (and BOOTP) client messages being broadcast on a subnet and then forwards those DHCP messages to a DHCP server on a remote subnet. The DHCP server sends DHCP response messages back to the relay agent, which then broadcasts them onto the local subnet for the DHCP client. Using DHCP relay agents eliminates the need to have a DHCP server on every subnet.

To support and use the DHCP service across multiple subnets, routers connecting each subnet should comply with the DHCP/BOOTP relay agent capabilities described in RFC 1542. To comply with RFC 1542 and provide relay agent support, each router must be able to recognize BOOTP and DHCP protocol messages and relay them appropriately. Because routers typically interpret DHCP messages as BOOTP messages, a router with only BOOTP relay agent capability relays DHCP packets and any BOOTP packets sent on the network.

The DHCP relay agent is configured with the address of a DHCP server. The DHCP relay agent listens for DHCPDISCOVER, DHCPREQUEST, and DHCPINFORM messages that are broadcast from the client. The DHCP relay agent then waits a previously configured amount of time and, if no response is detected, sends a unicast message to the configured DHCP server. The server then acts on the message and sends the reply back to the DHCP relay agent. The relay agent then broadcasts the message on the local subnet, allowing the DHCP client to receive it. This is depicted in Figure 1-2.

Figure 1-2

DHCP messages are forwarded by a DHCP relay agent

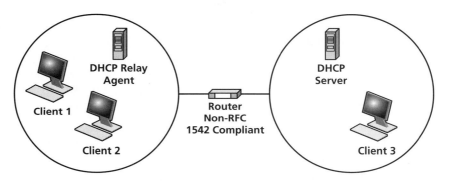

1. Client 1 Broadcasts a DHCPDISCOVER packet
2. Relay agent forwards DHCPDISCOVER packet to DHCP server
3. Server sends a DHCPOFFER packet to the DHCP relay agent
4. Relay agent broadcasts the DHCPOFFER packet
5. Client 1 broadcasts a DHCPREQUEST packet
6. Relay agent forwards the DHCPREQUEST packet to the DHCP server
7. Server broadcasts a DHCPACK packet which is picked up by the DHCP relay agent
8. Relay agent broadcasts the DHCPACK packet

CONFIGURING CLIENTS WITHOUT DHCP

Client systems need to obtain an IP address in order to join the network. DHCP is the usual solution, but it is possible that no DHCP server would be accessible (for example, a remote server could become inaccessible if the relay agent went down). As mentioned previously, clients can be configured automatically determine their IP configuration in cases where they cannot access an external DHCP server. This automatic configuration facility is called *Automatic Private IP Addressing (APIPA)*.

In most cases, DHCP clients find a server either on a local subnet or through a relay agent. To allow for the possibility that a DHCP server is unavailable, Windows Vista, Windows Server 2008, Windows Server 2003, Windows XP, Windows 2000, and Windows 98 provide Automatic Private IP Addressing (APIPA). APIPA is a facility of the Windows TCP/IP implementation that allows a computer to determine IP configuration information without a DHCP server or manual configuration.

APIPA avoids the problem of IP hosts being unable to communicate if for some reason the DHCP server is unavailable. Figure 1-3 illustrates different IP address assignment outcomes

Figure 1-3

How IP addresses are assigned using APIPA or an alternate configuration

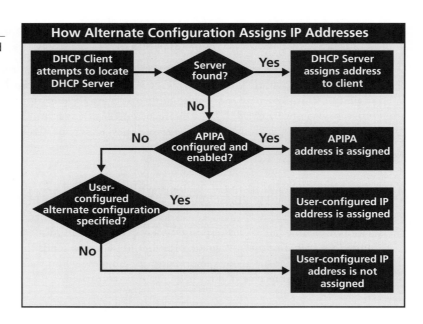

when a DHCP client attempts to find a DHCP server. In the case where a DHCP server is not found and APIPA is configured and enabled, an APIPA address is assigned. APIPA is useful for small workgroup networks where no DHCP server is implemented. Because autoconfiguration does not support a default gateway, it works only with a single subnet and is not appropriate for larger networks.

If the DHCP client is unable to locate a DHCP server and is not configured with an alternate configuration (as shown in Figure 1-4), the computer configures itself with an IP address randomly chosen from the Internet Assigned Numbers Authority (IANA)–reserved class B network 169.254.0.0 and with the subnet mask 255.255.0.0. The autoconfigured computer then tests to verify that the IP address it has chosen is not already in use by using a gratuitous ARP broadcast. If the chosen IP address is in use, the computer randomly selects another address. The computer makes up to ten attempts to find an available IP address.

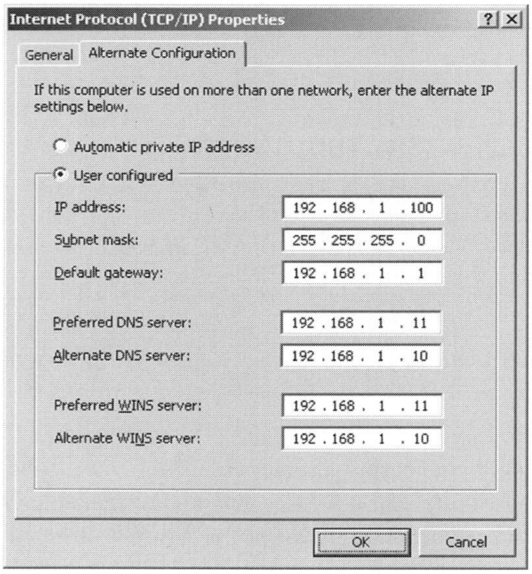

Figure 1-4

Alternate configuration properties page

Once the selected address has been verified as available, the client is configured to use that address. The DHCP client continues to check for a DHCP server in the background every five minutes, and if a DHCP server is found, the configuration offered by the DHCP server is used.

Windows Vista, Windows XP, Windows Server 2008, and Windows Server 2003 clients can be configured to use an alternate configuration, which the DHCP client uses if a DHCP server cannot be contacted. The alternate configuration includes an IP address, a subnet mask, a default gateway, DNS, and additional configuration information.

One purpose of the alternate configuration is as a solution for portable computers that move between a corporate, DHCP-enabled network and a home network where static IP addressing is used. For example, Janice has a portable computer she uses at work and at home. At work, her portable computer obtains IP address information using DHCP, but she does not use a DHCP server at home. Janice can use alternate configuration to hold her home IP address, subnet mask, default gateway, and DNS server information so that when she connects her portable computer to her home network, it is configured automatically.

If you use DHCP with an alternate configuration, and the DHCP client cannot locate a DHCP server, the alternate configuration is used to configure the network adapter. No additional discovery attempts are made except under the following conditions:

- The network adapter is disabled and then enabled again.
- Media (such as network cabling) is disconnected and then reconnected.
- The TCP/IP settings for the adapter are changed, and DHCP remains enabled after these changes.

If a DHCP server is found, the network adapter is assigned a valid DHCP IP address lease.

To display the Alternate Configuration tab shown in Figure 1-4, the network adapter must be configured to obtain an IP address automatically. To view the Alternate Configuration tab, follow these steps:

1. Open the Control Panel, and double-click Network and Internet.
2. Double-click Network and Sharing Center.
3. In the Network Connections window, right-click Local Area Connection, and then click Properties.
4. In the Local Area Connection Properties page, click Internet Protocol (TCP/IP), and then click Properties.
5. In the Alternate Configuration tab, specify your IP address settings.

■ Using the Routing and Remote Access Service (RRAS)

THE BOTTOM LINE

Routing, or the process of transferring data across a network from one LAN to another, provides the basis for TCP/IP communications on the Internet and nearly all other corporate networks. Routing plays a key role in every organization that is connected to the Internet or that has more than one network segment. Routing can be a complex process, but if you understand some key concepts such as authentication, authorization, static routing, and policies, you can effectively configure, monitor, and troubleshoot routing and remote access for your organization.

As the name implies, the RRAS server role provides two key services for your network clients:

- Routing—By configuring two network interface cards (NICs) within a Windows Server 2008 server, the server can provide a means of transmitting data from one network to another.

TAKE NOTE*

For larger networks, the processing demands of network routing are typically handled by dedicated hardware-based routers. The routing service included with Windows Server 2008 is better suited for a smaller network or one with a small amount of network traffic that needs to pass between subnets.

The Routing and Remote Access server role is discussed further in Lesson 5.

• Remote Access—A Windows Server 2008 computer can act as a remote access server, which can allow remote network clients to access resources on a network as though they were physically connected to the LAN. The Windows Server 2008 remote access server can provide remote access using either dial-up connections via a modem, or else through a Virtual Private Network (VPN) connection over the Internet or another public network.

■ Introducing Network Access Protection (NAP)

THE BOTTOM LINE

One of the principal challenges in corporate networks is the ability to secure networks against unwarranted access. In addition to configuring perimeter firewalls, network administrators also need to protect the network against "inside threats," laptop computers that are physically brought inside the corporate network or that gain access to the company network through remote access technologies such as Virtual Private Networks (VPNs.) For network administrators, this creates a challenge of enforcing corporate security standards such as up-to-date anti-virus protection definitions and a consistent firewall configuration. To assist with this endeavor, Windows Server 2008 provides the Network Access Protection platform, which provides a policy enforcement mechanism to control access to a 2008 network.

Network Access Protection is discussed at length in Lesson 10.

Network Access Protection is a new feature in Windows Server 2008 that allows network administrators to specify one or more policies that define the conditions under which network access will or will not be permitted. For example, consider a user who brings his home laptop into the office, and this laptop does not have anti-virus software installed. By connecting this laptop to the corporate network, this user runs the risk of propagating a network virus or worm throughout the corporate network, because the perimeter firewall does not offer any protection against a computer that is located inside of the perimeter. If Network Access Protection is in place, this laptop can be placed into a "quarantine" area where it cannot cause harm to the remainder of the computers on the network.

SUMMARY SKILL MATRIX

IN THIS LESSON YOU LEARNED:

• Network protocols create a logical language that allows computers to communicate.

• The most commonly used network protocol on modern networks is the Transmission Control Protocol/Internet Protocol (TCP/IP) protocol suite.

• There are currently two implementations of TCP/IP: TCP/IP version 4, or IPv4, and TCP/IP version 6, or IPv6.

• Each host on a TCP/IP network needs to be configured with a unique IP address.

• TCP/IP networks use the Domain Name System (DNS) to map human-readable machine names to IP addresses and vice versa, such as mapping the *www.cpandl.com* host name to the 10.10.1.104 IP address.

• Network administrators can use the Dynamic Host Configuration Protocol (DHCP) to automatically assign IP addresses to multiple client computers.

• The Routing and Remote Access service provides the ability to use a Windows Server 2008 computer as a router, which passes network traffic from one TCP/IP network to another, as well as remote access capabilities using either dial-up or VPN technology.

• To allow administrators to enforce network security policies such as mandatory anti-virus or firewall configurations, Windows Server 2008 has introduced the Network Access Protection (NAP) enforcement platform.

• Network addressing is fundamental to successful communication between systems.

- DNS provides name resolution to allow meaningful names to be used to refer to network addresses.

- DHCP is a simple, standard protocol that makes TCP/IP network configuration much easier for the administrator by dynamically assigning IP addresses and providing additional configuration information to DHCP clients automatically.

- Clients may be configured to use APIPA or an alternate static IP address configuration if DHCP is unavailable.

■ Knowledge Assessment

Fill in the Blank

Complete the following sentences by writing the correct word or words in the blanks provided.

1. The most widely used IP addressing scheme is _____.

2. The most recent and largest address space IP addressing scheme is _____.

3. To distribute IP addresses automatically, a network administrator would configure the _____ service.

4. The first attempt at breaking up IP address space used _____ to provide address ranges of differing sizes.

5. Prior to the introduction of the Domain Name System, computers used _____ to map human-readable names to IP addresses.

6. A(n) _____ is used to separate the host address portion of an IP address from the network address.

7. The subnet mask within the TCP/IP configuration is used to distinguish the _____ from the host address.

8. In dotted-decimal notation, each IPv4 address is broken up into four _____.

9. Server computers and other systems that need to be accessed reliably by network clients should be configured with a(n) _____.

10. The method of breaking up IP address space into address ranges of flexible size is called _____.

Multiple Choice

Circle the correct choice.

1. What must each host on a TCP/IP network be configured with in order to communicate with other hosts?
   a. Preferred DNS server
   b. Preferred WINS server
   c. IP address
   d. Default gateway

2. What is the process of transmitting TCP/IP traffic from one IP subnet to another?
   a. Subnetting
   b. Routing
   c. Transmitting
   d. Broadcasting

3. An IP network that is formatted such as 192.168.1.0/24 is referred to as what type of notation?
   a. CIDR notation
   b. NAT notation
   c. IPv4 notation
   d. IPv6 notation

4. What is the default network protocol of the Internet and most modern corporate networks?
   a. IPX/SPX
   b. NetBEUI
   c. AppleTalk
   d. TCP/IP

5. What was used by TCP/IP networks to perform name resolution prior to the introduction of the Domain Name System (DNS)?
   a. HOSTS files
   b. HOST files
   c. LM files
   d. WINS files

6. What is the process of dividing a large TCP/IP address space into multiple smaller networks called?
   a. Routing
   b. NATting
   c. Subnetting
   d. Supernetting

7. What technology is used by private network ranges that has extended the useful life of IPv4 addressing and slowed the adoption rate of IPv6?
   a. Subnetting
   b. NAT
   c. Routing
   d. CIDR

8. Which TCP/IP configuration item allows client computers to communicate with other computers that are located on remote networks?
   a. Default gateway
   b. Router
   c. Hub
   d. Switch

9. On a TCP/IP network that uses the Domain Name System (DNS) for name resolution, what unique configuration item must each TCP/IP host possess?
   a. HOSTS file
   b. LMHOSTS file
   c. Fully-qualified domain name
   d. UNC name

10. In what format are IPv4 IP addresses most commonly written?
    a. Hexadecimal
    b. Binary
    c. Dotted-decimal
    d. Dotted-hexadecimal

■ Case Scenarios

Scenario 1-1: Designing Windows Server 2008 Network Services

Lucerne Publishing is a publishing company based in New York City, New York, which produces science textbooks for colleges and medical schools. In recent months, Lucerne Publishing has been planning a move towards a "virtual office," where over 300 writers, editors, and graphics personnel will transition to working out of their homes instead of working in traditional "brick-and-mortar" offices. The main office in New York City will continue to house roughly 200 employees working in centralized functions such as Payroll, Accounting, and Human Resources. Each of these departments maintains a number of file and application servers that house sensitive personal and financial data, all of which require extensive security for their sensitive data. As the network administrator for Lucerne Publishing, you are tasked with configuring remote access for these new virtual office employees, while still maintaining the overall security of the Lucerne Publishing network.

Based on this information, answer the following questions:

1. In order to support access for remote employees, you have been authorized to upgrade Internet access at the Lucerne Publishing corporate office. You expect a significant increase in both inbound and outbound traffic as Lucerne Publishing makes the transition to a virtual office environment. You need to choose a method for routing traffic to and from the Internet and the corporate offices. Should you configure a Windows Server 2008 computer to act as your Internet router, or select another option?

2. What types of access can you support for virtual office staff members to access corporate resources, and how will you provide this access?

3. Lucerne Publishing's Chief Security Officer has expressed a concern over the security risks posed by allowing access to internal networks by virtual office computers, given that these computers will not be closely monitored by corporate IT staff. What can you do to minimize the risks to Lucerne Publishing's internal resources?

Installing Microsoft Windows Server 2008

KEY TERMS

basic disks
boot volume
dynamic disks
GPT (GUID Partition Table)
Initial Configuration Tasks
Internet Connection Sharing (ICS)
Key Management Service (KMS)
MBR (Master Boot Record)
mirrored volume

mount point
Multiple Activation Key (MAK)
NetBIOS
Network and Sharing Center
network discovery
network location
RAID-5 volume
repair mode
Server Core
simple volume
spanned volume

striped volume
system volume
volume
Volume Activation
Volume Activation Management Tool (VAMT)
Windows Firewall
Windows Server Backup
WINS Server
Wireless Networking

Engulf & Devour (E&D) is preparing to deploy new Windows Server 2008 computers to upgrade the network infrastructure of several small companies they have recently acquired. In order to facilitate this process, E&D's IT department must determine the appropriate server installation option for each server as well as manage the process of licensing and activating the new operating system licenses.

In this lesson, we will describe the activities associated with installing the Microsoft Windows Server 2008 operating system. We will begin by describing the steps involved in installing the Windows Server 2008 software. Next we will take a look at Server Manager, a new administrative console that provides a "one-stop shop" for server administration tasks in Windows Server 2008. We will then examine configuring hard disk storage options in Windows Server 2008, as well as the new Server Core installation option in Windows Server 2008. Finally, we will describe the new process of Windows Activation, which is used to manage software licensing and activation within an enterprise environment.

■ Installing the Software

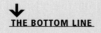
THE BOTTOM LINE

Installing the Microsoft Windows Server 2008 operating system software is the cornerstone to building a working network environment. Any unresolved errors or other issues during the installation process can cause significant problems and headaches both immediately and in the future. A good grasp of the fundamentals is important for a smooth installation.

Installation of Windows Server 2008 software can produce a system configuration containing only the specific facilities required for a specific role, called *Server Core,* or a full server installation containing all of the available Windows Server 2008 functionality.

When installing Windows Server 2008, you have the option of installing onto fresh media that has never been used before or onto previously used media containing existing files. If

Windows Server 2008 is installed onto a disk partition containing a previous version of Windows, the files will be preserved but the software may or may not be usable.

Software installation is an essential step in preparing a new hardware system for use. To accomplish this, the Windows Server 2008 software distribution media includes a completely self-contained installation procedure that will run in a standalone manner without requiring any additional resources. The standalone installation software also provides a *repair mode,* which provides a minimal execution environment to allow running software that may be required or useful in attempting to recover a damaged Windows system.

When Windows Server 2008 is installed onto previously used media, the contents may be preserved or the media may be reinitialized and treated as though it is new, which will result in the previous contents being irretrievably destroyed. If the contents of previously used media are preserved, some of the initialization to prepare new hardware for use is not required, and some additional provisions to protect and preserve existing file contents are required.

When Windows Server 2008 software is installed onto previously unused hardware (or previously used hardware that is being completely reinitialized), several actions must be taken to initialize the hardware and prepare it for use. At the lowest level, a partition structure must be created on the physical hard drive to provide a logical addressing structure that organizes it into usable storage areas, and then a file volume structure must be created to manage the contents of a partition to allow storing files within it.

Traditionally, a disk could contain up to four primary partitions, one of which could be designated as an extended partition containing logical partitions (or logical drives). Originally the partition structure was associated with a single physical disk with a maximum of four logical partitions in the extended partition, but most modern systems have extended these limitations. Although some low-level disk utilities do allow modifying existing partition parameters, this entails a high risk of data loss, so in practice it is safest to assume that all disk partitions should be backed up before attempting to perform any type of modification such as deleting or extending them. Deleting a partition destroys the contents, so any files or data stored in it will be lost. Partitions provide a convenient mechanism for isolating different file systems. For example, legacy FAT and modern NTFS file systems can both be provided on a single disk, or one partition can be used to contain data files with another containing system software.

Windows Server 2008 software will be installed into a single partition designated during the installation process. Because the software is installed into a single partition, the specified minimum storage requirements actually apply to the space within the partition being used, not the total drive size. The installation process will allow installation to any hard drive attached to the system. It will also allow deleting previously existing partitions and creating new ones on any hard drive.

 INSTALL WINDOWS SERVER 2008

GET READY. This exercise assumes that you have configured a physical computer (or a virtual guest using virtualization software such as Microsoft Virtual Server 2005 R2 or Microsoft Virtual PC) with a single hard drive configured as a single partition.

1. Insert a bootable Windows Server 2008 media and power on the physical or virtual server.

2. You can see the opening installation screen in Figure 2-1. Here you are prompted to configure the following three items:
   - Language to install—for example, English or German
   - Time and currency format—for example, English (United States) or French (Switzerland)
   - Keyboard or input method—for example, US or United Kingdom

Figure 2-1

Beginning the Windows Server 2008 installation

3. Click **Next**, followed by **Install Now**.

4. Next you will see the screen shown in Figure 2-2, where you will be prompted to enter the Windows product key. Enter a legitimate Windows product key and click **Next**.

Figure 2-2

Entering the Windows product key

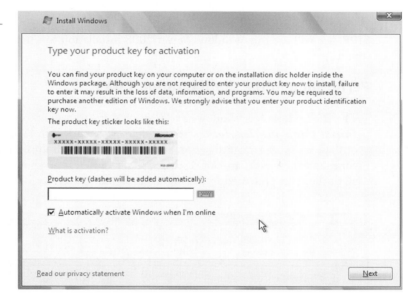

5. Next you will be prompted either to install the full version of Windows Server 2008 or perform a Server Core installation. For now, select a **full install**; we'll discuss Server Core in a later section. Click **Next** to continue.

6. On the following screen, you'll be prompted to accept the Windows Server 2008 license terms. Read the license terms and then place a check mark next to **I accept the license terms**. Click **Next** to continue the installation.

7. Next you'll see the screen shown in Figure 2-3, which will prompt you to select between an upgrade installation or a clean install. Since we are installing Windows onto brand-new hardware, notice that the Upgrade option is grayed out and only the Custom option is available. Select the **Custom** installation option.

Figure 2-3

Selecting an installation
method

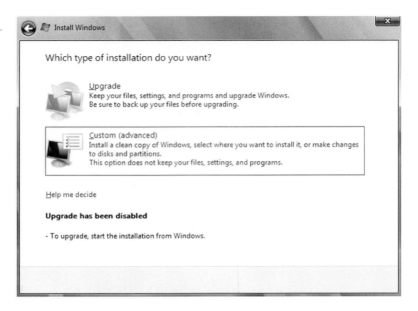

8. On the following screen, you'll be prompted to select the hard drive partition on which you wish to install Windows. Select the appropriate partition and click **Next**.

9. At this point the installation process will begin. The remainder of the installation will run largely automated until it completes.

10. To improve the security of a Windows Server 2008 installation, on final reboot you will be prompted to establish a complex password.

STOP. We will use this Windows Server 2008 installation for future exercises in this and other lessons.

Performing Initial Configuration Tasks

The freshly installed Windows Server 2008 software will automatically launch the *Initial Configuration Tasks* screen at startup, as shown in Figures 2-4 and 2-5. Many of these tasks are straightforward, such as setting the administrator password or the time zone, and these tasks are not discussed in detail here. You should, however, step through all of the tasks presented in the initial configuration screen for your system.

Figure 2-4

Viewing the Initial
Configuration Tasks screen

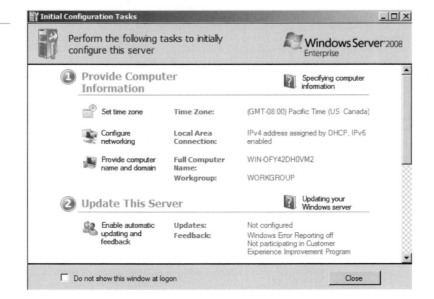

It is especially important to download and apply any updates that have been released since the installation media was created, as shown in the second section of the configuration tasks in Figure 2-5.

Figure 2-5

Viewing additional Initial Configuration Tasks

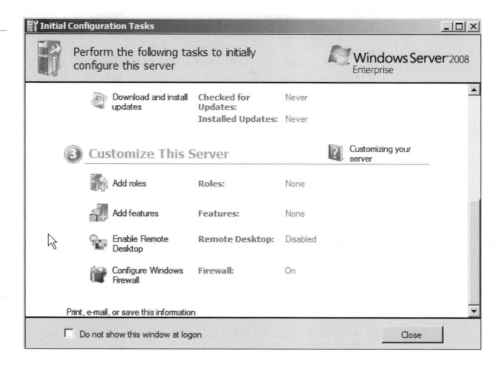

Configuring Basic Network Settings

To simplify the configuration process, Windows Server 2008 introduces the Initial Configuration Tasks screen, which will appear by default on each newly configured 2008 computer. As you've seen, this interface provides a single administrative point to configure common items such as the server clock, time zone, Windows Update settings, and basic network settings before moving on to more advanced configuration options. On any Windows Server 2008 computer that will participate on a corporate network, it is critical to configure network settings correctly to allow it to communicate with other hosts on local or remote networks.

X REF

For more information on TCP/IP addressing, refer to Lesson 1.

As discussed in Lesson 1, each host on a TCP/IP network should be configured with a number of mandatory and optional configuration items, including:

- IPv4 or IPv6 address
- Subnet mask
- Default gateway
- DNS/WINS servers

The option to configure networking allows you to view and set the networking parameters for your Windows Server 2008 system and the network it serves. This is where you set the IP address or specify the system is to be a DHCP client, and the DNS servers it will use. If this system will be a DHCP server, you should set a static IP address, because that will be required when you try to set up the DHCP server role. If the system is used on multiple networks, you can set an alternate configuration to be used when a DHCP server is unavailable (by using either Automatic Private IP Addressing, or providing a fixed IP address as a fallback option). To set these values, open the Properties screen for the connection you want to set, choose the item for TCP/IPv4, and click the Properties button. This allows you to set the IP addressing mechanism for the system, and when DHCP is used (*Obtain an IP address automatically* is selected), a tab is provided to allow the alternate configuration to be specified as a fallback option.

If you set the IP address manually, you will also need to provide DNS server information manually. Otherwise, the DHCP server will provide the DNS server information as part of setting the client parameters.

You can also use the Connection Properties screen to control ***Internet Connection Sharing (ICS),*** which allows other users on your network to access the Internet through your computer. This requires your computer to have two network connections, one to the Internet and the other to a local network. Essentially, ICS turns your computer into a router so that other computers on the local network can access its Internet connection. You should note that the default setting allows other network users to control or disable the shared Internet connection. This avoids the need for them to have access to your computer in order to manage the shared Internet connection, but it could allow anybody on your network to manage the connection (unless you take care to set up other security facilities).

The *View Status* display for the connection provides access to many details of the connection, including DHCP lease details, network gateway information, the device Media Access Control (MAC) or physical address, and much more, as shown in Figure 2-6.

Figure 2-6

Viewing the status of a network connection

You can configure network settings on a Windows Server 2008 computer using a number of different tools, including the Initial Configuration Tasks or the new Server Manager consoles, as well as the Windows command line.

 CONFIGURE BASIC NETWORK SETTINGS

GET READY. This exercise will use a mixture of GUI interfaces and command-line utilities to configure network settings.

1. Log onto the Windows Server 2008 computer using administrative credentials.
2. On a newly installed server, the Initial Configuration Tasks screen appears. To configure the IP address, subnet mask, and default gateway from the Initial Configuration Tasks screen, click **Configure Networking**. The Network Connections screen will open. Right-click the **Local Area Connection** icon and click **Properties** as shown in Figure 2-7.

Figure 2-7

Local Area Network
Connection Properties

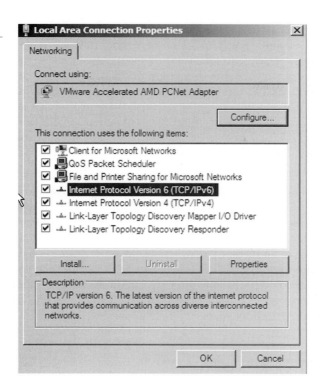

3. Double-click **Internet Protocol version 4 (IPv4)**. To configure the server with a static IP address, select **Use the following IP address**. Enter an appropriate IP address, subnet mask, and default gateway for your environment. Click **OK**, and then click **OK** again.

4. To add a preferred and alternate DNS server from the command line, click the **Start** button, then click **All Programs→Accessories→Command Prompt**.

5. Key the command **netsh interface ipv4 add dnsserver "Local Area Connection"** **<DNS server IP address>.address>.address>,** using the IP address of your preferred DNS server, and then press (**Enter**). Repeat this command, inserting the IP address of your alternate DNS server, and then press (**Enter**).

6. Key **exit** and press (**Enter**) to close the command prompt window.

PAUSE. You can log off of the Windows Server 2008 computer, or remain logged on for the next exercise.

Configuring the Windows Firewall

The final task in the initial configuration task list is to configure the *Windows Firewall*. Initially, the Windows Firewall is on by default, and this allows you to turn it off (not recommended!) or to change the settings.

The **network location** setting characterizes the network environment to which you are connected—for example "work" or "public network." The important effect of this setting is to control network discovery, which is the process by which other computers on the network can find (and perhaps access) your computer, and the shared resources it provides. **Network discovery** finds and accesses other computers and shared resources on the network. File and printer sharing would be examples of a service affected by this setting. If you inappropriately allowed network discovery in a public network environment (for example, an Internet café), you would allow total strangers to see and access any file shares on your system. The **Network and Sharing Center** allows you to set the network location, and the Windows Firewall screen has a link to access the Network Center.

The Windows Firewall Settings screen shown in Figure 2-8 allows you to turn the firewall on or off, and to control the connections it will allow when it is running. The most restrictive option is to block all incoming connections when Windows Firewall is on. This prevents any inbound connection attempts from succeeding, and it is intended for situations in which you are connected to an insecure network and inbound connections are more likely to be attacks from malicious users or hackers. There will be no notification of blocked attempts to connect, even for connections that you have indicated should be allowed normally. The normal mode for Windows Firewall is on, which blocks all connection requests except those explicitly allowed on the Exceptions tab.

Figure 2-8

Configuring the Windows Firewall

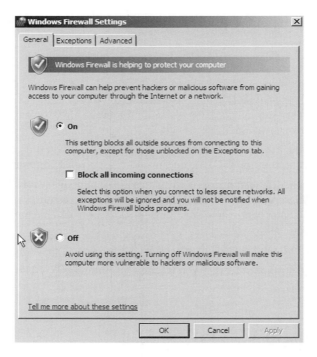

The Exceptions tab lists some of the exceptions that are frequently encountered in network environments, so that they can be explicitly allowed through the Windows Firewall. This is useful for enterprise environments in which the network itself is protected by firewalls and other security measures. In such an environment, the facilities listed would commonly be needed for asset management, distributed applications, and other business imperatives, so allowing them through the Windows Firewall is necessary. For maximum security, however, you should enable only those required in your particular environment. The Exceptions tab also allows enabling access by a specific program, or by specifying a particular port. Specifying a particular port is less desirable because it opens that port permanently, whereas specifying a program allows access only when that program is running.

Configuring Server Roles

> To improve the security and manageability of Windows Server 2008 computers, you can use the Server Manager console to install one or multiple Server Roles, which define a particular duty that a server might perform on a 2008 network. For example, installing the Active Directory Domain Services role will step you through adding all of the services needed to configure a server as an Active Directory domain controller. To reduce the attack surface on Windows Server 2008 computers, system files (such as executables and DLL files) associated with a particular role will not be installed on a server until the role is installed, instead of leaving unused software lying dormant on the server as a potential target for a network virus or worm.

The default installation of Windows Server 2008 Enterprise Edition allows you to install 17 different server roles:

- Active Directory Certificate Services
- Active Directory Domain Services
- Active Directory Federation Services
- Active Directory Lightweight Directory Services
- Active Directory Rights Management Services
- Application Server
- DHCP Server
- DNS Server
- Fax Server
- File Services
- Network Policy and Access Services
- Print Services
- Terminal Services
- UDDI Services
- Web Server (IIS)
- Windows Deployment Services
- Windows SharePoint Services

When adding a server role using Server Manager, you are presented with a number of informational screens describing the role being installed, as well as any prerequisites to install the role and checklists to follow to configure the role once it has been installed. You can also use Server Manager to cleanly remove a role if it is no longer in use on a particular server.

 CONFIGURE SERVER ROLES ON WINDOWS SERVER 2008

GET READY. This exercise assumes that you have installed Windows Server 2008, Enterprise Edition, and are logged on as a local Administrator of the server.

1. If the Server Manager screen does not appear automatically, click the **Start** button and then click **Server Manager**.
2. In the left-hand pane, double-click the **Roles** node.
3. In the right-hand pane, click **Add role**. Click **Next** to bypass the initial Welcome Screen.

4. You will see the Select Server Roles screen shown in Figure 2-9. Here you will select the role that you want to install on the server. For this exercise we will install the DNS Server role. Place a check mark next to DNS Server and click **Next**.

Figure 2-9

Selecting Server Roles to install

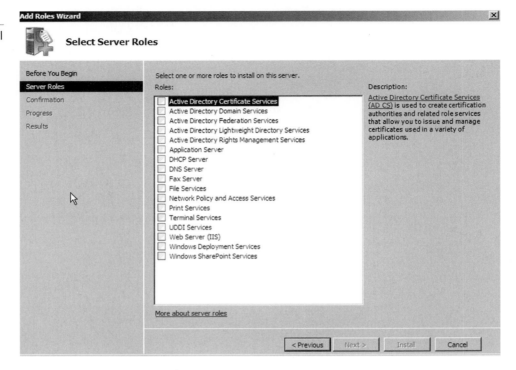

5. On the following screen you will see an introduction to the DNS Server role, including links to additional information in the Windows Help files. Click **Next** to continue.

6. The Confirm Installation Selections screen appears. Click **Install** to begin the installation.

7. After a few minutes, the Installation Results screen will appear. Click **Close** to return to the Server Manager console, shown in Figure 2-10. Notice that the DNS Server role is now listed in the Roles Summary section.

Figure 2-10

Viewing Server Manager

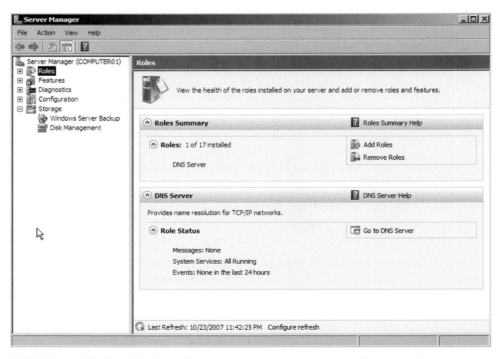

PAUSE. Log off of the Windows Server 2008 computer, or remain logged on for the next exercise.

In the previous exercise, you configured the DNS Server role using the Server Manager console. The following section describes configuring hard drives and storage options for Windows Server 2008.

Adding Windows Server 2008 Features

The Add features option allows adding various features and facilities that may be useful or necessary, depending on your network environment and requirements..

Some of the features that may be relevant in the context of this tutorial include:

- Remote Server Administration Tools—The Remote Server Administration Tools allow the Windows Server 2008 system to be used to remotely administer another server. Installation of these tools installs the ability to administer the remote server's software, not to use the remote server's software. This enables outbound connections from your system to manage other servers.
- *Windows Server Backup*—The Windows Server Backup feature allows recovery of operating system state, files, folders, and application data by periodically creating a snapshot of the full server, or selected volumes.
- *WINS Server*—The WINS Server feature provides the ability to run a WINS (Windows Internet Name Service) server, which provides a *NetBIOS* Name Server facility. NetBIOS name resolution was the primary means of name resolution prior to the introduction of Active Directory in Windows 2000 Server, which relied on DNS as its primary means of resolving human-readable names to IP addresses. Essentially, WINS is to NetBIOS names as DNS is to domain names, providing a mapping of a computer's NetBIOS name to a corresponding IP address.
- *Wireless Networking*—The Wireless Networking feature installs and configures wireless connections and wireless LAN profiles.

Configuring Storage in Windows Server 2008

Once you have installed the Windows Server 2008 operating system, you can add and remove physical hard disks and logical partitions to increase or modify the available storage on your server. Similar to other administrative tasks in Windows Server 2008, you can manage storage options using either a Graphical User Interface or a command-line interface. In this section we will discuss the terminology that you will need to understand to manage storage on a Windows Server 2008 computer, as well as the tools that you can use to do so.

Windows Server 2008 (and all Microsoft operating systems going back to Windows 2000) supports two types of hard disks:

- *Basic disks* use partition tables that are recognized and supported by older operating systems such as MS-DOS, Windows 95, Windows 98, and Windows Me. Basic disks do not support advanced storage options such as striped volumes, spanned volumes, and RAID-5 volumes. All disk drives in a Windows Server 2008 computer begin as basic disks until they are converted to dynamic disks.
- *Dynamic disks* provide access to more advanced configuration features. Once a basic disk is converted to a dynamic disk, that disk can be accessed only by operating systems that support dynamic disks: Windows 2000 Professional, Windows XP Professional, Windows Vista Business, Enterprise or Ultimate, Windows 2000 Server, Windows Server 2003, and Windows Server 2008.

When working with dynamic disks, you will need to be familiar with the following terms:

- A *volume* describes a logical unit of disk space that is made up of space contained on one or more physical disks. Volumes on a dynamic disk can be configured as simple, spanned, mirrored, striped, or RAID-5 volumes.
- A *simple volume* consists of free space contained on a single physical disk. You can configure all of the available space on a disk as a simple volume, or you can configure multiple simple volumes using the space on a single disk.
- A *spanned volume* is made up of free space from multiple physical disks. For example, if you have two physical disks in a server that are each 500GB in size, you can combine them into a single spanned volume that is 1TB in size. Spanned volumes are not fault-tolerant, which means that if you lose one disk in the volume, you will lose all data contained on all disks. A spanned volume can be created on a minimum of 2 disks and a maximum of 32 disks.
- A *striped volume* is similar to a spanned volume in that it is made up of free space from multiple disks. Unlike a spanned volume, though, a striped volume uses RAID-0 striping to interleave the data across the disks, thus improving the read performance of the volume. Striped volumes are also not fault-tolerant and will not withstand the loss of a disk in the volume. A striped volume can be created on a minimum of 2 disks and a maximum of 32 disks.
- A *mirrored volume* is a fault-tolerant volume consisting of two physical disks, in which the data on one disk is copied exactly onto the second disk. This provides data redundancy, such that if one disk in the mirror fails, the other disk will continue to function without loss of data.
- A *RAID-5 volume* is a fault-tolerant volume where data is interleaved across three or more disks much in the same way as in a striped volume, but with additional information known as *parity*. If one disk in a RAID-5 volume fails, the data contained on the failed disk can be rebuilt using the parity information stored on the disks in the rest of the volume. A RAID-5 volume can be created using a minimum of three disks and a maximum of 32 disks.

When you create a new partition, you can either assign the partition a drive letter, or else you can configure it as a *mount point* that will appear as a folder within an existing drive letter. For example, creating a 500MB partition and assigning it to a mount point to the E:\EXCHANGE\DATA directory will add a folder called DATA containing 500MB of space.

You can manage disks and partitions in Windows Server 2008 using the Disk Management GUI tool, or the diskpart command-line utility. In the following exercise, we will perform various tasks associated with managing storage in Windows Server 2008.

Before you can manage a disk drive in Windows Server 2008, the disk needs to be initialized. All new disks are initialized as basic disks, and can be initialized using one of two partition styles:

- *MBR (Master Boot Record)*—This partition style is recognized by down-level operating systems.
- *GPT (GUID Partition Table)*—This partition style is recommended for disks larger than 2TB, or disks that are used in Itanium computers.

⊙ CONFIGURE STORAGE IN WINDOWS SERVER 2008

GET READY. This exercise assumes that you have added three additional disks to your Windows Server 2008 computer, each with unallocated space available to create new partitions. If you are using a virtual environment to perform these steps, you can add additional disks using the administrative console of your virtualization software.

1. Log onto the Windows Server 2008 computer using credentials that have administrative rights to the local computer.

2. If the Server Manager console does not appear automatically, click the **Start** button, and then click **Server Manager**.

3. In the left-hand pane, drill down to **Storage→Disk Management**.

4. You will see a screen similar to Figure 2-11. If the new disks are listed as *Offline*, right-click each disk and click **Online**. The disk status will change to *Not Initialized*.

Figure 2-11

Viewing Disk Management

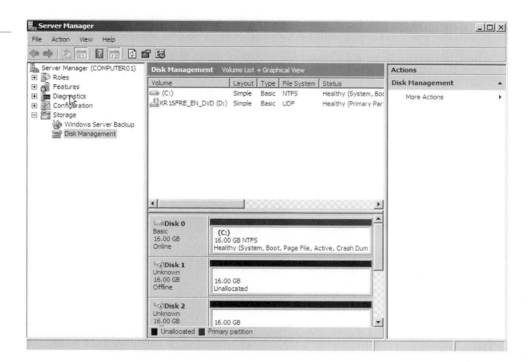

5. Right-click one new disk and click **Initialize Disk**. You will see the screen shown in Figure 2-12. Select the **MBR** partition style and click **OK**. All new disks will list a status of *Online* and are initialized as basic disks.

Figure 2-12

Initializing a newly installed disk

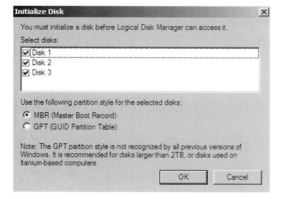

6. Right-click a newly added disk and click **Convert to dynamic disk**. Select one or more disks to convert. Click **OK**.

7. To demonstrate creating a new partition in Disk Management, we will create a simple volume. Right-click a disk containing unallocated space and click **New Simple Volume**. The New Simple Volume Wizard appears. Click **Next**.

8. The Specify Volume Size screen appears. Enter **50** to create a 50MB partition and click **Next**.

9. The Assign Drive Letter or Path screen appears. Assign the new partition an available drive letter and click **Next**.

10. The Format Partition screen appears. Select the option to format this drive using the NTFS file system and click **Next**.

11. Click **Finish** to create the partition. The new partition will show a status of *Formatting*, followed by a status of *Healthy* when the format has completed.

Next we will create a RAID 5 partition using the diskpart command-line utility.

12. Click **Start**, key **cmd** in the Run line, and click **OK**.

13. To create a 50MB RAID-5 partition across three disks, enter the command **diskpart create volume raid size=50 disk=1,2,3** and then press (Enter).

14. Key **exit** and press (Enter) to close the command prompt.

15. Confirm that the newly configured RAID partition is displayed in the Disk Management console.

PAUSE. You can close Server Manager or leave it open for a subsequent exercise.

Installing Server Core

Windows Server 2008 introduces a new option for installing only the services required for a specific function, creating a server installation that possesses an extremely small installation footprint. This feature is called Server Core and it provides only the services required to perform specific roles such as the DHCP, DNS, file server, or domain controller roles.

Rather than being a separate product (or SKU in licensing terms), Server Core is simply an installation option that is available with all Windows Server 2008 media; you can use the 2008 media to install either Server Core or a full installation of the operating system as your needs dictate. Server Core creates a small installation footprint as well as a limited attack surface from a network security perspective. Since it does not install nonessential services and applications, it includes only a limited GUI. For example, a Server Core computer will allow you to launch the Windows Registry Editor, Notepad, and a number of Control Panel applets; but it does not include a Start Menu and it does not allow you to install or run any of the MMC consoles such as Computer Management or Active Directory Users and Computer. Even more interesting from a security standpoint is that a Server Core installation does not include programs that were previously standard components on a server operating system, such as Windows Explorer and Outlook Express, since their presence created additional opportunities for security compromises of the server.

There are several advantages to installing Server Core. Because it includes only what is required for the designated roles, a Server Core installation will typically require less maintenance and fewer updates as there are fewer components to manage. Security is improved. Since there are fewer programs and components installed and running on the server, there are fewer attack vectors exposed to the network, resulting in a reduced attack surface. Because there are fewer components installed, the minimum resources required will be less than for a full installation, and there may be less overhead during normal processing.

On the other hand, there are some disadvantages associated with the Server Core configuration. Most noticeable is the inconvenience of not having the familiar GUI options available during system administration. Server Core installations are also designed for a specific set of limited roles, so they might not be as well suited for small networks where a single server might be used for several roles.

The installation process for Server Core is identical to the installation of a full version of Windows Server 2008. Once a Server Core computer is installed, however, it can be managed

locally using only command-line utilities and the limited GUI facilities installed on a Server Core computer. When a computer running Windows Server 2008 Server Core is initially installed, you will see the interface shown in Figure 2-13. As you can see, there is only a command prompt available to you to begin administering the computer.

Figure 2-13

Administering a Server Core computer

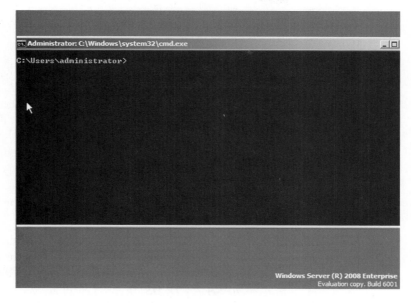

Managing Server Core from the Command Line

Since a Server Core installation includes only the most limited GUI capabilities, local administration of a Server Core computer requires a thorough knowledge of the command-line utilities that are available within Windows Server 2008. Using these utilities, you can perform an almost identical set of administrative functions as you can using the graphical user interface in a full installation of 2008, including modifying network settings, joining a Server Core computer to an Active Directory domain, and more.

 MANAGE SERVER CORE FROM THE COMMAND LINE

GET READY. This exercise assumes that you have configured a Windows Server 2008 Server Core using the default installation settings, using the steps described in the "Install Windows Server 2008" exercise.

1. To list the current TCP/IP configuration, key the command string **netsh interface ipv4 show config** in the command prompt and press ⟨**Enter**⟩.

2. To configure a static IPv4 IP address, key the command string **netsh interface ipv4 add address "Local Area Connection"** *<IP Address> <Subnet Mask> <Default Gateway>* and press ⟨**Enter**⟩.

3. To add a DNS resolver, key the command string **netsh interface ipv4 add dns server "Local Area Connection"** *<DNS Server IP Address>* and press ⟨**Enter**⟩.

4. To confirm that your changes were made, key **netsh interface ipv4 show config** again and press ⟨**Enter**⟩.

5. To set the correct time zone for the Server Core computer, ⟨**Enter**⟩ **timedate .cpl.** and press ⟨**Enter**⟩. The familiar Date and Time Control Panel applet appears.

6. To see the limited GUI functionality of Server Core in action, key **explorer.exe a**nd press ⟨**Enter**⟩. Notice that the Server Core installation does not recognize explorer. exe as a valid command.

STOP. You have completed the exercise.

In the previous exercise, you performed some common administrative tasks on a Server Core computer using both command-line tools and limited GUI functionality that is available within Server Core. For a full listing of command-line utilities at your disposal, search the Microsoft TechNet Web site for the phrase "Command-Line Reference A-Z."

Configuring Windows Activation

To help address the ongoing issue of software piracy, Windows Vista and Windows Server 2008 include tools to assist administrators in automating and managing the licensing process for operating system software on their network. In particular, *Volume Activation* is used to manage the licensing process for volume licenses of both Vista as well as Windows Server 2008. Volume Activation can eliminate the need to manually enter a product key when the operating system software is installed, and it allows you to protect and manage volume license keys throughout an organization.

Microsoft offers two types of software keys for a Windows Vista or Windows Server 2008 network, depending on the needs of your specific situation:

- A *Multiple Activation Key (MAK)* is used for a one-time activation with Microsoft's hosted activation service. A MAK key can be activated via the Internet, over the phone, or by using the *Volume Activation Management Tool (VAMT)*.
- A *Key Management Service (KMS)* license key allows you to host an activation service locally within your own network. Rather than contacting the Microsoft-hosted activation service each time a new instance of Vista or Windows Server 2008 needs to be activated on your network, KMS allows you to contact the Microsoft activation service one time to activate your KMS host, after which all activation traffic is managed locally. The minimum number of physical computers required to allow you to use a KMS key is 25 Vista computers and five Windows Server 2008 computers. Any computer on your network that has been activated by an internal KMS host will attempt to "check in" with the KMS host every seven days, and will be required to connect to that host at least once every 180 days to maintain its license.

When working in a corporate network or other production environment, you can obtain more information about Microsoft Licensing from the Microsoft Web site, or by contacting an authorized reseller of Microsoft products.

SUMMARY SKILL MATRIX

IN THIS LESSON YOU LEARNED:

- The Windows Server 2008 distribution media contains a bootable system that can be used for a standalone software installation or to repair an existing installation.

- Windows Server 2008 will be installed on a single partition specified at the start of the installation process.

- Existing files may be preserved, or they can be destroyed by reinitializing the partition to which Windows Server 2008 is installed.

- Initial configuration tasks must be performed after the Windows Server 2008 software is installed, to finish preparing it for use. These tasks include setting system parameters and passwords, adding server roles, adding server features, and setting up Windows Firewall.

- Network addressing is fundamental to successful communication between systems.

- DNS provides name resolution to allow meaningful names to be used to refer to network addresses.

- DHCP is a simple, standard protocol that makes TCP/IP network configuration much easier for the administrator by dynamically assigning IP addresses and providing additional configuration information to DHCP clients automatically.

- Clients may be configured to use APIPA or an alternate static IP address configuration if DHCP is unavailable.

- Windows Server 2008 allows you to configure various types of storage, including RAID-0, RAID-1, and RAID-5 storage arrays.

- Windows Vista and Windows Server 2008 use activation technology to help combat piracy of Microsoft software.

■ Knowledge Assessment

Fill in the Blank

Complete the following sentences by writing the correct word or words in the blanks provided.

1. The ability to use the installation process to fix problems with an existing Windows Server system is called _____.

2. Installation of just the necessary components for a particular server role, without the GUI and other software features, is called _____.

3. The _____ screen appears by default when the Windows Server 2008 operating system is first installed.

4. A _____ offers the best performance of any multi-disk configuration option within the Disk Management MMC, but does so at the expense of fault tolerance.

5. The feature that allows users on different computers to access the Internet through a single connection is called _____.

6. The _____ provides a single point of administration to configure networking and firewall configuration tasks on a Windows Server 2008 computer.

7. The setting describing the network environment, such as home or public network, is called the _____.

8. Unsolicited inbound traffic can be blocked through the use of the _____.

9. The network location setting controls the behavior of _____.

10. Once a disk is converted from a basic disk to a(n) _____, it can be accessed only by operating systems that support dynamic disks: Windows 2000 Professional, Windows XP Professional, Windows Vista Business, Enterprise or Ultimate, Windows 2000 Server, Windows Server 2003, and Windows Server 2008.

Multiple Choice

Circle the correct choice.

1. What type of license key allows you to host an activation service locally within your own network?
   a. Multiple Activation Key (MAK)   b. Key Management System (KMS)
   c. Key Activation System (KAS)   d. Multiple Management System (MMS)

2. What type of volume uses 50% of available drive space to provide fault tolerance for the volume?
   a. RAID-0   b. RAID-1
   c. RAID-5   d. RAID-6

3. Which disk formatting option will cause a disk to appear as a folder within an existing volume?
   a. Mount point
   b. Mirrored volume
   c. Striped volume
   d. GPT point

4. Which Windows Server 2008 feature installs and configured wireless connections and wireless LAN profiles?
   a. Network and Sharing Center
   b. Windows Firewall with Advanced Security
   c. Wireless Networking
   d. Network Access Protection

5. What was the primary means of name resolution on Windows networks prior to the introduction of Windows 2000 and Active Directory?
   a. AppleTalk
   b. Domain Name System (DNS)
   c. HOSTS files
   d. NetBIOS

6. Which feature is used to perform backups and restores of Windows volumes?
   a. NTBackup
   b. Windows Server Backup
   c. Windows Backup
   d. Windows NT Backup

7. Which networking service is used to automatically associate NetBIOS names with IP addresses?
   a. DNS
   b. NetBEUI
   c. WINS
   d. AppleTalk

8. Which disk partition style is recommended for disks larger than 2TB, or disks that are used in Itanium computers?
   a. Master Boot Record (MBR)
   b. GUID Partition Table (GPT)
   c. Master Partition Table (MPT)
   d. GUID Boot Record (GBR)

9. What is used to manage the licensing process for volume licenses of Windows Vista and Windows Server 2008?
   a. Volume Activation
   b. Activation keys
   c. Microsoft Select
   d. Enterprise Agreement

10. Which volume contains the operating system files on a Windows computer?
    a. System volume
    b. Boot volume
    c. Mirrored volume
    d. Striped volume

■ Case Scenarios

Scenario 2-1: Planning for Windows Server 2008

Contoso, Ltd. is a research company located in Palo Alto, California. It is in the midst of a significant upgrade to its network infrastructure, including an upgrade of all server computers to Windows Server 2008. The team leader for the server upgrade project is gathering information to determine the optimum configuration for each server computer. Based on the information in this lesson, answer the following questions.

1. You have a SQL Server 2005 database against which clients perform numerous read-intensive operations. You have been tasked with optimizing the performance of this database as much as possible. Based on this requirement, how should you configure the disks on which the database files will be installed?

2. Contoso, Ltd. has a number of satellite offices where researchers work locally on client projects. These offices are minimally staffed and do not usually have on-site IT staff available to administer any locally housed servers. You are concerned with installing only the minimum necessary services and creating the most secure possible installation footprint on servers that are housed at these remote offices. What new feature of Windows Server 2008 can you use to increase the security of these servers?

Configuring and Managing the DHCP Server Role

OBJECTIVE DOMAIN MATRIX

Technology Skill	Objective Domain	Objective Domain Number
Configuring the DHCP Server Role	Configure Dynamic Host Configuration Protocol (DHCP)	1.2

KEY TERMS

Address Resolution Protocol (ARP)
Application Layer
authorize
automatic restores
available address pool
checkpoint file
class options
compacted
DHCPACK
DHCPDECLINE
DHCPDISCOVER

DHCPINFORM
DHCPNACK
DHCPOFFER
DHCPRELEASE
DHCPREQUEST
exclusion range
Joint Engine Technology (JET)
Media Access Control (MAC)
multinets
Open System Interconnection (OSI)
reconciliation

Request for Comments (RFC)
reservations
rogue DHCP server
superscope
T1
T2
Trivial File Transfer Protocol (TFTP)
User Datagram Protocol (UDP)

Adventure Works (*http://www.adventure-works.com*) is a worldwide company specializing in providing hiking, scuba, and other outdoor excursions. Their corporate headquarters, located in Boulder, Colorado, has just undergone a significant upgrade to its network infrastructure to support recent expansion in the number of administrative staff required in Boulder to support the efforts of the tour organizers and leaders. Before the infrastructure upgrade, Adventure Works' network administrators configured each server and workstation with a static IP address, using a Microsoft Access database to keep track of which IP addresses were assigned to which computers. To improve the efficiency of managing the recent staff expansion, Adventure Works IT management has decided to deploy a DHCP server using Microsoft Windows Server 2008.

By the end of this lesson, you will have a detailed understanding of the Dynamic Host Configuration Protocol (DHCP) server role within Microsoft Windows Server 2008. DHCP can be used to automatically assign a computer's IP address, subnet mask, and default | gateway, as well as such optional configuration items as a preferred and alternate DNS server or WINS server. This lesson will cover the steps required to install and configure the DHCP server as well as related components such as the DHCP Relay Agent.

■ Configuring the DHCP Server Role

THE BOTTOM LINE

In order to communicate with other hosts on a network, all Transmission Control Protocol/Internet Protocol (TCP/IP) hosts must be correctly configured. Each host must have an Internet Protocol (IP) address and a subnet mask, and if communicating outside the local subnet, each must also have a default gateway. Each IP address must be valid and unique within the host's internetwork. This requirement can present a challenge for network administrators. If it is done manually, accurate and timely records must be kept of each host, noting where the host is located and what IP address and subnet mask have been assigned to it. This can quickly become a daunting, tedious task. Organizations with large numbers of workstations requiring IP addresses would have great difficulty managing IP addressing manually. The Dynamic Host Configuration Protocol (DHCP) simplifies this process by automating the assigning, tracking, and reassigning of IP addresses.

CERTIFICATION READY?
Configure Dynamic Host Configuration Protocol (DHCP)
1.2

IP addressing is complex, in part because each host (a computer, printer, or other device with a network interface) connected to a TCP/IP network must be assigned at least one unique IP address and subnet mask in order to communicate on the network. Additionally, most hosts will require additional information, such as the IP addresses of the default gateway and the DNS servers. DHCP frees system administrators from manually configuring each host on the network. The larger the network, the greater the benefit of using a dynamic address assignment. Without this, each host must be configured manually and IP addresses must be carefully managed to avoid duplication or misconfiguration.

Since the advent of TCP/IP, several solutions have been developed to address the challenge of configuring TCP/IP settings for organizations with a large number of workstations. The *Reverse Address Resolution Protocol (RARP)* was designed for diskless workstations that had no means of permanently storing their TCP/IP settings. RARP, as its name suggests, was essentially the opposite of **Address Resolution Protocol (ARP)**. ARP was used to discover the Media Access Control (MAC) address (an address unique to a Network Interface Card) that corresponds to a particular IP address. RARP clients broadcast the MAC address. A RARP server then responds by transmitting the IP address assigned to the client computer.

Because RARP failed to provide other much-needed settings to the client, such as a subnet mask and a default gateway, it gave way to another solution, the Bootstrap Protocol (BOOTP). BOOTP, which is still in use today, enables a TCP/IP workstation to retrieve settings for all the configuration parameters it needs to run, including an IP address, a subnet mask, a default gateway, and Domain Name System (DNS) server addresses. Using *Trivial File Transfer Protocol (TFTP)*, a lightweight version of FTP that uses the UDP protocol, a workstation also can download an executable boot file from a BOOTP server. The major drawback of BOOTP is that an administrator still must specify settings for each workstation on the BOOTP server. A better way to administer TCP/IP would be to automatically assign unique IP addresses while preventing duplicate address assignment and while providing other important settings such as the default gateway, subnet mask, DNS, Windows Internet Naming Service (WINS) server, and so on. Ideally, this would be accomplished without having to manually list every device on the network. To address this issue, server administrators can deploy DHCP.

DHCP is based heavily on BOOTP, but rather than pushing preconfigured parameters to expected clients, DHCP can dynamically allocate an IP address from a pool of addresses and then reclaim it when it is no longer needed. Because this process is dynamic, no duplicate addresses are assigned by a properly configured DHCP server, and administrators can move computers between subnets without manually configuring them. In addition, a large number of standard configuration and platform-specific parameters can be specified and dynamically delivered to the client. DHCP is an open, industry-standard protocol that reduces

the complexity of administering networks based on TCP/IP. It is defined by the *Internet Engineering Task Force (IETF)* in **Requests for Comments (RFCs)** 2131 and 2132.

Managing IP addresses and host options is much easier when configuration information can be managed from a single location rather than coordinating information across many locations. DHCP can automatically configure a host while it is booting on a TCP/IP network, as well as change settings while the host is connected to the network. All of this is accomplished using settings and information from a central DHCP database. Because settings and information are stored centrally, you can quickly and easily add or change a client setting (for example, the IP address of an alternate DNS server) for all clients on your network from a single location. Without a centralized database of configuration information, it is difficult to maintain a current view of the host settings or to change them.

Each Microsoft Windows Server 2008 edition (the Standard Edition, Enterprise Edition, and Datacenter Edition) include the DHCP Server service, which is an optional installation. All Microsoft Windows clients automatically install the DHCP Client service as part of TCP/IP, including Windows Server 2008, Windows Server 2008, Microsoft Windows Vista, and Microsoft Windows XP.

In brief, DHCP provides four key benefits to those managing and maintaining a TCP/IP network:

- Centralized administration of IP configuration—DHCP IP configuration information can be stored in a single location and enables the administrator to centrally manage all IP configuration information. A *DHCP server* tracks all leased and reserved IP addresses and lists them in the DHCP console. You can use the DHCP console to determine the IP addresses of all DHCP-enabled devices on your network. Without DHCP, not only would you need to manually assign addresses, you would also need to devise a method of tracking and updating them.

- Dynamic host configuration—DHCP automates the host configuration process for key configuration parameters. This eliminates the need to manually configure individual hosts when TCP/IP is first deployed or when IP infrastructure changes are required.

- Seamless IP host configuration—The use of DHCP ensures that DHCP clients get accurate and timely IP configuration parameters, such as the IP address, subnet mask, default gateway, IP address of the DNS server, and so on, without user intervention. Because the configuration is automatic, troubleshooting of misconfigurations, such as mistyped numbers, is largely eliminated.

- Flexibility and scalability—Using DHCP gives the administrator increased flexibility, allowing the administrator to more easily change IP configurations when the infrastructure changes. DHCP also scales from small to large networks. DHCP can service networks with ten clients as well as networks with thousands of clients. For very small, isolated networks, Automatic Private IP Addressing (APIPA) can be used. (APIPA is discussed later in this lesson.)

Understanding How DHCP Works

The core function of DHCP is to assign addresses. DHCP functions at the **Application Layer** of the **Open System Interconnection (OSI)** reference model, as defined by the International Organization for Standardization (ISO) and the Telecommunication Standards Section of the International Telecommunications Union (ITU-T). The OSI model is used for reference and teaching purposes; it divides computer networking functions into seven layers. From top to bottom, the seven layers are application, presentation, session, transport, network, data-link, and physical. For more information about the OSI reference model, see the *Network + Certification Training Kit,* Second Edition (Microsoft Press, 2001).

As discussed previously, the key aspect of the DHCP process is that it is dynamic. What this means to the network administrator is that the network can be configured to allocate an IP address to any device that is connected anywhere on the network. This allocation of addresses is achieved by sending messages to, and receiving application layer messages (messages from the Application Layer of the OSI model) from, a DHCP server. All DHCP messages are carried in *User Datagram Protocol (UDP)* datagrams using the well-known port numbers 67 (from the server) and 68 (to the client). UDP operates at the Transport Layer of the OSI model and is a low-overhead protocol because it does not use any type of packet acknowledgement.

Before learning how address allocation works, you should understand some terminology related to the DHCP server role: DHCP clients, servers, and leases. These terms are defined as follows.

- *DHCP client*—A computer that obtains its configuration information from DHCP.
- *DHCP server*—A computer that provides DHCP configuration information to multiple clients; the IP addresses and configuration information that the DHCP server makes available to the client are defined by the DHCP administrator.
- *DHCP lease*—This defines the duration for which a DHCP server assigns an IP address to a DHCP client. The lease duration can be any amount of time between 1 minute and 999 days, or it can be unlimited. The default lease duration is eight days.

In addition to this terminology, you should also be familiar with the various *DHCP message types* that are used by DHCP clients and servers on a TCP/IP network.

- ***DHCPDISCOVER***—Sent by clients via broadcast to locate a DHCP server. Per RFC 2131, the DHCPDISCOVER message may include options that suggest values for the network address and lease duration.
- ***DHCPOFFER***—Sent by one or more DHCP servers to a DHCP client in response to DHCPDISCOVER, along with offered configuration parameters.
- ***DHCPREQUEST***—Sent by the DHCP client to signal its acceptance of the offered address and parameters. The client generates a DHCPREQUEST message containing the address of the server from which it is accepting the offer, along with the offered IP address. Because the client has not yet configured itself with the offered parameters, it transmits the DHCPREQUEST message as a broadcast. This broadcast notifies the server that the client is accepting the offered address and also notifies the other servers on the network that the client is rejecting their offers.
- ***DHCPDECLINE***—Sent by a DHCP client to a DHCP server, informing the server that the offered IP address has been declined. The DHCP client will send a DHCPDECLINE message if it determines that the offered address is already in use. After sending a DHCPDECLINE, the client must begin the lease or renewal process again.
- ***DHCPACK***—Sent by a DHCP server to a DHCP client to confirm an IP address and to provide the client with those configuration parameters that the client has requested and the server is configured to provide.
- ***DHCPNACK***—Sent by a DHCP server to a DHCP client to deny the client's DHCPREQUEST. This might occur if the requested address is incorrect because the client was moved to a new subnet or because the DHCP client's lease expired and cannot be renewed. After receiving a DHCPNACK message, the client must begin the lease or renewal process again.
- ***DHCPRELEASE***—Sent by a DHCP client to a DHCP server to relinquish an IP address and cancel the remaining lease. This message type is sent to the server that provided the lease.
- ***DHCPINFORM***—Sent from a DHCP client to a DHCP server to ask only for additional local configuration parameters; the client already has a configured IP address. This message type is also used to detect unauthorized DHCP servers.

The initial DHCP lease process is accomplished using a series of exchanges between a DHCP client and DHCP server that utilize four messages, DHCPDISCOVER, DHCPOFFER,

DHCPREQUEST, and DHCPACK, as shown in Figure 3-1. You can remember this four-step sequence of the DHCP lease process with the acronym DORA, for "Discover, Offer, Request, Acknowledgement," as described here:

Figure 3-1

The DHCP lease process

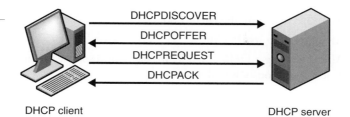

DHCP client   DHCP server

1. DHCPDISCOVER. The client broadcasts a DHCPDISCOVER message to find a DHCP server. Because the client does not already have an IP address or know the IP address of the DHCP server, the DHCPDISCOVER message is sent as a local area broadcast, with 0.0.0.0 as the source address and 255.255.255.255 as the destination address. The DHCPDISCOVER message is a request for the location of a DHCP server and IP addressing information. The request contains the client's MAC address and computer name so that the DHCP servers know which client sent the request. After broadcasting its DHCPDISCOVER message, the DHCP client waits 1 second for an offer. If an offer is not received, the client will not be able to initialize, and the client will rebroadcast the request three times (at 9-, 13-, and 16-second intervals, plus a random offset between 0 milliseconds and 1 second). If an offer is not received after four tries, the client continuously retries in five-minute intervals. If DHCP fails, Windows Server 2008, Windows Vista, Windows XP, and Windows Server 2003 can use APIPA to obtain a dynamically assigned IP address and subnet mask. Clients can also use an alternate configuration, which assigns predefined settings if a DHCP server cannot be located. APIPA and alternate configurations are described in the "Using APIPA and Alternate Configurations" section later in this lesson.

2. All DHCP servers that receive the DHCPDISCOVER message and that have a valid configuration for the client will broadcast a DHCPOFFER message with the following information:
   - Source (DHCP server) IP address
   - Physical (MAC) address of the requesting client (this is sent to the broadcast IP address of 255.255.255.255 because the client has not yet been configured with IP information)
   - An offered IP address
   - Client hardware address
   - Subnet mask
   - Length of lease
   - A server identifier (the IP address of the offering DHCP server)

3. After the client receives an offer from at least one DHCP server, it broadcasts a DHCPREQUEST message to all DHCP servers with 0.0.0.0 as the source address and 255.255.255.255 as the destination address. The broadcast DHCPREQUEST message contains the following information:
   - The IP address of the DHCP server chosen by the client
   - The requested IP address for the client
   - A list of requested parameters (subnet mask, router, DNS server list, domain name, vendor-specific information, WINS server list, NetBIOS node type, NetBIOS scope)

TAKE NOTE＊

When DHCP servers whose offers were not accepted receive the DHCPREQUEST message, they retract their offers.

4. The DHCP server with the accepted offer sends a successful acknowledgement to the client in the form of a DHCPACK message. This message contains a valid lease for an IP address, including the renewal times (T1 and T2, which are discussed next) and the duration of the lease (in seconds).

A DHCP client will perform the initial lease process in the following situations:

- The very first time the client boots
- After releasing its IP address
- After receiving a DHCPNACK message, in response to the DHCP client attempting to renew a previously leased address

Because each DHCP lease has a finite lifetime, the client must periodically renew the lease after obtaining it. Windows DHCP clients attempt to renew the lease either at each reboot or at regular intervals after the DHCP client has initialized. The lease renewal involves just two DHCP messages, as shown in Figure 3-2—DHCPREQUEST (either broadcast or unicast) and DHCPACK. If a Windows DHCP client renews a lease while booting, these messages are sent through broadcast IP packets. If the lease renewal is made while a Windows DHCP client is running, the DHCP client and the DHCP server communicate using unicast messages. (In contrast with broadcast messages, unicast messages are point-to-point messages between two hosts.)

Figure 3-2

The DHCP lease renewal process

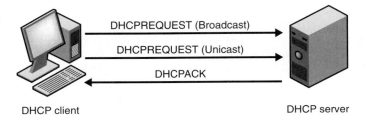

DHCP client   DHCP server

A DHCP client first attempts to reacquire its lease at half the lease time, which is known as **T1**. The DHCP client obtains the value of T1 from the DHCPACK message that confirmed the IP lease. If the lease reacquisition fails at T1, the DHCP client attempts a further lease renewal at 87.5 percent of the lease time, which is known as **T2**. Like T1, T2 is specified in the DHCPACK message. If the lease is not reacquired before it expires (if, for example, the DHCP server is unreachable for an extended period of time), the client immediately releases the IP address as soon as the lease expires and attempts to acquire a new lease.

If the DHCP client requests a lease through a DHCPREQUEST message that the DHCP server cannot fulfill (for example, when a portable computer is moved to a different subnet, as shown in Figure 3-3), the DHCP server sends a DHCPNACK message to the client. This informs the client that the requested IP lease will not be renewed. The client then begins the acquisition process again by broadcasting a DHCPDISCOVER message. When a Windows DHCP client boots in a new subnet, it broadcasts a DHCPREQUEST message to renew its lease. The DHCP renewal request is broadcast on the subnet so all DHCP servers that provide DHCP addresses will receive the request. This DHCP server responding on the new subnet is different from the server that provided the initial lease. When the DHCP server receives the broadcast, it compares the address the DHCP client is requesting with the scopes configured on the server and the subnet.

Figure 3-3

A DHCP client booting in a
new subnet

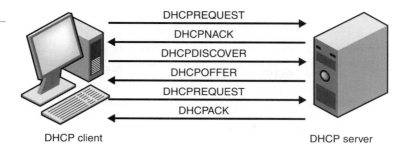

If it is not possible to satisfy the client request, the DHCP server issues a DHCPNACK message, and the DHCP client then begins the lease acquisition process again. If the DHCP client is unable to locate any DHCP server when rebooting, it issues an ARP broadcast for the default gateway that was previously obtained, if one was provided. If the IP address of the gateway is successfully resolved, the DHCP client assumes that it remains located on the same network from which it obtained its current lease and continues to use its lease. Otherwise, if the IP address of the gateway is not resolved, the client assumes that it has been moved to a network that has no DHCP services currently available (such as a home network), and it configures itself using either APIPA or an alternate configuration. Once it configures itself, the DHCP client tries to locate a DHCP server every five minutes in an attempt to renew its lease.

Using the DHCP Relay Agent

DHCP relies heavily on broadcast messages. Broadcast messages are generally limited to the subnet in which they originate and are not forwarded to other subnets. This poses a problem if a client is located on a different subnet from the DHCP server. A *DHCP relay agent* is either a host or an IP router that listens for DHCP (and BOOTP) client messages being broadcast on a subnet and then forwards those DHCP messages to a DHCP server. The DHCP server sends DHCP response messages back to the relay agent, which then broadcasts them onto the subnet for the DHCP client. Using DHCP relay agents eliminates the need to have a DHCP server on every subnet.

To support and use the DHCP service across multiple subnets, routers connecting each subnet should comply with the DHCP/BOOTP relay agent capabilities described in RFC 1542. To comply with RFC 1542 and provide relay agent support, each router must be able to recognize BOOTP and DHCP protocol messages and relay them appropriately. Because routers typically interpret DHCP messages as BOOTP messages, a router with only BOOTP relay agent capability relays DHCP packets and any BOOTP packets sent on the network.

The DHCP relay agent is configured with the address of a DHCP server. The DHCP relay agent listens for DHCPDISCOVER, DHCPREQUEST, and DHCPINFORM messages that are broadcast from the client. The DHCP relay agent then waits a previously configured amount of time and, if no response is detected, sends a unicast message to the configured DHCP server. The server then acts on the message and sends the reply back to the DHCP relay agent. The relay agent then broadcasts the message on the local subnet, allowing the DHCP client to receive it.

Using APIPA and Alternate Configurations

In most cases, DHCP clients find a server either on a local subnet or through a relay agent. To allow for the possibility that a DHCP server is unavailable, Windows clients can obtain their IP configuration using Automatic Private IP Addressing (APIPA). APIPA is a feature of the Windows TCP/IP implementation that allows a computer to determine IP configuration information without a DHCP server without relying on manual configuration of the TCP/IP stack.

APIPA avoids the problem of IP hosts being unable to communicate if for some reason the DHCP server is unavailable. In the case where a DHCP server is not found and APIPA is configured and enabled, an APIPA address is assigned. APIPA is useful for small workgroup networks where no DHCP server is implemented.

If the DHCP client is unable to locate a DHCP server and is not configured with an alternate configuration (discussed next), the computer configures itself with an IP address randomly chosen from the Internet Assigned Numbers Authority (IANA)–reserved class B network 169.254.0.0 and with the subnet mask 255.255.0.0. The auto-configured computer then tests to verify that the IP address it has chosen is not already in use by using a gratuitous ARP broadcast. If the chosen IP address is in use, the computer randomly selects another address. The computer makes up to ten attempts to find an available IP address.

Once the selected address has been verified as available, the client is configured to use that address. The DHCP client continues to check for a DHCP server in the background every five minutes, and if a DHCP server is found, the configuration offered by the DHCP server is used.

Windows clients can also be configured to use an alternate configuration, which the DHCP client uses instead of APIPA if a DHCP server cannot be contacted. The alternate configuration includes an IP address, a subnet mask, a default gateway, DNS, and WINS server addresses.

One purpose of the alternate configuration is as a solution for portable computers that move between a corporate, DHCP-enabled network and a home network where static IP addressing is used. For example, Janice has a portable computer she uses at work and at home. At work, her portable computer obtains IP address information using DHCP, but she does not use a DHCP server at home. Janice can use alternate configuration to hold her home IP address, subnet mask, default gateway, and DNS server information so that when she connects her portable computer to her home network, it is configured automatically.

If you use DHCP with an alternate configuration and the DHCP client cannot locate a DHCP server, the alternate configuration is used to configure the network adapter. No additional discovery attempts are made except under the following conditions:

- The network adapter is disabled and then enabled again
- Media (such as network cabling) is disconnected and then reconnected
- The TCP/IP settings for the adapter are changed, and DHCP remains enabled after these changes

If a DHCP server is found, the network adapter is assigned a valid DHCP IP address lease.

To display the Alternate Configuration tab in Windows Server 2008, as shown in Figure 3-4, the network adapter must be configured to obtain an IP address automatically. To view the Alternate Configuration tab, follow these steps:

1. Open the Control Panel, and double-click Network and Sharing Center. In the Network and Sharing section, click Manage Network Connections.
2. In the Network Connections window, right-click Local Area Connection, and then click Properties.
3. In the Local Area Connection Properties page, click Internet Protocol version 4 (TCP/IPv4), and then click Properties.
4. Ensure that the Obtain an IP Address Automatically radio button is selected. In the Alternate Configuration tab, specify your IP address settings.

Figure 3-4

Viewing the Alternate
Configuration screen

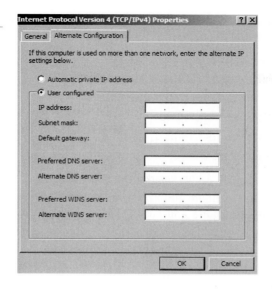

Installing the DHCP Server Role

Windows Server 2008 has introduced the Server Manager utility as a single point of reference for managing all components of the Windows operating system, as well as installing, managing, and uninstalling various server roles such as Active Directory Domain Services, DHCP, DNS, and others. Adding the DHCP server role is largely wizard-driven, and allows you to configure basic DHCP settings at the same time that you install the role.

 INSTALL THE DHCP SERVER ROLE

GET READY. This exercise assumes that you have installed Windows Server 2008, Enterprise Edition, and that you have local administrator access to the computer. In Part A we will add the DHCP server role on a full installation of Windows Server 2008. In Part B we will add the DHCP server role on a Server Core installation of Windows Server 2008.

PART A—Adding the DHCP Server Role on a Full Installation of Windows Server 2008

1. Press (Ctrl) + (Alt) + (Del) on the Windows Server 2008 computer and log on as the default administrator of the local computer.
2. The Server Manager screen will appear automatically. Expand the Server Manager window to full-screen if necessary.
3. In the left-hand pane of Server Manager, double-click **Roles**.
4. Click **Add Role**. Click **Next** to bypass the initial Welcome screen.
5. The Select Server Roles screen appears. Place a checkmark next to **DHCP Server**. Click **Next**.
6. The Introduction to DHCP Server screen appears. Read the information about the DHCP Server role and click **Next**.
7. The Specify IPv4 DNS Server Settings screen appears. Enter the appropriate information for your network configuration and click **Next**.
8. The Specify IPv4 WINS Server Settings screen appears. Select the appropriate configuration for your network and click **Next**.
9. The Add or Edit DHCP Scopes screen appears. Click **Add** to create a DHCP scope for your network.

10. The Add Scope screen appears. Enter the appropriate information for your network configuration, for example:

- *Name:* 70-642 Lab Network
- *Starting IP Address:* 192.168.1.100
- *Ending IP Address:* 192.168.1.254
- *Subnet Mask:* 255.255.255.0
- *Default Gateway:* 192.168.1.1
- *Subnet type:* Wired

11. Ensure that there is a checkmark next to **Activate this scope**, and then click **OK**.

12. Click **Next**. The Configure DHCPv6 Stateless Mode screen appears. Select **Enable DHCPv6 stateless mode** and click **Next**.

13. The Specify IPv6 DNS Server Settings screen appears. Enter the appropriate information for your network configuration and click **Next**.

14. The Authorize DHCP Server screen appears. Select **Skip authorization of this DHCP server in AD DS** and click **Next**.

15. The Confirm Installation Selections screen appears. Click **Install**.

PART B—Adding the DHCP Server Role on a Server Core Installation of Windows Server 2008

1. Press (Ctrl) + (Alt) + (Del) on the Server Core computer and log on as the default administrator of the local computer.

2. From the command prompt, enter the following command and press **Enter**:

    Start /w ocsetup DHCPServerCore

STOP. When the installation is completed, log off of the Windows Server 2008 computer.

In the previous exercise, you installed the DHCP Server role on a Windows Server 2008 computer. In the next section, we will discuss the process of authorizing DHCP servers within Active Directory.

Authorizing a DHCP Server

In implementations of DHCP prior to Windows 2000, any user could create a DHCP server on the network, an action that could lead to conflicts in IP address assignments. For example, if a client obtains a lease from an incorrectly configured DHCP server, the client might receive an invalid IP address, which prevents it from communicating on the network. This can prevent users from logging on. In Windows Server 2000 and later, an unauthorized DHCP server (also referred to as a *rogue DHCP server*) is simply a DHCP server that has not been explicitly listed in the Active Directory Domain Service as an authorized server. You must *authorize* a DHCP server in Active Directory before the server can issue leases to DHCP clients.

At the time of initialization, the DHCP server contacts Active Directory to determine whether it is on the list of servers that are currently authorized to operate on the network. One of the following actions then occurs:

- If the DHCP server is authorized, the DHCP Server service starts.
- If the DHCP server is not authorized, the DHCP Server service logs an error in the system event log, does not start, and, of course, will not respond to client requests.

Let's examine two scenarios. In the first scenario, the DHCP server is part of a domain and is authorized. In the second scenario, the DHCP server is not in a domain and, consequently, not authorized.

In the first scenario, the DHCP server initializes and determines if it is part of the directory domain. Since it is, it contacts the directory service to verify that it is authorized. The directory service confirms the server is authorized. After receiving this confirmation, the server broadcasts a DHCPINFORM message to determine if other directory services are available and repeats the authorization process with each directory service that responds. After this is completed, the server begins servicing DHCP clients accordingly.

In the second scenario, the server is not a part of a domain. When the server initializes, it checks for DHCP member servers. If no DHCP member servers are located, the server begins servicing DHCP clients and continues to check for member servers by sending a DHCPINFORM message every five minutes. If a DHCP member server is located, the server shuts down its DHCP service and, of course, stops servicing DHCP clients.

Active Directory must be present to authorize DHCP servers and block unauthorized servers. If you install a DHCP server on a network without Active Directory, no authorization will take place. If you subsequently add Active Directory, the DHCP server will sense the presence of Active Directory; however, if it has not been authorized, the server will shut itself down. DHCP servers are not authorized by default; they must be explicitly authorized.

When a DHCP server that is not a member server of the domain (such as a member of a workgroup) initializes, the following happens:

1. The server broadcasts a DHCPINFORM message on the network.
2. Any other server that receives this message responds with a DHCPACK message and provides the name of the directory domain it is part of.
3. If a workgroup DHCP server detects a member DHCP server of a domain on the network, the workgroup DHCP server assumes itself to be unauthorized on that network and shuts itself down.
4. If the workgroup DHCP server detects the presence of another workgroup server, it ignores it; this means multiple workgroup servers can be active at the same time as long as there is no directory service.

Even when a workgroup server initializes and becomes authorized (because no other domain member server or workgroup server is on the network), it continues to broadcast DHCPINFORM every five minutes. If an authorized domain member DHCP server initializes later, the workgroup server becomes unauthorized and stops servicing client requests.

TAKE NOTE *

To authorize a DHCP server, a user must be a member of the Enterprise Admins group, which exists in the root domain of the forest.

⊙ AUTHORIZE A DHCP SERVER

GET READY. This exercise assumes that you have installed the DHCP Server role on a Windows Server 2008 computer in an Active Directory domain, and that you have local administrator rights to the DHCP server.

1. Press (Ctrl) + (Alt) + (Del) on the Windows Server 2008 computer and log on as the default administrator of the local computer.
2. Click **Start→Administrative Tools→DHCP**.
3. In the console tree, right-click **DHCP**, and then click **Manage Authorized Servers**.
4. In the Manage Authorized Servers dialog box, select **Authorize**.
5. In the Authorize DHCP Server dialog box, key the name or IP address of the DHCP server to be authorized, and then click **OK**.
6. The computer will list the IP and full computer name and then ask for confirmation. Click **OK** to continue.

STOP. You can close the DHCP administrative console or leave it open for a subsequent exercise. To authorize a DHCP server from a Server Core computer, use the netsh command using the following syntax: **netshdhcp add server <Server IP Address>**

In this exercise, you authorized a DHCP server within an Active Directory domain. In the next section we will discuss creating and configuring DHCP scopes to issue specific DHCP configurations to your network clients.

Configuring DHCP Scopes

A DHCP scope determines which IP addresses are allocated to clients. A scope defines a set of IP addresses and associated configuration information that can be supplied to a DHCP client. A scope must be defined and activated before DHCP clients can use the DHCP server for dynamic TCP/IP configuration. You can configure as many scopes on a DHCP server as needed for your network environment.

A DHCP administrator can create one or more scopes on one or more Windows Server 2008 servers running the DHCP Server service. However, because DHCP servers do not communicate scope information with each other, you must be careful to define scopes so that multiple DHCP servers are not assigning the same IP address to multiple clients or assigning addresses that are statically assigned to existing IP hosts.

The IP addresses defined in a DHCP scope must be contiguous and are associated with a subnet mask. If the addresses you want to assign are not contiguous, you must create a scope encompassing all the addresses you want to assign and then exclude specific addresses or address ranges from the scope. You can create only one scope per subnet on a single DHCP server. To allow for the possibility that some IP addresses in the scope might have been already assigned and are in use, the DHCP administrator can specify an *exclusion range*—one or more IP addresses in the scope that are not handed out to DHCP clients. An exclusion range is a limited sequence of IP addresses within a scope range that are to be excluded from DHCP service offerings. Where exclusion ranges are used, they ensure that any addresses within the defined exclusion range are not offered to clients of the DHCP server. You should exclude all statically configured IP addresses within a particular IP address range.

Once a DHCP scope is defined and exclusion ranges are applied, the remaining addresses form what is called an *available address pool* within the scope. Pooled addresses can then be dynamically assigned to DHCP clients on the network.

 CONFIGURE A DHCP SCOPE

GET READY. This exercise assumes that you have installed the DHCP Server role on a Windows Server 2008 computer, and that you have administrative rights to that server.

1. Press (Ctrl) + (Alt) + (Del) on the Windows Server 2008 computer and log on as the default administrator of the local computer.
2. Click **Start→Administrative Tools→DHCP**.
3. To configure an IPv4 DHCP scope, drill down to the server name, followed by IPv4.
4. Right-click **IPv4** and select **New scope**. Click **Next** to bypass the initial Welcome screen.
5. The Scope Name screen appears. Enter a name and description for the DHCP scope and then click **Next**.
6. The IP Address Range screen appears. Enter the starting and ending IP address and the subnet mask for the scope and then click **Next**.
7. The Add Exclusions screen appears. Enter any necessary exclusions and then click **Next**.
8. The Lease Duration screen appears. Enter the length of the DHCP lease and click **Next**.

9. The Configure DHCP Options screen appears. Click **Yes, I want to configure these options now** and click **Next**.

10. The Router (Default Gateway) screen appears. Enter the default gateway for the scope, click **Add,** and then click **Next**.

11. The Domain Name and DNS Servers screen appears. Enter the DNS domain and DNS servers as appropriate for the scope. Click **Next**.

12. The WINS Servers screen appears. Enter the WINS servers as appropriate for the scope and then click **Next**.

13. The Activate Scope screen appears. Click **Yes, I want to activate this scope now** and then click **Next**.

14. Click **Finish** to complete creating the DHCP scope.

PAUSE. You can close the DHCP management console or else leave it open for a subsequent exercise. To configure a DHCP scope from a Server Core computer, use the netsh command.

In the previous exercise you created and configured a DHCP server on a Windows Server 2008 computer. In the next section we will discuss creating DHCP reservations within a DHCP scope.

> **TAKE NOTE***
>
> A DHCP *superscope* is an administrative grouping of scopes that is used to support *multinets*, or multiple logical subnets (subdivisions of an IP network) on a single network segment (a portion of the IP internetwork bounded by IP routers). Multinetting commonly occurs when the number of hosts on a network segment grows beyond the capacity of the original address space. By creating a logically distinct second scope and then grouping these two scopes into a single superscope, you can double your physical segment's capacity for addresses. (In multinet scenarios, routing is also required to connect the logical subnets.) In this way, the DHCP server can provide clients on a single physical network with leases from more than one scope. Superscopes contain only a list of member scopes or child scopes that can be activated together; they are not used to configure other details about scope use.

Configuring a DHCP Reservation

> Network administrators can use DHCP *reservations* for DHCP-enabled hosts that need to have static IP addresses on your network. Examples of hosts that require static IP addresses are e-mail servers and application servers. File and print servers may also require static or reserved IP addresses if they are accessed by their IP addresses.

DHCP reservations enable permanent address lease assignment by the DHCP server. Where reservations are used, they ensure that a specified hardware device on the network can always use the same IP address. Reservations must be created within a scope and must not be excluded from the scope. Excluded addresses are not available for assignment to clients even if reserved for a client. An IP address is set aside, or reserved, for a specific network device that has the *Media Access Control (MAC)* address (the hard-coded hexadecimal hardware address associated with a Network Interface Card) associated with that IP address. Therefore, when creating a reservation, you must know the MAC address for each device for which you are reserving an address. The MAC address can be obtained by keying **ipconfig /all** at the command line, which will result in output similar to the following:

Ethernet adapter Wireless Network Connection:

Connection-specific DNS Suffix.:

Description........................: Dell Wireless 1390 WLAN Mini-Card

Physical Address.................: 00-1A-92-9F-D7-DC

Dhcp Enabled......................:	Yes
Autoconfiguration Enabled...:	Yes
IP Address..........................:	192.168.1.100
Subnet Mask.......................:	255.255.255.0
Default Gateway..................:	192.168.1.1
DHCP Server.......................:	192.168.1.1
DNS Servers.......................:	192.168.1.210
	192.168.1.215
Lease Obtained..................:	Sunday, December 02, 2007 4:54:47 PM
Lease Expires....................:	Monday, December 03, 2007 4:54:47 PM

The MAC address in this example is 00-1A-92-9F-D7-DC.

 CONFIGURE A DHCP RESERVATION

GET READY. This exercise assumes that you have configured a DHCP Server on a Windows Server 2008 computer and have configured at least one DHCP scope.

1. Press (Ctrl) + (Alt) + (Del) on the Windows Server 2008 computer and log on as the default administrator of the local computer.
2. Click **Start→Administrative Tools→DHCP**.
3. To configure an IPv4 DHCP scope, drill down to the server name, followed by IPv4, followed by the scope name, and then expand the **Reservations** node.
4. Right-click the **Reservations** node and click **New Reservation....**
5. The New Reservation screen appears. Enter a descriptive name for the reservation, followed by the desired IP address.
6. Enter the MAC address of the computer that should receive this reservation, and an optional description.
7. Click **Add** and then click **Close**.

PAUSE. You can close the DHCP administration console, or else leave it open for a subsequent exercise. To configure a DHCP scope from a Server Core computer, use the netsh command.

In the previous exercise, you configured a DHCP reservation within a DHCP scope. In the next exercise, we will discuss configuring DHCP options to fine-tune the configuration of computers receiving their IP address configuration from a Windows Server 2008 DHCP server.

Configuring DHCP Options

DHCP options are additional client-configuration parameters that a DHCP server can assign when serving leases to DHCP clients. DHCP options are configured using the DHCP console and can apply to scopes and reservations. For example, IP addresses for a router or default gateway, WINS servers, or DNS servers are commonly provided for a single scope or globally for all scopes managed by the DHCP server.

Many DHCP options are predefined through RFC 2132, but the Microsoft DHCP server also allows you to define and add custom options. Table 3-1 describes some of the options that can be configured.

Table 3-1

DHCP Options

OPTION	DESCRIPTION
Router (default gateway)	The addresses of any default gateway or router. This router is commonly referred to as the default gateway.
Domain name	A DNS domain name defines the domain to which a client computer belongs. The client computer can use this information to update a DNS server so that other computers can locate the client.
DNS and WINS servers	The addresses of any DNS and WINS servers for clients to use for network communication.

DHCP options can be assigned to all scopes, one specific scope, or to a specific machine reservation. There are four types of DHCP options in Windows Server 2008:

- *Server options*—apply to all clients of the DHCP server. Use these options for parameters common across all scopes on the DHCP server.
- *Scope options*—apply to all clients within a scope and are the most often used set of options. Scope options override server options.
- **Class options**—provide DHCP parameters to DHCP clients based on type—either vendor classes or user classes.
- *Client options*—apply to individual clients. Client options override all other options (server, scope, and class).

User classes are created at the discretion of the DHCP administrator. Vendor classes are defined by the machine's vendor and cannot be changed. Using vendor and user classes, an administrator can then configure the DHCP server to assign different options, depending on the type of client receiving them. For example, an administrator can configure the DHCP server to assign different options based on type of client, such as desktop or portable computer. This feature gives administrators greater flexibility in configuring clients. If client class options are not used, default settings are assigned. Vendor class and vendor options are described in RFC 2132 and can be looked up at *http://www.rfc-editor.org/rfcsearch.html*.

Configuring the DHCP Relay Agent

When the DHCP client and the DHCP server are on the same subnet, the DHCPDISCOVER, DHCPOFFER, DHCPREQUEST, and DHCPACK messages are sent by means of broadcast traffic. When the DHCP server and DHCP client are not on the same subnet, the connecting router or routers must support the forwarding of DHCP messages between the DHCP client and the DHCP server, or a BOOTP/DHCP relay agent must be installed on the subnet where the client is located. This is because BOOTP and DHCP protocols rely on network broadcasts to perform their work, and routers in normal routed environments do not automatically forward broadcasts from one interface to another.

In this section, we will discuss the two options available to you to allow a DHCP server on one subnet to service client requests from remote subnets. First, if the routers separating the DHCP server and clients are RFC 1542 compliant, the routers can be configured for BOOTP forwarding. Through BOOTP forwarding, routers forward DHCP broadcasts between clients and servers and inform servers on the originating subnet of the DHCP requests. This process allows DHCP servers to assign addresses to the remote clients from the appropriate scope.

The second way to allow remote communication between DHCP servers and clients is to configure a DHCP relay agent on the subnet containing the remote clients. DHCP relay agents intercept DHCPDISCOVER packets and forward them to a remote DHCP server whose address has been pre-configured. A DHCP relay agent is either a router or a host computer configured to listen for DHCP/BOOTP broadcast messages and direct them to a specific DHCP server or servers. Using relay agents eliminates the necessity of having a DHCP server on each physical network segment or having RFC 2131–compliant routers. Relay agents not only direct local DHCP client requests to remote DHCP servers, but also return remote DHCP server responses to the DHCP clients. Although the DHCP relay agent is configured through the Routing and Remote Access server role, the computer that is hosting the agent does not need to be functioning as an actual router between subnets. RFC 2131–compliant routers (supersedes RFC 1542) contain relay agents that allow them to forward DHCP packets.

Let's examine a scenario in which a DHCP client on Subnet 2 attempts to obtain its IP address from a DHCP server on Subnet 1:

1. The DHCP client broadcasts a DHCPDISCOVER message on Subnet 2 as a UDP datagram over UDP port 67, which is the port reserved and shared for BOOTP and DHCP server communication.

2. The relay agent, in this case a DHCP/BOOTP relay–enabled router, examines the gateway IP address field in the DHCP/BOOTP message header. If the field has an IP address of 0.0.0.0, the relay agent fills it with its own IP address and forwards the message to Subnet 1, where the DHCP server is located.

3. When the DHCP server on Subnet 1 receives the DHCPDISCOVER message, it examines the gateway IP address field for a DHCP scope to determine whether it can supply an IP address lease. If the DHCP server has multiple DHCP scopes, the address in the gateway IP address field identifies the DHCP scope from which to offer an IP address lease.

For example, if the gateway IP address field has an IP address of 192.168.45.2, the DHCP server checks its DHCP scopes for a scope range that matches the Class C IP network that includes the gateway IP address of the computer. In this case, the DHCP server checks to see which scope includes addresses between 192.168.45.1 and 192.168.45.254. If a scope exists that matches this criterion, the DHCP server selects an available address from the matched scope to use in an IP address lease offer (DHCPOFFER) response to the client. The DHCP Relay Agent process continues as follows:

4. The DHCP server sends a DHCPOFFER message directly to the relay agent identified in the gateway IP address field.

5. The router relays the address lease offer (DHCPOFFER) to the DHCP client as a broadcast since the client's IP address is still unknown.

After the client receives the DHCPOFFER, a DHCPREQUEST message is relayed from client to server, and a DHCPACK message is relayed from server to client in accordance with RFC 1542.

Managing the DHCP Database

DHCP plays a key role in an organization's network infrastructure. Without an accessible DHCP server, most clients completely lose network connectivity. Therefore, like any key resource in your organization, you must carefully manage the DHCP server. Proper management of a DHCP server helps prevent server downtime and aids in quick recovery after a server failure.

Your network is constantly changing. New servers are added and existing servers are changing roles or are removed from the network altogether. Because of this, you must both monitor and manage the DHCP service to ensure it is meeting the needs of the organization. Specifically, you must manage the DHCP database by performing the following database functions:

- Backup and restore
- Reconciliation
- Compacting the database
- Removing the database

The DHCP server database is a dynamic database, which is a data store that is updated as DHCP clients are assigned or as they release their TCP/IP configuration parameters. Because the DHCP database is not a distributed database like the DNS server database, maintaining the DHCP server database is less complex. DNS is stored hierarchically across many different servers, with each server containing a part of the overall database. DHCP, by contrast, is contained in a few files on one server.

The DHCP server database in the Windows Server 2008 family uses the ***Joint Engine Technology (JET)*** storage engine. When you install the DHCP service, the files shown in Table 3-2 are automatically created in the %systemroot%\System32\Dhcp directory.

Table 3-2

DHCP Service Database Files

FILE	DESCRIPTION
Dhcp.mdb	The DHCP server database file.
Temp.edb	A file used by the DHCP database as a temporary storage file during database index maintenance operations. This file sometimes resides in the %systemroot%\System32\Dhcp directory after a system failure.
J50.log and J50#####.log	A log of all database transactions. The DHCP database uses this file to recover data when necessary.
J50.chk	A ***checkpoint file*** indicates the location of the last information that was successfully written from the transaction logs to the database. In a data recovery scenario, the checkpoint file indicates where the recovery or replaying of data should begin. The checkpoint file is updated when data is written to the database file (Dhcp.mdb).

There is virtually no limit to the number of records a DHCP server stores; the size of the database is primarily dependent upon the number of DHCP clients on the network. The size of the DHCP database is not directly proportional to the number of active client lease entries, though, because over time some DHCP client entries become obsolete or deleted. This space is not immediately reclaimed and therefore some space remains unused. To recover the unused space, the DHCP database must be ***compacted***; that is, the database must be optimized to reclaim unused space that has been left by adding and removing records. Dynamic database compaction occurs on DHCP servers as an automatic background process during idle time or after a database update.

Backing Up and Restoring the DHCP Database

Windows Server 2008 DHCP servers support automatic and manual backups. To provide fault tolerance in the case of a failure, it is important to back up the DHCP database. This enables you to restore the database from the backup copy if the hardware fails.

When you perform a backup, the entire DHCP database is saved, including the following:

- Scopes, including superscopes and multicast scopes
- Reservations
- Leases
- Options, including server options, scope options, reservation options, and class options

By default, the DHCP service automatically backs up the DHCP database and related registry entries to a backup directory on the local drive. This occurs every 60 minutes. By default, automatic backups are stored in the %systemroot%\System32\Dhcp\Backup directory. The administrator can also change the backup location. Automatic backups can use only *automatic restores*, which are performed by the DHCP service when corruption is detected.

You can also back up the DHCP database manually. By default, manual backups are stored in the %systemroot%\System32\Dhcp\Backup\ directory, or you can specify an alternate location. You can manually back up the DHCP database while the DHCP service is running. The backup destination must be on the local disk; remote paths are not allowed, and the backup directory is created automatically if it does not already exist. The administrator can then copy the backed up DHCP files to an offline storage location such as a tape or a disk.

 BACK UP AND RESTORE THE DHCP DATABASE

GET READY. This exercise assumes that you have installed the DHCP Server role on a Windows Server 2008 computer, and that you have administrative rights to that server.

1. In the DHCP console, in the console tree, select the appropriate DHCP server.
2. Right-click the server and click **Backup**.
3. In the Browse For Folder dialog box, select the appropriate folder to back up to, and then click **OK**.
4. To restore the DHCP database, right-click the server and click **Restore**.
5. In the Browse For Folder dialog box, select the folder where the backup resides and then click **OK**.
6. In the DHCP dialog box, click **Yes** to stop and then restart the service.
7. If the status of the service does not update, press **F5** to refresh the DHCP console.

PAUSE. You can close the DHCP administrator console, or else leave it open for subsequent exercises.

In the previous exercise you performed a manual backup and restore of the DHCP database. Next we will discuss reconciling the DHCP database.

Reconciling the DHCP Database

When you reconcile a server or a scope, the DHCP service uses both the summary information in the registry and the detailed information in the DHCP database to reconstruct the most current view of the DHCP service. You can choose to reconcile all scopes on the server by selecting the DHCP server, or you can reconcile one scope by selecting the appropriate scope.

Reconciliation is the process of verifying DHCP database values against DHCP registry values. You should reconcile your DHCP database in the following scenarios:

- The DHCP database values are configured correctly, but they are not displayed correctly in the DHCP console.
- After you have restored a DHCP database, but the restored DHCP database does not have the most recent values.

For example, assume your existing database was deleted and you have to restore an older version of the database. If you start DHCP and open the console, you will notice that the scope and options display, but the active leases do not. Reconciliation populates the client lease information from the registry to the DHCP database.

Before using the Reconcile feature to verify client information for a DHCP scope from the registry, the server computer needs to meet the following criteria:

- You must restore the DHCP server registry keys, or they must remain intact from previous service operations on the server computer.
- You must generate a fresh copy of the DHCP server database file in the %systemroot%\ System32\Dhcp folder on the server computer.

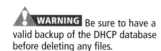 **WARNING** Be sure to have a valid backup of the DHCP database before deleting any files.

You can generate a fresh copy of the DHCP server database file by stopping the DHCP server service, deleting all of the database files in the current database path folder, and then restarting the DHCP server service.

Once the registry and database meet the previous criteria, you can restart the DHCP service. Upon opening the DHCP console, you might notice that scope information is present, but that there are no active leases displayed. To regain your active leases for each scope, use the Reconcile feature. You can reconcile a single scope or the entire server by right-clicking on the appropriate node and then clicking Reconcile.

When viewing properties for individual clients displayed in the list of active leases, you might notice client information displayed incorrectly. When the scope clients renew their leases, the DHCP Manager corrects and updates this information.

SUMMARY SKILL MATRIX

IN THIS LESSON YOU LEARNED:

- DHCP is a simple, standard protocol that makes TCP/IP network configuration much easier for the administrator by dynamically assigning IP addresses and providing additional configuration information to DHCP clients automatically.

- Additional configuration information is provided in the form of options and can be associated with reserved IPs, to a vendor or user class, to a scope, or to an entire DHCP server.

- Because DHCP is a key component in your organization, you must manage and monitor it.

- DHCP management consists of backing up and restoring the database as well as reconciling, compacting, and, in some cases, removing the database.

- APIPA is useful for providing addresses to single-segment networks that do not have a DHCP server.

■ Knowledge Assessment

Matching

Match the term in Column 1 to its description in Column 2.

   a. authorize
   b. automatic restore
   c. class options
   d. DHCPDECLINE

e. DHCPRELEASE

f. exclusion range

g. Joint Engine Technology (JET)

h. reservation

i. rogue DHCP server

j. T2

_E_ 1. This DHCP message type is sent by a DHCP client when it no longer requires the use of an IP address that it has leased from a DHCP server.

_H_ 2. You can configure one of these to ensure that a DHCP client always eceives the same IP address from a particular DHCP server.

_F_ 3. This is used to ensure that a particular address or block of addresses within a scope is not assigned to DHCP clients by a DHCP server.

_A_ 4. You must do this to any DHCP server that needs to function within an Active Directory domain.

_D_ 5. A DHCP client will send this message type if it determines that an IP address offered by a DHCP server is already in use.

_B_ 6. This is performed by a DHCP server when corruption is detected within the DHCP database.

_G_ 7. The DHCP database is based on this database technology.

_I i_ 8. Authorizing DHCP servers in Active Directory is designed to prevent against these.

_C_ 9. These provide DHCP parameters to DHCP clients based on vendor or user type.

_j_ 10. This defaults to 87.5% of the total DHCP lease.

Multiple Choice

Select all answers that apply for the following questions.

1. Which of the following DHCP message types is sent first in the process of obtaining an address lease?
   a. DHCPOFFER
   b. DHCPACK
   c. DHCPDISCOVER
   d. DHCPREQUEST

2. At which layer of the OSI model does DHCP operate?
   a. Session layer
   b. Network layer
   c. Application layer
   d. Presentation layer

3. What protocol is used by the Trivial File Transfer Protocol (TFTP)?
   a. User Datagram Protocol (UDP)
   b. Transmission Control Protocol (TCP)
   c. Internet Protocol (IP)
   d. Internet Message Control Protocol (ICMP)

4. A DHCP client first attempts to reacquire its lease at half the lease time, which is known as:
   a. DHCP reservation
   b. T1
   c. T2
   d. DHCP lease

5. The _____ is composed of the remaining addresses within a DHCP scope once all exclusion ranges have been applied.
   a. total address pool
   b. available address pool
   c. net address pool
   d. remaining address pool

6. The following is a lightweight version of FTP that uses the UDP protocol, which is used by the BOOTP protocol to transmit network configuration information:
   a. TCP
   b. IP
   c. TFTP
   d. SNMP

7. The following process will populate DHCP client lease information from the registry to the DHCP database:
   a. Backup
   b. Automatic restore
   c. Reconciliation
   d. Discovery

8. The following is an administrative grouping of scopes that is used to support multiple logical subnets on a single network segment:
   a. host
   c. superscope
   b. scope
   d. multinet

9. This indicates the location of the last information that was successfully written from transaction logs to a database file such as a DHCP database.
   a. Log file
   b. JET file
   c. Checkpoint file
   d. Check file

10. The following is a hexadecimal address that is uniquely associated with a specific Network Interface Card (NIC):
    a. MAC
    b. JET
    c. BOOTP
    d. IETF

■ Case Scenarios

Scenario 3-1: Obtaining an IP Address

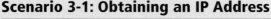

Last month, a server was configured for DHCP and was functioning normally. Five days ago, a test server on the same network segment was promoted to be the first domain controller on the network. Today several users on the same subnet as the original DHCP server have complained that they are unable to obtain an IP address using DHCP. What is the most likely reason users are unable to obtain an IP address?

a. The users' IP address leases have expired.

b. A DHCP relay agent is missing or incorrectly configured.

c. There are duplicate IP addresses on the network.

d. The DHCP server must be authorized and is not.

Scenario 3-2: Maximizing Lease Availability

You are configuring DHCP scope options for Contoso, Ltd. The company has a limited number of IP addresses available for clients, and it wants to configure DHCP to maximize IP address availability. Choose all of the following actions that will accomplish this objective:

a. Set long lease durations for IP addresses.

b. Set short lease durations for IP addresses.

c. Configure a DHCP option to automatically release an IP address when the computer shuts down.

d. Create DHCP reservations for all portable computers.

Configuring and Managing the DNS Server Role

OBJECTIVE DOMAIN MATRIX

Technology Skill	Objective Domain	Objective Domain Number
Installing the DNS Server Role	Configure a Domain Name System (DNS) server	2.1
Introducing DNS Zones	Configure DNS zones	2.2
Configuring Active Directory–Integrated Zones	Configure DNS replication	2.4
Configuring DNS Resource Records	Configure DNS records	2.3
Introducing the DNS Name Resolution Process	Configure name resolution for client	2.5

KEY TERMS

authoritative
authoritative answer
canonical name (CNAME) resource record
conditional forwarder
country code
discretionary access control list (DACL)
DomainDNSZones
file-backed zone
ForestDNSZones

forward lookup zone
forwarder
forwarding-only server
full zone transfer (AXFR)
host (A)
host (AAAA) resource record
incremental zone transfer (IXFR)
in-addr.arpa domain
ip6.arpa domain
mail exchanger (MX) resource record

PTR resource record
reverse lookup zone
root hints
second-level domains
secure dynamic updates
standard zone
stub zone
Time to Live (TTL)
top-level domains
zone transfer

Contoso, Ltd. is a global manufacturer of computer peripherals, with locations in Guadalajara, Mexico; Austin, Texas; and Tallinn, Estonia. Each location contains several hundred PCs that are frequently rebuilt using different machine names to emulate various testing environments. As the network administrator of Contoso, you have been tasked with configuring a name resolution solution that will allow users in each location to maintain consistent access to resources. To enable this functionality, you have decided to deploy the Domain Name System (DNS) server role using a Microsoft Windows Server 2008 computer in each company location.

In this lesson we will discuss the Domain Name System (DNS), the primary means of name resolution in Active Directory and on major TCP/IP networks such as the Internet. We will begin with a discussion of the components of DNS. Once you have a grounding in the overall concepts of DNS, we will walk through the steps required to implement this service on a Windows Server 2008 network.

■ Configuring the Domain Name System (DNS) Service

↓ THE BOTTOM LINE

This lesson introduces fundamental concepts related to Domain Name System (DNS) name resolution in Microsoft Windows Server 2008. The lesson also explains key DNS concepts such as the DNS namespace, DNS zones, types of DNS servers, DNS resource records, and DNS resolvers. Also discussed is the process of configuring DNS servers, the types and process of DNS queries, and forwarding. Because DNS plays such a key role in Windows Server 2008, it is critical that you have a strong grasp of its concepts, processes, and methods of configuration. Without DNS, your network will most likely not function—clients won't be able to resolve names to Internet Protocol (IP) addresses. In addition, Active Directory clients use DNS to locate domain controllers; therefore, it is important that you understand key DNS concepts and how to properly configure DNS for your network.

For network devices such as computers and printers to communicate on the Internet or within your organization's network, they must be able to locate one another. In a Windows Server 2008 network, the primary means of locating network devices and network services is through the use of the Domain Name System, or DNS. For example, in order for COMPUTERA to communicate with COMPUTERB over a Transmission Control Protocol/Internet Protocol (TCP/IP) network, COMPUTERA must obtain the IP address of COMPUTERB. The process of mapping an IP address to a computer name (for example, COMPUTERA) is called *name resolution*. Windows Server 2008 includes both the DNS and Windows Internet Naming System (WINS) name resolution services to allow 2008 computers to translate between human-readable names, which are easy for users to understand, and numerical IP addresses, which are difficult for users to comprehend but are necessary for TCP/IP communications.

Before you can design and configure DNS for your Windows Server 2008 network, it is important to have an understanding of how DNS name resolution was developed for use on TCP/IP networks. Before the growth of the ARPANET into what we now know as the Internet, name resolution was handled through the use of text files called *HOSTS files* that were stored locally on each computer. The HOSTS file listed each name of the host and its corresponding IP address. Whenever a new host was added to the network, an administrator would manually update the HOSTS file with the new host name or IP address information. Periodically, all ARPANET users would then download and use the updated HOSTS file. Because the HOSTS file was flat, rather than hierarchical, it was impossible to organize hosts into separate domain structures. There was no method for creating hierarchical namespaces such as domains.

Another problem with HOSTS files was the size of the file and the inability to distribute the workload that resulted from parsing this file across multiple computers. Every HOSTS file listed every available ARPANET host, which meant that every computer that parsed the HOSTS file did 100 percent of the work to resolve client names into IP addresses. Clearly, this was inefficient and a better name resolution system had to be devised. In 1984, when the number of hosts on ARPANET reached 1,000, DNS was introduced. Because DNS is designed as a distributed database with a hierarchical structure, it can serve as the foundation for host name resolution in a TCP/IP network of any size, including the Internet. The distributed nature of DNS enables the name resolution workload to be shared among many computers. Today, most internetworking software, such as electronic mail programs and Web browsers, uses DNS for name resolution.

Although DNS is most commonly associated with the Internet, private networks also use DNS because of the following benefits:

- Scalability—Because DNS is capable of distributing workload across several databases or computers, it can scale to handle any level of name resolution required.

- Constancy—Host names remain constant even when associated IP addresses change, which makes locating network resources much easier.

- Ease of Use—Users access computers using easy-to-remember names such as *www. microsoft.com* rather than a numerical IP address, such as 192.168.1.100.

- Simplicity—Users need to learn only one naming convention to find resources on either the Internet or an intranet.

To understand the importance of DNS and how it functions within a Windows Server 2008 environment, you must understand a number of different components within DNS.

Introducing DNS Namespaces

A *DNS namespace* is a hierarchical, tree-structured list of DNS host names, starting at an unnamed root that is used for all DNS operations. Each domain can have additional child domains: a typical DNS namespace might be the *contoso.com* domain, which contains the *us.contoso.com* and *ee.contoso.com* child domains within the same namespace, and host names (also called *leaf objects*) representing individual TCP/IP-enabled devices such as *server1.austin.us.contoso.com*, *hplaserjet.sales.ee.contoso.com*, or *www.us.contoso.com*. Figure 4-1 illustrates the structure of a typical DNS namespace that you might find on the Internet.

Figure 4-1

Viewing a typical DNS namespace

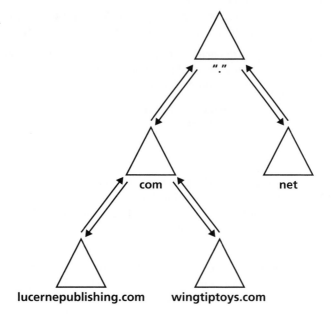

The DNS namespace has a hierarchical structure, and each DNS domain name is unique within a namespace. In Figure 4-1, at the top of the Internet DNS namespace is the root domain. The root domain is represented by "." (a period). Under the DNS root domain, the **top-level domains**, or first-level domains, are organizational types such as .org, .com, and .edu. There are three types of top-level domains:

- Generic—See Table 4-1 for examples of generic, top-level domain names.
- *Country code*—Examples of country code domain names are .uk., .jp, and .us.
- Infrastructure domain—.arpa is the Internet's infrastructure domain name.

Table 4-1

Generic Top-Level Domain Names

DOMAIN NAME	USE
.aero	Exclusively reserved for the aviation community
.biz	A top-level domain that is aimed at large and small companies around the world
.com	Commercial organizations, such as *microsoft.com* for the Microsoft Corporation
.coop	A top-level domain for cooperatives
.edu	Educational institutions, now mainly four-year colleges and universities, such as *wustl.edu* for Washington University in St. Louis.
.gov	Agencies of the U.S. federal government, such as *fbi.gov* for the U.S. Federal Bureau of Investigation
.info	An unrestricted domain aimed at providing information for worldwide consumption
.int	Organizations established by international treaties, such as *nato.int* for NATO
.mil	U.S. military, such as *af.mil* for the U.S. Air Force
.museum	A domain restricted to museums and related organizations and individuals
.name	A global domain for use by individuals that possibly develops into a global digital identity for users
.net	Computers of network providers, organizations dedicated to the Internet, Internet service providers (ISPs), and so forth, such as *internic.net* for the Internet Network Information Center (InterNIC)
.org	A top-level domain for groups that do not fit anywhere else, such as non-governmental or nonprofit organizations (for example, *w3.org*, which is the World Wide Web Consortium)
.pro	A top-level domain for professionals, such as doctors, lawyers, and accountants

DNS uses the fully qualified domain name (FQDN) to map a host name to an IP address. An FQDN describes the exact relationship between a host and its DNS domain. For example, *computer1.sales.microsoft.com* represents a fully qualified domain name: the computer1 host, located in the sales domain, located in the Microsoft second-level domain, located in the .com top-level domain.

Second-level domains are registered to individuals or organizations, such as *microsoft.com*, the Microsoft Corporation domain; or *wustl.edu*, which is Washington University in the St. Louis domain; or *gov.au*, the domain for the Australian government. Second-level DNS domains can have many *subdomains*, and any domain can have hosts. A host is a specific computer or other network device within a domain, such as *computer1* in the *sales* subdomain of the *microsoft.com* domain.

One benefit of the hierarchical structure of DNS is that it is possible to have two hosts with the same host name that are in different locations in the hierarchy. For example, two hosts named *computer1*—*computer1.sales.microsoft.com* and *computer1.cpandl.microsoft.com*—can both exist without conflict because they are in different locations in the namespace hierarchy.

Deploying DNS Servers

As you might expect from the name, *DNS servers* are Windows Servers that host the DNS server role and are classified by the type of zones that they host. A DNS server can host primary zones, secondary zones, stub zones, or no zones. (A DNS *zone* is a collection of host name–to–IP address mappings for hosts in a contiguous portion of the DNS namespace, such as *contoso.com* or *austin.contoso.com*.) A DNS server is called the *primary name server* for any primary zones it hosts and a *secondary name server* for the secondary zones it hosts. A *caching-only server* hosts no zones.

 REF   DNS zones will be discussed more fully in the next section: "Introducing DNS zones."

DNS server types are determined by the type of zone or zones they host, and by the functions they perform. A DNS server may host either primary or secondary zones or both. If the server doesn't host any zones, it is referred to a *caching-only server*. A server is said to be ***authoritative*** for a particular zone if it hosts a primary or secondary zone for a particular DNS domain. These three types of servers are supported in Windows Server 2003 and Windows Server 2008, and are discussed as follows:

- Primary name server—Primary name servers have been configured with one or more primary DNS zones. In the case of standard or file-backed zones, when a change is made to the zone data, such as adding resource records to the zone, the changes must be made on the primary server for that zone; these changes will then propagate to secondary name servers. In the case of AD-integrated zones, there is no distinction between primary and secondary servers.

- Secondary name server—A secondary name server hosts one or more secondary zone databases. Because a zone transfer is used to create a secondary zone, the primary name server and zone already must exist to create a secondary name server.

- Caching-only server—Caching-only servers do not host any zones and are not authoritative for any domain. Caching-only DNS servers start with an empty cache, and then add resource record entries as the server fulfills client requests. This information is then available from its cache when answering subsequent client queries. A caching-only DNS server is valuable at a site when DNS functionality is needed locally but when creating a separate domain or zone is not desirable.

Installing the DNS Server Role

CERTIFICATION READY?
Configure a Domain Name System (DNS) server
2.1

To enjoy the benefits of DNS, you must, of course, install DNS. Before you install DNS, it is recommended that you configure your computer to use a static IP address. If the DNS server is assigned its IP address from Dynamic Host Configuration Protocol (DHCP), its IP address may change. If the DNS server's IP address changes, queries sent by DNS clients configured with the old IP address will fail. Windows Server 2008 provides several wizards and other tools to install DNS quickly and easily. One method of installing DNS is by using the Server Manager page. The Server Manager page enables you to add or remove server roles, such as file server, print server, DHCP server, and DNS server. The following procedure explains how to use the Server Manager console to add the DNS server role. It will also cover the steps needed to create a zone and one or more resource records within a zone, now that we have covered the theory behind each of these concepts.

➜ INSTALL THE DNS SERVER ROLE

GET READY. This exercise assumes that you are logged onto a Windows Server 2008 computer that has been configured with a static IP address, and that the Initial Configuration Tasks for this server have already been completed.

Install the DNS server role

1. Log onto the server using administrative credentials.
2. Click the **Start** button, and then click **Server Manager**. Expand the Server Manager console to full-screen, if necessary.
3. In the left-hand pane, click **Roles**. In the right-hand pane, click **Add Roles**.
4. The Before You Begin screen appears. Read the preliminary information and click **Next**.
5. The Select Server Roles screen appears. Place a checkmark next to **DNS Server** and click **Next**.
6. The DNS Server screen appears. Read the information presented about the DNS server role and click **Next**.
7. The Confirm Installation Selections screen appears. Click **Install** to install the DNS server role.
8. After a few minutes, the Installation Results screen will appear. Click **Close**.

PAUSE. Close the DNS console and log off of the Windows Server 2008 server.

In the previous exercise, you installed the DNS server role. In upcoming exercises you will configure DNS zones, create DNS resource records, and perform a number of other common configuration tasks on a Windows Server 2008 DNS server.

Introducing DNS Zones

CERTIFICATION READY?
Configure DNS zones
2.2

As previously noted, another benefit of the DNS hierarchical structure is that workload for name resolution is distributed across many different resources. For administrative purposes, DNS domains can be organized into zones. A zone is a collection of host name–to–IP address mappings for hosts in a contiguous portion of the DNS namespace. Just like DNS resource records, DNS zones can be created and configured using the Windows Server 2008 DNS MMC snap-in, or else the *dnscmd* DNS management command-line utility.

A DNS zone can hold the resource records for one domain, or it can hold the resource records for multiple domains. A zone can host more than one domain only if the domains are contiguous—that is, connected by a direct parent-child relationship. One reason to divide a namespace into zones is to delegate authority for different portions of it, as one very large domain could be difficult to administer if contained in a single zone.

For each DNS domain name included in a zone, the zone becomes the authoritative source for information about that domain. When a zone is authoritative over a portion of the namespace, it means that it hosts the resource records for that portion of the namespace. It does not necessarily mean, however, that the server can update or modify the zone.

DNS zones are classified by where they are stored, whether they are writable, and by what information they receive and return. Zones can be stored either in text files or in Active Directory. When you configure a DNS server, you can configure it either with several zone types or with none at all, depending on the type of role that the DNS server has in the network. By using different zones, you can configure your DNS solution to best meet your needs. For example, it is recommended that you configure a primary zone and a secondary zone on separate DNS servers to provide fault tolerance should one server fail. You can also configure a stub zone if the zone is maintained on a separate DNS server to allow local DNS servers to stay up-to-date whenever remote DNS server information for a particular zone is updated.

In brief, zone data is maintained on a DNS name server and is stored in one of two ways:

- As a text-based zone file containing lists of mappings, called a ***standard zone*** or a ***file-backed zone***
- Within an Active Directory database, called an *Active Directory–integrated zone*

In terms of the types of queries that a DNS zone (either standard or AD-integrated) can respond to, each zone can be either a ***forward lookup zone*** or a ***reverse lookup zone***. In turn, each forward or reverse lookup zone can be one of three types:

- Primary zone
- Secondary zone
- Stub zone

As you can see, there are numerous possible combinations of each zone type that you can configure on a DNS server. For example, a single DNS server can host:

- A standard primary forward lookup zone
- A standard secondary forward lookup zone
- An Active Directory–integrated stub zone
- A standard secondary reverse lookup zone

…and so on.

When configuring a DNS server, you can configure a single server to host multiple zones if desired, and you can mix and match between different zone types. For example, a single DNS server might host a primary zone for *contoso.com*, as well as a secondary zone for *lucernepublishing.com* to allow improved name resolution for a remote network's resources, as might be necessary in the case of cross-departmental or cross-organizational projects that require access to resources across multiple organizations.

Configuring Standard Zones

You can configure DNS zones in a number of different ways to meet the requirements of your network topology, administrative model, and the size of your DNS namespace. Typical DNS server operation involves three standard zones (primary, secondary, and in-addr.arpa). Windows Server 2003 and Windows Server 2008 provide a fourth option, stub zones.

Let's look at each of the standard zone types that can be configured on a Windows Server 2008 server.

- Standard primary zone—A standard primary zone hosts a read/write copy of the DNS zone in which resource records are created and managed. Only one server can host and load the master copy of the zone; no additional primary servers for the zone are permitted, and only the server hosting the primary zone is allowed to accept dynamic updates and process zone changes. When setting up DNS servers to host the zones for a domain, the primary server normally is located where it will be accessible for administering the zone file.
- Standard secondary zone—A copy of the zone file may be stored on one or more servers to balance network load, provide fault tolerance, or avoid forcing queries across a slow, wide area network (WAN) link. This standard secondary zone is a read-only copy of the standard primary DNS zone. In standard zones, information from a primary zone is transmitted to a secondary zone by performing a **zone transfer**, which is done by copying the zone file from the primary server to a secondary server. A zone transfer can be a **full zone transfer** (called an **AXFR**), in which the entire contents of the zone is copied from the primary server to the secondary server during each zone transfer, or an **incremental zone transfer** (called an **IXFR**), in which only changed information is transmitted after an initial AXFR, in order to cut down on bandwidth usage between

TAKE NOTE*

When preparing for
your certification exams,
remember the difference
between a secondary
zone and a stub zone:
a secondary zone holds
a read-only copy of
every record contained
in the primary zone; a
stub zone contains only
the Start of Authority
(SOA) record and the
Name Server (NS)
records contained in the
Primary zone. (We will
discuss SOA, NS, and
other record types later
in this lesson.)

TAKE NOTE*

You will need to have
the primary zone in
place and online before
you will be able to add
the secondary zone or
the stub zone; there are
no prerequisites for add-
ing the primary zone.

primary and secondary servers. When a secondary zone is created, you must specify the IP address of one or more master DNS servers from which you want to copy the zone; these can be the Primary DNS server for the zone or another Secondary DNS server. These copies are referred to as *secondary zone database files*. The secondary zone database files are updated regularly from the primary zone database.

• Reverse lookup zone—Most queries sent to a DNS server are forward queries; that is, they request an IP address based on a DNS name. DNS also provides a reverse lookup process, which enables a host to determine another host's name based on its IP address. For example, a query contains the equivalent of "What is the DNS domain name of the host at IP address 192.168.100.1?" To answer this query, the **in-addr.arpa domain** is consulted in combination with the IP address in question. As you read the IP address from left to right, the network portion is some number of bits on the left, and the host portion is some number of bits on the right, based on the subnet mask. For example, 192.168.100.2, with a default subnet mask of 255.255.255.0, means the network portion is 192.168.100, and the host address is 2. Because the higher-level portion of the address is on the right, it must be reversed when building the domain tree. In short, because FQDNs go from specific to general, and IP addresses go from general to specific, that is, reading left to right, to facilitate reverse lookup, the IP address is reversed when concatenated with the in-addr.arpa domain. For example, the reverse lookup zone for the subnet 192.168.100.0 is 100.168.192.in-addr.arpa. The in-addr.arpa domain tree makes use of the *pointer (PTR) resource record*, which is used to associate the IP address with the host name. This lookup should correspond to an *address (A) resource record* for the host in a forward lookup zone. Reverse lookup queries often are used by network applications for verification rather than identification or as a tool for monitoring and troubleshooting the DNS service. The in-addr.arpa domain is used only for Internet Protocol version 4 (IPv4)-based networks. In the DNS console for Windows Server 2003, the DNS server's New Zone Wizard uses this domain when it creates a new reverse lookup zone. Internet Protocol version 6 (IPv6)-based reverse lookup zones are based on the **ip6.arpa domain**, which provides the same functionality as the in-addr.arpa domain for IPv6 networks.

• Stub zone—A DNS server running Windows Server 2003 or Windows Server 2008 also supports a new type of zone called a **stub zone**. A stub zone is a copy of a zone that contains only those resource records necessary to identify the authoritative DNS servers for that zone. A stub zone is a pointer to the DNS server that is authoritative for that zone, and it is used to maintain or improve DNS resolution efficiency. The stub zone contains a subset of zone data consisting of an SOA, an NS, and an A record. Like a standard secondary zone, resource records in the stub zone cannot be modified; they must be modified at the primary zone. Stub zones enable a DNS server to resolve DNS queries by using the stub zone's list of name servers without needing to query the Internet or internal root server for the DNS namespace. Using stub zones throughout your DNS infrastructure enables you to distribute a list of the authoritative DNS servers for a zone without using secondary zones. However, stub zones do not serve the same purpose as secondary zones and should not be considered as a solution to address redundancy and load sharing.

In the following exercises, we will configure a standard primary zone, secondary zone, and stub zone.

CONFIGURE A STANDARD PRIMARY ZONE

GET READY. This exercise assumes that you have installed the DNS server role as described in a previous exercise, and that you are logged onto the Windows Server 2008 computer with administrative privileges. In this exercise, we will create a forward lookup zone for the *contoso. com* domain on a server named DNSPRI.

1. Click the **Start** button, then click **Administrative Tools** and then **DNS**.
2. Expand the DNS console to full-screen, if necessary.
3. Drill down to **DNSPRI→Forward Lookup Zones**.

4. Right-click **Forward Lookup Zones** and click **New Zone**....

5. The Welcome to the New Zone Wizard screen appears. Click **Next**.

6. The Zone Type screen appears. Select the **Primary zone** radio button and click **Next**.

7. The Zone Name screen appears. In the *Zone name:* text box, enter **contoso.com** and then click **Next**.

8. The Zone File screen appears. Ensure that the *Create a new file with this file name:* radio button is selected and then click **Next**.

9. The Dynamic Update screen appears. Ensure that the *Do not allow dynamic updates* radio button is selected and then click **Next**.

10. The Completing the New Zone Wizard appears. Click **Finish**.

PAUSE. Close the DNS MMC snap-in and log off of the DNSPRI Windows Server 2008 server.

In the previous exercise, you configured a standard primary zone for the *contoso.com* DNS domain. In the next exercise, you will configure a secondary zone for load balancing on a second Windows Server 2008 computer called DNSSEC.

 CONFIGURE A STANDARD SECONDARY ZONE

GET READY. This exercise assumes that you have installed the DNS server role on a Windows Server 2008 computer called DNSSEC that has been configured with a static IP address, and that the Initial Configuration Tasks for this server have already been completed, This exercise assumes that you are logged onto DNSSEC with administrative privileges. You must also have the IP address of the DNSPRI server available.

1. Click the **Start** button, then click **Administrative Tools** and then **DNS**.

2. Expand the DNS console to full-screen, if necessary.

3. Drill down to **DNSSEC→Forward Lookup Zones**.

4. Right-click **Forward Lookup Zones** and click **New Zone**....

5. The Welcome to the New Zone Wizard screen appears. Click **Next**.

6. The Zone Type screen appears. Select the **Secondary zone** radio button and click **Next**.

7. The Zone Name screen appears. In the *Zone name:* text box, enter **contoso.com** and then click **Next**.

8. The Zone File screen appears. Ensure that the *Create a new file with this file name:* radio button is selected and then click **Next**.

9. The Master DNS Servers screen appears. Key the IP address of **DNSPRI** and then press (**Enter**). Ensure that the Validated column shows a status of "OK," and then click **Next**.

10. The Completing the New Zone Wizard appears. Click **Finish**.

PAUSE. Close the DNS MMC snap-in and log off of the DNSSEC Windows Server 2008 server.

In the previous exercise, you configured a standard secondary zone for the *contoso.com* DNS domain. In the next exercise, you will configure a stub zone on a Windows Server 2008 computer called DNSSEC.

 CONFIGURE A STUB ZONE

GET READY. This exercise assumes that you have installed the DNS server role on a Windows Server 2008 computer called DNSSEC that has been configured with a static IP address, and that the Initial Configuration Tasks for this server have already been completed, This exercise assumes that you are logged onto DNSSEC with administrative privileges. You must also have the IP address of the DNSPRI server available.

1. Click the **Start** button, then click **Administrative Tools** and then **DNS**.
2. Expand the DNS console to full-screen, if necessary.
3. Drill down to **DNSSEC→Forward Lookup Zones**.
4. Right-click **Forward Lookup Zones** and click **New Zone...**.
5. The Welcome to the New Zone Wizard screen appears. Click **Next**.
6. The Zone Type screen appears. Select the **Stub zone** radio button and click **Next**.
7. The Zone Name screen appears. In the *Zone name:* text box, enter **contoso.com** and then click **Next**.
8. The Master DNS Servers screen appears. Key the IP address of **DNSPRI** and then press (**Enter**). Ensure that the Validated column shows a status of "OK," and then click **Next**.
9. The Completing the New Zone Wizard appears. Click **Finish**.

PAUSE. Close the DNS MMC snap-in and log off of the DNSSEC Windows Server 2008 server.

In the previous exercise, you configured a standard stub zone for the *contoso.com* DNS domain. In the next section, we will discuss configuring Active Directory–integrated DNS zones to improve the replication efficiency and security of your DNS data.

Configuring Active Directory–Integrated Zones

Storing zones in Active Directory is a Microsoft proprietary method of managing, securing, and replicating DNS zone information. An Active Directory–integrated zone is a DNS zone contained within Active Directory. Zones stored in text files are typically referred to as *standard* or *file-backed zones*, while zones that are stored in Active Directory are referred to as *Active Directory–integrated zones*.

Storing a zone in Active Directory has the following benefits:

- Fault tolerance—Redundant copy of DNS zone information can be stored on multiple servers.
- Security—DNS zones stored in Active Directory can take advantage of increased security by modifying its *discretionary access control list (DACL)*. The DACL enables you to specify which users and groups may modify the DNS zones. You can also configure *secure dynamic updates* for Active Directory–integrated zones, which will only allow records to be updated by the client that first registered the record.
- Zones are multimaster—This means that zones can be updated in more than one location, i.e., from more than one server. All domain controllers where the zone is stored can modify the zone, and changes to the zone are then replicated to the other domain controllers that contain the zone file.
- Efficient replication—Zone transfers are replaced by more efficient Active Directory replication. This can be especially important over networks with slow links because Active Directory compresses replication data that passes between sites.
- Maintain use of secondary zones—Zones that are stored in Active Directory can also be transferred to standard secondary servers to create secondary zones in the same way that file-backed secondary zones are transferred.

Windows Server 2003 and Windows Server 2008 provide a more efficient method of replicating DNS zone information than does Microsoft Windows 2000 Server. In Microsoft

Windows 2000, updates to Active Directory zones were replicated to all domain controllers in that domain, whether or not they were also configured as DNS servers.

With Windows Server 2003 and Windows Server 2008, Active Directory–integrated zones can be configured with one of three different *replication scopes*, which is to say that their information can be replicated in three different ways:

- To all domain controllers in the domain (this is the only replication scope available that was available in Windows 2000)
- To all domain controllers that are DNS servers in the local domain, also known as the **DomainDNSZones** application partition
- To all domain controllers that are also DNS servers in the entire forest, also known as the **ForestDNSZones** application

You can create two types of Active Directory–integrated zones: forward lookup zones and reverse lookup zones.

An *Active Directory–integrated forward lookup zone* is similar to a standard primary zone. Outside of Active Directory, primary and secondary servers are necessary because they follow a single-master update model, where only one server contains a writable copy of the zone database. However, Active Directory–integrated zones follow a multimaster update model, meaning all Active Directory–integrated zones contain a read/write copy of the zone and can make changes to the zone information. Therefore, primary and secondary distinctions are not necessary.

An *Active Directory–integrated reverse lookup zone* is used for resolving an IP address to a name and is similar to the standard in-addr.arpa zone. The reverse lookup zone is stored and updated in the same manner as the Active Directory–integrated forward lookup zone.

Configuring DNS Delegation

Initially, a zone stores information about a single DNS domain name. As other domains are added, you must make a decision about whether or not the domain will be part of the same zone. If you choose to add the subdomain, you may manage the subdomain as part of the original zone, or else delegate management of the subdomain to a different zone.

For example, Figure 4-2 shows the *contoso.com* domain, which contains domain names for Contoso, Ltd. When the *contoso.com* domain is first created at a single server, it is configured as a single zone for all of the Contoso DNS namespace. If, however, the *contoso.com* domain needs to use subdomains, those subdomains must be included in the zone or delegated away to another zone.

Figure 4-2

Viewing a DNS zone configuration

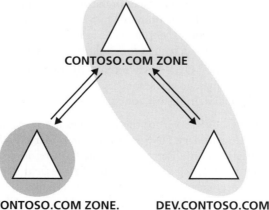

CONTOSO.COM ZONE

SALES.CONTOSO.COM ZONE.   DEV.CONTOSO.COM

In this example, the *contoso.com* domain shows a new subdomain—the *sales.contoso.com* domain—delegated away from the *contoso.com* zone and managed in its own zone. However, the *contoso.com* zone needs to contain a few resource records to provide the delegation information that references the DNS servers that are authoritative for the delegated *sales.contoso.com* subdomain. If the *contoso.com* zone does not use delegation for a subdomain, the data for the subdomain remains part of the *contoso.com* zone. For example, the subdomain *dev.contoso.com* is not delegated away, but is managed by the *contoso.com* zone.

Configuring DNS Zone Transfers

Zone transfers are the complete or partial transfer of all data in a zone from the primary DNS server hosting the zone to a secondary DNS server hosting a copy of the zone. The copy of the zone hosted on a secondary DNS server is initially created using a zone transfer. When changes are made to the zone on a primary DNS server, the primary DNS server notifies the secondary DNS servers that changes have occurred and the changes are replicated to all the secondary DNS servers for that zone using zone transfers.

In the original DNS specifications, only one form of zone transfer was available, the full zone transfer (AXFR). Windows 2000, Windows Server 2003, and Windows Server 2008 DNS also support incremental zone transfers in addition to full zone transfers. This section describes both types of zone transfers, as well as the notification process known as *DNS Notify*.

The following events trigger zone transfers:

- A transfer is manually initiated using the console at the secondary server.
- The zone refresh interval expires.
- The DNS Server service is started at the secondary server.
- The master server notifies the secondary server of a zone change or changes.

Zone transfers are always initiated at the secondary server for a zone and sent to the server's configured master server, which acts as its source for the zone. A master server can be any other DNS server that loads the zone, such as either the primary server for the zone or another secondary server. When the master server receives the request for the zone, it can reply with either an incremental (IXFR) or full (AXFR) transfer of the zone to the secondary server.

In a full zone transfer, the primary DNS server hosting the primary zone transfers a copy of the entire zone database to the secondary DNS server hosting a copy of the zone. Whether a full or incremental transfer, the following process takes place:

X REF

See the "Configuring DNS Resource Records" section of this lesson for information about the Start of Authority (SOA) record.

1. When the value of the Refresh field in the Start of Authority (SOA) resource record for the zone hosted on the secondary DNS server expires, the secondary DNS server queries the primary DNS server for the SOA record of the primary zone.

2. The primary DNS server for the zone replies to the query with the SOA resource record.

3. The secondary DNS server for the zone compares the serial number in the returned SOA record to the serial number in the SOA record for the local copy of the zone. If the serial number sent by the primary DNS server for the zone is higher than the serial number for its local zone, the zone needs to be updated, and the secondary DNS server sends an AXFR request (a request for a full zone transfer) to the primary DNS server.

4. The primary DNS server receives the request for the zone transfer and sends the full zone database to the secondary DNS server, essentially re-creating the copy of the zone while maintaining any zone settings.

If the primary DNS server for the zone does not respond to the request for a zone transfer sent from the secondary DNS server, the secondary DNS server continues to retry for the interval specified in the Retry field in the SOA resource record for the zone. If there is still no answer after the interval specified in the Expire field in the SOA resource record for the zone expires, the secondary DNS server discards its zone.

Incremental zone transfers were designed to reduce the amount of network traffic generated by full zone transfers. Rather than sending a copy of the entire zone file, an incremental zone transfer sends only records that have changed since the last zone update. Windows 2000, Windows Server 2003, and Windows Server 2008 all support incremental zone transfers.

Although an incremental zone transfer saves network bandwidth, it uses additional disk space on the server to record the version history. The primary DNS server for the zone maintains a recent version history of the zone, which observes any record changes that occurred in the most recent version updates of the zone. To conserve disk space, DNS servers store only the most recent updates. The Windows Server 2008 DNS Server service stores these updates in a log file that resides in *the %systemroot%\System32\Dns* folder. The log file is named by using the name of the zone file with .log appended. For example, if the zone file for the *contoso.com* domain is stored in the file *Contoso.com.dns,* the log file is named *Contoso.com.dns.log.*

An incremental zone transfer uses the following process:

1. Initially, when a secondary server is first configured, it sends a full zone transfer request (AXFR) to its master DNS server. The master (source) server responds by sending a full copy of the zone to the secondary (destination) server.

2. Each zone delivery has a version indicated by a serial number in the properties of the SOA resource record and a refresh interval (by default, 900 seconds). The refresh interval indicates at what interval the secondary server should request another copy of the zone from the source server.

3. After the interval expires, the destination server submits an SOA query to request an incremental zone transfer.

4. The source server answers the query by sending its SOA record, which contains the aforementioned serial number.

5. The destination server compares the serial number from the SOA record to its current local serial number. If the numbers are equal, no transfer is requested, and the refresh interval is reset.

6. If the value of the serial number in the SOA response is higher than its current local serial number, records on the source are newer than the local records and an IXFR query is sent to the source server. This query contains the local serial number so the source server can determine which records the destination server needs.

7. Depending on several factors, the source server responds with either an incremental or full transfer of the zone. The primary DNS server for a zone is not required to perform an incremental zone transfer. It can choose to perform a full zone transfer under the following conditions:

   • The primary DNS server does not support incremental zone transfers.

   • The primary DNS server does not have all the necessary data for performing an incremental zone transfer.

   • An incremental zone transfer uses more network bandwidth than a full zone transfer.

When the secondary DNS server receives an incremental zone transfer, it creates a new version of the zone and begins replacing outdated resource records with the updated resource records from the source server, applying oldest to newest. When all the updates are completed, the secondary DNS server replaces its old version of the zone with the new version of the zone.

By default, Windows Server 2008 will only permit zone transfers on standard zones to those servers that have been configured as name servers for the zone in question. Before you can configure an additional name server, it must be configured with a valid FQDN that is resolvable by the server in question.

In the following exercise, we will configure DNSPRI to permit zone transfers to take place to the secondary zone configured on DNSSEC, and we will then force a zone transfer to take place between DNSPRI and DNSSEC.

➔ CONFIGURE A STANDARD SECONDARY ZONE

GET READY. This exercise assumes that you have configured DNSPRI with a primary zone for the *contoso.com* domain, and DNSSEC with a secondary zone for the *contoso.com* domain. This exercise assumes that you are logged onto DNSPRI and DNSSEC with administrative privileges. Parts A and C of this exercise will be performed on DNSSEC; Part B will be performed on DNSPRI. You must have the IP address of both servers available.

PART A—Confirm that zone transfers are not currently functional on DNSSEC

1. Log onto DNSSEC as a local administrator on the computer.
2. Click the **Start** button, then browse to **Administrative Tools→DNS**.
3. The DNS MMC snap-in opens. Browse to **DNSSEC→Forward Lookup Zones**.
4. Click the plus sign next to contoso.com. Notice that a red 'X' appears next to the zone name in the left-hand column, and the right-hand pane indicates that the DNS zone was not loaded by the server.

PART B—Configure zone transfers to DNSSEC from DNSPRI.

1. Log onto DNSPRI as a local administrator on the computer.
2. Click the **Start** button, then browse to **Administrative Tools→DNS**.
3. The DNS MMC snap-in opens. Browse to **DNSSEC→Forward Lookup Zones**.
4. Click the plus sign next to contoso.com. Right-click **contoso.com** and click **New Host (A or AAAA)....** The New Host screen appears.
5. In the Name (uses parent domain name if left blank): field, enter **DNSSEC**. In the IP address: field, enter the IP address of the DNSSEC server.
6. Click **Add Host** and then click **OK** followed by **Done**. Notice that an A record for DNSSEC now appears in the contoso.com zone.
7. Right-click **contoso.com** and click **Properties**. The **contoso.com** Properties screen appears.
8. Click the **Name Servers** tab. You will see the screen shown in Figure 4-3. Notice that only DNSPRI is listed as a Name Server for the contoso.com zone.

Figure 4-3

Configuring DNS name servers

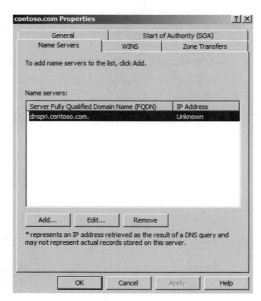

9. Click **Add**. The New Name Server Record screen appears.

10. In the Server fully qualified domain name (FQDN): text box, enter **DNSSEC.contoso.com**. Click **Resolve**.

11. Click **OK** twice to save your changes.

PART C—Confirm that zone transfers are now taking place on DNSSEC

1. Log onto DNSSEC as a local administrator on the computer.

2. Click the **Start** button, then browse to **Administrative Tools→DNS**.

3. The DNS MMC snap-in opens. Browse to **DNSSEC→Forward Lookup Zones**.

4. Click the plus sign next to contoso.com. Notice that the contents of the contoso .com zone have been transferred to DNSSEC.

PAUSE. Close the DNS MMC snap-in on each server, and then log off of both servers.

Using DNS Notify

Windows-based DNS servers support DNS Notify, an update to the original DNS protocol specification that permits a means of initiating notification to secondary servers when zone changes occur (RFC 1996). Servers that are notified can then initiate a zone transfer as described previously to request zone changes from their master servers and update their local replicas of the zone. This process improves consistency of zone data.

The list of secondary DNS servers that a primary DNS server will notify is maintained in the notify list, which is a list of the IP addresses for those secondary servers. When the zone is updated, the primary DNS server for the zone notifies only DNS servers on the notify list. For secondary DNS servers to be notified by the DNS server acting as their configured source for a zone, each secondary server must first have its IP address in the notify list of the source server. In Windows Server 2008 DNS, you can use the DNS Notify dialog box to set the notify list.

In addition to notifying the listed servers, the DNS console permits you to use the contents of the notify list as a means to restrict or limit zone transfer access to only those secondary servers specified in the list. This can help prevent an undesired attempt by an unknown or unapproved DNS server to pull, or request, zone updates.

When the zone on a primary DNS server is updated, the following events occur:

- The Serial Number field in the SOA record is incremented to indicate that a new version of the zone is written to a disk.

- The primary DNS server sends a notify message to the DNS servers that are specified in its notify list.

- A secondary DNS server for the zone that receives the notify message responds by sending an SOA-type query back to the notifying primary DNS server to determine if the zone on the primary DNS server is a later version than the copy of the zone currently stored on the secondary DNS server.

- If a notified secondary DNS server determines that the serial number specified in the SOA record of the zone on the primary DNS server is higher than the serial number specified in the SOA record for its current zone copy (the zone contains more recent updates), the notified secondary DNS server requests a zone transfer (AXFR or IXFR).

Configuring DNS Resource Records

A DNS *resource record* is information that is related to a DNS domain; for example, the host record defining a host IP address. Resource records are represented in binary form in packets when queries and responses are made using DNS. In DNS zone files, however, resource records are represented as text entries. In Windows Server 2008, resource records can be created using the DNS console or the dnscmd command-line utility.

Most resource records are represented as single-line text entries. If an entry is going to span more than one line, you can use parentheses to encapsulate the information. For readability, blank lines and comments often are inserted in the zone files and are ignored by the DNS server. Comments always start with a semicolon (;) and end with a carriage return.

Resource records have the following syntax:

Owner [TTL] Class Type RDATA

Table 4-2 describes the common set of information in resource records.

Table 4-2

Typical Resource Record Fields

NAME	DESCRIPTION
Owner	Identifies the host or the DNS domain to which this resource record belongs.
TTL (Time to Live)	A 32-bit integer representing the maximum time, in seconds, that a DNS server or client caches this resource record before it is discarded. This field is optional, and if it is not specified, the client uses the minimum TTL in the SOA record.
Class	Defines the protocol family in use, which is IN for the Internet system.
Type	Identifies the type of resource record. For example, A indicates that the resource record stores host address information.
Resource Record Data (RDATA)	Contains RDATA. The RDATA field is a variable-length field that represents the information being described by the resource record. For example, in an A resource record, the data contained in this field is the 32-bit IP address that represents the host identified by the owner.

The DNS database consists of resource records that relate different information about the names in the database. A resource record for a DNS name can identify a single resource within the network, such as the network host that uses that name, or that there is a service running on that network host, such as electronic mail.

Different types of resource records provide DNS data about computers on a TCP/IP network. The most common resource records are described in Table 4-3 and in detail in the following sections. This discussion includes resource records specific to Windows 2000, Windows Server 2003, and Windows Server 2008 DNS implementations.

Table 4-3

Resource Record Types

DESCRIPTION	CLASS	TTL	TYPE	DATA
Start of Authority (SOA record)	Internet (IN)	60 minutes	SOA	Owner name, primary name server FQDN, serial number, refresh interval, retry interval, expire time, and minimum TTL
Host (A) Record	Internet (IN)	TTL of the SOA in the same zone	A	Owner name (host DNS name) and host IPv4 address
Host (AAAA) Record	Internet (IN)	TTL of the SOA in the zone	AAAA	Owner name (host DNS name) and host IPv6 address
Name Server (NS Record)	Internet (IN)	TTL of the SOA in the same zone	NS	Owner name and DNS server name

(continued)

Table 4-3 (continued)

Description	Class	TTL	Type	Data
Mail Exchanger (MX Record)	Internet (IN)	TTL of the SOA in the same zone	MX	Owner name, Mail Exchanger (MX) server DNS name, and preference number
Canonical Name (CNAME Record, alias record)	Internet (IN)	TTL of the SOA in the same zone	CNAME	Owner name (alias name) and host DNS name
Service Locator Record (SRV)	Internet (IN)	TTL of the SOA in the same zone	SRV	Domain name associated with the service, Service Name (LDAP, KDC, etc.), Protocol, Weight, Priority, Port number

Start of Authority (SOA) Resource Record

Every zone contains an SOA resource record at the top of the zone file. An SOA resource record indicates the starting point or original point of authority for information stored in a zone. It contains all the zone-specific information for the DNS server to use when maintaining the zone. The SOA resource record is the first resource record that is created when creating a new zone.

The RDATA field for the SOA resource record contains the fields shown in Table 4-4.

Table 4-4

RDATA Fields for the SOA Resource Record

RDATA Fields	Description
Authoritative server	Contains the name of the primary DNS server authoritative for the zone.
Responsible person	Shows the e-mail address of the administrator who is responsible for the zone. This field takes a period (.) instead of an at (@) sign.
Serial number	Shows how many times the zone is updated. When a zone's secondary server contacts its master server to determine whether it needs to initiate a zone transfer, the zone's secondary server compares its own serial number with that of the master. If the serial number of the master server is higher, the secondary server initiates a zone transfer.
Refresh	Shows how often the secondary server for the zone checks to see whether the zone data is changed.
Retry	After sending a zone transfer request, shows how long (in seconds) the zone's secondary server waits before sending another request.
Expire	After a zone transfer, shows how long (in seconds) the zone's secondary server continues to respond to zone queries before discarding its own zone as invalid.
Minimum TTL	Applies to all the resource records in the zone whenever a TTL value is not specified in a resource record or is shorter than the minimum TTL specified in the zone's SOA record. Whenever a DNS client queries the server, the server sends back resource records containing a record-specific TTL or the minimum TTL. Negative responses are cached for the minimum TTL of the SOA resource record of the authoritative zone.

The following output is an example of an SOA resource record:

```
na.contoso.com. IN SOA (
nadc1.na.contoso.com.; authoritative server for the zone
administrator.na.contoso.com.; zone admin e-mail;
(responsible person)
5099;    serial number
3600;    refresh (1 hour)
600;     retry (10 mins)
86400;   expire (1 day)
60 );    minimum TTL (1 min)
```

Name Server (NS) Resource Record

The name server (NS) resource record identifies a DNS server that is authoritative for a zone; that is, a DNS server that hosts a primary or secondary copy of the DNS zone in question. The name of the DNS server that is authoritative for a zone is stored in the RDATA field. NS records are used to indicate both primary and secondary DNS servers for the zone specified in the SOA resource record and to indicate the DNS servers for any delegated zones. If a zone has multiple authoritative servers (for example, a primary server and one or more secondary servers), you need to have an NS record for each server.

TAKE NOTE *

Every zone must contain at least one NS record.

The Windows Server 2008 DNS Server service automatically creates the first NS record for a zone when the zone is created. You can add additional NS records by using DNS or the dnscmd command-line tool.

For example, if the administrator for *contoso.com* delegates authority for the *us.contoso.com.* subdomain to the *usdc1.us.contoso.com* server, the following line is added to the *contoso.com* and *na.contoso.com* zones:

```
us.contoso.com. IN NS usdc1.us.contoso.com.
```

Using Delegation and Glue Records

Delegation and glue records are resource records that you add to a zone to delegate a subdomain to a separate zone hosted on a different DNS server. A delegation record is represented by the NS record in the parent zone that lists the authoritative DNS server hosting the child zone for the delegated subdomain. A glue record is the A record in the parent zone for the authoritative DNS server hosting the child zone for the delegated subdomain.

For example, the DNS server that hosts the zone for the domain *contoso.com* will delegate authority for the subdomain *us.contoso.com* to the DNS server *ns2.us.contoso.com*, which is where a zone for the domain *us.contoso.com* is hosted. To create this delegation, the following records are added to the parent zone *contoso.com*:

```
us.contoso.com.         IN NS ns2.us.contoso.com
ns2.us.contoso.com.     IN A 172.16.54.1
```

When a DNS client submits a query for a name in the child zone to the DNS server that is authoritative for the parent zone, the authoritative DNS server for the parent zone checks its zone. The delegation resource records tell it which DNS server is authoritative for the child zone. The authoritative DNS server for the parent zone can then return a referral containing the delegation records to the DNS client.

A glue record is necessary in this example because *ns2.us.contoso.com* is a member of the delegated domain *us.contoso.com*. However, if it was a member of a different domain, such as *lucernepublishing.com*, the DNS client can perform standard name resolution to resolve the name of the authoritative DNS server to an IP address, in which case a glue record is not required. Separate domain configurations are less common.

Incorrect delegations are a major source of name resolution failure for DNS because an incorrect delegation removes a branch of the DNS namespace tree, and the other nodes in the tree cannot locate the DNS names in and under the branch. For this reason, it is recommended that you verify delegations periodically, and that administrators responsible for parent and child zones communicate any modifications that can affect delegation.

IPv4 Host Records (A) and IPv6 Host Records (AAAA)

The IPv4 **host (A)** resource record maps a FQDN to an IPv4 address. The IPv6 **host (AAAA) resource record** performs the same function, except that it maps an FQDN to an IPv6 address.

For example, the following A resource record is located in the zone *us.contoso.com* and maps the FQDN of a server to its IP address:

```
usdc1.us.contoso.com.    IN A 172.16.48.1
```

The A resource record contains the following fields:

- The Owner, TTL, Class, and Type fields, which are described in Table 4-2, "Typical Resource Record Fields," earlier in this lesson.
- The RDATA field is the IP address of the owner.

PTR Resource Record

The **PTR resource record** performs the reverse function of the A resource record by mapping an IP address to an FQDN. For example, the following PTR resource record maps the IP address 172.16.48.1 of *usdc1.us.contoso.com* to its FQDN:

```
1.48.16.172.in-addr.arpa. IN PTR usdc1.us.contoso.com.
```

PTR resource records contain the following fields:

- The Owner, TTL, Class, and Type fields, which are described in Table 4-2, "Typical Resource Record Fields," earlier in this lesson.
- The RDATA field is the host name of the host with the IP address contained in the Owner field.

Canonical Name (CNAME) Resource Record

The **canonical name (CNAME) resource record** creates an alias for a specified FQDN. You can use CNAME records to hide the implementation details of your network from the clients that connect to it. For example, if you want to put a File Transfer Protocol (FTP) server named *ftp1.us.contoso.com* on your *us.contoso.com* subdomain, but you know that in six months you might move it to a computer named *ftp2.us.contoso.com* and you do not want your users to have to know about the change, do the following: create an alias called *ftp.us.contoso.com* that points to *ftp1.us.contoso.com*. When you move your computer, you need to change only the CNAME record to point to *ftp2.us.contoso.com*.

For example, the following CNAME resource record creates an alias for *ftp1.na.contoso.com*:

```
ftp.us.contoso.com. IN CNAME ftp1.us.contoso.com.
```

After a DNS client queries for the name for *ftp.na.contoso.com*, the DNS server finds the CNAME resource record, resolves the query for *ftp1.us.contoso.com*, and returns both the A and CNAME resource records to the client.

CNAME resource records contain the following fields:

- The Owner, TTL, Class, and Type fields. The Owner field for CNAME records is the alias.
- The RDATA field is the name of the host to which the alias points. (A CNAME record cannot be created unless the A record that it is pointing to already exists.)

Mail Exchanger (MX) Resource Record

The ***mail exchanger (MX) resource record*** specifies a server that is configured to act as a mail server for a DNS name. The mail server identified by an MX record is a host that either processes or forwards mail for a DNS domain name. Processing the mail means either delivering it to the addressee or passing it to a different type of mail transport. Forwarding the mail means sending it to its final destination server, sending it by using Simple Mail Transfer Protocol (SMTP) to another mail exchange server that is closer to the final destination, or queuing it for a specified amount of time.

To improve the reliability of the mail service for a domain, you can designate secondary mail servers that can store mail for a domain. If the primary mail server stops responding, the secondary servers can hold the mail and then forward it when the mail server comes back into service. An SMTP smart host (a host capable of using MX records) uses multiple mail servers, provided you configure multiple MX resource records.

The following example shows MX resource records for the mail servers for the domain *na.contoso.com*:

```
@ IN MX 5 mailserver1.us.contoso.com.
@ IN MX 10 mailserver2.us.contoso.com.
@ IN MX 20 mailserver3.us.contoso.com.
```

MX resource records contain the following fields:

- The Owner, TTL, Class, and Type fields, which are described in Table 4-2, "Typical Resource Record Fields," earlier in this lesson.

The following data is stored in the RDATA field of the MX resource record:

- The fourth field in the MX record is the mail server preference value. The preference value specifies the preference given to the MX record among other MX records. Records with lower priority numbers (which are higher priority) are preferred. Thus, when a mail client needs to send mail to a certain DNS domain, it first contacts a DNS server for that domain and retrieves all the MX records. It then contacts the mailer with the lowest preference value.
- The final field is the name of the mail server to contact.

For more information about how mail is routed in the domain system, see RFC 974, which can be accessed at *http://www.rfc-editor.org/rfcsearch.html*.

For example, suppose Holly Holt sends an e-mail message to *loviatt@us.contoso.com* on a day that mailserver1 is down, but mailserver2 is working. Her e-mail client tries to deliver the message to mailserver1 because it has the lowest preference value, but it fails because mailserver1 is down. In this case, Holly's e-mail client chooses mailserver2 because its preference value is the second lowest. If mailserver2 is operating, the mail is successfully delivered to mailserver2.

To prevent mail loops, if the e-mail client is on a host that is listed as an MX for the destination host, the e-mail client can deliver only to an MX with a lower preference value than its own host. If a mail server receives multiple MX records with equal priority, the choice of which MX record to use depends on implementation.

Service Locator (SRV) Resource Record

Service locator (SRV) resource records enable you to specify the location of servers that provide a specific network service over a specific protocol and in a specific domain. SRV records allow you to have several servers offering a network service and to move services between servers without changing the client configuration. For example, if you have two application servers in your domain, you can create SRV resource records in DNS that specify which hosts serve as application servers. Client applications that support SRV records will use DNS to retrieve the SRV resource records for the application servers.

Active Directory is an example of an application that relies on SRV resource records. An example of an application that supports SRV resource records is the Windows 2000, Windows Server 2003, and Windows Server 2008 Netlogon service. On Windows 2000, Microsoft Windows XP, Windows Server 2003, Windows Server 2008, and Windows Vista, client computers use SRV resource records to locate domain controllers for an Active Directory domain.

The format for an SRV record is as follows:

`_Service_Protocol.Name [TTL] Class SRV Priority Weight Port Target`

Table 4-5 outlines the SRV resource record fields.

Table 4-5

SRV Resource Record Fields

FIELD NAME	DESCRIPTION
Service	Specifies the name of the service, such as http or telnet.
Protocol	Specifies the protocol, such as Transmission Control Protocol (TCP) or User Datagram Protocol (UDP).
Name	Specifies the domain name to which the resource record refers.
TTL	Uses a 32-bit integer to represent the maximum time, in seconds, that a DNS server or client caches this entry before it is discarded. This field is optional, and if it is not specified, the client uses the minimum TTL in the SOA record.
Class	Defines the protocol family in use, which is usually IN for the Internet system. The other value defined in RFC 1034 is CH for the Chaos system, which was used experimentally at the Massachusetts Institute of Technology.

Table 4-6 describes the data stored in the RDATA field of the SRV resource record.

Table 4-6

SRV Record RDATA Fields

FIELD NAME	DESCRIPTION
Priority	Specifies the priority of the host. Clients attempt to contact the host with the lowest priority number.
Weight	Performs load balancing. When the Priority field is the same for two or more records in the same domain, clients must try records with higher weights more often, unless the clients support some other load-balancing mechanism.
Port	Shows the port for the service on this host.
Target	Shows the FQDN for the host providing the service.

The following example shows SRV records for two domain controller servers:

```
_ldap._tcp.contoso.com. IN SRV 0 0 389 dc1.contoso.com.
_ldap._tcp.contoso.com. IN SRV 10 0 389 dc2.contoso.com.
```

This example does not specify a TTL. Therefore, the DNS client uses the minimum TTL specified in the SOA resource record.

If a computer needs to locate a Lightweight Directory Access Protocol (LDAP) server in the *contoso.com* domain, the DNS client sends an SRV query for the following name:

```
_ldap._tcp.contoso.com.
```

The DNS server replies with the SRV records listed in the previous example. The DNS client then chooses between DC1 and DC2 by looking at their priority values. Because DC1 has the lower priority value, the LDAP client chooses DC1. In this example, if the priority values were the same but the weight values were different, the client would choose a domain controller randomly with a probability proportional to the Weight field value.

Next, the DNS client requests the A record for *DC1.contoso.com*, and the DNS server sends the A record. Finally, the client attempts to contact the domain controller using the IP address in the A record.

Using Wildcard Resource Records

In some DNS designs, you might need to use a large number of resource records in a zone. However, you might find it difficult to manually add the records. In such cases, you can define a wildcard DNS resource record.

The following is an example of a wildcard address from the *contoso.com* domain:

```
* IN A 172.16.54.1
```

If the preceding A record is in DNS, all queries for a host in the *contoso.com* domain not explicitly defined in the zone file receive a reply for 172.16.54.1. Windows 2000, Windows Server 2003, and Windows Server 2008 DNS support wildcard resource records.

 CONFIGURE DNS RESOURCE RECORDS

GET READY. This exercise assumes that you have configured DNSPRI with a primary zone for the *contoso.com* domain. This exercise assumes that you are logged onto DNSPRI with administrative privileges.

1. In the DNS console, drill down to **DNSPRI→Forward Lookup Zones→contoso.com**.
2. Right-click **contoso.com** and click **New Host Record (A or AAAA)....**
3. The New Host window appears. In the Name (uses parent domain name if blank): field, enter **SERVER1**. In the IP Address field, enter an IP address appropriate for your environment, such as *192.168.52.150*.
4. Click **Add Host**. Read the DNS window that appears. Click **OK** and then click **Done**.
5. Right-click **contoso.com** and click **New Mail Exchanger (MX)....**
6. The New Resource Record window appears. In the host or child domain: text box, enter **mail.** In the Fully Qualified Domain Name (FQDN) of mail server: text box, enter *SERVER1.contoso.com*.
7. Click **OK**.

PAUSE. Close the DNS MMC snap-in and log off of the Windows Server 2008 computer before continuing.

In the previous exercise, you configured DNS resource records on a Windows Server 2008 computer. In the following section, you will learn about the process of allowing clients to dynamically update their own resource records on a Windows Server 2008 DNS server.

Configuring DNS Dynamic Updates

Windows Server 2008 DNS supports the DNS dynamic update protocol (RFC [Request for Comments] 2136), which enables DNS clients to dynamically update their resource records in DNS zones. You can specify that the DHCP server in your network dynamically update DNS when it configures a DHCP client computer. This reduces the administration time that is necessary when manually administering zone records. You use the dynamic update feature in conjunction with DHCP to update resource records when a computer releases or updates its IP address.

Client computers running Windows 2000 or later attempt to update address (A) resource records directly, but they utilize the DHCP server to dynamically update their pointer (PTR) resource records. DHCP-enabled client computers running earlier versions of Microsoft operating systems are unable to update or register their DNS resource records directly. These DHCP clients must use the DHCP service provided with Windows 2000, Windows Server 2003, and Windows Server 2008 to register and update both their A and PTR resource records on behalf of these down-level clients.

Although dynamic updates allow clients to update DNS resource records, this is not a secure method. A more secure way of updating DNS resource records is using secure dynamic updates. The server attempts the update only if the client can prove its identity and has the proper credentials to make the update. Secure dynamic updates are available only through Active Directory domain service and when Active Directory–integrated DNS is enabled. By default, Active Directory–integrated zones only allow secure dynamic updates, though this setting can be modified when you create the zone. If you created the zone as a standard primary zone, and then you converted it into an Active Directory–integrated zone, it preserves the primary zone dynamic update configuration, which can be changed using the DNS MMC console.

You can configure dynamic updates for a DNS zone to use one of the following options:

- None—No dynamic updates permitted, all DNS entries must be created manually. This is the default dynamic updates setting for a standard DNS zone.
- Nonsecure and secure—Allows clients to first attempt a nonsecure dynamic update, and only if that fails to attempt a secure dynamic update. Because clients will attempt a nonsecure update first, configuring this setting is effectively the same as permitting all dynamic updates to occur in a nonsecure fashion.
- Secure only—This option is only available on DNS zones that have been configured on Active Directory domain controllers.

Configuring Aging and Scavenging of DNS Records

Traditionally, the DNS administrator manually added or deleted resource records from DNS zone files as required. With dynamic update, individual computers and services are able to automatically add, update, and delete DNS resource records. For example, the Windows XP, Windows Vista, Windows 2000, Windows Server 2003, and Windows Server 2008 DNS Client services register their clients' A and pointer (PTR) resource records in DNS at start time and every 24 hours thereafter. Dynamic update ensures that the records are up-to-date and guards against accidental deletion of resource records by the DNS administrator.

Over time, stale resource records accumulate in the DNS database. Records become stale, for example, when computers, especially those of mobile users, abnormally disconnect from the network. Stale records provide outdated and inaccurate information to clients, take up unnecessary space, and can possibly degrade server performance. Windows Server 2008 provides a mechanism called *scavenging* to remove these records as they become out-of-date.

Windows Server 2008 adds a time stamp to dynamically added resource records in primary zones where aging and scavenging are enabled. Records added manually are time stamped with a value of zero, which indicates those records should be excluded from the aging and scavenging process. Since secondary name servers receive a read-only copy of the zone data from primary name servers, only primary zones are eligible to participate in this process (or Active Directory–integrated zones, in the case of AD-integrated DNS). Servers can be configured to perform recurring scavenging operations automatically, or you can initiate a manual and immediate scavenging operation at the server.

DNS Scavenging depends on the following two settings:

- No-Refresh Interval—The time between the most recent refresh of a record time stamp and the moment when the time stamp may be refreshed again. When scavenging is enabled, this is set to 7 days by default.
- Refresh Interval—The time between the earliest moment when a record time stamp can be refreshed and the earliest moment when the record can be scavenged. The refresh interval must be longer than the maximum record refresh period. When scavenging is enabled, this is set to 7 days by default.

A DNS record becomes eligible for scavenging after both the no-refresh and refresh intervals have elapsed, for a total of 14 days by default. Scavenging is enabled on a per-zone basis, and is disabled by default. You should not enable DNS resource record scavenging unless you are absolutely certain that you understand all the parameters and have configured them correctly. Otherwise, you might accidentally configure the server to delete records that it should retain. If a name is accidentally deleted, not only do users fail to resolve queries for that name, but also a different user can create and own that name, even on zones configured for secure dynamic update.

Introducing the DNS Name Resolution Process

The DNS *resolver* refers to the DNS client software that exists on a Windows computer regardless of whether it is running a client or a server operating system. In this way it is important not to confuse the notion of a DNS client resolver with a client operating system such as Windows XP or Windows Vista; a Windows Server 2008 computer contains DNS client software and will often function as a DNS client when attempting to resolve DNS queries. When any DNS client needs to look up a fully qualified domain name to obtain its corresponding IP address, it forms a *DNS query* that contains the DNS domain name (stated as an FQDN), the query type specifying the resource records to be returned (A, SRV, and so on), and the DNS domain name class, which is IN for the Internet system. The query is first passed to the local DNS resolver client service for resolution. If the query cannot be resolved locally, it is sent to the preferred DNS server as configured in the client's TCP/IP properties. If the query does not match an entry in the cache, the resolution process continues with the client querying a DNS server to resolve the name.

CERTIFICATION READY?
Configure name
resolution for clients
2.5

When a query is sent to a DNS server, the server can respond in a number of ways. Following are the most common responses to DNS queries:

- An *authoritative answer*—An authoritative answer is a positive answer returned to the client and delivered with the authority bit set in the DNS message to indicate the answer was obtained from a server with direct authority for the queried name.
- A positive answer—A positive answer can consist of the queried resource record or a list of resource records (also known as a *resource record set*) that fits the queried DNS domain name and record type specified in the query message. Positive answers may or may not be authoritative.

- A referral answer—A referral answer contains additional resource records not specified by the name or type in the query. This type of answer is returned to the client if the recursion process is not supported. The records are meant to act as helpful reference answers that the client can use to continue the query using iteration. A referral answer contains additional data, such as resource records, that are other than the type queried. For example, if the queried host name was "www" and no A resource records for this name were found in this zone, but a CNAME resource record for "www" was found instead, the DNS server can include that information when responding to the client. If the client is able to use iteration, it can make additional queries using the referral information in an attempt to fully resolve the name.

- A negative answer—A negative answer from the server can indicate that one of two possible results was encountered while the server attempted to process and recursively resolve the query fully and authoritatively: An authoritative server reported that the queried name does not exist in the DNS namespace, or an authoritative server reported that the queried name exists but no records of the specified type exist for that name. The resolver passes the query response back to the requesting program and caches the response.

In addition to the zones configured on a DNS server, a server can also use two additional methods to respond to a client query. These additional name resolution methods involve the use of root hints, and the *DNS server cache,* described in the following sections.

Using Root Hints

DNS servers resolve DNS queries using local authoritative or cached data. But if the server does not contain the requested data and is not authoritative for the name in a query, it may perform recursive resolution or return a referral to another DNS server depending on whether the client requested recursion. The DNS Server service must be configured with ***root hints*** to resolve queries for names that it is not authoritative for or for which it contains no delegations. Root hints contain the names and IP addresses of the DNS servers authoritative for the root zone. You can use the DNS console to manage the list of root servers, as well as the dnscmd command-line utility.

By default, DNS servers use a root hints file, called *cache.dns,* on Microsoft DNS servers. The cache.dns file is stored in the *%systemroot%\System32\Dns* folder on the server computer. When the server starts, cache.dns is preloaded into server memory. By using root hints to find root servers, a DNS server is able to complete recursive queries. This process is designed to enable any DNS server to locate the servers that are authoritative for any other DNS domain name used at any level in the namespace tree.

When you use the Windows Server 2008 GUI to configure a DNS server, it sends an NS query for the root domain (.) to the preferred and alternate DNS servers for the server. The query response is placed into the root hints of the DNS server. If no root servers are detected, the wizard sends the same query to the DNS servers specified in the cache.dns file that correspond to the root servers on the Internet. If no root servers are detected, the wizard prompts the user to either make the server a root server or to manually specify root hints. Updating root hints enables the server to function more efficiently. You should update root hints whenever a new server is added or changed.

Configuring Name Server Caching

As DNS servers make recursive queries on behalf of clients, they temporarily cache resource records. Cached resource records contain information obtained from DNS servers that are authoritative for DNS domain names learned while making iterative queries (discussed in the next section) to search and fully answer a recursive query performed on behalf of a client. Later, when other clients place new queries that request resource record information matching cached resource records, the DNS server can use the cached resource record information to answer them.

Caching provides a way to speed the performance of DNS resolution for subsequent queries of popular names, while substantially reducing DNS-related query traffic on the network. When information is cached, a **_Time to Live (TTL)_** value applies to all cached resource records. As long as the TTL for a cached resource record does not expire, a DNS server can continue to cache and use the resource record again when answering queries by its clients that match these resource records. Caching TTL values used by resource records in most zone configurations are assigned the minimum (default) TTL, which is set in the zone's SOA resource record. By default, the minimum TTL is 3,600 seconds (one hour) but can be adjusted, or, if needed, individual caching TTLs can be set at each resource record.

To reduce the amount of traffic to the DNS server or servers, the DNS resolver on each client will cache resource records that are obtained from query responses. These resource records are used to resolve repeated client queries and reduce redundant queries to the DNS server. Each entry in the cache has a specified TTL, typically set by the query response. When the TTL expires, the entry is purged from the cache. When the resolver is unable to answer a query using its own cache, the resolver sends the query to one or more DNS servers configured in the TCP/IP properties of the server. If a HOSTS file is configured on the client, it is preloaded into the resolver cache.

To view the DNS resolver cache on any Windows computer, key the following at a command prompt:

`ipconfig /displaydns`

To purge the cache, key the following at a command prompt:

`ipconfig /flushdns`

Using Iterative and Recursive DNS Queries

Queries from DNS resolvers (whether originating from a client or a server-based operating system) can take one of two forms: an _iterative query_ or a _recursive query_. An iterative query is a DNS query sent to a DNS server in which the querying host requests it to return the best answer it can provide using its own information, and without seeking further assistance from other DNS servers.

⚠ WARNING Do not confuse _recursion_, which is used by _iterative queries_, with _recursive queries_, which are discussed next!

For example, in Figure 4-4, a host queries the primary DNS server, which checks its records and refers the client to Server A. Server A checks its names cache, does not find an answer, and sends a referral to Server B instead. The host receives the response and submits a query to Server B, which responds with a referral to Server C. The original host queries Server C and receives a response. The process of a DNS server performing this "tree-walking" of DNS servers to locate the answer to a query is referred to as _recursion_.

As shown in Figure 4-4, the querying host is responsible for issuing additional queries until it obtains a definitive answer. In the example that follows, the host issues three queries before receiving the requested information. The process is as follows:

1. The first step of the query process is to convert a name request into a query and then pass it to the DNS Client service for resolution that uses locally cached information.

Figure 4-4

Viewing a typical iterative query

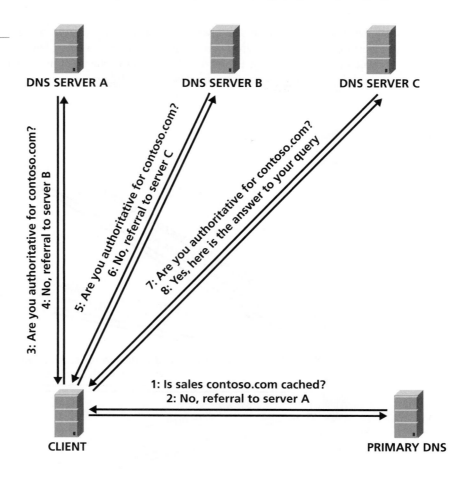

If the query can be answered from the local cache, the process is complete. Otherwise, the client submits an iterative query to its preferred DNS server.

2. The primary DNS server checks to see if it has authority for that domain. In this example, it does not have authority, but it does contain information that points to the .com top-level domain DNS servers. The primary server responds with a referral to the .com top-level domain servers.

3. The DNS client submits an iterative query to DNS Server A.

4. DNS Server A responds with a referral to DNS Server B.

5. The client submits an iterative query to DNS Server B for *sales.contoso.com*.

6. DNS Server B responds with a referral to DNS Server C.

7. The client submits an iterative query to DNS Server C.

8. DNS Server C is authoritative for the *sales.contoso.com* domain and responds with a definitive answer to the client query (in this case, the A record for *sales.contoso.com*).

A recursive query is a DNS query sent to a DNS server in which the querying host asks the DNS server to provide a definitive answer to the query, even if that means contacting other servers to provide the answer. When sent a recursive query, the DNS server iteratively queries other DNS servers to obtain an answer. In Figure 4-5, the querying host issues only one query before receiving the requested information.

To centralize the workload and reduce network traffic, host computers typically issue recursive queries to DNS servers. A network of 1,000 clients iteratively querying DNS servers is clearly less efficient than centralizing queries to a handful of DNS servers. Centralizing queries means each client sends a single recursive query rather than each client sending multiple iterative queries. DNS servers generally issue iterative queries against other DNS servers if they are unable to answer a recursive query from cached information. By using recursive queries, the workload of resolving DNS names can be concentrated to a few servers and thereby achieve much greater efficiency. Figure 4-5 illustrates the client submitting a recursive query and receiving a definitive answer. The process is as follows:

Figure 4-5

Viewing the recursive query process

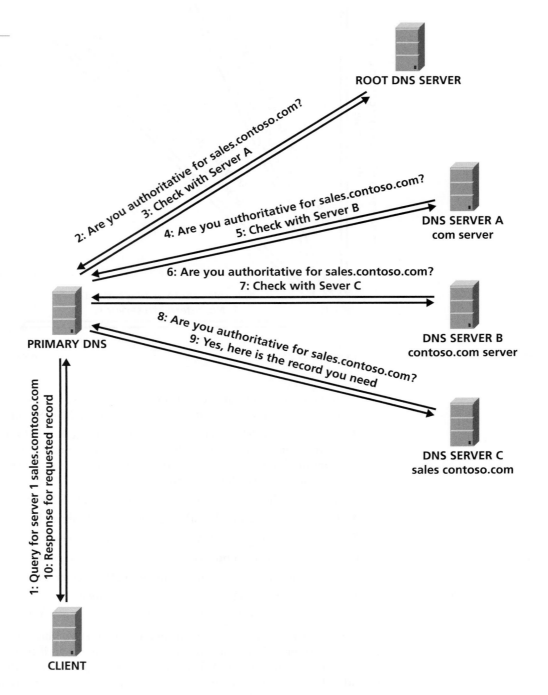

1. The first step of the query process is to convert a name request into a query and then pass it to the DNS Client service for resolution using locally cached information. If the query can be answered from the local cache, the process is complete. Otherwise, the query is passed to the local DNS server.

2. The local name server checks to see if it has authority for that domain. In this example, it does not have authority, but it does contain root hints. The local name server uses the root hints to begin a search for the name server that has authority for the domain *sales.contoso.com*. It then queries the root name server.

3. The root name server sends IP addresses of name servers for the .com top-level domain back to the local DNS server.

4. The local DNS server submits an iterative query to DNS Server A (.com) for *sales .contoso.com.*

5. DNS Server A responds with a referral to the *contoso.com* name server, DNS Server B.

6. The local DNS server submits another iterative query to DNS Server B, *contoso.com.*

7. DNS Server B responds with the IP address for the authoritative server, DNS Server C.

8. The local DNS server submits an iterative query to DNS Server C.

9. DNS Server C responds with a definitive answer (in this case the A record).

10. The local DNS server responds to the DNS client with a definitive answer. The client can now establish a TCP/IP connection with *sales.contoso.com.* From the client's perspective, one request was submitted to and fulfilled by the local DNS server. The information obtained by the local DNS server is cached to answer subsequent queries.

By default, DNS servers use timings for retry intervals and time-out intervals. These are as follows:

- A recursion retry interval of three seconds. This is the length of time the DNS service waits before retrying a query made during a recursive lookup.

- A recursion time-out interval of 15 seconds. This is the length of time the DNS service waits before failing a recursive lookup that has been retried.

Configuring Forwarders

A *forwarder* is a DNS server on a network used to forward DNS queries for external DNS names to DNS servers outside of that network. A *conditional forwarder* forwards queries on the basis of domain name; for example, by forwarding queries for hosts within the *contoso.com* DNS domain to one set of DNS servers, but forwarding queries for the *lucernepublishing.com* domain to a different set of servers.

A DNS server on a network is designated as a forwarder by having the other DNS servers in the network forward the queries they cannot resolve locally to that DNS server. By using a forwarder, you can manage name resolution for names outside of your network, such as names on the Internet, and you improve the efficiency of name resolution for the computers in your network. For example, to use forwarders to manage the DNS traffic between your network and the Internet, configure the firewall used by your network to allow only one DNS server to communicate with the Internet. When you have configured the other DNS servers in your network to forward queries they cannot resolve locally to that DNS server, it will act as your forwarder. Because external network traffic is going through a single DNS server, that server builds up a large cache of DNS data, which, over time, decreases Internet traffic and provides faster response times to clients.

Without having a specific DNS server designated as a forwarder, all DNS servers can send queries outside of a network using their root hints. As a result, a lot of internal, and possibly critical, DNS information can be exposed on the Internet. In addition to this security and privacy issue, this method of resolution can result in a large volume of external traffic that is costly and inefficient for a network with a slow Internet connection or a company with high Internet service costs.

A DNS server configured to use a forwarder will behave differently than a DNS server that is not configured to use a forwarder. A DNS server configured to use a forwarder behaves as follows:

1. When the DNS server receives a query, it attempts to resolve this query by using the primary and secondary zones that it hosts and by using its cache.

TAKE NOTE *

When preparing for certification exams, take note of which DNS settings are configured at the server level as opposed to the zone level. Forwarding is configured for each DNS server, whereas dynamic updates are configured per DNS zone.

2. If the query cannot be resolved using this local data, it will forward the query to the DNS server designated as a forwarder.

3. The DNS server will wait briefly for an answer from the forwarder before attempting to contact the DNS servers specified in its root hints.

4. Rather than send the standard iterative query, when a DNS server forwards a query to a forwarder, by default, it sends a recursive query to the forwarder.

Each domain name used for forwarding on a DNS server is associated with the IP addresses of one or more DNS servers. A DNS server configured for forwarding will use its forwarders list after it has determined that it cannot resolve a query using its authoritative data (primary or secondary zone data) or cached data. If the server cannot resolve a query using forwarders, it may attempt recursion to the root hint servers.

The order of the IP addresses listed determines the sequence in which the IP addresses are used. After the DNS server forwards the query to the forwarder with the first IP address associated with the domain name, it waits a short period for an answer from that forwarder (according to the DNS server's time-out setting) before resuming the forwarding operation with the next IP address associated with the domain name. It continues this process until it receives a positive answer from a forwarder or until it has tried all addresses in the list.

When a DNS server configured to use conditional forwarding receives a query for a domain name, it compares that domain name with its list of domain name conditions and uses the longest domain name condition that corresponds to the domain name in the query. For example, a DNS server receives a query for *www.qualitycontrol.research.wingtiptoys.com*.

It compares that domain name with both *wingtiptoys.com* and *research.wingtiptoys.com*. The DNS server determines that *research.wingtiptoys.com* is the domain name that more closely matches the original query.

Conditional forwarding enables a DNS server to forward queries to other DNS servers based on the DNS domain names in the queries. With conditional forwarding, a DNS server could be configured to forward all the queries it receives for names ending with *research.wingtiptoys.com* to a specific DNS server's IP address or to the IP addresses of multiple DNS servers.

For example, when two companies, *fabrikam.com* and *wingtiptoys.com*, merge or collaborate, they may want to allow clients from the internal namespace of one company to resolve the names of the clients from the internal namespace of another company.

The administrators from one organization (*fabrikam.com*) may inform the administrators of the other organization (*wingtiptoys.com*) about the set of DNS servers that they can use to send DNS queries for name resolution within the internal namespace of the first organization. In this case, the DNS servers in the *wingtiptoys.com* organization will be configured to forward all queries for names ending with *fabrikam.com* to the designated DNS servers.

One important configuration item to note is that a DNS server cannot perform conditional forwarding for any domain names for which that server is authoritative. For example, the authoritative DNS server for the zone *widgets.microsoft.com* cannot forward queries according to the domain name *widgets.microsoft.com*. If the DNS server were allowed to do this, it would nullify the server's capability to respond to queries for the domain name *widgets.microsoft.com*. The DNS server authoritative for *widgets.microsoft.com* can forward queries for DNS names that end with *hr.widgets.microsoft.com*, if *hr.widgets.microsoft.com* is delegated to another DNS server.

The conditional forwarder setting consists of the following:

- The domain names for which the DNS server will forward queries
- One or more DNS server IP addresses for each domain name specified

A DNS server can also be configured as a ***forwarding-only server***, which will not perform recursion after the forwarders fail; if it does not get a successful query response from any of the servers configured as forwarders, it sends a negative response to the DNS client. This option to prevent recursion can be set for each conditional forwarder in Windows Server 2008. For

example, a DNS server can be configured to perform recursion for the domain name *research .wingtiptoys.com*, but not to perform recursion for the domain name *wingtiptoys.com*.

A new feature of Windows Server 2008 is that conditional forwarder information can be integrated into Active Directory when DNS is installed on a domain controller. This allows you to replicate conditional forwarder information among multiple DNS servers on your network. A conditional forwarder in an Active Directory environment can be replicated to any of the following:

- All DNS servers in the forest
- All DNS servers in the domain
- All domain controllers in the domain

In the following exercise, we will configure both forwarders and conditional forwarders on a Windows Server 2008 DNS server.

 CONFIGURE FORWARDERS

GET READY. This exercise assumes that you have configured DNSPRI with a primary zone for the *contoso.com* domain. This exercise assumes that you are logged onto DNSPRI with administrative privileges. In Part A you will configure a DNS forwarder; in Part B you will configure conditional forwarders based on domain name.

PART A—Configure a forwarder for a DNS Server

1. Click the **Start** button, then browse to **Administrative Tools→DNS**.
2. Click the plus sign (+) next to DNSPRI. Right-click **DNSPRI** and select **Properties**.
3. Click the **Forwarders** tab. You will see the screen shown in Figure 4-6.

Figure 4-6

Configuring DNS forwarders

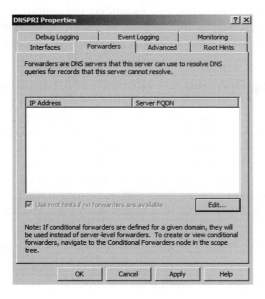

4. Click **Edit**. Enter the IP address of a remote DNS server and click **OK**.
5. To prevent this DNS server from using recursion, remove the checkmark next to Use root hints if no forwarders are available, and then click **OK**.

PART B—Configure a conditional forwarder

1. In the left-hand pane of the DNS MMC snap-in, select the **Conditional Forwarders** node.

2. Right-click the **Conditional Forwarders** node and click **New Conditional Forwarder....** You will see the screen shown in Figure 4-7.

Figure 4-7

Configuring conditional forwarders

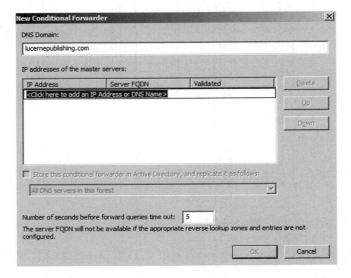

3. In the DNS Domain: text box, enter the name of the remote domain for which you wish to set up conditional forwarding; for example, enter *lucernepublishing.com*.

4. In the IP addresses of the master servers: field, enter the IP address of a server that is authoritative for the lucernepublishing.com zone and press (Enter).

5. Click **OK** to save your changes.

PAUSE. Close the DNS MMC snap-in and log off of the Windows Server 2008 computer before continuing.

In the previous exercise, you configured forwarders and conditional forwarders on a Windows Server 2008 DNS server. In the next section, we will discuss the ongoing administration and troubleshooting of the DNS server role using both graphical user interface (GUI) and command-line tools.

Troubleshooting DNS and the Name Resolution Process

DNS is a key service in Microsoft Windows Server 2008 networks. If DNS fails, clients often lose connectivity to the Internet or to other clients and Active Directory fails. Effective management and monitoring procedures mitigate the possibility of DNS server failure. This section introduces you to the tools, concepts, and procedures necessary to manage and monitor DNS name resolution. Topics in this lesson include securing DNS, monitoring and troubleshooting DNS with tools such as the DNS Event Viewer and DNS debug log, and using tools such as Nslookup and Dnscmd.

Several tools are useful for managing and monitoring DNS services. These tools include the following:

- The DNS MMC snap-in, which is part of Administrative Tools. The DNS console is the primary tool for configuring DNS.
- Nslookup, which can be used to query DNS zone information to verify existing and proper configuration of resource records.
- Logging features, such as DNS events that are logged to the Windows Event Viewer, which you can view with the DNS MMC snap-in, Server Manager, or the Windows Event Viewer. File-based logs also can be used temporarily as an advanced debugging option to log and trace selected service events.
- Dnscmd, which enables you to use the command line to perform most of the tasks you can perform using the DNS console.

You can use the DNS console to manually or automatically test DNS servers by submitting two different types of queries:

- A simple query, or iterative query. The DNS resolver (client) on the server computer queries the local DNS servers, which are located on the same computer.
- A recursive query to other DNS servers. The DNS resolver (client) on the server computer queries the local DNS server, but instead of submitting an iterative query, it submits a recursive query. Specifically, the client asks the server to use recursion to resolve a name server (NS)–type query for the root of the DNS domain namespace. This type of query typically requires additional recursive processing and can be helpful in verifying that server root hints or zone delegations are properly set.

These settings are accessed by clicking the Monitoring tab in the DNS server properties window. You can perform the test by clicking the Test Now button or specify an interval for performing the test.

Using NsLookup

Nslookup is a command-line tool built into TCP/IP that is available in Windows Server 2008 to perform DNS queries and enable examination of the content of zone files on local and remote servers. Nslookup is often used to verify the configuration of DNS zones and to diagnose and solve name resolution problems. In order for Nslookup to be used to troubleshoot DNS name resolution, a reverse lookup zone must be configured for the DNS domain that is being queried.

Nslookup can be run at the command prompt (in command prompt mode) or as a program that accepts serial commands and queries (in interactive mode). To look up a single host name, you would typically enter a single command at the command prompt. For example, executing the following command at the command prompt returns the Internet Protocol (IP) addresses associated with the fully qualified domain name (FQDN) *www.microsoft.com* (output results will vary):

```
C:\.nslookup www.microsoft.com
Server: usdc1.us.contoso.com
Address: 192.168.0.100
Non-authoritative answer:
Name: www.microsoft.akadns.net
Addresses: 207.46.134.155,   207.46.134.190, 207.46.249.222,
207.46.249.27
207.46.249.190
Aliases: www.microsoft.com
```

To resolve the query, the Nslookup utility submits the name to the DNS server specified for the primary connection on the local client computer. This DNS server can then answer the query from its cache or through recursion.

If you submit a query for a host name that does not exist, you receive the following response:

```
C:\.nslookup thisdoesnotexist.contoso.com
Server: usdc1.us.contoso.com
Address: 192.168.0.100
*** usdc1.us.contoso.com can't find thisdoesnotexist.contoso.com:
Non-existent domain
```

If you troubleshoot a specific DNS server instead of the one specified for the primary connection on the local client computer, you can specify that DNS server using the Nslookup command. For example, the following command executed at the command prompt queries the DNS server at 192.168.52.141 for the name *www.microsoft.com*:

```
C:\.nslookup www.microsoft.com 192.168.52.141
```

You can also use Nslookup to resolve IP addresses to host names. For example, the following command executed at the command prompt returns the FQDN associated with the address 192.168.141.22, as shown in this output:

```
C:\.nslookup 192.168.141.22
Server: localhost
Address: 127.0.0.1

Name: www.contoso.com
Address: 192.168.141.22
```

Use the following syntax for Nslookup in the command prompt mode:

```
nslookup [-opt...] [{Host| [Server]}]
```

The Nslookup command uses the following switches:

- -opt—Specifies one or more Nslookup subcommands as a command-line option.
- Host—Looks up information for Host using the current default DNS name server (NS), if no other server is specified. To look up a computer not in the current DNS domain, append a period to the name.
- Server—Specifies to use this server as the DNS name server. If you omit Server, the default DNS name server is used.

When issuing multiple Nslookup commands, it is generally more efficient to use Nslookup in interactive mode. To enter interactive mode, open a command prompt, key nslookup, and press Enter. In interactive mode, Nslookup accepts commands that allow the program to perform a variety of functions, such as displaying the specific contents of messages included in DNS exchanges, simulating a zone transfer, or searching for records of a specific type on a given server. These commands can be displayed by keying the help or ? command.

When you are in interactive mode, you can also use the Set command to configure Nslookup options that determine how the resolver carries out queries. One option is to use the debug command. By default, Nslookup is set to nodebug. Keying set debug while in interactive mode enters debug mode, which enables Nslookup to display the DNS response messages communicated from the DNS server. You can view the options currently configured for Nslookup by running the *set all* command.

⚠️ **WARNING** Nslookup commands entered while in interactive mode are case-sensitive and must be keyed in lowercase.

Table 4-7 describes the most common options configured with the Set command.

Table 4-7

Command-Line Options Available with the Set Command

OPTION	PURPOSE	EXAMPLE (INTERACTIVE MODE)
set all	Shows the configuration status of all options.	>set all
set [no]debug	Puts Nslookup in debug mode. With debug mode turned on, more information is printed about the packet sent to the server and the resulting answer.	>set debug Or >set nodebug
set [no]d2	Puts Nslookup in verbose debug mode so you can examine the query and response packets between the resolver and the server.	>set d2 Or >set nod2

(continued)

Table 4-7 *(continued)*

Option	Purpose	Example (Interactive Mode)
set domain=\<domain name\>	Tells the resolver which domain name to append for unqualified queries (for example, sales is an unqualified query as opposed to *sales.fabrikam.com*), including all queried names not followed by a trailing dot.	>set domain=bottinc.com
set timeout=\<time-out value\>	Tells the resolver what time-value to use, in seconds. This option is useful for slow links on which queries frequently time out and the wait time must be lengthened.	>set timeout=5
set type=\<record type\> or set querytype=\<record type\> or set q=\<record type\>	Tells the resolver which type of resource records to search for (for example, address [A], pointer [PTR], or service locator [SRV] records). If you want the resolver to query for all types of resource records, key set type=all.	>set type=A >set q=MX

By default, names queried for in Nslookup return only matching host address (A) resource records. To look up different data types within the domain namespace, use the Set Type command or set querytype (set q) command at the command prompt. For example, to query for mail exchanger (MX) resource records only instead of A resource records, key set q=mx. To query for a record of any type, execute the Nslookup command set q=any.

TAKE NOTE*

The first time a query is made for a remote name, the answer is authoritative, but subsequent queries are nonauthoritative. This pattern appears for the following reason: the first time a remote host is queried, the local DNS server contacts the DNS server that is authoritative for that domain. The local DNS server then caches that information so that subsequent queries are answered nonauthoritatively out of the local server's cache.

To query another name server directly, use the *server* or *lserver* commands to switch to that name server. The *lserver* command uses the local server to get the address of the server to switch to, whereas the *server* command uses the current default server to get the address.

After you execute either of these commands, all subsequent lookups in the current Nslookup session are performed at the specified server until you switch servers again. The following syntax illustrates what you would key to initiate a server switch:

```
C:\> nslookup
Default Server: nameserver1.contoso.com
Address: 10.0.0.1
> server nameserver2
Default Server: nameserver2.contoso.com
Address: 10.0.0.2
```

You can use the Nslookup subcommand ls to list information for a DNS domain. However, when you issue an Nslookup command with the ls subcommand, you effectively are requesting a zone transfer, so if the DNS server does not permit zone transfers to the IP address that you are running Nslookup from, this command will fail. The syntax for the ls command is as follows:

```
ls [- a | d | t type] domain [> filename]
```

Table 4-8 lists valid options for the ls subcommand.

Table 4-8

Nslookup ls Options

OPTION	PURPOSE	EXAMPLE
-t QueryType	Lists all records of a specific type.	>ls –t cname contoso.com
-a	Lists aliases of computers in the DNS domain (equivalent to -t CNAME).	>ls –a contoso.com
-d	Lists all records for the DNS domain (equivalent to -t ANY).	>ls –d contoso.com
-h	Lists central processing unit (CPU) and operating system information for the DNS domain (equivalent to—t HINFO).	>ls –h contoso.com
-s	Lists well-known services of computers in the DNS domain (equivalent to -t WKS).	>ls –s contoso.com

The following output demonstrates the use of the ls command in interactive mode:

```
>ls contoso.com
[nameserver1.contoso.com]
nameserver1.contoso.com.    NS server = ns1.contoso.com
nameserver2.contoso.com     NS server = ns2.contoso.com
nameserver1                 A 10.0.0.1
nameserver2                 A 10.0.0.2
```

Using Dnscmd

You can use the Dnscmd command-line tool to perform most of the tasks that you can do from the DNS console. This tool can be used to script batch files, to help automate the management and updates of existing DNS server configurations, or to perform setup and configuration of DNS servers.

Dnscmd is provided as a built-in command-line tool for managing DNS servers in Windows Server 2008. The Dnscmd command allows you to perform a large number of DNS-related tasks, including the following:

- Create, delete, and view zones and records.
- Reset server and zone properties.
- Perform zone maintenance operations, such as updating the zone, reloading the zone, refreshing the zone, writing the zone back to a file or to Active Directory, and pausing or resuming the zone.
- Clear the cache.
- Stop and start the DNS service.
- View statistics.

For example, to display a complete list of the zones configured on a DNS server by using Dnscmd, at the command prompt, key dnscmd [ComputerName] /enumzones. A sample output of this command follows:

```
C:\>dnscmd localhost /enumzones
Enumerated zone list:
Zone count = 5
```

Zone name	Type	Storage Properties
.	Cache	AD-Legacy
_msdcs.contoso01.com	Primary	AD-Forest Secure
1.1.10.in-addr.arpa	Primary	AD-Legacy Secure Rev
computer01.contoso.com	Primary	AD-Legacy
contoso01.com	Primary	AD-Domain Secure

Command completed successfully.

To display information about a specific zone that is configured on a DNS server by using Dnscmd, at the command prompt, key the following:

dnscmd [ComputerName] /zoneinfo [zone]

Sample output of this command follows below:

```
C:\>dnscmd localhost /zoneinfo contoso01.com
Zone query result:
Zone info:
        ptr                     = 00083050
        zone name               = contoso01.com
        zone type               = 1
        update                  = 2
        DS integrated           = 1
        data file               = (null)
        using WINS              = 0
        using Nbstat            = 0
        aging                   = 0
        refresh interval        = 168
        no refresh              = 168
        scavenge available      = 3529116
        Zone Masters
        NULL IP Array.
        Zone Secondaries
        NULL IP Array.
        secure secs             = 3
        directory partition     = AD-Domain flags 00000015
        zone DN                 = DC=contoso01.com,cn=MicrosoftDNS,
                                  DC=DomainDnsZones, DC=contoso01,
                                  DC=com


                        Command completed successfully.
```

Configuring Advanced DNS Server Properties

Advanced DNS server properties refer to the settings that can be configured in the Advanced tab of the DNS Server Properties dialog box (shown in Figure 4-8). These properties relate to server-specific features, such as disabling recursion, handling resolution of multi-homed hosts, and achieving compatibility with non-Microsoft DNS servers.

Figure 4-8

Viewing advanced DNS server
properties

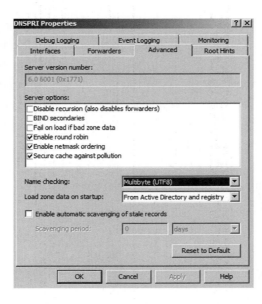

The default installation settings of the DNS server role include six server options, which are
either on or off, and three other server features with various selections for configuration. Table
4-9 shows the default settings for all nine features.

Table 4-9

Default DNS Installation Settings

PROPERTY	SETTING
Disable Recursion (also disables forwarders)	Off
BIND Secondaries	Off
Fail On Load If Bad Zone Data	Off
Enable Round Robin	On
Enable Netmask Ordering	On
Secure Cache Against Pollution	On
Name Checking	Multibyte (UTF-8)
Load Zone Data On Startup	From Active Directory And Registry
Enable Automatic Scavenging Of Stale Records	Off (requires configuration when enabled)

In most situations, these installation defaults are acceptable and do not require modification.
However, when needed, you can use the DNS console to modify these advanced parameters and
accommodate special deployment needs and situations. You can restore these default settings at
any time using the Advanced tab by clicking the Reset To Default button on the Advanced tab.

We'll now describe each available configuration option in more detail.

- Disable Recursion—The Disable Recursion server option is disabled by default (meaning
  that recursion is enabled). When the Disable Recursion option is enabled, the DNS Server
  service does not answer queries for which it is not authoritative or which it has not already
  answered and placed in its cache. Instead, the DNS Server service provides the client with
  referrals, which are resource records that allow a DNS client to perform iterative queries to
  resolve an FQDN. Do not disable recursion on a server if any other name servers are using
  this server as a forwarder. You should only disable recursion when you want to create a
  server that does not query any other servers to resolve client DNS queries.

TAKE NOTE *

BIND version 9.1 was released January 17, 2001, so this option should not see much use on a production network.

- BIND Secondaries—The BIND Secondaries option controls whether a fast transfer format is used during a DNS zone transfer. Berkeley Internet Name Domain (BIND) is a common implementation of DNS written and ported to most available versions of the UNIX operating system. Fast transfer format is an efficient means of transferring zone data that provides data compression and allows multiple records to be transferred per individual Transmission Control Protocol (TCP) message. Fast zone transfer is always used among Windows-based DNS servers, so the BIND Secondaries option does not affect communications among Windows servers. However, only BIND versions 4.9.4 and later can handle these fast zone transfers. For BIND versions earlier than 4.9.4, DNS servers running Windows Server 2003 can be configured to transfer a zone using the slower, uncompressed transfer format. When you select the BIND Secondaries check box in the Advanced tab of the Server Properties dialog box, no fast transfers are made. If you know your DNS server will be performing zone transfers with DNS servers using BIND version 4.9.4 or later, you should disable this option to allow fast zone transfers to occur.

- Fail On Load If Bad Zone Data—DNS servers running on Windows Server 2008 will, by default, load a zone even if that zone contains errors. In that scenario, errors are logged and ignored. Enabling Fail On Load If Bad Zone Data prevents a zone with errors from being loaded.

- Enable Round Robin—*DNS round robin* is a load balancing mechanism used by DNS servers to share and distribute network resource loads. If multiple resource records satisfy a query, you can use round robin to rotate the order of resource record types returned to the client. By default, DNS uses round robin to rotate the order of resource record data returned in query answers in which multiple resource records of the same type exist for a queried DNS domain name. This feature provides a simple method for load balancing client use of Web servers and other frequently queried multi-homed computers.

Consider this example of DNS round robin: The Web server named *server1.contoso.com* has three network adapters and three distinct IP addresses. In the stored zone (either in a database file or in Active Directory), the three A resource records mapping the host name to each of its IP addresses appear in this fixed order:

```
server1 IN A 10.0.0.1
server1 IN A 10.0.0.2
server1 IN A 10.0.0.3
```

The first DNS client—Client1—that queries the server to resolve this host's name receives the list in this default order. However, when a second client—Client2—sends a subsequent query to resolve this name, the list is rotated as follows:

```
server1 IN A 10.0.0.2
server1 IN A 10.0.0.3
server1 IN A 10.0.0.1
```

When you clear the Enable Round Robin check box, round robin is disabled for the DNS server. If round robin is disabled for a DNS server, the order of the response for these queries is based on a static ordering of resource records in the answer list as they are stored in the zone (either its zone file or Active Directory).

- Enable Netmask Ordering—Netmask ordering is a method DNS uses to give ordering and preference to IP addresses on the same network when a requesting client queries for a host name that has multiple A resource records. This is designed so that the client program will attempt to connect to a host using the closest (and, therefore, presumably fastest) IP address available. When returning more than one IP address to a client when Netmask Ordering is enabled, IP addresses most closely matching the client's subnet mask are placed at the top of the response list. The Enable Netmask Ordering option is selected by default.

For an example of netmask ordering in action, consider the following scenario: a multihomed computer, *server1.contoso.com*, has three A resource records for each of its three IP addresses in the *contoso.com* zone. These three records appear in the following order in the zone—either in the zone file or in Active Directory:

```
server1 IN A 192.168.1.27
server1 IN A 10.0.0.14
server1 IN A 172.16.20.4
```

When a DNS client resolver at IP address 10.4.3.2 queries the server for the IP addresses of the host *server1.contoso.com*, the DNS Server service notes that the originating IP network address (10.0.0.0) of the client matches the network (class A) ID of the 10.0.0.14 address in the answer list of resource records. The DNS Server service then reorders the addresses in the response list as follows:

```
server1 IN A 10.0.0.14
server1 IN A 192.168.1.27
server1 IN A 172.16.20.4
```

If the network ID of the IP address of the requesting client does not match any of the network IDs of the resource records in the answer list, the list is not reordered.

- Secure Cache Against Pollution—By default, the Secure Cache Against Pollution option is enabled. This setting allows the DNS server to protect its cache against referrals that are potentially polluting or nonsecure. When the setting is enabled, the server caches only those records with a name that corresponds to the domain for which the original queried name was made. Any referrals received from another DNS server along with a query response are simply discarded. For example, if a query is originally made for the name *example.lucernepublishing.com*, and a referral answer provides a record for a name outside the *lucernepublishing.com* domain name tree (such as *msn.com*), that name is discarded if the Secure Cache Against Pollution option is enabled. This setting helps prevent unauthorized computers from impersonating another network server. When this option is disabled, however, the server caches all the records received in response to DNS queries—even when the records do not correspond to the queried-for domain name.
- Name Checking—By default, the Name Checking dropdown list box in the Advanced tab of the DNS Server Properties dialog box is set to Multibyte (UTF-8). Thus, the DNS service, by default, verifies that all domain names handled by the DNS service conform to the UCS Transformation Format (UTF). Unicode is a 2-byte encoding scheme, compatible with the traditional 1-byte American Standard Code for Information Interchange (ASCII) format, that allows for binary representation of most human languages. Table 4-10 lists and describes the four name-checking methods.

Table 4-10

Name-Checking Methods

METHOD	DESCRIPTION
Strict RFC (American National Standards Institute [ANSI])	Uses strict checking of names. These restrictions, set in Request for Comments (RFC) 1123, include limiting names to uppercase and lowercase letters (A–Z, a–z), numbers (0–9), and hyphens (-). The first character of the DNS name can be a number.
Non RFC (ANSI)	Permits names that are nonstandard and that do not follow RFC 1123 Internet host naming specifications.
Multibyte (UTF-8)	Permits recognition of characters other than ASCII, including Unicode, which is normally encoded as more than one octet (8 bits) in length.
	With this option, multibyte characters can be transformed and represented using UTF-8 support, which is provided with Windows Server 2003.

(continued)

Table 4-10 (continued)

METHOD	DESCRIPTION
	Names encoded in UTF-8 format must not exceed the size limits stated in RFC 2181, which specifies a maximum of 63 octets per label and 255 octets per name. Character count is insufficient to determine size because some UTF-8 characters exceed one octet in length. This option allows for domain names using non-English alphabets.
All Names	Permits any naming conventions.

Despite the flexibility of the UTF-8 name-checking method, you should consider changing the Name Checking option to Strict RFC when your DNS servers perform zone transfers to non-Windows servers that are not UTF-8-aware. Although DNS server implementations that are not UTF-8-aware might be able to accept the transfer of a zone containing UTF-8-encoded names, these servers might not be capable of writing back those names to a zone file or reloading those names from a zone file.

You should use the other two name-checking options, Non RFC and All Names, only when a specific application requires them.

- Load Zone Data On Startup—By default, the Load Zone Data On Startup property is set to the From Active Directory And Registry option. Thus, by default, DNS servers in Windows Server 2003 initialize with the settings specified in the Active Directory database and the server registry. You can also load zone data using two other settings: From Registry and From File. The From Registry option forces the DNS server to initialize by reading parameters stored in the Windows registry. The From File option forces the DNS server to initialize by reading parameters stored in a boot file. The boot file must be a text file named Boot located on the local computer in the *%systemroot%\ System32\Dns* folder. When a boot file is used, settings in the file are applied to the server, overriding the settings stored in the registry on the DNS server. However, for parameters that are not configurable using boot file directives, registry defaults (or stored reconfigured server settings) are applied by the DNS Server service.

TAKE NOTE*

Windows Server 2008 has made improvements in the way that Active Directory–integrated zones are loaded when a domain controller that's running the DNS Server role starts up. This improvement, called *background zone loading*, allows DNS servers in large organizations to begin responding to DNS queries much earlier in the boot process than in previous versions of the Windows server operating systems.

SUMMARY SKILL MATRIX

IN THIS LESSON YOU LEARNED:

- DNS names and the DNS protocol are required for Active Directory domains and for compatibility with the Internet.

- The DNS namespace is hierarchical and based on a unique root that can have any number of subdomains. An FQDN is the name of a DNS host in this namespace that indicates the host's location relative to the root of the DNS domain tree. An example of an FQDN is *host1.subdomain.microsoft.com.*

- A DNS zone is a contiguous portion of a namespace for which a server is authoritative. A server can be authoritative for one or more zones, and a zone can contain one or more contiguous domains. A DNS server is authoritative for a zone if it hosts the zone, either as a primary or secondary DNS server. Each DNS zone contains the resource records it needs to answer queries for its portion of the DNS namespace.

- There are several types of DNS servers: primary, secondary, master name, and caching-only.

  - A DNS server that hosts a primary DNS zone is said to act as a primary DNS server. Primary DNS servers store original source data for zones. With Windows Server 2003, you can implement primary zones in one of two ways: as standard primary zones, in which zone data is stored in a text file, or as an Active Directory–integrated zone, in which zone data is stored in the Active Directory database.

- A DNS server that hosts a secondary DNS server is said to act as a secondary DNS server. Secondary DNS servers are authoritative backup servers for the primary server. The servers from which secondary servers acquire zone information are called masters.

- A caching-only server forwards requests to other DNS servers and hosts no zones, but builds a cache of frequently requested records.

- Recursion is one of the two process types for DNS name resolution. A DNS client will request that a DNS server provide a complete answer to a query that does not include pointers to other DNS servers, effectively shifting the workload of resolving the query from the client to the DNS server. For the DNS server to perform recursion properly, the server needs to know where to begin searching for names in the DNS namespace. This information is provided by the root hints file, *cache.dns,* which is stored on the server computer.

- A DNS server on a network is designated as a forwarder by having the other DNS servers in the network forward the queries they cannot resolve locally to that DNS server. Conditional forwarding enables a DNS server to forward queries to other DNS servers based on the DNS domain names in the queries.

■ Knowledge Assessment

Fill in the Blank

Complete the following sentences by writing the correct word or words in the blanks provided.

1. A(n) ___Zone XFer___ will transfer all records within a zone from a primary server to a secondary server.

2. A(n) ___CNAme___ creates an alias for an existing A record.

3. A(n) ___mx record___ is used by e-mail systems such as Microsoft Exchange to locate mail servers in different networks.

4. The _____ allows IPv6 hosts to map host names to IP addresses.

5. *contoso.com* is an example of a(n) _____ within the .com top-level domain.

6. The _____ application scope will replicate DNS data to all DNS servers within a domain.

7. A(n) _____ stores DNS data in a text file on the server hard drive, rather than as part of Active Directory.

8. Each DNS record has a(n) _____ that indicates the maximum time that a record will be cached by a DNS server before it is discarded.

9. A DNS server is considered _____ for each zone that it hosts.

10. A DNS domain name like.*uk* or.*it* is an example of a(n) _____ domain.

Multiple Choice

Select all answers that apply for the following questions.

1. This DNS configuration item will forward DNS queries to different servers based on the domain name of the query.
   a. Iterative forwarder
   b. Recursive forwarder
   c. Conditional forwarder
   d. IPv6 forwarder

2. This type of zone takes human-readable FQDNs and translates them into IP addresses.
   a. Standard zone
   b. Forward lookup zone
   c. Reverse lookup zone
   d. Inverse lookup zone

3. This zone is used in conjunction with IPv4 IP addresses to resolve queries for IPv4 IP addresses to resolve queries for FQDNs.
   a. In.addr-arpa
   b. In.addr-ipv4
   c. In.addr-ipv4.arpa
   d. In.ipv4.arpa

4. The IPv6 DNS host record is referred to as a(n):
   a. A record
   b. AA record
   c. AAA record
   d. AAAA record

5. A DNS server that hosts a primary or secondary zone containing a particular record can issue the following response to a query for that record:
   a. Authoritative answer
   b. Non-authoritative answer
   c. Referral answer
   d. Non-referral answer

6. You can secure an Active Directory–integrated DNS server, zone, or record by applying the following to it:
   a. System Access Control List
   b. Security Access Control List
   c. Discretionary Access Control List
   d. Distributed Access Control List

7. This zone type contains only SOA, name server, and glue records for the relevant zone.
   a. Secondary zone
   b. Stub zone
   c. Primary zone
   d. Caching-only zone

8. Data from a primary zone is transmitted to secondary zones using the following:
   a. Zone transfer
   b. Zone transmission
   c. DNS Zone
   d. Active Directory replication

9. These contain the names and IP addresses of the DNS servers authoritative for the root zone.
   a. "." zone
   b. Top-level zone
   c. Root Hints
   d. Root Cache

10. The following feature is available only on Active Directory–integrated DNS zones:
    a. Dynamic updates
    b. Incremental zone transfers
    c. Reverse lookup zones
    d. Secure dynamic updates

■ Case Scenarios

Scenario 4-1: Enabling Network Users to Connect to Internet Host Names

You are the network administrator for Contoso, Ltd. The Contoso network consists of a single domain, *contoso.com*, which is protected from the Internet by a firewall. The firewall runs on a computer named NS1 that is directly connected to the Internet. NS1 also runs the DNS Server service, and its firewall allows DNS traffic to pass between the Internet and the DNS Server service on NS1 but not between the Internet and the internal network. The DNS Server service on NS1 is configured to use round robin. Behind the firewall, two computers are running Windows Server 2003—NS2 and NS3, which host a primary and secondary DNS server, respectively, for the *contoso.com* zone.

Users on the company network report that, although they use host names to connect to computers on the local private network, they cannot use host names to connect to Internet destinations, such as *www.microsoft.com*.

Which of the following actions requires the least amount of administrative effort to enable network users to connect to Internet host names?

  a. Disable recursion on NS2 and NS3.
  b. Enable netmask ordering on NS1.
  c. Configure NS2 and NS3 to use NS1 as a forwarder.
  d. Disable round robin on NS1.

Scenario 4-2: Implementing DNS Updates

You are the system administrator for Contoso, Ltd. The company has grown rapidly over the past year, and currently Contoso is using only a single DNS zone. Recently, the Marketing department has made several requests for DNS changes that were delayed. Users would like the ability to make their own DNS updates.

What should you do to try to address this problem?

  a. Create a secondary server in the Marketing department so that users can manage their own zone.
  b. Delegate the marketing domain to a DNS server in the Marketing department.
  c. Place a domain controller running DNS in the Marketing department so that people in the department can make changes.
  d. Upgrade the network infrastructure to improve network performance.

Configuring Routing and Remote Access (RRAS) and Wireless Networking

OBJECTIVE DOMAIN MATRIX

Technology Skill	Objective Domain	Objective Domain Number
Configuring Routing	Configure routing	1.3
Configuring Remote Access	Configure remote access	3.1
Configuring Wireless Access	Configure wireless access	3.4

KEY TERMS

authenticator
Authorization Server (AS)
bits
default route
Dial-Up Networking (DUN)
directly attached network
  routes
EAP-Logoff
frames
host routes
hub

Layer 3 device
limited broadcast address
loopback address
metric
network access control
Network Policy Server (NPS)
Open Shortest Path First
  (OSPF)
packets
Physical Layer
remote network routes

router
routing protocols
Set by Caller
software-based router
Strongest Encryption (MPPE
  128-bit)
supplicant
switch
Virtual Private Network
  (VPN)

Wingtip Toys, a toy manufacturing company based in Taiwan, maintains manufacturing plants and business centers in multiple cities around the world. In addition to these physical locations, Wingtip Toys employs a large base of sales and marketing staff that split time between home offices and travelling to conferences and customer locations. In order to provide access for these remote staff to resources on the Wingtip Toys network, Wingtip Toys management has decided to deploy remote access servers, using a combination of dial-up and virtual private networking (VPN) technologies.

In this lesson, we discuss the concepts and tasks required to configure Routing and Remote Access (RRAS) for a Windows Server 2008 computer. We will begin with an overall discussion of routing, including routing tables, manually-assigned static routes, and the use of dynamic routing protocols. We will then cover the steps required to configure a Windows Server 2008 computer to provide a number of inter-connected routing services, including remote access using VPN or dial-up networking, allowing wireless access, and configuring Network Address Translation (NAT).

■ Configuring Routing

Routing, or the process of transferring data across an internetwork from one LAN to another, provides the basis for the Internet and nearly all TCP/IP network communications between multiple organizations. It plays a key role in every organization that is connected to the Internet or that has more than one network segment. Routing can be complex, but if you understand some key concepts and terminology, you can effectively configure, monitor, and troubleshoot routing and remote access for your organization.

CERTIFICATION READY?
Configure routing
1.3

Most enterprise networks employ several common network devices: hubs, switches, and routers. This section focuses on the routing capabilities of Microsoft Windows Server 2008. Before examining that topic, however, let's review some common physical network devices and clearly identify the role of the router.

X REF

For more information about OSI layers, see the *Network+ Certification Training Kit*, Second Edition (Microsoft Press, 2003).

A **hub** (sometimes called a *multi-port repeater*) operates at Open Systems Interconnection (OSI) reference model layer 1, which organizes data into **bits**, which are binary sequences of 0s and 1s used to transmit data across a wired or wireless network. Because a hub operates at layer 1 (the **Physical Layer**), it does not perform any sort of processing against the data it receives; instead, it simply receives the incoming signal and recreates it for transmission on all of its ports. Using a hub extends the size of a network by joining multiple segments together into a larger segment. A hub is invisible to all nodes on a LAN on which it is deployed.

Unlike a hub, a **switch** examines the destination and source address of an incoming data frame, and forwards the frame to the appropriate destination port according to the destination address. Most switches operate at OSI layer 2 (the *Data-link Layer*), which organizes data into **frames**.

As its name suggests, a **router** determines routes from a source network to a destination network: where to send network packets based on the addressing in the packet. Routers operate at OSI layer 3 (the *Network Layer*), which groups data into **packets**. Because routers operate at this level, they are referred to as **Layer 3 devices**.

Routers can be used as follows:

- To join networks together over extended distances or WANs. WAN traffic often travels over multiple routes, and the routers choose the fastest or cheapest route between a source computer and destination.
- To connect dissimilar LANs, such as an Ethernet LAN, to a Fiber Distributed Data Interface (FDDI) backbone.

You can use routers in many different topologies (the physical layout of a network) and network configurations. Figure 5-1 shows a simple network routing configuration with a server running Routing and Remote Access and connecting two LAN segments (LAN Segment 1 and LAN Segment 2). In this configuration, the router joins the two segments. Because the router is directly connected to both networks for which it would have to route packets, there is no need to create *static routes* to manually instruct the router where packets need to be directed.

Figure 5-1

Viewing a simple routed network

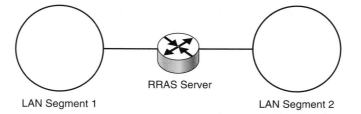

RRAS Server

LAN Segment 1   LAN Segment 2

Figure 5-2 shows a more complex router configuration. In this scenario, three networks (LAN Segments 1, 2, and 3) are connected by two routers (Routers 1 and 2). In a more complex routing scenario such as this one, **routing protocols** can be used to automatically transmit information about the routing *topology*, and which segments can be reached via which router. The following are some of the more common routing protocols:

- Routing Information Protocol (RIP) is one of the most long-standing routing protocols; it has been in use since the earliest days of routed networks. Routers that run the RIP protocol will broadcast information about available networks on a regular basis, as well as when the network topology changes. Because RIP is broadcast-based—that is, it sends out routing information in broadcast packets that are transmitted to every router that is connected to the same network—it is designed for use only on smaller networks.

- RIP v2 is version 2 of the Routing Information Protocol, and was designed to improve the amount of routing information that was provided by RIP, as well as to increase the security of the routing protocol.

- ***Open Shortest Path First (OSPF)*** was designed to address the scalability limitations of RIP, to create a routing protocol that could be used on significantly larger networks. Rather than using broadcasts to transmit routing information, each OSPF router maintains a database of routes to all destination networks that it knows of; when it receives network traffic destined for one of these destination networks, it routes the traffic using the best (shortest) route that it has information about in its database. OSPF routers share this database information only with those OSPF routers that it has been configured to share information with, rather than simply broadcasting traffic across an entire network.

Figure 5-2

Viewing a more complex router configuration

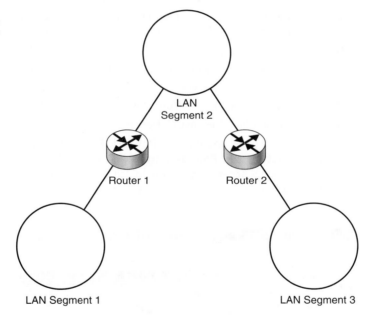

In Figure 5-2, Router 1 is directly connected to Segments 1 and 2, and Router 2 is directly connected to Segments 2 and 3. Router 1 must notify Router 2 that Segment 1 can be reached through Router 1, and Router 2 must notify Router 1 that Segment 3 can be reached through Router 2. This notification is automatically communicated if a routing protocol such as RIP or OSPF is used. Without routing protocols, the network administrator must manually configure routing tables for the different segments to reach each other by adding static routes. Static routes are often the best option for small, simple networks; however, they are difficult to implement in larger networks and they do not automatically adapt to changes in the internetwork topology.

When routing is configured properly and a user on Segment 1 wants to communicate with a user on Segment 3, the user's computer on Segment 1 forwards the packet to Router 1. Router 1 then forwards the packet to Router 2. Router 2 then forwards the packet to the user's computer on Segment 3.

One of the many roles that Windows Server 2008 can play is that of a network router. A ***software-based router***, such as a Windows Server 2008 computer that is running the Routing and Remote Access server role, can be used to route traffic between lightly-trafficked subnets on a small network. On a larger, more complex network with heavy network traffic between subnets, a *hardware-based router* might be a more appropriate choice to improve network performance.

 CONFIGURE ROUTING

GET READY. This exercise assumes that you have installed a Windows Server 2008 computer named RRAS using default installation settings. This exercise additionally assumes that you have installed two network interface cards (NICs) in this server, each attached to a separate network segment.

1. Press **Ctrl**+**Alt**+**Del** Log onto the RRAS computer using the default administrator username and password. If the Initial Configuration Tasks screen appears, click **Close**.

2. If the Server Manager console does not appear automatically, click the **Start** button, then click **Server Manager**. Expand the Server Manager window to full-screen if necessary.

3. In the left window pane, expand the **Roles** node. In the right window pane, click **Add role**. Click **Next** to bypass the initial Welcome screen. The Select Server Roles screen appears.

4. Place a checkmark next to **Network Policy and Access Services** and then click **Next**. The Network Policy and Access Services screen appears.

5. Read the informational screen concerning the Network Policy and Access Services role and then click **Next**. The Select Role Services screen appears.

6. Place a checkmark next to **Routing**. The Add Roles Wizard screen appears.

7. Click **Add Required Role Services** and then click **Next**. The Confirm Installation Selections screen appears.

8. Click **Install**. The Installation Progress screen appears.

9. Click **Close** when the installation is complete.

10. In the left pane, expand the **Network Policy and Access Services** node. Right-click **Routing and Remote Access** and then click **Configure and Enable Routing and Remote Access**, as shown in Figure 5-3. The Welcome to the Routing and Remote Access Server Setup Wizard screen appears.

Figure 5-3

Configuring routing and remote access

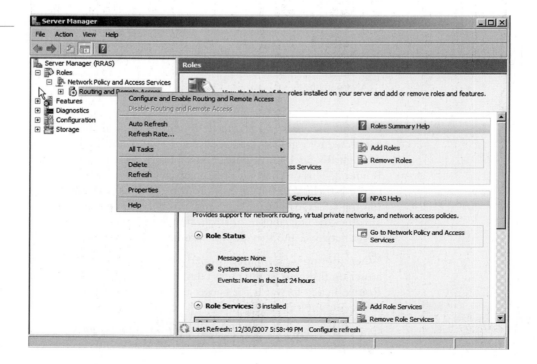

11. Click **Next**. The Configuration screen appears, as shown in Figure 5-4.

Figure 5-4

Select a routing and remote access configuration

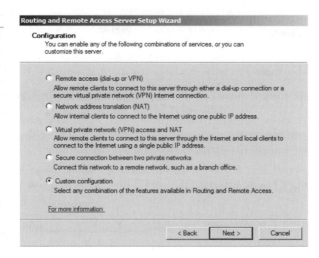

12. Click the **Custom configuration** radio button and then click **Next**. The Custom Configuration screen appears.

13. Place a checkmark next to **LAN routing** and then click **Next**. The Completing the Routing and Remote Access Server Setup Wizard screen appears.

14. Click **Finish**. The Routing and Remote Access screen appears. Click **Start service**.

PAUSE. To prepare for subsequent exercises, right-click **Routing and Remote Access**, click **Disable Routing and Remote Access**, and then click **Yes** to reset the configuration of the RRAS server.

In the previous exercise, you installed and configured the Routing role service on a Windows Server 2008 computer. In upcoming sections, we will discuss additional configuration items for the Routing role service, such as configuring static routes and dynamic routing protocols.

Configuring Routing Protocols

To successfully forward packets to networks to which they are not directly connected, a router must have routing table entries for these networks. In a small network where routes change infrequently, manually configuring static routes in the routing table is sufficient. In networks where information changes more frequently, you should consider configuring a routing protocol to automatically configure route information between networks.

In order to configure routers to transmit traffic from one network to another, the router must "learn" how to find remote hosts that are located on network subnets. This can happen in one of two ways:

- Static routes can be manually configured by a router administrator to specify the route to take to a remote network. Static routes do not add any processing overhead on the router and so can be useful on a small network with very few routes. But because static routes must be manually configured, they do not scale well in larger and more complex environments.

- Routing protocols allow routers to automatically "learn" about remote networks from other routers on the network. Some common routing protocols include the *Router Information Protocol version 2 (RIPv2)* as well as Open Shortest Path First (OSPF).

WARNING Whereas both RIPv2 and OSPF were supported under Windows Server 2003, only RIPv2 is supported by Windows Server 2008.

A static-routed IP environment is best suited to small, single-path, static IP internetworks. By definition, static-routed networks do not use routing protocols such as RIP or OSPF to communicate routing information between routers. For best results, the internetwork should be limited to fewer than 10 subnets with an easily predicted traffic pattern (such as arranged consecutively in a straight line). Of course, a static-routed IP environment is appropriate only as long as the routes in the environment remain the same.

For environments in which static routes are insufficient, Windows Server 2008 includes the following three routing protocols that can be added to the Routing and Remote Access service:

- Router Information Protocol, version 2 (RIPv2)—As described previously, this protocol is designed for exchanging routing information within a small to medium-sized network. It enables routers to determine the appropriate paths along which to send traffic.
- *IGMP Router And Proxy*—Used for multicast forwarding.
- DHCP Relay Agent—Also considered a routing protocol in Routing and Remote Access; this service relays DHCP information between DHCP servers to provide an IP configuration to computers on different subnets.

Managing Routing Tables

A routing table (see Figure 5-5) contains entries called *routes* that provide directions toward destination networks or hosts. The IP routing table serves as a decision tree that enables IP to decide the *interface* and *gateway* through which it should send the outgoing traffic. The routing table contains many individual routes; each route consists of a destination, network mask, gateway interface, and metric.

Figure 5-5

Viewing a routing table using a Graphical User Interface

RRAS - IP Routing Table						
Destination	Network mask	Gateway	Interface	Metric	Protocol	
127.0.0.0	255.0.0.0	127.0.0.1	Loopback	51	Local	
127.0.0.1	255.255.255.255	127.0.0.1	Loopback	306	Local	
192.168.52.0	255.255.255.0	0.0.0.0	Local Area C...	266	Network management	
192.168.52.134	255.255.255.255	0.0.0.0	Local Area C...	266	Network management	
192.168.52.255	255.255.255.255	0.0.0.0	Local Area C...	266	Network management	
192.168.53.0	255.255.255.0	0.0.0.0	Local Area C...	266	Network management	
192.168.53.128	255.255.255.255	0.0.0.0	Local Area C...	266	Network management	
192.168.53.255	255.255.255.255	0.0.0.0	Local Area C...	266	Network management	
224.0.0.0	240.0.0.0	0.0.0.0	Local Area C...	266	Network management	
255.255.255.255	255.255.255.255	0.0.0.0	Local Area C...	266	Network management	

You can view the IP routing table by using the Routing And Remote Access console or the command prompt. In the Routing And Remote Access console, expand the IP Routing node, right-click the Static Routes node, and then click Show IP Routing Table, as shown in Figure 5-5. To view the routing table from the command prompt, at the command prompt, key route print, and then press Enter, as shown in Figure 5-6.

Figure 5-6

Viewing a routing table from the command prompt

Reading the IP Routing Table

> Routers use routing tables to determine where to send packets. When IP packets are sent to an IP router, the router reads the destination address of the packet and compares that destination address to the entries in the routing table. One of these entries is used to determine the interface to which to send the packet and the gateway to which the packet will be sent next.

As shown previously in Figure 5-5 and 5-6, each routing table entry includes the following five columns that are described in this section.

The first column in the routing table indicates the *network destination.* As the name suggests, this indicates the destination network that this route entry is used to reach. The router compares the destination address of every received IP packet to entries in this column. Entries in this column that are common to most routing tables include the following:

- 0.0.0.0—represents the default route, which is used when no other matches are found in the routing table. (This is the route that is used by the default gateway configured on a client computer's network interface card.)
- 127.0.0.0—points to the ***loopback address*** of 127.0.0.1, which corresponds to the local machine.
- 224.0.0.0—entries refer to a separate multicast route.
- *w.x.y.*255—represents a *broadcast address.* Broadcast addresses include specific subnet broadcast addresses, such as 192.168.0.255.
- 255.255.255.255—is the ***limited broadcast address***, which is general for all networks and routers.

Second, the *netmask* column refers to the subnet mask of the destination network. This information is important because the largest match determines the route or table entry that is applied to the packet. For instance, suppose a router receives two packets, the first destined for the address 192.168.0.82 and the second destined for the address 192.168.0.87. If the router contains a single routing table entry for the 192.168.0.0 destination network with a netmask of 255.255.0.0, both packets would be routed using this information. If, however, the router has a second entry for a destination network of 192.168.0.82 with a netmask of 255.255.255.255, this second entry would be used to route the 192.168.0.82 packet, while the 192.168.0.87 packet would be routed using the first entry. In this way, a routing table is parsed from the most specific to the most general, so that a packet is routed using the table entry that most closely matches the packet's destination.

The third column indicates the gateway value for each routing table entry. When a particular route or table entry is applied to a packet, the gateway value determines the next address or hop that the packet should be sent to.

Next you can see the interface value for each routing table entry. When a particular route (table entry) is applied to a packet, the interface value specified in that route determines which local network interface card is used to forward the packet to the appropriate gateway.

The final column in the routing table corresponds to the routing table entry's ***metric.*** This column indicates the *cost* of using a route. If two routes are identical, the route with the lower metric or cost is chosen over the route with the higher metric/cost. Lower (smaller) metrics have precedence over higher (larger) metrics, so that a route with a metric of 2 will be chosen over a route with a metric of 10. For the routing protocol RIP, the number of hops before the network destination determines the metric. However, you can use any algorithm to determine the metric if you are configuring a route manually.

Four types of routes can be found in a routing table:

- ***Directly attached network routes***—Routes for subnets to which the node is directly attached. For directly attached network routes, the Gateway column in the routing table

TAKE NOTE ★

In the case of a tie, one of the routes is arbitrarily selected.

can either be blank or can contain the IP address of the interface on that subnet. If the address is local, delivery requires little additional effort. Address Resolution Protocol (ARP) resolves the IP address into a hardware address, which represents the Media Access Control (MAC) address for the destination Ethernet card.

- **Remote network routes**—Routes for subnets that are available across routers and that are not directly attached to the node. For remote network routes, the Next-Hop field is a local router's IP address. If the address is remote, the next step is to determine the gateway through which to reach the remote address. In a network with only a single router acting as an external connection, no determination needs to be made. In any network with more than one router, determining which gateway to use requires routing table consultation.

- **Host routes**—A route to a specific IP address. Host routes allow routing to occur on a per-IP address basis. For host routes, the network ID is a specific IP address, and the network mask is 255.255.255.255.

- **Default route**—The default route is used when a more specific network or host route is not found. The default route destination is 0.0.0.0 with the network mask 0.0.0.0. The next-hop address of the default route is typically the node's default gateway.

To configure the routing table from the command line, use the route command-line utility. The Route utility syntax is as follows:

```
route [-f] [-p] [Command [Destination] [mask Netmask]
[Gateway] [metric Metric] [if Interface]
```

Table 5-1 lists the available commands, their functions, and an example of how to use each command. Key route /? at the command prompt for additional usage information.

Table 5-1

Route Command-Line Utility Commands

COMMAND	FUNCTION	EXAMPLE
Print	Displays the routing table.	**route print**
Add	Adds a route to the routing table. By default, routes do not persist (they are discarded) when the system reboots. Use the -p switch to make a route persist across system restarts. Persistent routes are stored in the registry location HKEY_LOCAL_MACHINE\SY TEM \CurrentControlSet\ Services\Tcpip \Parameters\PersistentRoutes.	**route add -p 10.0.0.1 mask 255.0.0.0 192.168.0.1**
Change	Modifies an existing route.	**route change 10.0.0.1 mask 255.255.0.0 10.27.0.25**
Delete	Deletes an existing route. To delete a route, you need only provide the IP address of the route.	**route delete 10.0.0.1**

Configuring Demand-Dial Routing

Routing and Remote Access also includes support for *demand-dial routing* (also known as *dial-on-demand routing*). When the router receives a packet, the router can use demand-dial routing to initiate a connection to a remote site. The connection becomes active only when data is sent to the remote site. The link is disconnected when no data has been sent over the link for a specified amount of time. Because demand-dial connections for low-traffic situations can use existing dial-up telephone lines instead of leased lines, demand-dial routing can significantly reduce connection costs.

The first step in deploying demand-dial routing is to configure a demand-dial interface on each computer you wish to function as a demand-dial router. You can configure these interfaces by using the Demand-Dial Interface Wizard when you initially set up Routing and Remote Access or as an option after the Routing and Remote Access service has already been configured and enabled.

If you have previously configured and enabled the Routing and Remote Access service without demand-dial functionality, you must enable this functionality before you create any demand-dial interfaces.

To enable demand-dial functionality, select the LAN And Demand-Dial Routing option in the General tab of the Routing and Remote Access Properties dialog box, as shown in Figure 5-7.

Figure 5-7

Configuring demand-dial routing

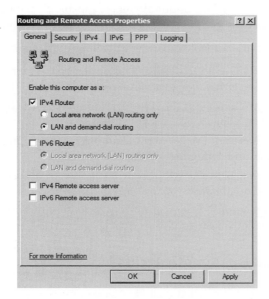

Configuring Remote Access

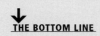

THE BOTTOM LINE

A Windows Server 2008 computer that runs the Routing and Remote Access server role can provide a number of different types of remote access connectivity for your network clients. This includes remote access for clients, either using dial-up or VPN access. The RRAS service also allows you to configure a Windows Server 2008 computer to act as a *Network Address Translation (NAT)* device, which allows internal network clients to connect to the Internet using a single shared IP address; you can configure a 2008 server to function solely as a NAT device, or else to provide both NAT and VPN services simultaneously. Finally, you can configure a Windows Server 2008 computer to create a secure site-to-site connection between two private networks, such as two branch offices that need to connect securely to one another over a public network such as the Internet.

CERTIFICATION READY?
Configure remote access
3.1

When configuring the Routing and Remote Access server role, you can provide connectivity for remote access clients using one of the following technologies:

- *Dial-Up Networking (DUN)*—creates a physical connection between a client and a remote access server using a dedicated device such as an analog or an ISDN modem. An example of Dial-Up Networking is a laptop that has a modem installed, which the client uses to dial the phone number of a remote access server. Once the modem creates a dedicated connection to the server, the remote access server allows the caller to access resources within the corporate network. Since Dial-Up Networking uses a dedicated physical connection, DUN connections often use unencrypted traffic.

- *Virtual Private Network (VPN)*—connectivity creates a secure point-to-point connection across either a private network or a public network such as the Internet. VPNs rely on secure TCP/IP-based protocols called *tunneling protocols* to create a secured VPN connection. The best example of virtual private networking is that of a *VPN client* that makes a VPN connection to an Internet-facing remote access server. The remote access server authenticates the VPN client and creates a secured connection between the VPN client and the internal corporate network that is tunneled over a public Internet connection. In contrast to Dial-Up Networking, a VPN is a logical connection between the VPN client and the VPN server over a public network like the Internet. In order to secure any data sent over the public network, VPN data must be encrypted.

As shown in Figure 5-4, the Routing And Remote Access Server Setup Wizard presents you with a configuration page from which you can select services. The final option on the list is Custom Configuration. Use this option if you are capable of manually configuring the server and if none of the services match your routing and remote access needs exactly.

There are several options available to you when configuring remote access:

- Remote Access (Dial-Up Or VPN)—This option enables remote clients to connect to the server by using either a dial-up connection or a secure VPN.
- Network Address Translation (NAT)—This option enables internal clients to connect to the Internet using a single, external IP address.
- Virtual Private Network (VPN) Access And NAT—This option configures NAT for the internal network and configures VPN connections.
- Secure Connection Between Two Private Networks—This option is useful when, for example, setting up a *router-to-router VPN*.
- Custom Configuration—As noted previously, you use this option when none of the service combinations meet your exact needs.

Configuring Dial-Up Remote Access

Dial-up remote access, also called Dial-Up Networking, enables remote computers that have a modem to connect to the organization's network as if the remote computers were connected locally, although at slower data transfer speeds. Windows Server 2008 remote access servers can allow connections from clients that run Windows Server 2008, Windows Server 2003, Microsoft Windows Vista, Microsoft Windows XP Professional, Microsoft Windows NT, Microsoft Windows 95, Microsoft Windows 98, Microsoft Windows for Workgroups, or MS-DOS. Typically, the client connects through a standard phone line—Plain Old Telephone Service (POTS line), Integrated Services Digital Network (ISDN), digital subscriber line (DSL), or cable modem.

To enable multiple dial-up users to connect to your network simultaneously, you must have a *modem bank* (also called *modem-pooling equipment*), appropriate connections to the local telecommunications provider, and a means of connecting the modem bank (such as an adapter installed on the computer that runs Windows Server 2008).

CONFIGURE DIAL-UP REMOTE ACCESS

GET READY. This exercise assumes that you have installed a Windows Server 2008 computer named RRAS using default installation settings. This exercise additionally assumes that you have installed at least one hardware modem.

1. Log onto the RRAS computer using the default administrator credentials.
2. In the left pane, expand the Network Policy and Access Services node. Right-click **Routing and Remote Access** and then click **Configure and Enable Routing and**

Remote Access. The Welcome to the Routing and Remote Access Server Setup Wizard screen appears.

3. Click **Next.** The Configuration screen appears. Select the **Remote access (dial-up or VPN)** radio button and then click **Next.** The Remote Access screen appears.

4. On the Remote Access page, select the **Dial-Up** check box and then click **Next.**

5. If your server has more than one network interface, on the Network Selection page, click the interface to which you wish to assign remote clients and then click **Next.**

6. On the IP Address Assignment page, select either **Automatically (to use a DHCP server to assign addresses)** or **From A Specified Range Of Addresses (addresses are supplied by the routing and remote access server)** and then click **Next.**

7. In the Managing Multiple Remote Access Servers dialog box, select the option to **not use a _RADIUS server._**

8. Click **Next** and then click **Finish.** The Routing and Remote Access service starts and initializes automatically.

PAUSE. To prepare for subsequent exercises, right-click **Routing and Remote Access,** click **Disable Routing and Remote Access,** and then click **Yes** to reset the configuration of the RRAS server.

In the previous exercise, you configured a Windows Server 2008 computer to provide dial-up remote access services. In the next section, we will discuss configuring additional remote access scenarios.

Configuring VPNs

Another means of connecting remote users is by using a VPN, which is an extension of a private network across a public network, such as the Internet. Like dial-up remote access, after the user is connected to the organization's network, it is as if the user is physically located at a computer that is local to the organization (with, however, slower data transfer speeds). Because a VPN can be established using the Internet, your organization's network can be accessed globally. Accessing your network can be done quickly, cheaply, and safely across the world. Dedicated private lines are not required, and security can be configured at very high levels.

Although VPNs are versatile and provide solutions to many different connectivity challenges, such as branch offices, telecommuters, and traveling employees, the following are situations in which a VPN does not provide the best solution:

- When performance at any price is the primary concern
- When most traffic is synchronous, as in voice and video transmissions
- When using an application with unusual protocols that are not compatible with TCP/IP

In these situations, you should consider a dedicated private line.

In a VPN, both ends of the connection make a link to a public internetwork, such as the Internet. The link can take the usual forms: a regular telephone line, an ISDN line, or a dedicated line of some sort. Rather than sending a packet as the originating node produces it, the VPN uses a tunneling protocol to encapsulate the packet in an additional _header._ The header provides routing information so that the encapsulated data can traverse the intermediate internetwork. The data is encrypted for privacy; if packets are intercepted, they cannot be unencrypted without encryption keys.

A VPN enables a remote user in Missouri, for example, to establish a dial-up connection with any Internet service provider (ISP) and, through that connection, to make a direct connection to a server on the company network in Texas. It is quick, cheap, and easy to set up. A VPN enables traveling employees, telecommuters in home offices, and employees in branch offices to connect to the main network at a company's headquarters. Each component connects to the ISP through a different type of communications channel, but they are all part of the same VPN.

Just as remote users can connect to their corporate network by utilizing an intermediate internetwork, two routers can also establish connection the same way to create a router-to-router VPN.

A VPN connection in Windows Server 2008 consists of the following components:

- A VPN server
- A VPN client
- A VPN connection (the portion of the connection in which the data is encrypted)
- A VPN tunnel (the portion of the connection in which the data is encapsulated)

The following two tunneling protocols provide this service and are installed with Routing and Remote Access:

- *Point-to-Point Tunneling Protocol (PPTP)*—An extension of the Point-to-Point Protocol (PPP) that was in use for many years, PPTP was first used in Windows NT 4. In Windows Server 2008, PPTP supports only the 128-bit RC4 encryption algorithm, which is supported by default. Less secure encryption algorithms can be enabled by modifying the Windows Registry, but this is not recommended by Microsoft.
- Layer Two Tunneling Protocol (L2TP)—An Internet Engineering Task Force (IETF) standard tunneling protocol that is used to encapsulate Point-to-Point Protocol (PPP) frames for transmission over TCP/IP, X.25, frame relay, or Asynchronous Transfer Mode (ATM) networks. LT2P combines the best features of PPTP, which was developed by Microsoft, and the Layer 2 Forwarding (L2F) protocol, which was developed by Cisco Systems. You can implement L2TP with IPSec to provide a secure, encrypted VPN solution. In Windows Server 2008, L2TP will support the Advanced Encryption Standard (AES) 256-bit, AES 192-bit, AES 128-bit, and 3DES encryption algorithms by default. Less secure encryption algorithms such as the Data Encryption Standard (DES) can be enabled by modifying the Windows Registry, but this is not recommended.

Configuring Network Access Translation (NAT)

Implemented by Windows Server 2008 Routing and Remote Access service, NAT is a protocol that enables private networks to connect to the Internet. The NAT protocol translates internal, private IP addresses to external, public IP addresses, and vice versa. This process reduces the number of public IP addresses required by an organization and thereby reduces the organization's IP address acquisition costs because private IP addresses are used internally and then translated to public IP addresses to communicate with the Internet. The NAT process also obscures private networks from external access by hiding private IP addresses from public networks. The only IP address that is visible to the Internet is the IP address of the computer running NAT.

When NAT is used to connect a private network user to a public network, the following process occurs:

1. The user's IP on the client computer creates an IP packet with specific values in the IP and Transmission Control Protocol (TCP) or User Datagram Protocol (UDP) headers. The client computer then forwards the IP packet to the computer running NAT.

2. The computer running NAT changes the outgoing packet header to indicate that the packet originated from the NAT computer's external address, but the computer running NAT does not change the destination; it then sends the remapped packet over the Internet to the Web server.

3. The external Web server receives the packet and sends a reply to the computer running NAT.

4. The computer running NAT receives the packet and checks its mapping information to determine the destination client computer. The computer running NAT changes the packet header to indicate the private address of the destination client, and then sends the packet to the client.

Authorizing Remote Access Connections

After a user submits credentials to create a remote access connection, the remote access connection must be authorized by a Windows Server 2008 server running the ***Network Policy Server (NPS)*** RRAS role service, or else a third-party authentication and authorization service such as a Remote Authentication Dial-In User Service (RADIUS) server. Remote access authorization consists of two steps: verifying the *dial-in properties* of the user account, and verifying any NPS Network Policies that have been applied against the Routing and Remote Access server. The Microsoft implementation of a RADIUS server is the Network Policy Server. Use a RADIUS server to centralize remote access authentication, authorization, and logging. When you implement RADIUS, multiple Windows Server 2008 computers running the Routing and Remote Access service can forward access requests to a single RADIUS server. The RADIUS server then queries the domain controller for authentication and applies NPS Network Policies to the connection requests.

The concepts of authentication and authorization are often blurred or misunderstood. Authentication is the process of verifying that an entity or object is who or what it claims to be. Examples include confirming the source and integrity of information, such as verifying a digital signature or verifying the identity of a user or computer. Authorization is the process that determines what a user is permitted to do on a computer system or network. Naturally, authorization occurs only after successful authentication. Additionally, most remote access systems will include an *accounting* component that will log access to resources. In short:

- Authentication proves that the user is who he or she claims to be.

- Authorization controls what resources an authorized user can and cannot access.

- Accounting keeps track of what resources a user has accessed or attempted to access.

Dial-in properties, which apply to both direct dial-up and VPN connections, are configured in the Dial-In tab of the User Account Properties dialog box. If a user is dialing in to a domain, a user account that corresponds to the name sent through the dial-up connection must already exist in the domain. Dial-in properties for this account can thus be configured in the Active Directory Users And Computers console.

If the user is dialing in to a stand-alone server, however, the account must already exist as a user account in the answering server's local Security Accounts Manager (SAM) database. SAM is a Windows service used during the logon process. SAM maintains user account information, including groups to which a user belongs. Dial-in properties for this account can thus be configured in the Local Users And Groups console in Computer Management.

Figure 5-8 shows the Dial-In tab of a local user account properties, which is described in the next section.

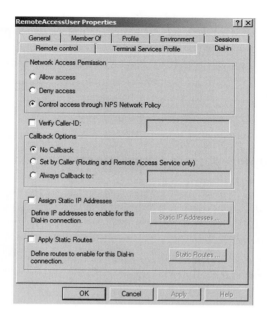

In Windows Server 2008, the Control Access Through NPS Network Policy option is enabled by default. You can set the remote access permission for user accounts to any one of the following three levels:

- Control Access Through NPS Network Policy—This particular option neither blocks nor allows dial-up access for the user. Instead, it specifies that the user's access permissions be determined by first matching the NPS Network Policy applied to the connection. (By default, NPS Network Policies block all remote access connections.)

- Deny Access—When you select the Deny Access option, dial-up access for the user account is blocked, regardless of other settings or policies that are applied to the account.

- Allow Access—When you select the Allow Access option, dial-up remote access for the user account is permitted, thereby overriding the remote access permission setting in NPS Network Policies. Note that the Allow Access setting does not always prevent NPS Network policies from blocking remote access; an NPS Network policy can still restrict the account's remote access through the NPS Network Policy profile. For example, dial-up hours specified in an NPS Network policy profile might prevent a user account from connecting in the evening hours, even when the Allow Access option has been set for the user account's dial-in properties. However, the Allow Access option specifies that the Deny Remote Access Permission setting in NPS Network Policies is ignored.

If the Verify Caller ID check box is selected, the server verifies the caller's phone number; if the phone number does not match the configured phone number, the connection attempt is denied. The caller, the phone system between the caller and the server, and the remote access server must support caller ID. On a computer running the Routing and Remote Access service, caller ID support consists of call-answering equipment that provides caller ID information and the appropriate Windows driver to pass the information to the Routing and Remote Access service. If you configure a caller ID phone number for a user and you do not have support for the passing of caller ID information from the caller to the Routing and Remote Access service, connection attempts are denied.

By default, the Callback Options setting is configured as No Callback. If the Set By Caller option is selected, the server calls the caller back at a number specified by the caller. If the Always Callback To: option is selected, an administrator must specify a number that the server always uses during the callback process.

Additionally, you can configure a static IP address and/or static IP addresses that should apply to this user whenever he or she connects to a Remote Access server.

Applying NPS Network Policies

An NPS Network Policy is a set of permissions or restrictions that is read by a remote access authenticating server that applies to remote access connections. Remote access permissions were simple to understand and implement in Windows NT 4 and Windows NT 3.51. Remote access permissions were granted directly on the user's account using User Manager or the Remote Access Administration utility. Although this was simple and easy to understand, it worked well only when a small number of users required permission for remote access. In Windows Server 2008, Windows Server 2003, and Windows 2000 Server, remote access authorization is more complicated and consequently requires more effort to understand; however, it is also much more powerful and can be precisely configured to meet the security and access needs of both small and very large organizations.

TAKE NOTE * NPS Network Policies in Windows Server 2008 are analogous to Remote Access Policies in Windows Server 2003 and Windows 2000 Server.

As mentioned previously, authorization is determined by a combination of the dial-in properties for the user account and the NPS network policies. With remote access policies, connections can be authorized or denied based on user attributes, group membership, the time of day, the type of connection being requested, and many other variables.

Using the Network Policy Server, a Windows Server 2008 computer can also function as a Remote Authentication Dial-In User Service (RADIUS) server, to provide *authentication*, authorization, and accounting for access to network resources.

Configuring an NPS Network Policy

An NPS Network Policy, which is a rule for evaluating remote connections, consists of three components: conditions, constraints, and settings. You can think of an NPS Network Policy as a rule for allowing or disallowing remote access: Windows Server 2008 will compare any incoming connection attempt against the rules configured within each NPS Network Policy. If the conditions and constraints defined by the connection attempt match those configured in the Network Policy, the remote access server will either allow or deny the connection, and configure additional settings, as defined by the policy. Every remote access policy has an Access Permissions setting, which specifies whether connections matching the policy should be allowed or denied.

When a user attempts to connect to a remote access server, the following process takes place, as illustrated in Figure 5-9:

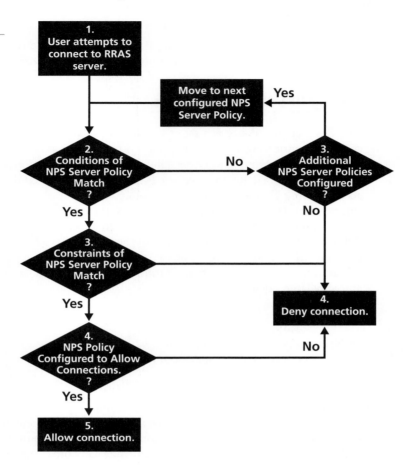

1. User attempts to initiate a remote access connection.
2. Remote Access server checks the conditions in the first configured NPS Network Policy.
3. If the conditions of this NPS Network Policy do not match, the Remote Access server checks any remaining configured NPS Network Policies until it finds a match.
4. Once the Remote Access Server finds an NPS Network Policy with conditions that match the incoming connection attempt, the Remote Access server checks any constraints that have been configured for the policy.
5. If the connection attempt does not match any configured constraints—time of day, minimum encryption level, etc.—the Remote Access server denies the connection.
6. If the connection attempt matches both the conditions and the constraints of a particular NPS Network Policy, the remote access server will allow or deny the connection, based on the Access Permissions configured for that policy.

NPS Network Policies are ordered on each Remote Access server, and each policy is evaluated in order from top to bottom. It is important to place these policies in the correct order, because once the RRAS server finds a match, it will stop processing additional policies. For example, if you have an NPS Network Policy of "deny all connections between the hours of 8 A.M.–5 P.M." set as the first configured policy, the RRAS server will deny all connections within that timeframe even if you have a more specific NPS Network Policy configured lower in the list. As a best practice, NPS Network Policies should be ordered so that more specific policies are higher in the list, and less specific policies are lower in the list, so that policies can be processed in the correct order.

For example, you might have two policies configured in the following order:

1. If a user is a member of the "Remote Consultant" group, allow the connection regardless of time of day.
2. Deny all connections between 8 A.M.–5 P.M., Monday through Friday, regardless of any other conditions.

In this scenario, a member of the "Remote Consultant" group would be able to connect to the RRAS server at 10 A.M. on a Tuesday because he/she is a match to Policy #1, which is processed before Policy #2. If a user is not a member of the "Remote Consultant" group, he/she will not be a match to Policy #1, and Policy #2 will take effect.

By default, two NPS Network Policies are preconfigured in Windows Server 2008. The first default policy is Connections To Microsoft Routing And Remote Access Server, as shown in Figure 5-10, which is configured to match every remote access connection to the Routing and Remote Access service. When Routing and Remote Access is reading this policy, the policy naturally matches every incoming connection. However, if a RADIUS server or a third-party authentication mechanism is reading this policy, network access might be provided by a non-Microsoft vendor. Consequently, this policy will not match those connections.

Figure 5-10

Configuring NPS Network Policies

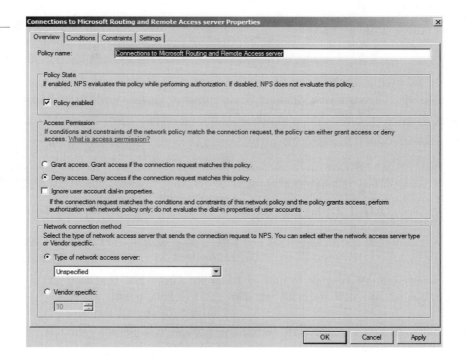

The second default remote access policy is Connections To Other Access Servers. This policy is configured to match every incoming connection, regardless of network access server type. Because the first policy matches all connections to a Microsoft Routing and Remote Access server, this policy will take effect only if an incoming connection is being authenticated by a RADIUS server or some other authentication mechanism.

Configuring Policy Conditions

Each NPS Network policy is based on policy conditions that determine when the policy is applied. For example, a policy might include a condition that Windows Groups matches WINGTIPTOYS\Telecommuters. This policy would then match a connection for a user who belongs to the Telecommuters security group.

By clicking the Add button in the Select Attribute dialog box on the Conditions tab, you can add a new category for a remote access policy condition, as shown in Figure 5-11.

Figure 5-11

Adding a new policy condition

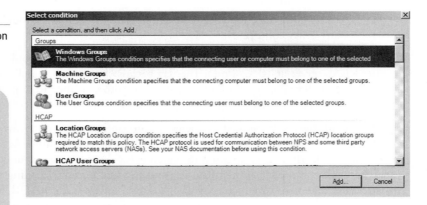

TAKE NOTE*

Only membership in global security groups can serve as a remote policy condition. You cannot specify membership in universal or domain local security groups as the condition for a remote access policy.

Configuring Policy Settings

An NPS Network policy profile consists of a set of settings and properties that can be applied to a connection. You can configure an NPS profile by clicking the Settings tab in the policy Properties page, as shown in Figure 5-12.

Figure 5-12

Configuring NPS policy server settings

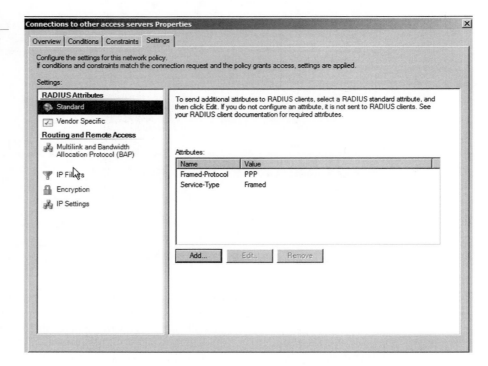

One example of an NPS Policy Setting includes IP properties that specify IP address assignment behavior. You have the following options:

- Server Must Supply An IP Address.
- Client May Request An IP Address.
- Server Settings Determine IP Address Assignment (the default setting).
- Assign A Static IP Address. The assigned IP address is typically used to accommodate vendor-specific attributes for IP addresses.

In addition, you can set *multilink* properties that enable a remote access connection to use multiple modem connections for a single connection and determine the maximum number of ports (modems) that a multilink connection can use, and set *Bandwidth Allocation Protocol (BAP)* policies that determine BAP usage and specify when extra BAP lines are dropped. The multilink and BAP properties are specific to the Routing and Remote Access service. By default, multilink and BAP are disabled. The Routing and Remote Access service must have multilink and BAP enabled for the multilink properties of the profile to be enforced.

Finally, there are four encryption options available in the Encryption tab:

- *Basic Encryption (MPPE 40-Bit)*—For dial-up and PPTP-based VPN connections, MPPE is used with a 40-bit key. For L2TP/IPSec VPN connections, 56-bit DES encryption is used.
- *Strong Encryption (MPPE 56-Bit)*—For dial-up and PPTP VPN connections, MPPE is used with a 56-bit key. For L2TP/IPSec VPN connections, 56-bit DES encryption is used.
- ***Strongest Encryption (MPPE 128-Bit)***—For dial-up and PPTP VPN connections, MPPE is used with a 128-bit key. For L2TP/IPSec VPN connections, 168-bit Triple DES encryption is used.
- *No Encryption*—This option allows unencrypted connections that match the remote access policy conditions. Clear this option to require encryption.

Choosing an Authentication Protocol

To authenticate the credentials submitted by the dial-up connection, the remote access server must first negotiate a common authentication protocol with the remote access client. Most authentication protocols offer some measure of security so that user credentials cannot be intercepted. Authentication protocols in Windows clients and servers are assigned a priority based on this security level.

Following is a complete list of the authentication protocols supported by Routing and Remote Access in Windows Server 2008 (listed in order from most secure to least secure):

- *EAP-TLS*—A certificate-based authentication that is based on EAP, an extensible framework that supports new *authentication method*s. EAP-TLS is typically used in conjunction with smart cards. It supports encryption of both authentication data and connection data. Note that stand-alone servers do not support EAP-TLS. The remote access server that runs Windows Server 2008 must be a member of a domain.
- *MS-CHAP v2*—A mutual authentication method that offers encryption of both authentication data and connection data. A new cryptographic key is used for each connection and each transmission direction. MS-CHAP v2 is enabled by default in Windows 2000, Windows XP, Windows Server 2003, and Windows Server 2008.
- *MS-CHAP v1*—A one-way authentication method that offers encryption of both authentication data and connection data. The same cryptographic key is used in all connections. MS-CHAP v1 supports older Windows clients, such as Windows 95 and Windows 98.
- *Extensible Authentication Protocol-Message Digest 5 Challenge Handshake Authentication Protocol (EAP-MD5 CHAP)*—A version of CHAP (see the following bullet) that is ported to the EAP framework. EAP-MD5 CHAP supports encryption of authentication data through the industry-standard MD5 hashing scheme and provides compatibility with non-Microsoft clients, such as those running Mac OS X. It does not support the encryption of connection data.
- *Challenge Handshake Authentication Protocol (CHAP)*—A generic authentication method that offers encryption of authentication data through the MD5 hashing scheme. CHAP provides compatibility with non-Microsoft clients. The group policy that is applied to

accounts using this authentication method must be configured to store passwords using reversible encryption. (Passwords must be reset after this new policy is applied.) It does not support encryption of connection data.

- *Shiva Password Authentication Protocol (SPAP)*—A weakly encrypted authentication protocol that offers interoperability with Shiva remote networking products. SPAP does not support the encryption of connection data.
- *Password Authentication Protocol (PAP)*—A generic authentication method that does not encrypt authentication data. User credentials are sent over the network in plaintext. PAP does not support the encryption of connection data.
- *Unauthenticated access*—Not an authentication protocol, but a configuration option that—when set on the NAS and remote access policy is applied to the connection—allows remote access connections to connect without submitting credentials. Can be used to troubleshoot or test remote access connectivity. Unauthenticated access does not support the encryption of connection data.

Table 5-2 provides information to help you map your requirements to the appropriate protocol.

Table 5-2 Selecting an Authentication Protocol

Requirement	Select
Encrypted authentication support for Windows 95, Windows 98, Microsoft Windows Millennium Edition (Me), or Windows NT 4 remote access clients (native support)	MS-CHAP v1
Encrypted authentication support for Windows 95, Windows 98, Windows Millennium Edition (Me), or Windows NT 4 remote access clients (with the latest Dial-Up Networking upgrade)	MS-CHAP v2 (VPN only for Windows 95)
Encrypted authentication support for certificate-based **public key infrastructure (PKI)**, such as those used with smart cards (when the remote access server is a member of a Windows 2000 server or Windows Server 2003 domain)	EAP-TLS
Encrypted authentication support for other Windows 2000, Windows XP, and Windows Server 2003 remote access clients	MS-CHAP v2
Mutual authentication (client and server always authenticate each other)	EAP-TLS and MS-CHAP v2
Support for encryption of connection data	MS-CHAP v1, MS-CHAP v2, and EAP-TLS
Encrypted authentication report for remote access clients that use other operating systems	CHAP
Encrypted authentication report for remote access clients running Shiva LAN Rover software	SPAP
Unencrypted authentication when the remote access clients do not support any other protocol	PAP
Authentication credentials are not supplied by the remote access client	Unauthenticated access

As a final step in configuring the Network Policy Server to provide authentication, authorization, and accounting for your remote access clients, you will also need to configure Accounting, as shown in Figure 5-13. By default, all remote access attempts are logged to text files stored in the *C:\Windows\system32\LogFiles* directory, but you can also configure logging to a SQL database for better reporting and event correlation.

Figure 5-13

Configuring Network Policy
Server Accounting

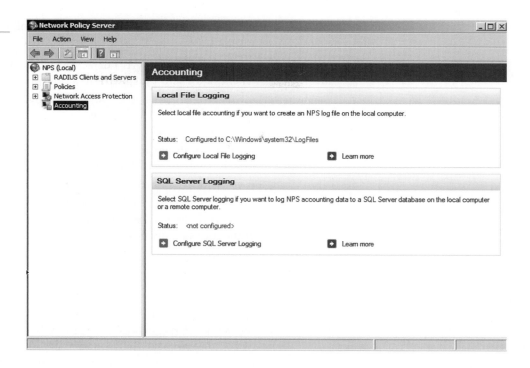

■ Configuring Wireless Access

THE BOTTOM LINE

In addition to the challenges of allowing remote access into your corporate network, recent advances in mobile computing technology have created a need to secure other types of network access. Whether the concern is securing wireless access points against unauthorized use, or preventing visitors or consultants from plugging into an unsecured network switch in a conference room to attempt to access sensitive resources, there is a clear need to secure access to a corporate network even beyond the typical username and password authentication protections that were previously sufficient.

CERTIFICATION READY?
Configure wireless access

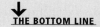
3.4

To help secure network access for both wired and wireless connections, the Institute of Electrical and Electronics Engineers (IEEE) developed the 802.1X standard for ***network access control***. 802.1X is *port-based*, which means that it can allow or deny access on the basis of a *physical port*, such as someone plugging into a single wall jack using an Ethernet cable, or a *logical port*, such as one or more people connecting to a wireless access point using the WiFi cards in one or more laptops or handheld devices.

802.1X provides port-based security through the use of the following three components:

- ***Supplicant***—This is the device that is seeking access to the network, such as a laptop attempting to access a wireless access point.
- ***Authenticator***—This is the component that requests authentication credentials from supplicants, most commonly the port on a switch for a wired connection or a wireless access point. Despite its name, the authenticator does not actually verify the user or computer credentials; rather, the authenticator forwards the supplicant's credentials to the Authentication Server (AS).
- ***Authentication Server (AS)***—As just mentioned, this is the server that verifies the supplicant's authentication credentials, and informs the authenticator whether to allow or disallow access to the 802.1X-secured network port. The Authentication Server role in an 802.1X infrastructure can be performed by a Windows Server 2008 computer that is running the Network Policy Server role, as well as any third-party RADIUS servers.

When a wired or wireless port is secured through 802.1X, the following process takes place before network access is permitted:

1. The authenticator (switch port or WAP) detects an access attempt by a new supplicant (a wireless client or a client plugging into a physical port).
2. The authenticator sets the port (whether physical or logical) to an "unauthorized" state so that only 802.1X traffic can be passed.
3. The authenticator sends an *EAP-Request* packet to the supplicant, requesting their EAP information. The supplicant responds with an *EAP-Response* to the authenticator, which the authenticator forwards to the Authentication Server (AS).
4. If the AS accepts the EAP-Response, it instructs the authenticator to set the port to an "authorized" state so that traffic can pass normally across the port.
5. When the supplicant is no longer using the secured port, it sends an ***EAP-Logoff*** message to the authenticator, which instructs the authenticator to place the port back into an unauthorized state.

To configure a Windows Server 2008 server to allow wireless access, you will need to do the following:

1. Install and configure *RADIUS clients*. In this case, the RADIUS client is not a Windows Vista or Windows XP client computer; rather, the RADIUS clients consist of network access servers such as 802.1X-capable switches and wireless access points.
2. Select one or more authentication methods. For 802.1X wired and wireless connections, you can select one or more of the following authentication methods:
   a. *Extensible Authentication Protocol (EAP)* with *Transport Layer Security (TLS)* (also called *EAP-TLS*)
   b. Protected EAP (PEAP) with Microsoft Challenge Authentication Protocol version 2 (MS-CHAP v2), or PEAP-MS-CHAP v2
   c. PEAP with EAP-TLS (also called PEAP-TLS)
3. Configure a Windows Server 2008 NPS Server as a RADIUS server. This consists of the following three steps:
   a. Within the NPS MMC snap-in, add each switch or wireless access point as a RADIUS client.
   b. Configure NPS Network Policies as described earlier to define the conditions under which you will allow or disallow network access.
   c. Configure accounting on the NPS server, either to a text file or to a SQL Server database.

> **WARNING** Both EAP-TLS and PEAP-TLS require you to configure a Public Key Infrastructure (PKI) such as one using Active Directory Certificate Services (AD CS). Deploying Active Directory and the AD CS role is outside of the scope of this text; you can find full coverage of these topics in the textbook *Planning, Implementing, and Maintaining Windows Server Active Directory Infrastructure*.

SUMMARY SKILL MATRIX

IN THIS LESSON YOU LEARNED:

- By using the Routing and Remote Access service, Windows Server 2008 can be configured as a router and remote access server. A significant advantage of using Windows Server 2008 in this manner is that it is integrated with Windows features such as Group Policy and the Active Directory service. The Routing And Remote Access console is the principal tool used for configuring and managing this service.

- Routing and Remote Access can be automatically configured for several options: Remote Access (Dial-Up or VPN), Network Address Translation (NAT), Virtual Private Network (VPN) Access And NAT, and Secure Connection Between Two Private Networks. Or, if none of the standard options match your requirements, you can also manually configure Routing and Remote Access.

- Without dynamic routing protocols such as RIPv2, network administrators must add static routes to connect to non-neighboring subnets when those subnets do not lie in the same direction as the default route.

- Routers read the destination addresses of received packets and route those packets according to directions that are provided by routing tables. In Windows Server 2008, you can view the IP routing table through the Routing And Remote Access console or through the Route Print command.

- Windows Server 2008 provides extensive support for demand-dial routing, which is the routing of packets over physical point-to-point links, such as analog phone lines and ISDN, and over virtual point-to-point links, such as PPTP and L2TP. Demand-dial routing allows you to connect to the Internet, connect branch offices, or implement router-to-router VPN connections.

- The remote access connection must be authorized after it is authenticated. Remote access authorization begins with the user account's dial-in properties; the first matching remote access policy is then applied to the connection.

- The Microsoft implementation of a RADIUS server is the Network Policy Server. Use a RADIUS server to centralize remote access authentication, authorization, and logging. When you implement RADIUS, multiple Windows Server 2008 computers running the Routing and Remote Access service forward access requests to the RADIUS server. The RADIUS server then queries the domain controller for authentication and applies remote access policies to the connection requests.

- The 802.1X IEEE standard allows for port-level network access control of both wired and wireless connections.

- A Windows Server 2008 server running the NPS role can also secure 802.1X connectivity for 802.1X-capable network switched and wireless access ports.

■ Knowledge Assessment

Matching

Match the following definitions with the appropriate term.

   a. authenticator
   b. frames
   c. Layer 3 device
   d. loopback address
   e. network access control
   f. Network Policy Server (NPS)
   g. Open Shortest Path First (OSPF)
   h. Physical Layer
   i. Software-based router
   j. Strongest Encryption (MPPE 128-bit)

_____ **1.** This type of router is well-suited for a small organization with low levels of network traffic utilization.

_____ **2.** Network data at the Data Link Layer is organized into these.

_____ **3.** This is used as the Windows Server 2008 implementation of a RADIUS server.

_____ **4.** This routing protocol was supported in Windows Server 2003 but is no longer available with the Routing and Remote Access server role in Windows Server 2008.

_____ **5.** This address corresponds to the 127.0.0.1 address used for TCP/IP diagnostics and troubleshooting.

_____ **6.** This is the 802.1X component that sends an EAP-Request message to any clients attempting to gain network access.

_____ **7.** Network hubs operate at this layer of the OSI model.

_____ **8.** This is the strongest level of encryption that you can configure as part of an NPS Network Policy setting.

_____ **9.** This is another term to describe a network router.

_____**10.** 802.1X is used to configure this for both wired and wireless network connections.

Multiple Choice

Select all answers that apply for the following questions.

1. The IP address 255.255.255.255 represents _____ in the IP Routing table.
   a. Loopback address
   b. Limited broadcast address
   c. Directly-attached network route
   d. Default route

2. To allow users to specify a call-back number when they connect to a remote access server via modem, you will enable the following setting:
   a. No Callback
   b. Set by Caller
   c. Always Callback To
   d. Verify Caller ID

3. Routing Information Protocol v2 (RIPv2) is an example of a:
   a. Routing table
   b. Routing prompt
   c. Routing chart
   d. Routing protocol

4. Windows Server 2008 can provide remote access services through a Virtual Private Network (VPN) or through:
   a. Dial-Up Networking (DUN)
   b. Remote Callback
   c. Demand-Dial Routing
   d. X.25

5. When a workstation ends a session with an 802.1X-secured network port, it sends the following to inform the network access server to set the port back to an "Unauthorized" status:
   a. EAP-Inform
   b. EAP-Discover
   c. EAP-Logoff
   d. EAP-Request

6. If an IP Routing Table contains two routes to the same destination network, the route with the lowest _____ will be selected first.
   a. Weight
   b. Metric
   c. GUID
   d. Priority

7. Network information at the Network Layer of the OSI model is organized into:
   a. Bits
   b. Frames
   c. Datagrams
   d. Packets

8. In an 802.1X infrastructure, an NPS or RADIUS server performs the role of the:
   a. Applicant
   b. Supplicant
   c. Authorization Server (AS)
   d. Authenticator

9. The following RRAS service allows multiple computers on an internal network to share a single public IP address to access the Internet:
   a. Network Access Control
   b. Network Address Translation (NAT)
   c. Network Access Protection
   d. Network Address Control

10. The following route is used by a computer's default gateway to send traffic to remote networks:
   a. Default route
   b. Limited broadcast address
   c. Broadcast address
   d. Default interface

■ Case Scenarios

Scenario 5-1: Configuring Remote Access Connectivity

You are a network consultant for Humongous Insurance, a health insurance provider based in New York City, NY. Humongous Insurance supports small offices for its agents in cities across the United States, and has recently deployed a farm of centralized database servers containing customer information for all of Humongous' customers. The management of Humongous Insurance has tasked you with determining the best way for the remote sales offices to access these new centralized servers. Some sales offices have dedicated broadband Internet connectivity, while other smaller offices still rely on modems and telephone lines.

1. What technology can you use to provide connectivity for those smaller offices that do not have broadband Internet?

2. Humongous Insurance management is concerned about sales agents dialing into the Humongous network during non-working hours solely to gain access to the Internet. How can you prevent this from occurring?

3. Management has hired a rotating group of insurance claims representatives who will be available to assist customers between the hours of 5 P.M. and midnight, Eastern time. How can you allow these representatives access to the Humongous network while preventing casual use of company resources by other employees?

6 LESSON

Configuring File Services

OBJECTIVE DOMAIN MATRIX

TECHNOLOGY SKILL	OBJECTIVE DOMAIN	OBJECTIVE DOMAIN NUMBER
Configuring a File Server	Configure a file server	4.1
Using the Distributed File System	Configure Distributed File System (DFS)	4.2

KEY TERMS

client failback
Distributed File System (DFS)
extended partition
full mesh topology
hub/spoke topology
member
multiple master replication

namespace
namespace server
primary partition
referral
Remote Differential
  Compression (RDC)

replication group
Server service
single master replication
targets

Lucerne Publishing is a publisher of medical textbooks, with offices in Chicago, New York City, San Francisco, and Seattle. Lucerne Publishing has numerous file servers located in each office, and is continually adding and removing servers as they take on new clients and new publishing projects. In order to ease file access for the Lucerne Publishing user population, Lucerne Publishing IT has recently begun an endeavor to overhaul its file sharing technologies. As a consultant for Lucerne Publishing, you have been tasked with recommending solutions to improve file sharing for the Lucerne Publishing network.

This lesson provides an overview of the File Server role in Windows Server 2008. We will begin with the tasks necessary to deploy one or more file servers in your organization, including working with disk drives, creating shares and assigning permissions, and designing a file sharing strategy for your users. We will then examine the Distributed File System (DFS) role service, which allows users to access files residing on multiple physical servers using a single unified namespace.

■ Planning a File Server Deployment

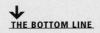
THE BOTTOM LINE

Time spent planning a file server deployment before actually configuring the computer is never wasted. In its most basic form, configuring a Microsoft Windows Server 2008 computer to function as a file server is the simplest role to implement. All you have to do is share a folder or a drive and, technically speaking, you have a file server. However, on an enterprise network, things are almost never that simple.

Planning for file sharing on a large network requires you to assess a number of factors, including:

- Scalability—How much storage space do your users need, and how much more will they need a year from now?
- Navigation—On a large network with many shares, how are users expected to find the files that they need?
- Protection—How do you control access to network file shares?
- Abuse—How do you prevent users from consuming too much server storage space?
- Diversity—How do you provide file sharing support for users running operating systems other than Windows?
- Fault tolerance—How quickly can you recover from the failure of a hard drive, a server, or an entire facility?
- Availability—How can you make sure that users have continuous local access to critical files, even on remote networks?

The File Services role and the other storage-related features included with Windows Server 2008 provide tools that enable system administrators to address all of these problems on a scale appropriate to a large enterprise network. However, before you implement the role or begin using these tools, you should spend some time thinking about your users' needs and how they affect their file storage and sharing practices. The process of implementing technologies such as the Distributed File System, discussed later in this lesson, and storage quotas, discussed in Lesson 11, requires you to have some idea of how you intend to use the technologies on your enterprise network. Therefore, a period of planning and design is recommended before you start the implementation. Whether you are planning to deploy a single large file server or multiple file servers across an enterprise, you must take into account the inherent storage limitations of Windows Server 2008, which are listed in Table 6-1.

Table 6-1

Windows Server 2008 Storage Limitations

STORAGE CHARACTERISTIC	LIMITATION
Maximum basic volume size	2 terabytes
Maximum dynamic volume size (simple and mirrored volumes)	2 terabytes
Maximum dynamic volume size (spanned and striped volumes)	64 terabytes (2 terabytes per disk, with a maximum of 32 disks
Maximum dynamic volume size (RAID-5 volumes)	62 terabytes (2 terabytes per disk, with a maximum of 32 disks, and 2 terabytes reserved for parity information)
Maximum NTFS volume size	2^{32} clusters minus 1 cluster (Using the default 4 kilobyte cluster size, the maximum volume size is 16 terabytes minus 64 kilobytes. Using the maximum 64 kilobyte cluster size, the maximum volume size is 256 terabytes minus 64 kilobytes.)
Maximum number of clusters on an NTFS volume	2^{32} (4,294,967,296)
Maximum NTFS file size	2^{44} bytes (16 terabytes) minus 64 kilobytes
Maximum number of files on an NTFS volume	2^{32} minus 1 file (4,294,967,295)
Maximum number of volumes on a server	Approximately 2,000 (1000 dynamic volumes and the rest basic)

Another factor that can affect your plans is how many sites your enterprise network encompasses and what technologies you use to provide network communications between those sites. If, for example, your organization has branch offices scattered around the world and uses relatively expensive wide area networking (WAN) links to connect them, it would probably be more economical to install a file server at each location, rather than have all of your users access a single file server using the WAN links.

Within each site, the number of file servers you need can depend on how often your users work with the same files and how much fault tolerance and high availability you want to build into the system. For example, if each department in your organization typically works with its own documents and rarely needs access to the files of other departments, deploying individual file servers to each department might be preferable. If everyone in your organization works with the same set of files, a single server might be a better choice.

The need for high availability and fault tolerance can also lead you to deploy additional servers, whether you initially configure them all as file servers or not. Distributing roles among multiple servers enables you to redeploy roles as needed, in the event of a hardware failure or other catastrophe.

■ Configuring a File Server

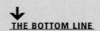
THE BOTTOM LINE

Implementing basic file server functions requires only a default Windows Server 2008 installation; the File Server role is available on all versions of the Windows Server 2008 software. The process of deploying and configuring a simple file server using Windows Server 2008 includes many of the most basic server administration tasks, including installing disks, creating shares, assigning permissions, and mapping drive letters. The following sections describe the procedures for these administration tasks, which form the basis of all file server implementations.

CERTIFICATION READY?
Configure a file server

4.1

Working with Disks

When preparing a hard disk for use, Windows Server 2008 file servers often require different settings than workstations. When you install Windows Server 2008 on a computer, the setup program automatically performs all of the preparation tasks for the hard disks in the system. However, when you install additional hard disk drives on a file server, or when you want to use settings that differ from the system defaults, you must perform a number of tasks manually.

When you install additional storage on a Windows Server 2008 computer, you must address the following tasks:

- Select a partitioning style—Windows Server 2008 supports two hard disk partition styles, on both x86- and x64-based computers: the master boot record (MBR) partition style and the GUID (globally unique identifier) partition table (GPT) partition style. You must choose one of these partition styles for a drive; you cannot use both.

- Select a disk type—Windows Server 2008 supports two disk types: basic disks and dynamic disks. You cannot use both disk types on the same disk drive, but you can mix disk types in the same computer.

- Divide the disk into partitions or volumes—Although many professionals use the terms *partition* and *volume* interchangeably, it is correct to refer to creating partitions on basic disks, and volumes on dynamic disks.

- Format the partitions or volumes with a file system—Windows Server 2008 supports the NTFS file system and the FAT file system (including the FAT16 and FAT32 variants).

UNDERSTANDING DISK TYPES

Most personal computers use basic disks because they are the easiest to manage. A basic disk uses primary partitions, extended partitions, and logical drives to organize data. A primary partition appears to the operating system as though it is a physically separate disk and can host an operating system, in which case it is known as the *active partition*.

During the installation of Windows Server 2008, the setup program creates both a system partition and a boot partition. The system partition contains hardware-related files that the computer uses to boot. The boot partition contains the operating system files, which are stored in the Windows directory. In most cases, these two partitions are one and the same, comprising the active primary partition that Windows uses when starting. The active partition tells the computer which system partition and operating system it should use to start Windows.

When you work with basic disks in Windows Server 2008, you can create up to four ***primary partitions***; that is, a partition that can be used to load an operating system. For the fourth partition, you have the option of creating an ***extended partition*** instead (one on which you cannot load an operating system), on which you can create as many logical drives as you need. You can format and assign drive letters to logical drives, but they cannot host an operating system. Table 6-2 compares some of the characteristics of primary and extended partitions.

Table 6-2

Primary and Extended Partition Comparison

PRIMARY PARTITIONS	EXTENDED PARTITIONS
A primary partition functions as though it is a physically separate disk and can host an operating system.	Extended partitions cannot host an operating system.
A primary partition can be marked as an active partition. You can have only one active partition per hard disk. The system BIOS looks to the active partition for the boot files it uses to start the operating system.	You cannot mark an extended partition as an active partition.
You can create up to four primary partitions or three primary partitions and one extended partition.	A basic disk can contain only one extended partition, but unlimited logical drives within the partition.
You format each primary partition and assign a unique drive letter.	You do not format the extended partition itself, but the logical drives it contains. You assign a unique drive letter to each of the logical drives.

The alternative to using a basic disk is to convert it to a dynamic disk. The process of converting a basic disk to a dynamic disk creates a single partition that occupies the entire disk. You can then create an unlimited number of volumes out of the space in that partition. The advantage of using dynamic disks is that they support several different types of volumes, as described in the next section.

UNDERSTANDING VOLUME TYPES

A dynamic disk can contain an unlimited number of volumes that function a lot like primary partitions on a basic disk, but you cannot mark an existing dynamic disk as an active partition.

When you create a volume on a dynamic disk in Windows Server 2008, you must choose from the following five volume types:

- Simple volume—Consists of space from a single disk. Once you have created a simple volume, you can later extend it to multiple disks to create a spanned or striped volume, as long as it is not a system volume or boot volume. You can also extend a simple volume into any adjacent unallocated space on the same disk, or shrink the volume by de-allocating any unused space in the volume.

- Spanned volume—Consists of space from 2 to 32 physical disks, all of which must be dynamic disks. A spanned volume is essentially a method for combining the space from multiple dynamic disks into a single large volume. Windows Server 2008 writes to the spanned volume by filling all of the space on the first disk, and then proceeds to fill each of the additional disks in turn. You can extend a spanned volume at any time by adding additional disk space. Creating a spanned volume does not increase the disk's read/write performance, nor does it provide fault tolerance. In fact, if a single physical disk in the spanned volume fails, all of the data in the entire volume is lost.

- Striped volume—Consists of space from 2 to 32 physical disks, all of which must be dynamic disks. The difference between a striped volume and a spanned volume is that in a striped volume, the system writes data one stripe at a time to each successive disk in the volume. Striping provides improved performance because each disk drive in the array has time to seek the location of its next stripe while the other drives are writing. Striped volumes do not provide fault tolerance, however, and you cannot extend them after creation. If a single physical disk in the striped volume fails, all of the data in the entire volume is lost.

- Mirrored volume—Consists of an identical amount of space on two physical disks, both of which must be dynamic disks. The system performs all read and write operations on both disks simultaneously, so they contain duplicate copies of all data stored on the volume. If one of the disks should fail, the other one continues to provide access to the volume until it is repaired or replaced.

- RAID-5 volume—Consists of space on three or more physical disks, all of which must be dynamic disks. The system stripes data and parity information across all of the disks, so that if one physical disk fails, the missing data can be recreated using the parity information on the other disks. RAID-5 volumes provide improved read performance, because of the disk striping, but write performance suffers, due to the need for parity calculations.

CHOOSING A VOLUME SIZE

Although Windows Server 2008 can support dynamic volumes as large as 64 terabytes, this does not mean that you should create volumes that big, even if you have a server with that much storage. To facilitate the maintenance and administration processes, it is usually preferable to split your file server's storage into volumes of manageable size, rather than create a single, gigantic volume.

One common practice is to choose a volume size based on the capacity of your network backup solution. For example, if you perform network backups using tape drives with an 80 gigabyte capacity, creating volumes that can fit onto a single tape can facilitate the backup process. Creating smaller volumes will also speed up the restore process, in the event that you have to recover a volume from a tape or other backup medium.

Another factor to consider is the amount of down time your business can tolerate. If one of your volumes should suffer a file system error, and you do not have a fault tolerance mechanism in place to take up the slack, you might have to bring it down, so that you can run Chkdsk.exe or some other disk repair utility. The larger the volume, the longer the Chkdsk process will take, and longer your users will be without their files.

Using the Disk Management Snap-in

Before you can configure a Windows Server 2008 computer as a file server, you must prepare your disks by selecting a partition type, a volume type, and a file system. You will perform this task using the Disk Management MMC snap-in that you can use to perform disk-related tasks such as initializing disks, selecting a partition style, converting basic disks to dynamic disks, and more.

ANOTHER WAY

You can also use the DiskPart.exe command prompt utility to perform disk management tasks.

To access the Disk Management Snap-in, use any one of the following procedures:

- From the Administrative Tools program group, select Computer Management, and then click the Disk Management node.
- Click the Start button, right-click Computer, and then click Manage. When the Computer Management console appears, select the Disk Management node.
- Open the Run dialog box and execute the compmgmt.msc file.

In the Disk Management snap-in shown in Figure 6-1, the two center panes, the Top view and the Bottom view, display disk and volume information, respectively. Although Disk Management can display only two views at any one time, three views are available:

Figure 6-1

The Disk Management snap-in

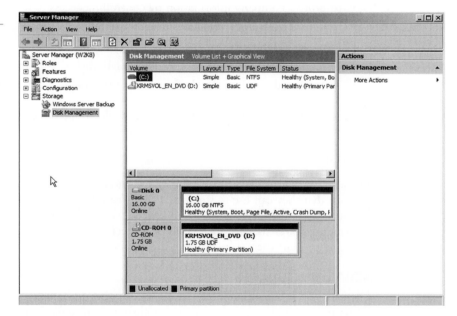

- Disk List—This view provides a summary about the physical drives in the computer. This information includes the disk number; disk type, such as Basic or DVD; disk capacity; size of unallocated space; the status of the disk device, such as online, offline, or no media; the device type, such as SCSI or IDE; and the partition style, such as MBR or GPT.
- Volume List—This view provides a more detailed summary of all the drives on the computer. This information includes the volume name; the volume layout, such as Simple, Spanned, or Striped; the disk type, such as Basic or Dynamic; the file system in use, such as FAT32 or NTFS; the hard disk status, such as Healthy, Failed, or Formatting; the disk capacity; the disk available free space; the percentage of the hard disk that is free; whether the hard disk is fault tolerant; and the disk overhead percentage.
- Graphical View—This view displays a graphical representation of all the physical disks, partitions, volumes, and logical drives available on the computer. The graphical view is divided into two columns: the disk status column (located on the left) and the volume status column (located on the right). The disk status column displays the number, type, capacity, and status of each disk. The volume status column displays the name, size, file system, and status of each volume.

By default, the Top pane contains the Volume List view, and the Bottom pane contains the Graphical View. You can change the views to suit your purposes by clicking the View menu, selecting either Top or Bottom, and then selecting the desired view. You can hide the Bottom view by clicking the Hidden menu option.

Designing a File Sharing Strategy

Once you have configured disk drives and installed a Windows Server 2008 file server, you will need to decide how users should store their files on that server and who should be permitted to access them. This process includes designing a strategy for offering file shares on one or more servers on your network, securing those shares against unwanted access, and determining how your user base will access the information in question.

Why should the administrators of an enterprise network want users to store their files on shared server drives, rather than their local workstation drives? The answers to this question typically include the following:

- To enable users to collaborate on projects by sharing access to files
- To back up document files more easily
- To protect company information by controlling access to documents
- To reduce the number of shares needed on the network
- To prevent having to share access to workstations
- To monitor users' storage habits and regulate their disk space consumption
- To insulate users from the sharing and permission assignment processes

If it was not for these problems, file sharing would simply be a matter of creating a share on each user's workstation and granting everyone full access to it. Because of these problems, however, this practice would lead to chaos, in the form of lost files, corrupted workstations, and endless help calls from confused users.

The idea of creating server-based file shares is to provide users with a simplified data storage solution that they can use to store their files, share files with other users, and easily locate the files shared by their colleagues. Behind the scenes, and unbeknown to the users, administrators can use server-based storage tools to protect everyone's files, regulate access to sensitive data, and prevent users from abusing their storage privileges.

ARRANGING SHARES

The first step in designing a file sharing strategy begins before you even install the server operating system, by projecting your anticipated storage needs and procuring the correct server hardware and disk arrays to meet your needs. Once you are ready to begin configuring file sharing, you will then decide how many shares to create and where to create them. Simply installing a big hard drive in a server and giving everyone access to it would be as chaotic as sharing everyone's workstation drives. Depending on the size of your organization, you might have one single file server, or many servers scattered around the network.

For many large organizations, departmental or workgroup file servers are a viable solution. Each user has his or her "local" server, the directory layout of which becomes familiar to them. If you have separate file servers for the various departments or workgroups in your organization, it is a good idea to develop a consistent directory structure and duplicate it on all of the servers, so that if users have to access a server in another department, they can find their way around.

Generally speaking, a well-designed sharing strategy provides each user with three resources:

- A private storage space, such as a home folder, to which the user has exclusive access
- A public storage space, where each user can store files that they want colleagues to be able to access
- Access to a shared work space for communal and collaborative documents

CONTROLLING ACCESS

On most enterprise networks, the principle of "least privilege" should apply. This principle states that users should have only the privileges they need to perform their required tasks, and no more. A user's private storage space should be exactly that, private and inaccessible, if not invisible, to other users. This is a place in which each user can store his or her private files, without exposing them to other users. Each user should therefore have full privileges to his or her private storage, with the ability to create, delete, read, write, and modify files. Other users should have no privileges to that space at all.

 The easiest way to create private folders with the appropriate permissions for each user is to create a home folder through each Active Directory user object.

In the shared work space for collaborative documents, users should have privileges based on their individual needs. Some users might need only read access to certain files, while others might have to modify them as well. Even more restricted should be the ability to create and delete files, which you should limit to managers or supervisors.

Administrators, of course, must have the privileges required to exercise full control over all users' private and public storage spaces, as well as the ability to modify permissions as needed.

To assign these privileges on a Windows Server 2008 file server, the most common practice is to use NTFS permissions. There is no compelling reason to use the FAT (File Allocation Table) file system in Windows Server 2008. NTFS not only provides the most granular user access control, it also provides other advanced storage features, including file encryption and compression.

To simplify the administration process, you should always assign permissions to security groups, and not to individual users. Assigning permissions to groups enables you to add new users or move them to other job assignments without modifying the permissions themselves. On a large Active Directory network, you might also consider the standard practice of assigning the NTFS permissions to a domain local group, placing the user objects to receive the permissions in a global (or universal) group, and making the global group a member of a domain local group.

Except in special cases, it is usually not necessary to explicitly deny NTFS permissions to users or groups. Some administrators prefer to use this capability, however. When various administrators use different permission assignment techniques on the same network, it can become extremely difficult to track down the sources of certain effective permissions. Another way to simplify the administration process on an enterprise network is to establish specific permission assignment policies, so that everyone performs tasks the same way.

X REF For more information on NTFS permission assignments, see "Assigning Permissions," later in this lesson.

Creating Shares

Sharing folders makes them accessible to network users. Once you have configured the disks on a file server, you must create shares for network users to be able to access those disks. As noted in the planning discussions earlier in this lesson, you should have a sharing strategy in place by the time you are ready to actually create your shares.

Regardless of the size of your network, your strategy for creating shared folders should consist of the following information:

- What folders you will share
- What names you will assign to the shares
- What permissions you will grant users to the shares
- What Offline Files settings you will use for the shares

You can share a folder on a Windows Server 2008 computer by right-clicking the folder in any Windows Explorer window, selecting Share from the context menu, and following the instructions in the File Sharing dialog box, as shown in Figure 6-2.

Figure 6-2

The File Sharing dialog box

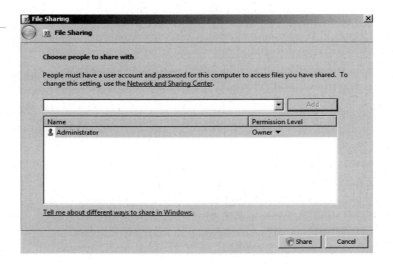

This method of creating shares provides a simplified interface that contains only limited control over elements such as share permissions. To create multiple shares, and exercise more granular control over their properties, you can use the Shared Folders snap-in, as shown in the following procedure.

 TAKE NOTE For the users on the network to be able to see the shares you create on the file server, you must make sure that the Network Discovery and File Sharing settings are turned on in the Network and Sharing Center control panel on the server.

➔ SHARE A FOLDER

GET READY. Log on to Windows Server 2008 using an account with administrative privileges. When the logon process is completed, close the Initial Configuration Tasks window and any other windows that appear.

1. Click **Start→Administrative Tools→Computer Management**. The Computer Management console appears.

 **ANOTHER WAY** If you have installed the File Services role on the Windows Server 2008 computer, you can also use the Sharing and Storage Management console to create and manage shares.

2. In the scope (left) pane, expand the Shared Folders snap-in and select **Shares**. All of the folder shares on the computer appear in the detail (center) pane, as shown in Figure 6-3.

Figure 6-3

The Shared Folders snap-in

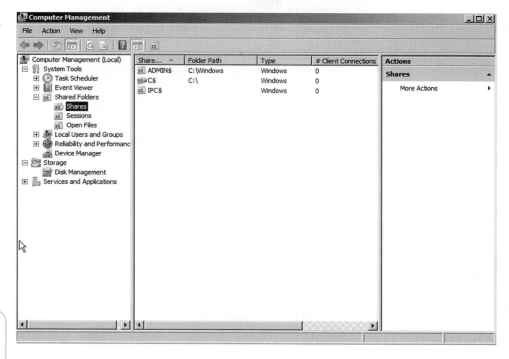

+ MORE INFORMATION

Every disk in the computer has a root share, for administrative purposes. These shares, along with the default ADMIN and IPC shares, appear with a dollar sign ("$") following the name, which causes them to be hidden from users browsing the network. You can create your own hidden shares by appending a dollar sign to the end of any share name.

3. Right-click the **Shares** folder and, from the context menu, select **New Share**. The Create a Shared Folder Wizard appears.

4. Click **Next** to bypass the Welcome page. The Folder Path page appears.

5. In the Folder Path text box, key the name of or browse to the folder you want to share. Then click **Next**. The Name, Description, and Settings page appears.

6. In the Share Name text box, specify how you want the folder to appear to network users. By default, the Share Name value is the same as the folder name. In the Description text box, key any additional information about the share you want to display to network users.

7. Click the **Change** button. The Offline Settings dialog box appears, as shown in Figure 6-4.

Figure 6-4

The offline Settings dialog box

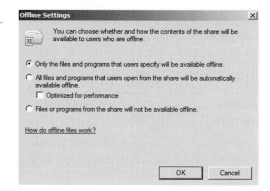

8. Select one of the three options to specify whether network users are permitted to save offline copies of the files in the shared folder. Then click **OK** to close the dialog box.

9. Back on the Name, Description, and Settings page, click **Next**. The Shared Folder Permissions page appears, as shown in Figure 6-5.

Figure 6-5

The Shared Folder Permissions page

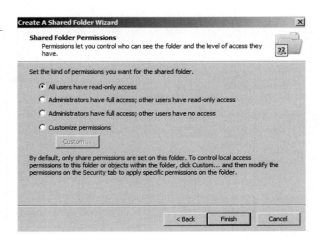

For more information on configuring share permissions, see "Assigning Permissions," later in this lesson.

10. Select one of the first three options to choose a pre-configured share permission configuration or select the **Customize Permissions** option and click **Custom** to open the Customize Permissions dialog box.
11. Assign permissions to the share as needed and click **OK** to close the Customize Permissions dialog box.
12. Back in the Shared Folder Permissions page, click **Next**. The Sharing was Successful page appears.
13. If you plan to create more shares, select the *When I click Finish, run the wizard again to share another folder* checkbox and click **Finish**.

STOP. The new share appears in the details pane of the console.

Assigning Permissions

Earlier in this lesson, you learned about controlling access to a file server, to provide network users with the access they need, while protecting other files against possible intrusion and damage, whether deliberate or not. To implement this access control, Windows Server 2008 uses permissions.

Permissions are privileges granted to specific system entities, such as users, groups, or computers, enabling them to perform a task or access a resource. For example, you can grant a specific user permission to read a file, while denying that same user the permissions needed to modify or delete the file.

Windows Server 2008 has several sets of permissions, which operate independently of each other. As a server administrator, you should be familiar with the operation of the following four permission systems:

- Share permissions—Control access to folders over a network. To access a file over a network, a user must have appropriate share permissions (and appropriate NTFS permissions, if the shared folder is on an NTFS volume).
- NTFS permissions—Control access to the files and folders stored on disk volumes formatted with the NTFS file system. To access a file, whether on the local system or over a network, a user must have the appropriate NTFS permissions.

- Registry permissions—Control access to specific parts of the Windows registry. An application that modifies registry settings or a user attempting to manually modify the registry must have the appropriate registry permissions.
- Active Directory permissions—Control access to specific parts of an Active Directory hierarchy. Although file servers typically do not also function as Active Directory domain controllers, server administrators might utilize these permissions when servicing computers that are members of a domain.

All of these permission systems operate independently of one another, and sometimes combine to provide increased protection to a specific resource. For example, an administrator might grant Ralph the NTFS permissions needed to access a spreadsheet stored on a file server volume. If Ralph sits down at the file server console and logs on as himself, he will be able to access that spreadsheet. However, if Ralph is working at his own computer, he will not be able to access the spreadsheet until the administrator creates a share containing the file and grants Ralph the proper share permissions as well.

While all of these permissions systems are operating all the time, server administrators do not necessarily have to work with them all on a regular basis. In fact, many administrators might not ever have to manually alter a Registry or Active Directory permission. However, many server administrators do have to work with NTFS and share permissions on a daily basis.

For network users to be able to access a shared folder on an NTFS drive, you must grant them both share permissions and NTFS permissions. As you saw earlier, you can grant share permissions as part of the share creation process, but you can also modify the permissions at any time afterwards.

Setting Share Permissions

In Windows Server 2008, shared folders have their own set of permissions that is completely independent from the other Windows permission systems. For network users to access shares on a file server, you must grant them the appropriate share permissions.

By default, the Everyone special identity receives the Allow Read share permission to any new shared folders you create. To set additional share permissions, use the following procedure.

 SET SHARE PERMISSIONS

GET READY. Log on to Windows Server 2008 using an account with domain administrative privileges. When the logon process is completed, close the Initial Configuration Tasks window and any other windows that appear. Make sure that Network Discovery and File Sharing are turned on in the Network and Sharing Center control panel.

1. Click **Start→Administrative Tools→Computer Management**. The Computer Management console appears.
2. In the scope (left) pane, expand the Shared Folders snap-in and select **Shares**. All of the folder shares on the computer appear in the detail (center) pane.

If you have installed the File Services role on the Windows Server 2008 computer, you can also use the Sharing and Storage Management console to create and manage shares.

3. Right-click the share whose permissions you want to modify and, from the context menu, select **Properties**. The Properties sheet for the share appears, as shown in Figure 6-6.

Figure 6-6

A shared folder's Properties sheet

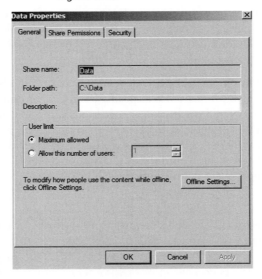

4. Click the **Share Permissions** tab. As with all of the Windows permission systems, the top half of the sheet lists the security principals that have been granted permissions, and the bottom half displays the permissions granted to the selected principal.

5. Click **Add**. The Select Users, Computers, or Groups dialog box appears.

6. In the *Enter the object names to select* text box, key the name of the user or group you want to add and click **OK**. (If you have not created your own user or group objects, enter the name of a built-in group such as Administrators.) The user or group is added to the Group or user names list.

7. In the Permissions list for the added user or group, select or clear the checkboxes to Allow or Deny any of the permissions shown in Table 6-3.

Table 6-3

Share Permissions and Their Functions

SHARE PERMISSION	ALLOWS OR DENIES SECURITY PRINCIPALS THE ABILITY TO:
Full Control	• Change file permissions • Take ownership of files • Perform all tasks allowed by the Change permission.
Change	• Create folders • Add files to folders • Change data in files • Append data to files • Change file attributes • Delete folders and files • Perform all actions permitted by the Read permission
Read	• Display folder names, file names, file data, and attributes • Execute program files • Access other folders within the shared folder

8. Click **OK** to close the Properties sheet.

STOP. You can log off of the Windows Server 2008 computer, or remain logged on for subsequent exercises.

As discussed later in this lesson, many file server administrators simply assign the Allow Full Control share permission to the Everyone special identity, essentially bypassing the share permission system, and rely solely on NTFS permissions for granular file system protection.

When assigning share permissions, be aware that they do not combine in the same way that NTFS permissions do. Consider an example of a hypothetical user named Alice: If you grant Alice the Allow Read and Allow Change permissions to the shared C:\Documents\Alice folder, and at a later time deny her all three permissions to the shared C:\Documents folder, the Deny permissions prevent her from accessing any files through the C:\Documents share, including those in the C:\Documents\Alice folder. However, she can still access her files through the C:\Documents\Alice share because of the Allow permissions. In other words, the C:\Documents\Alice share does not inherit the Deny permissions from the C:\Documents share.

Installing the File Services Role

↓ **THE BOTTOM LINE**

A default Windows Server 2008 installation includes all of the components needed for a basic file server deployment. You can manage the server's disk drives, share folders, map drives, and control access to those shares with no additional software installations. However, enterprise networks often have requirements that go beyond the basics and, to address those needs, Windows Server 2008 includes the File Services role, which implements the Distributed File System (DFS), a service that allows you to simplify the view of file shares located across multiple servers as they appear to your user base, as well as other useful technologies for implementing file sharing on a Windows Server 2008 network.

Selecting Role Services

When you install the File Services role using Server Manager, the Add Roles Wizard displays several pages that are specific to the File Services components. On the Select Role Services page, you choose the File Services components you want to install.

The role services for the File Services role are listed in Table 6-4, along with the names of the pages they add to the Add Roles Wizard and the system services they install on the computer.

Table 6-4

Role Service Selections for the File Services Role

ROLE SERVICE	WIZARD PAGES ADDED	SYSTEM SERVICES INSTALLED	DESCRIPTION
File Server	[None]	• Server (LanmanServer)	• Installs the Share and Storage Management console for Microsoft Management Console (MMC). • The only role service required to add the File Services role.
Distributed File System: DFS Namespaces	• DFS Namespaces • Namespace Type • Credentials	• DFS Namespace (DFS)	• Enables you to create virtual namespaces that consist of actual directories located on servers all over the network. • By default, the DFS Namespace system service is in the Stopped state after installation, with the Startup Type set to Auto.

(continued)

Table 6-4 *(continued)*

Role Service	Wizard Pages Added	System Services Installed	Description
Distributed File System: DFS Replication	[None]	• DFS Replication (DFSR)	• Implements a multimaster replication engine that can keep copies of files at remote locations updated on a regular basis.
File Server Resource Manager	• Storage Monitoring	• File Server Resource Manager (SRMSVC) • File Server Storage Reports Manager (SRMReports)	• Installs an MMC console that provides centralized management of quotas, file screening policies, and storage reports. • By default, the File Server Storage Reports Manager system service is in the Stopped state after installation, with the Startup Type set to Manual.
Services for Network File System	[None]	• Server for NFS (NFSSvc)	• Enables UNIX clients to access files on the server using NFS.
Windows Search Service	• Volumes to Index	• Windows Search (wsearch)	• Creates an index of the files on selected volumes, enabling qualified clients to perform rapid file searches.
Windows Server 2003 File Services: File Replication Service	[None]	• File Replication (NTFRS)	• Provides backwards compatibility enabling Windows Server 2008 computers to synchronize folders with Windows Server 2003 computers running the File Replication Service instead of DFS Replication.
Windows Server 2003 File Services: Indexing Service	[None]	• Indexing Service (cisvc)	• Provides backwards compatibility with the Windows Server 2003 Indexing Service, which catalogs files and their properties on computers throughout the network. • You cannot install the Windows Server 2003 Indexing Service on the same computer as the Windows Search Service.

The ***Server service***, which enables the computer to share files with network users, is installed on all Windows Server 2008 computers by default. This is why the wizard always selects the File Server role service by default when you install the File Services role. It is possible to remove the File Server role service, but doing so would prevent the computer from sharing its folders.

■ Using the Distributed File System

THE BOTTOM LINE

The larger the enterprise, the more file servers the network users are likely to need. There are a number of reasons why network administrators might prefer to install multiple, smaller servers, rather than one large server, including the desire to improve network performance and reduce internetwork bandwidth by keeping traffic local, a need to provide users at remote sites with local access to their files, the administrative convenience of giving individual departments or workgroups control over their own servers, and the ability to provide fault tolerance by using redundant servers.

Generally speaking, deploying multiple servers provides a number of benefits, but when discussing file servers in particular, large enterprise network deployments present administrators with several problems that smaller deployments do not.

First, using a large number of file servers often makes it difficult for users to locate their files. When administrators distribute shared folders among many servers, network users might be forced to browse through multiple domains, servers, and shares to find the files they need. For experienced users that understand something of how a network operates, this can be an exasperating inconvenience. For inexperienced users who are unfamiliar with basic networking principles, it can be an exercise in mystified frustration.

A second common problem for enterprise networks that have networks at multiple sites is providing users with access to their files, while minimizing the traffic passing over expensive wide area network (WAN) connections. One option for administrators is to store files at a central location and let the remote users access them over the WAN. However, this solution allows WAN traffic levels to increase without check, and if a WAN connection should fail, the remote users are cut off from their files. The other alternative is to maintain local copies of all of the files needed at each location. This provides users at every site with local access to their data, minimizes WAN traffic, and enables the network to tolerate a WAN link failure with a minimal loss of productivity. However, to make this solution feasible, it is necessary to synchronize the copies of the files at the different locations, so that changes made at one site are propagated to all of the others.

+ MORE INFORMATION

While the local area networks (LANs) installed within a company site are wholly owned by the company, the WAN links that connect remote sites together nearly always involve a third-party provider, such as a telephone company. The cost of a WAN connection is usually based on the amount of bandwidth needed between the sites, so it is in the company's best interest to minimize the amount of traffic passing over the WAN links as much as possible.

An additional problem for enterprise administrators is implementing a backup solution for small branch offices that do not have their own IT staffs. Even if the organization is willing to install a complete backup hardware and software solution at each site, the tasks of changing the media, running the backup jobs, monitoring their progress, and performing any restores that are needed would be left to untrained personnel. The alternative, backing up over the WAN connection to a centrally-located backup server, is likely to be slow, costly, and bandwidth-intensive.

The ***Distributed File System (DFS)*** implemented in the Windows Server 2008 File Services role includes two technologies: DFS Namespaces and DFS Replication, which address these problems and enable administrators to do the following:

- Simplify the process of locating files
- Control the amount of traffic passing over WAN links
- Provide users at remote sites with local file server access
- Configure the network to survive a WAN link failure
- Facilitate consistent backups

The architecture of the DFS technologies is discussed in the following section.

Introducing DFS

Each of the two role services that make up the Distributed File System role provides a service that can work together with the other to provide a DFS solution that is scalable to almost any size network. The DFS Namespaces role service provides a basic virtual directory functionality, and the DFS Replication role service enables administrators to deploy that virtual directory on multiple servers, all over the enterprise.

At its simplest, DFS is a virtual *namespace* technology that enables you to create a single directory tree that contains references to shared folders located on various file servers, all over the network. This directory tree is virtual; it does not exist as a true copy of the folders on different servers. It is instead a collection of references to the original folders, which users can browse as though it was an actual server share. The actual shared folders are referred to as the *targets* of the virtual folders in the namespace.

For example, Figure 6-7 shows three file servers, each with its own shared folders. Normally, a user looking for a particular file would have to search the folders on each server individually.

Figure 6-7

File server shares without DFS

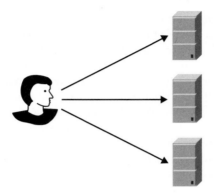

By creating a DFS namespace that contains a virtual representation of the shared folders on all three servers, as shown in Figure 6-8, the user can search through a single directory structure. When the user attempts to open a file in the DFS namespace, the *namespace server,* that is, the server responsible for maintaining the list of DFS shared folders and responding to user requests for those folders, forwards the access request to the file server where the file is actually stored, which then supplies it to the user.

Figure 6-8

User access requests are forwarded by the DFS server

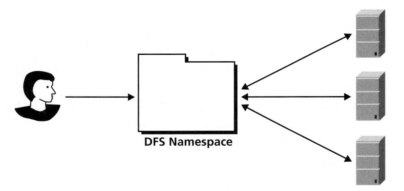

DFS Namespace

Creating a DFS namespace enables users to locate their files more easily, regardless of where they are actually located. You can create multiple namespaces on a single server, and also create additional namespace servers for a single namespace.

Replicating Shares

Creating a DFS namespace does not, by itself, affect the actual locations of the files and folders listed in the namespace, nor does it do anything to improve file services to remote sites. It is the DFS Replication role service that performs these tasks. DFS Replication is a multiple master replication engine that can create and maintain copies of shared folders on different servers throughout an enterprise network.

➕ **MORE INFORMATION**

The alternative to multiple master replication is ***single master replication***, a much simpler concept in which changes that users make to one copy of a file are propagated, in one direction only, to the other copies.

Multiple master replication is a technique in which duplicate copies of a file are all updated on a regular basis, no matter which copy changes. For example, if a file is duplicated on four different servers, a user can access any one of the four copies and modify the file as needed. The replication engine then takes the changes made to the modified copy and uses them to update the other three copies.

At its simplest, DFS Replication is simply a service that copies files from one location to another. However, DFS Replication also works in tandem with DFS Namespaces to provide unified services, such as the following:

- Data distribution—By replicating shared folders to multiple locations, DFS enables users to access the files they need from a local server, minimizing internetwork traffic and its accompanying delays due to network latency. In addition, by integrating the replicated copies into a DFS namespace, users all over the enterprise can browse the same directory tree. When a user attempts to access a file, the namespace server directs the request to the nearest replica.

- Load balancing—A DFS namespace by itself can simplify the process by which users locate the files they need, but if many people all over the network need access to the same file, all of the requests are still directed to the same file server, which can cause a performance bottleneck in the computer itself or on the subnet where the file server is located. By replicating shared folders to multiple servers, DFS can distribute the access requests among them, thus preventing any one server from shouldering the entire traffic load.

- Data collection—Instead of installing backup solutions at remote sites or performing backups over a WAN connection, DFS enables administrators to replicate data from remote file servers to a central location, where the backups can take place. Windows Server 2008 DFS includes a protocol called ***Remote Differential Compression (RDC)***, which conserves network bandwidth by detecting changes in files and transmitting only the modified data to the destination. This conserves bandwidth and also greatly reduces the time needed for the replication process.

Configuring DFS

Implementing DFS on a Windows Server 2008 computer requires more than simply installing the File Services role and the Distributed File System role services. Once the role and role services are in place, you have to perform at least some of the following configuration tasks: creating a namespace, adding folders to a namespace, configuring a DFS referral order, and creating a DFS replication group.

To create a DFS namespace, you must have a Windows Server 2008 or Windows Server 2003 computer with the Distributed File System role and the DFS Namespace role service installed. Once you have created a namespace, this computer will be known as the namespace server, and will be responsible for maintaining the list of shared folders represented in the virtual directory tree and responding to network user requests for access to those shared folders.

TAKE NOTE ✱

All versions of the Windows Server 2008 and Windows Server 2003 operating systems can function as DFS namespace servers. However, the Standard Edition and Web Edition products can host only a single DFS namespace, while the Enterprise Edition and Datacenter Edition versions can host multiple namespaces.

In essence, the namespace server functions just like a file server, except that when a user requests access to a file in the DFS directory tree, the namespace server replies, not with the file itself, but with a ***referral*** specifying the file's actual location. The DFS client on the user's computer then sends its access request to the file server listed in the referral, and receives the file in return.

TAKE NOTE ✱

To raise the domain functional level of a domain, you use the Active Directory Domains and Trusts console.

Although the DFS namespace does not include the actual data files of the shared folders that populate it, it does require some storage space of its own, to maintain the directory structure that forms the virtual directory tree. The namespace server must have an NTFS volume to create the shared folder that will host the namespace.

The DFS Namespaces role service supports two basic types of namespaces: stand-alone and domain-based, and domain-based namespaces come in two modes: Windows Server 2008 mode and Windows 2000 mode, which are based on the domain functional level of the domain hosting the namespace.

The differences between these three namespace configurations are summarized in Table 6-5.

Table 6-5

Comparison of Stand-alone and Domain-based DFS Namespaces

Stand-alone Namespace	Domain-based Namespace (Windows Server 2008
Path to namespace is \\server\root	Path to namespace is \\domain\root
Server name is exposed	Server name is hidden
Namespace can contain up to 50,000 folders	Namespace can contain up to 50,000 folders
Can be a domain controller, a member server in a domain, or a standalone server	Must be a domain controller or member server in the domain hosting the namespace
Namespace stored in system registry and memory cache	Namespace stored in Active Directory and memory cache on each namespace server
Supports the use of only one namespace server for a single namespace (except for clustered servers)	Supports the use of multiple namespace servers (in the same domain) for a single namespace
No Active Directory domain services required	Requires Active Directory using the Windows Server 2008 domain functional level
Supports DFS Replication of folders when namespace server is joined to an Active Directory domain	Supports DFS Replication of folders
Can be part of a server cluster	The namespace cannot be a clustered resource, although the namespace server can be part of a cluster

TAKE NOTE ✱

In Windows 2000 mode, a DFS domain-based namespace can contain a maximum of 50,000 folders.

In terms of which namespace type you should use for your network, consider the following factors:

- If you are deploying DFS on an Active Directory network, you should select the domain-based namespace, unless some of the computers that will be namespace servers are running Windows Server 2003 or earlier, and you intend to add more than 5,000 folders to the namespace.

- If all of the computers that will be namespace servers are running Windows Server 2008, a domain-based namespace in Windows Server 2008 mode will provide the most fault tolerance and scalability.

- If you are deploying DFS on a network that does not use Active Directory, your only choice is to create a stand-alone namespace. In this case, you are limited to one namespace server and no DFS replication.

To create a new namespace, use the following procedure.

 CREATE A NAMESPACE

GET READY. Log on to Windows Server 2008 using an account with administrative privileges. When the logon process is completed, close the Initial Configuration Tasks window if it appears. In this exercise we will install the File Services role with the DFS Namespaces role service, after which we will create a DFS Namespace.

Install the File Services Role

1. If the Server Manager console does not appear automatically, click **Start**, and then click **Server Manager.** In the left-hand pane, browse to **Roles.** In the right-hand pane, click **Add roles.**

2. Click **Next** to bypass the initial Welcome screen. The Select Services screen appears. Place a checkmark next to **File Services**, and click **Next** twice to continue.

3. The Select Role Services screen appears. Place a checkmark next to **Distributed File System.** Ensure that both the **DFS Namespaces** and **DFS Replication** **sub-sections** are selected, and click **Next.**

> **TAKE NOTE** * The DFS Management snap-in can run only on Windows Server 2008, Windows Server 2003 R2, and Windows XP SP2 computers.

4. The Create a DFS Namespace screen appears as shown in Figure 6-9. Ensure that the *Create a namespace now, using this wizard* radio button is selected.

Figure 6-9

Creating a DFS Namespace

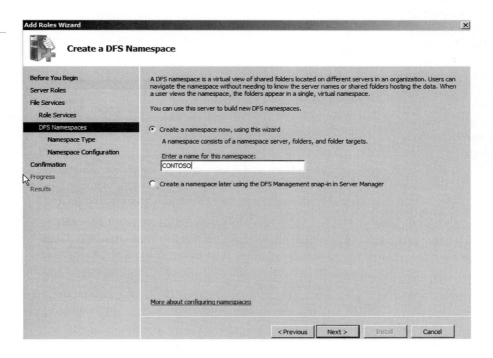

5. In the *Enter a name for this namespace* text box, key the name that will become the root of the namespace, such as *CONTOSO*. Click **Next.**

6. The root of the namespace is an actual share that the wizard will create on the namespace server, containing the referrals that point to the shared folders that populate the namespace. Users on the network will access the DFS namespace by browsing to this share or using its name in the form *\\server\root* or *\\domain\root*.

7. Click **Next**. The Select Namespace Type page appears, as shown in Figure 6-10.

Figure 6-10

The Select Namespace Type page

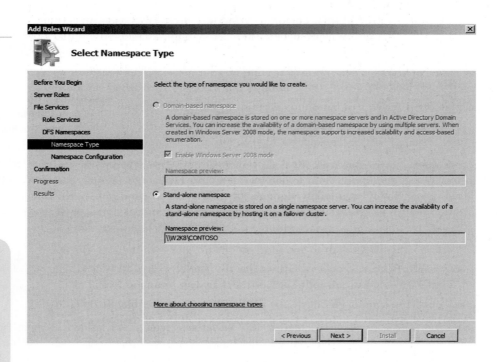

X REF

Windows Server 2008 mode in DFS also requires that the Active Directory domain be configured at the Windows Server 2008 domain functional level. More information about Active Directory and domain functional levels can be found in the Wiley MOAC series textbook *Planning, Implementing, and Maintaining Windows Server Active Directory Infrastructure*.

Since this server is configured in a workgroup, the only option available is to create a stand-alone namespace. In this example, clients will access this namespace using a syntax of *\\W2K8\contoso*. In an Active Directory environment, if you elect to create a domain-based namespace you will use the Enable Windows Server 2008 Mode checkbox to specify whether to create the namespace in Windows Server 2008 mode or Windows 2000 mode. Windows Server 2008 mode provides additional scalability and functionality for domain-based namespaces, but requires that all servers hosting the namespace as well as the Active Directory domain controllers be running Windows Server 2008.

8. Click **Next**. The Configure Namespace screen appears. From this screen you can add folders and folder targets during the process of creating the DFS namespace, or else add these after the namespace has been created. Click **Next** to continue without adding any DFS folders and folder targets.

9. The Confirm Installation Settings screen appears. Take note of any warnings and informational messages that appear, and then click **Install**.

After the process is completed, the Confirmation page appears, indicating that the wizard successfully created the namespace, and the namespace appears in the console's scope pane. Click **Close**.

STOP. You can log off of the Windows Server 2008 computer, or else remain logged on for subsequent exercises.

At any time after you create a domain-based namespace, you can add additional namespace servers, for load balancing or fault tolerance purposes, by right-clicking the namespace and, from the context menu, selecting Add Namespace Server. Every namespace server must have the DFS Namespaces role service installed and also must have an NTFS volume to store the namespace share.

TAKE NOTE*

Adding namespace servers to an existing namespace only replicates the virtual directory structure, not the target folders and files that the virtual folders refer to. To replicate the target folders, you must use DFS Replication, as discussed later in this lesson.

Once you have created a namespace, you can begin to build its virtual directory structure by adding folders. You can add two types of folders to a namespace, those with targets and those without. A folder with a target is one that points to one or more shared folders on the same or another server. Users browsing the namespace will see the folder you add, plus all of the subfolders and files that exist in the target folder beneath it. You can also create folders in the namespace that do not have targets, purely for organizational purposes.

You can add as many targets to a folder as you need. Typically, administrators add multiple targets to namespace folders to balance the server load and give users at different locations local access to the data. Adding multiple targets means that you will have identical copies of the target located on different servers. These duplicate targets must remain identical, so you will later configure DFS Replication to keep them updated.

To add folders to a DFS namespace, use the following procedure.

 ADD FOLDERS

GET READY. Log on to Windows Server 2008 using an account with administrative privileges. When the logon process is completed, close the Initial Configuration Tasks window and any other windows that appear.

1. Click **Start**, and then click **Administrative Tools→DFS Management**. The DFS Management console appears.

2. Right-click a namespace in the scope pane and, from the context menu, select **New Folder**. The New Folder dialog box appears.

3. In the Name text box, key the name of the folder such as *DATA*, as you want it to appear in the DFS virtual directory tree.

4. **Click Add**. The Add Folder Target dialog box appears.

5. Click **Browse**. The Browse For Shared Folders dialog box appears.

6. If you have not yet configured any shared folders on this server, select a server and click **New Shared Folder** to display the Create Share dialog box, which you can use to create a new shared folder and set its share permissions. Then click **OK** to close the Create Share dialog box. Then click **OK** to close the Browse for **Shared** Folders dialog box.

7. Click **OK** to close the Add Folder Target dialog box.

8. Repeat steps 2 through 7 to add additional targets to the folder. When you add multiple targets to a folder, the console prompts you to create a replication group, to keep the targets synchronized. Click **No**, as the process of configuring replication is covered later in this lesson.

9. Click **OK** to close the New Folder dialog box. The folder is added to the virtual directory tree in the scope pane.

STOP. You can log out of the Windows Server 2008 computer, or else remain logged on for subsequent exercises.

> **TAKE NOTE***
>
> When referring to folder targets, the term "server" refers to any Windows computer with one or more shared folders on it. Targets for a DFS namespace do not have to be running a Server version of Windows.

You can continue to populate the namespace by adding more folders to the virtual directory structure or by adding more targets to existing folders. When you select an untargeted folder in the scope pane, you can select New Folder from the context menu to create another folder (targeted or untargeted) subordinate to it. However, you can't add a subfolder to a targeted folder in this way. To do that, you must create the subfolder in the target share, and it will appear in the namespace.

Next we will discuss configuring the DFS referral order. When you add more than one target to a folder in a DFS namespace, the namespace server sends referrals containing all of the targets to clients attempting to access that folder. The client tries to connect to the first target in any referral it receives and, if the first target is unavailable, tries to access the second, and then the third, and so forth. As a result, the order of the targets in the referrals is critical, if the DFS implementation is to successfully provide users with local file access and control WAN traffic levels.

By default, when a DFS client attempts to access a folder with targets, the namespace server notes the site where the client is located and, in its referral, lists the targets at the same site first, in random order, followed by the targets at other sites, in order from the lowest to the highest cost. You can modify this default behavior in a variety of ways, by manipulating the referral controls found in the Properties sheet for every namespace, targeted folder, and target.

In a namespace's Properties sheet, on the Referral tab, you can change the Ordering Method value, which alters the way in which the server specifies the targets at different sites from the client, using the following values:

- Lowest cost
- Random order
- Exclude targets outside of the client's site

The fact that the targets in the same site as the client are supplied in random order by default effectively balances the client load among the servers at that site. Selecting the Random Order option for the Ordering Method value does the same load balancing for the targets at other sites. Selecting the *Exclude targets outside of the client's site* option prevents the clients from accessing targets at other sites, thus conserving WAN bandwidth. Note, however, that the Ordering Method value does not affect the order of the targets at the same site as the client, which always appear first in the referrals, and in random order.

In a targeted folder's Properties sheet, on the Referral tab, you can configure the name server to restrict its referrals for that folder only to servers at the same site as the client.

In a target's Properties sheet, on the Advanced tab, you can override the referral ordering values for the namespace and the folder containing the target by selecting one of the following options:

- First among all targets
- Last among all targets
- First among targets of equal cost
- Last among targets of equal cost

These individual target settings are most useful when you have copies of a target folder that you only want clients to access as a last resort. For example, you might have a hot standby file server on the network, in case another file server fails. To streamline the failover process, you add the shares on the standby server as targets to the appropriate DFS namespace folders, so that you don't have to take the time to do this if a server failure should occur. You don't want users to access the standby server unless there is a failure, so you configure all of the targets with the Last among all targets option, so that no matter what site clients are in, they will never access the standby shares unless all of the other copies of the shares are offline.

Next we will discuss **client failback**, which is the ability of DFS clients to revert to targets that were previously unavailable, when they become available again and are of lower cost that the target the client is using. For example, if a client cannot access the target at its same site, because the server is offline, it will access the lowest cost target at another site. When Client Failback is enabled, the client will revert to the target at its same site, when it becomes available.

You can enable Client Fallback for an entire namespace by selecting the *Clients fall back to preferred targets* checkbox on the Referrals page of the namespace's Properties sheet. You can also enable Client Fallback for an individual folder by selecting the checkbox of the same name on the Referrals tab of its Properties sheet.

Configuring DFS Replication

When a folder in a DFS namespace has multiple targets, the intention is for the targets to be identical, so that users can access the files from any one of the targets invisibly. However, in most cases, users modify the files in a folder as they work with them, which causes the targets to no longer be identical. To resynchronize the target folders, DFS includes a replication engine that automatically propagates changes from one target to all of the others.

To enable replication for a DFS folder with multiple targets, you must create a ***replication group***, which is a collection of servers, known as ***members***, each of which contains a target for a particular DFS folder. In its simplest form, a folder with two targets requires a replication group with two members: the servers hosting the targets. At regular intervals, the DFS Replication engine on the namespace server triggers replication events between the two members, using the RDC protocol, so that their target folders remain synchronized.

> **TAKE NOTE** ✱
>
> Although terms such as *group* and *member* are typically associated with Active Directory, DFS Replication does not use them to refer to Active Directory objects. In fact, unlike the File Replication Service (FRS) in Windows Server 2003, DFS Replication does not require Active Directory, and can function on stand-alone, as well as domain-based, namespace servers.

> ➕ **MORE INFORMATION**
>
> For each member server, the number of replication groups multiplied by the number of replicated folders multiplied by the number of simultaneous replication connections should not exceed 1,024. If you are having trouble keeping below this limit, the best solution is to schedule replication to occur at different times for different folders, thus limiting the number of simultaneous connections.

DFS Replication need not be so simple, however, as it is also highly scalable and configurable. A replication group can have up to 256 members, with 256 replicated folders, and each server can be a member of up to 256 replication groups, with as many as 256 connections (128 incoming and 128 outgoing). A member server can support up to one terabyte of replicated files, with up to eight million replicated files per volume.

In addition to scaling the replication process, you can also configure it to occur at specific times and limit the amount of bandwidth it can utilize. This enables you to exercise complete control over the WAN bandwidth utilized by the replication process.

The larger the DFS deployment, the more complicated the replication process becomes. By default, replication groups use a ***full mesh topology***, which means that every member in a group replicates with every other member. For relatively small DFS deployments, this is a satisfactory solution, but on larger installations, the full mesh topology can generate a huge amount of network traffic. In cases like this, you might want to opt for a ***hub/spoke topology***, which enables you to limit the replication traffic to specific pairs of members, as shown in Figure 6-11.

Figure 6-11

The full mesh and hub/spoke replication topologies

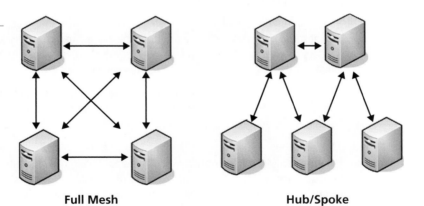

Full Mesh   **Hub/Spoke**

> **TAKE NOTE** ✱
>
> No matter which topology you use, DFS replication between two members is always bidirectional by default. This means that the Replicate Folder Wizard always establishes two connections, one in each direction, between every pair of computers involved in a replication relationship. This is true in a hub/spoke, as well as a full mesh, topology. To create unidirectional replication relationships, you can either disable selected connections between the members of a replication group in the DFS Management console, or use share permissions to prevent the replication process from updating files on certain member servers.

When you initially configure a DFS replication group, you will designate one server as the *primary member* of the replication group. During the replication process, the files from the server that you designate as the primary member will be copied to the other targets in the replication group. If any of the files in one target folder are different from their counterparts in the others, DFS Replication will use the primary member version to overwrite all other versions.

- Replicate continuously using a specified percentage of available bandwidth—this option allows you to specify how much bandwidth can be taken up by DFS replication, to prevent replication from overwhelming a link between multiple sites.

- Replicate only during specified days and times—this option allows you to specify the days of the week and the hours of the day that replication is permitted to occur.

Once you have created a replication group, it appears under the replication node in the scope pane of the DFS Management console.

SUMMARY SKILL MATRIX

IN THIS LESSON YOU LEARNED:

- Planning is a critical part of a file server deployment. Your deployment plan should specify how many file servers you need, what hardware they should have, how you will configure them, how you will share the server data, and how you will protect that data.

- Windows Server 2008 supports two hard disk partition types: MBR and GPT; two disk types: basic and dynamic; five volume types: simple, striped, spanned, mirrored, and RAID-5; and two file systems: NTFS and FAT.

- Creating folder shares makes the data stored on a file server's disks accessible to network users.

- Windows Server 2008 has several sets of permissions, which operate independently of one another, including NTFS permissions, share permissions, registry permissions, and Active Directory permissions.

- NTFS permissions enable you to control access to files and folders by specifying just what tasks individual users can perform on them. Share permissions provide rudimentary access control for all of the files on a network share. Network users must have the proper share and NTFS permissions to access file server shares.

- The File Services role includes several role services that you can choose to install, including Distributed File System and Services for Network File System. Selecting individual role services can add extra configuration pages to the Add Roles Wizard.

- The Distributed File System (DFS) includes two technologies: DFS Namespaces and DFS Replication, which can simplify the process of locating files, control the amount of traffic passing over WAN links, provide users at remote sites with local file server access, configure the network to survive a WAN link failure, and facilitate consistent backups.

- DFS is a virtual namespace technology that enables you to create a single directory tree that contains references to shared folders located on various file servers, all over the network.

- A namespace server functions just like a file server, except that when a user requests access to a file in the DFS directory tree, the namespace server replies, not with the file itself, but with a referral specifying the file's actual location.

- DFS Replication works in tandem with DFS Namespaces to provide unified services, such as data distribution, load balancing, and data collection.

- To enable replication for a DFS folder with multiple targets, you must create a replication group, which is a collection of servers known as members, each of which contains a target for a particular DFS folder.

Knowledge Assessment

Fill in the Blank

Complete the following sentences by writing the correct word or words in the blanks provided.

1. The DFS Replication engine uses a form of replication called _____.

2. In the Distributed File System, the actual shared folders referred to by the virtual folders in the namespace are known as _____.

3. DFS-Replication relies on a protocol called _____ for file replication.

4. A DFS replication topology in which every server replicates with every other server is called a(n) _____ topology.

5. The basic file sharing capabilities of a Windows server are provided by the _____ service.

6. To keep a DFS folder's multiple targets synchronized, you must create a(n) _____.

7. The _____ allows you to simplify the view of file shares located across multiple servers as they appear to your user base.

8. A(n) _____ appears to the operating system as though it is a physically separate disk and can host an operating system

9. A(n) _____ enables you to limit DFS replication traffic to specific pairs of members.

10. A DFS _____ enables you to create a single directory tree that contains references to shared folders located on multiple separate file servers.

Multiple Choice

Select all answers that apply for the following questions.

1. An alternative to the multimaster replication model used in DFS is:
   - **a.** Unilateral replication
   - **b.** Single master replication
   - **c.** Flat namespace replication
   - **d.** Hierarchical namespace replication

2. A server in a replication group is referred to as a:
   - **a.** Namespace
   - **b.** Namespace server
   - **c.** Member
   - **d.** Root target

3. This refers to the ability of DFS clients to revert back to folder targets that have been unavailable due to server or network outages.
   - **a.** Client failback
   - **b.** Server failback
   - **c.** Namespace failback
   - **d.** Target failback

4. A disk partition that can hold data but not an operating system is called a(n):
   - **a.** Primary partition
   - **b.** Boot partition
   - **c.** System partition
   - **d.** Extended partition

5. This DFS component is responsible for maintaining a list of DFS shared folders and responding to user requests for those folders.
   - **a.** Folder target
   - **b.** Member server
   - **c.** Namespace server
   - **d.** Root server

6. A DFS _____ contains a virtual representation of the shared folders on all DFS target servers.
   - **a.** Directory
   - **b.** Namespace
   - **c.** Target
   - **d.** Member

7. The Distributed File System uses the following replication model to keep servers in a replication group up to date:
   - **a.** Multiple Master Replication
   - **b.** Single Master Replication
   - **c.** Root Master Replication
   - **d.** Distributed Master Replication

8. In this topology, every member of a DFS replication group replicates with every other member, for full replication connectivity.
   - **a.** Hub and spoke replication
   - **b.** Complete replication
   - **c.** Direct replication
   - **d.** Full mesh replication

9. The following service is required on a Windows Server 2008 server in order to enable file sharing:
   - **a.** Workstation Service
   - **b.** SMB Service
   - **c.** IIS Service
   - **d.** Server Service

10. To enable replication for a DFS folder with multiple folder targets, you must create the following:
    - **a.** Replication group
    - **b.** Replication target
    - **c.** Replication folders
    - **d.** Replication servers

■ Case Scenarios

Scenario 6-1: Implementing Distributed File Sharing

You are the network administrator for a retail chain with support offices in multiple cities throughout the U.S. Upper management wishes to cut down on support costs in these offices by centralizing file backups of remote servers so that they are all performed from the corporate headquarters. However, remote IT staff is complaining that performing full backups of data over the WAN connections is taking too long, and is interfering with normal production work during the day if the backups do not finish in a timely manner. How can you improve the process of performing centralized backups using the technologies described in this lesson?

Configuring Print Services

OBJECTIVE DOMAIN MATRIX

TECHNOLOGY SKILL	OBJECTIVE DOMAIN	OBJECTIVE DOMAIN NUMBER
Deploying a Print Server	Configure and monitor print services	4.6

KEY TERMS

custom filters
Enhanced Metafile (EMF)
Everyone
Internet Printing Protocol (IPP)
local print device
locally-attached print device

Manage Documents
Manage Printers
network interface print device
network-attached print devices
Print
print device

print server
printer
printer driver
printer pool
XML Paper Specification
   (XPS)

Adventure Works, Inc. is a travel agency specializing in providing outdoor adventure vacations such as hiking and kayaking excursions. As a part of Adventure Works' marketing strategy, the company produces numerous color brochures describing the different vacation packages that they offer. In order to produce high-quality brochures, Adventure Works has invested in extremely expensive color laser printers for each office. Management is concerned that the use of these printers needs to be managed in order to control the cost of consumables, as well as being concerned about the overall management of printers throughout the Adventure Works network. As the network administrator for Adventure Works, you have been tasked with deploying the Print Services role in Microsoft Windows Server 2008 in order to control and manage printers on the Adventure Works network.

This lesson covers the concepts required to deploy the Print Services role on a Windows Server 2008 server. We begin with a discussion of the terminology used to describe local and network printers, including print servers, print queues, and printer pools. We then discuss the specific steps required to install, configure, and secure printers on a server that is running the Print Services role.

■ Deploying a Print Server

THE BOTTOM LINE

As with the file sharing functions discussed in the previous lesson, print device sharing is another one of the most basic applications for which local area networks were designed. Installing, sharing, monitoring, and managing a single network print device is relatively simple, but when you are responsible for dozens or even hundreds of print devices on a large enterprise network, these tasks can be overwhelming.

Printing in Microsoft Windows typically involves the following four components:

- **Print device**—A print device is the actual hardware that produces hard copy documents on paper or other print media. Windows Server 2008 supports both **local print devices**, which are directly attached to computer ports, and **network interface print devices**, which are connected to the network, either directly or through another computer.

- **Printer** —In Windows parlance, a printer is the software interface through which a computer communicates with a print device. Windows Server 2008 supports numerous physical interfaces, including Universal Serial bus (USB), IEEE 1394 (FireWire), parallel (LPT), serial (COM), Infrared Data Access (IrDA), and Bluetooth ports; and network printing services such as lpr, standard TCP/IP ports, and the **Internet Printing Protocol (IPP)**, which allows clients to print via HTTP traffic, either over an intranet or via the World Wide Web.

- **Print server**—A print server is a computer (or standalone device) that receives print jobs from clients and sends them to print devices that are either locally attached or connected to the network.

- **Printer driver**—A printer driver is a device driver that converts the print jobs generated by applications into an appropriate string of commands for a specific print device. Printer drivers are designed for a specific print device and provide applications with access to all of the print device's features.

These four components work together to process the print jobs produced by Windows applications and turn them into hard copy documents, as shown in Figure 7-1.

Figure 7-1

The Windows print architecture

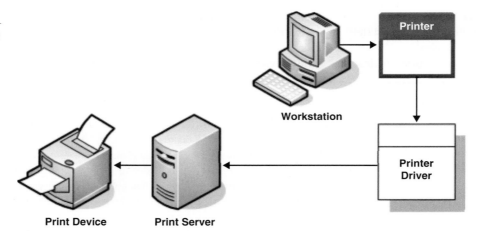

The flexibility of the Windows print architecture is manifested in the different ways that you can deploy the four printing components. A single computer can perform all of the roles (except for the print device, of course), or you can distribute them about the network. The following sections describe four fundamental configurations that are the basis of most Windows printer deployments. You can scale these configurations up to accommodate a network of virtually any size.

The simplest form of print architecture consists of one print device connected to one computer, also known as a **locally-attached print device**, as shown in Figure 7-2. When you connect a print device directly to a Windows Server 2008 computer and print from an application

Figure 7-2

A locally-attached print device

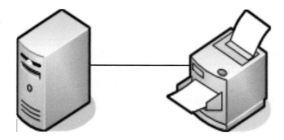

running on that system, the computer supplies the printer, printer driver, and print server functions.

However, in addition to printing from an application running on that computer, you can also share the printer (and the print device) with other users on the same network. In this arrangement, the computer with the locally-attached print device functions as a print server. The other computers on the network are the print clients, as shown in Figure 7-3.

Figure 7-3

Sharing a locally-attached printer

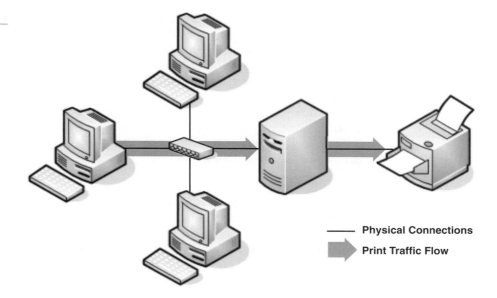

—— **Physical Connections**

→ **Print Traffic Flow**

In the default Windows Server 2008 printer sharing configuration, each client uses its own printer and printer driver. As before, the application, running on the client computer, sends the print job to the printer and the printer driver renders the job, based on the capabilities of the print device. In this arrangement, the printer driver creates a job file using one of two interim formats, as follows:

TAKE NOTE*

The format used depends on whether the client computer is running a newer XPS driver, or an older driver that uses the EMF interim format. In addition to Windows Server 2008 and Vista, XPS is also available for Windows Server 2003 and XP as part of the .NET Framework package.

- ***Enhanced Metafile (EMF)***—A standardized, highly portable print job format that is the default format used by the Windows 2000, Windows XP, and Windows Server 2003 print subsystems. The printer driver converts the application data into an EMF file, and the printer sends it to the print server, which stores it in the spooler. The spooler then uses the printer driver on the print server to render the job into the final PCL format understood by the print device.

- ***XML Paper Specification (XPS)***—A new, platform-independent document format included with Windows Server 2008 and Windows Vista, in which print job files use a single XPS format for their entire journey to the print device, rather than being converted first to EMF and then later to PCL.

The main advantage of this printing arrangement is that multiple users, located anywhere on the network, can send jobs to a single print device, connected to a computer functioning as a print server. The downside is that processing the print jobs for many users can impose a significant burden on the print server. Although any Windows computer can function as a print server, it is recommended that you only use a workstation for this purpose when you have no more than a handful of print clients to support, or a very light printing volume.

When you use a server computer as a print server, you must be conscious of the system resources that the print server role will require. Dedicating a computer solely to print server duties is only necessary when you have a lot of print clients or a high volume of printing to support. In most cases, Windows servers that run the Print Services role perform other functions as well. However, you must be judicious in your role assignments.

For example, it is common practice for a single server to run both the Print Services and File Services roles. The usage patterns for these two roles complement each other, in that they both tend to handle relatively brief transactions from clients. Running the Print Services role on a domain controller is seldom a good idea, however, because network clients are constantly accessing the domain controller; their usage patterns are more conflicting than complementary.

Using Networked Printers

The printing solutions discussed thus far all involve print devices that are connected directly to a computer, using a USB or other port. Print devices do not necessarily have to be attached to computers, however. You can connect a print device directly to the network instead. Many print device models are equipped with network interface adapters, enabling you to attach a standard network cable. Some others have expansion slots, into which you can install a network printing adapter purchased separately. Finally, for print devices with no networking capabilities, there are standalone network print servers available, to which you can attach one or more print devices and connect to the network. Print devices so equipped have their own IP addresses, and typically an embedded Web-based configuration interface, also.

With *network-attached print devices,* the primary deployment decision that the administrator must make is to decide which computer will function as the print server. One simple, but often less than practical, option is to let each print client function as its own print server, as shown in Figure 7-4. Each client processes and spools its own print jobs, connects to the print device using a TCP (Transmission Control Protocol) port, and sends the jobs directly to the device for printing.

Figure 7-4

A network-attached print device with multiple print servers

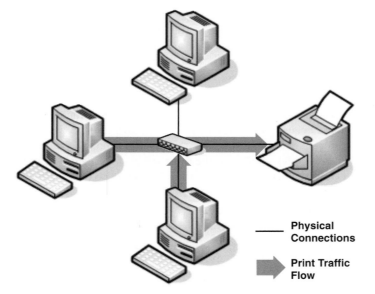

The advantage of this arrangement is that it is simple to set up, even by individual end users with no administrative assistance. However, the disadvantages are many, including the following:

- Users are oblivious of the other users accessing the print device. They have no way of knowing what other jobs have been sent to the print device, or how long it will be until the print device completes their jobs.
- Users examining the print queue see only their own jobs.
- Administrators have no way of centrally managing the print queue, because there are many print queues, one for each client.

- Administrators cannot implement advanced printing features, such as printer pools or remote administration.
- Error messages appear only on the computer that originated the job the print device is currently processing.
- All print job processing is performed by the client computer, rather than being partially offloaded to an external print server.

For these reasons, this arrangement is suitable only for small workgroup networks that do not have dedicated administrators supporting them.

The other, far more popular, option for network-attached printing is to designate one computer as a print server and use it to service all of the print clients on the network. To do this, you install a printer on one computer, the print server, and configure it to access the print device directly, through a TCP port. Then you share the printer, just as you would a locally-attached print device, and configure the clients to access the print share.

As you can see in Figure 7-5, the physical configuration is exactly the same as in the previous arrangement, but the logical path the print jobs take on the way to the print device is different. Instead of going straight to the print device, the jobs go to the print server, which spools them and sends them to the print device in order.

Figure 7-5

A network-attached print device with a single, shared print server

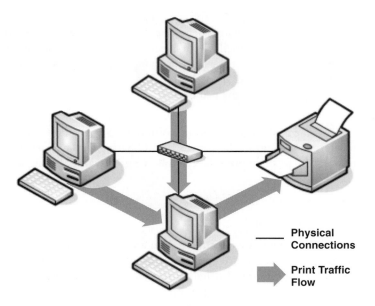

Physical
Connections

Print Traffic
Flow

With this arrangement, virtually all of the disadvantages of the multiple print server arrangement become advantages, as follows:

- All of the client jobs are stored in a single print queue, so that users and administrators can see a complete list of the jobs waiting to be printed.
- Part of the job rendering burden is shifted to the print server, returning control of the client computer to the user more quickly.
- Administrators can manage all of the queued jobs from a remote location.
- Print error messages appear on all client computers.
- Administrators can implement printer pools and other advanced printing features.
- Administrators can manage security, auditing, monitoring, and logging functions from a central location.

The printing configurations that we've just described are the building blocks that administrators can use to create printing solutions for their networks. There are a multitude of possible variations that you can use to create a network printing architecture that supports your organization's needs. Some of the more advanced possibilities are as follows:

- You can connect a single print server to multiple print devices, creating what is called a *printer pool.* On a busy network with many print clients, the print server can distribute large numbers of incoming jobs among several identical print devices to provide more timely service and fault tolerance.
- You can connect multiple print devices that support different forms and paper sizes to a single print server, which will distribute jobs with different requirements to the appropriate print devices.
- You can connect multiple print servers to a single print device. By creating multiple print servers, you can configure different priorities, security settings, auditing, and monitoring parameters for different users. For example, you can create a high-priority print server for company executives, while junior users send their jobs to a lower priority server. This ensures that the executives' jobs get printed first, even if the print servers are both connected to the same print device. Steps needed to modify print server priorities are discussed later in the lesson.

Sharing a Printer

Using Windows Server 2008 as a print server can be a simple or a complex matter, depending on how many clients the server has to support and how much printing they do. For a home or small business network, in which a handful of users need occasional access to the printer, no special preparation is necessary. However, if the computer must support heavy printer use, additional memory, hard drive space, and processing power may be required for the print server.

Before you can share a printer on a Windows Server 2008 computer, you must enable the appropriate settings in the Network and Sharing Center, just as you have to do to share files and folders. To share printers, the following Network Sharing and Discovery settings must be turned on:

- Network Discovery
- Printer Sharing

You can typically share a printer as you are installing it, or at any time afterwards. Older printers require you to initiate the installation process by launching the Add Printer Wizard from the Printers control panel. However, most of the print devices on the market today use either a USB connection to a computer or an Ethernet connection to a network.

In the case of a USB-connected printer, plugging the print device into a USB port on the computer and turning the device on initiates the installation process. Manual intervention is required only when Windows Server 2008 does not have a driver for the print device.

For network-attached print devices, an installation program is typically supplied with the product that locates the print device on the network, installs the correct drivers, creates a printer on the computer, and configures the printer with the proper IP address and other settings.

Once the printer is installed on the Windows Server 2008 computer that will function as your print server, you can share it with your network clients, using the following procedure.

 SHARE A PRINTER

GET READY. Log on to Windows Server 2008 using a domain account with Administrator privileges. When the logon process is completed, close the Initial Configuration Tasks window and any other windows that appear.

1. Click **Start**, and then click **Control Panel→Printers** The Printers window appears.

2. Right-click the icon for the printer you want to share and, from the context menu, select **Sharing**. The printer's Properties sheet appears, with the Sharing tab selected, as shown in Figure 7-6.

Figure 7-6

The Sharing tab of a printer's Properties sheet

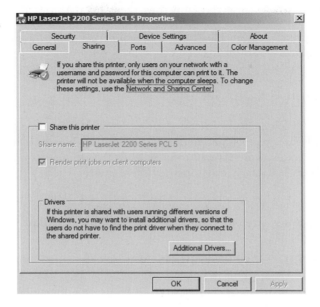

3. Select the **Share this printer** checkbox. The printer name appears in the Share name text box. You can accept the default name or supply one of your own.

4. Select one or both of the following optional checkboxes:

   • **Render print jobs on client computers**—Minimizes the resource utilization on the print server by forcing the print clients to perform the bulk of the print processing.

   • **List in the directory**—Creates a new printer object in the Active Directory database, enabling domain users to locate the printer by searching the directory. This option appears only when the computer is a member of an Active Directory domain, so your screen may differ slightly from Figure 7-6.

5. Click **Additional Drivers**. The Additional Drivers dialog box appears, as shown in Figure 7-7. This dialog box enables you to load printer drivers for the Itanium and $\times$ 64 versions of the operating system. When you install the alternate drivers, the print server supplies them to clients running those operating system versions automatically.

Figure 7-7

The Additional Drivers dialog box

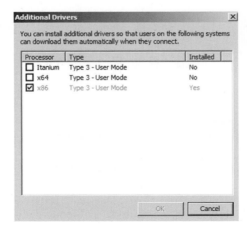

6. Select any combination of the available checkboxes and click **OK**. For each checkbox you selected, Windows Server 2008 displays a Printer Drivers dialog box.

7. In each Printer Drivers dialog box, key or browse to the location of the printer drivers for the selected operating system, and then click **OK**.

8. Click **OK** to close the Additional Drivers dialog box.

9. Click **OK** to close the Properties sheet for the printer.

STOP. The printer icon in the Printers control panel now includes a symbol indicating that it has been shared.

Configuring Printer Security

Just as with folder shares, clients must have the proper permissions to access a shared printer. Printer permissions are much simpler than NTFS permissions; they basically dictate whether users are allowed to merely use the printer, manage documents submitted to the printer, or manage the properties of the printer itself.

To assign permissions for a printer, use the following procedure.

 ASSIGN PRINTER PERMISSIONS

GET READY. Log on to Windows Server 2008 using a domain account with Administrator privileges. When the logon process is completed, close the Initial Configuration Tasks window and any other windows that appear.

1. Click **Start**, and then click **Control Panel.→Printers**. The Printers window appears.

2. Right-click one of the printer icons in the window and, from the context menu, select **Properties**. When the printer's Properties sheet appears, click the **Security** tab, as shown in Figure 7-8. The top half of the display lists all of the security principals currently possessing permissions to the selected printer. The bottom half lists the permissions held by the selected security principal.

Figure 7-8

The Security tab of a printer's Properties sheet

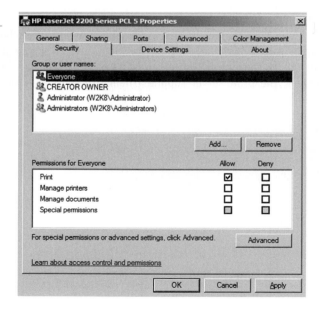

3. Click **Add**. The Select Users, Computers, or Groups dialog box appears, as shown in Figure 7-9.

Figure 7-9

The Select Users, Computers, or Groups dialog box

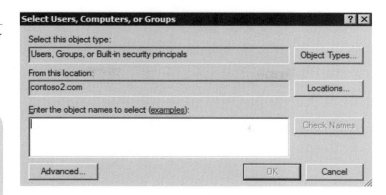

This procedure assumes that the Windows Server 2008 computer is a member of an Active Directory domain. When you assign printer permissions on a stand-alone server, you select local user and group accounts to be the security principals that receive the permissions.

4. In the *Enter the object names to select* text box, key a user or group name, and then click **OK**. (If you have not created any users or groups of your own, select a built-in group such as Administrators.) The user or group appears in the Group or user names list.

5. Select the user or group you added, and select or clear the checkboxes in the bottom half of the display to Allow or Deny the user any of the standard permissions shown in Table 7-1.

Table 7-1

Standard Printer Permissions

PERMISSION	CAPABILITIES	SPECIAL PERMISSIONS	DEFAULT ASSIGNMENTS
Print	• Connect to a printer • Print documents • Pause, resume, restart, and cancel the user's own documents	• Print • Read Permissions	Assigned to the Everyone special identity
Manage Printers	• Cancel all documents • Share a printer • Change printer properties • Delete a printer • Change printer permissions	• Print • Manage Printers • Read Permissions • Change Permissions • Take Ownership	Assigned to the Administrators group
Manage Documents	• Pause, resume, restart, and cancel all users' documents • Control job settings for all documents	• Manage Documents • Read Permissions • Change Permissions • Take Ownership	Assigned to the Creator Owner special identity

6. Click **OK** to close the Properties sheet.

STOP. You can log off of the Windows Server 2008 computer or remain logged on for subsequent exercises.

As with NTFS permissions, there are two types of printer permissions: standard permissions and special permissions. Each of the three standard permissions consists of a combination of special permissions.

WARNING If for any reason the Everyone special identity group is denied the print permission or even completely removed from a printer's permissions list, then users with the Manage Documents permission will not be able to print to that printer. This is because the Manage Documents permission does not include the Print permission, and it is only because of the default configuration of Everyone–Print that users with the Manage Documents permission have the print permission to the printer. The Manage Printers permission, on the other hand, includes the Print permission.

Managing Documents

By default, all printers assign the Allow Print permission to the *Everyone* special identity, which enables all users to access the printer and manage their own documents. Users that possess the Allow Manage Documents permission can manage any users' documents. Managing documents refers to pausing, resuming, restarting, and cancelling documents that are currently waiting in a print queue. Windows Server 2008 provides a print queue window for every printer, which enables you to view the jobs that are currently waiting to be printed.

To manage documents, use the following procedure.

 MANAGE DOCUMENTS

GET READY. Log on to Windows Server 2008 using any user account. When the logon process is completed, close the Initial Configuration Tasks window and any other windows that appear.

1. Click **Start**, and then click **Control Panel→Printers**. The Printers window appears.
2. Double-click one of the printer icons. A print queue window named for the printer appears, as shown in Figure 7-10.

Figure 7-10

A Windows Server 2008 print queue window

MS Publisher Color Printer						
Printer Document View						
Document Name	Status	Owner	Pages	Size	Submitted	Port
Test Page	Error - Print...	Administrator	1	77.7 KB	3:56:59 PM 9/19/2007	LPT2:
1 document(s) in queue						

3. Select one of the menu items listed in Table 7-2 to perform the associated function.
4. Close the print queue window.

STOP. You can log off of the Windows Server 2008 computer, or else remain logged on for subsequent exercises.

Table 7-2

Document Management Menu Commands

MENU ITEM	FUNCTION
Printer > Pause Printing	Causes the print server to stop sending jobs to the print device until you resume it by selecting the same menu item again. All pending jobs remain in the queue.
Printer > Cancel All Documents	Removes all pending jobs from the queue. Jobs that are in progress complete normally.
Printer > Use Printer Offline	Enables users to send jobs to the printer, where they remain in the queue, unprocessed, until you select the same menu item again.
Printer > Properties	Opens the Properties sheet for the printer.
Document > Pause	Pauses the selected document, preventing the print server from sending the job to the print device.
Document > Resume	Causes the print server to resume processing a selected document that has previously been paused.
Document > Restart	Causes the print server to discard the current job and restart printing the selected document from the beginning.
Document > Cancel	Causes the print server to remove the selected document from the queue.
Document > Properties	Opens the Properties sheet for the selected job.

TAKE NOTE*

When managing documents, keep in mind that the commands accessible from the print queue window affect only the jobs waiting in the queue, not those currently being processed by the print device. For example, a job that is partially transmitted to the print device cannot be completely cancelled. The data already in the print device's memory will be printed, even though the remainder of the job was removed from the queue. To stop a job that is currently printing, you must clear the print device's memory (by resetting it or power cycling the unit), as well as clear the job from the queue.

Managing Printers

Users with the Allow Manage Printers permission can go beyond just manipulating queued documents; they can reconfigure the printer itself. Managing a printer refers to altering the operational parameters that affect all users and controlling access to the printer.

Generally speaking, most of the software-based tasks that fall under the category of managing a printer are those you perform once, while setting up the printer for the first time. Day-to-day printer management is more likely to involve physical maintenance, such as clearing print jams, reloading paper, and changing toner or ink cartridges. However, the following sections examine some of the printer configuration tasks that typically are the responsibility of a printer manager.

SETTING PRINTER PRIORITIES

In some cases, you might want to give certain users in your organization priority access to a print device so that when print traffic is heavy, their jobs are processed before those of other users. To do this, you must create multiple printers, associate them with the same print device, and then modify their priorities, as described in the following procedure.

 SETTING A PRINTER'S PRIORITY

GET READY. Log on to Windows Server 2008 using an account with the Manage Printer permission. When the logon process is completed, close the Initial Configuration Tasks window and any other windows that appear.

1. Click **Start**, and then click **Control Panel→Printers**. The Printers window appears.
2. Right-click one of the printer icons and then, from the context menu, select **Properties**. The Properties sheet for the printer appears.
3. Click the **Advanced** tab, as shown in Figure 7-11.

Figure 7-11

The Advanced tab of a printer's Properties sheet

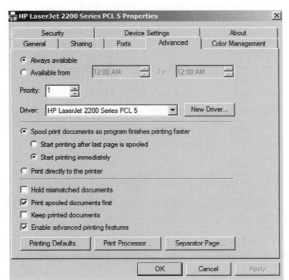

TAKE NOTE *

The values of the Priority spin box do not have any absolute significance; they are pertinent only in relation to each other. As long as one printer has a higher priority value than another, the server will process its print jobs first. In other words, it doesn't matter if the higher priority value is 9 or 99, as long as the lower priority value is less than 9.

4. Set the **Priority** spin box to a number representing the highest priority you want to set for the printer. Higher numbers represent higher priorities. The highest possible priority is 99.

5. Click the **Security** tab.

6. Add the users or groups that you want to provide with high-priority access to the printer and assign them the **Allow Print permission**.

7. Revoke the **Allow Print permission** from the Everyone special identity.

8. Click **OK** to close the Properties sheet.

9. Create an identical printer using the same printer driver and pointing to the same print device. Leave the Priority setting to its default value of 1 and leave the default permissions in place.

10. Rename the printers, specifying the priority assigned to each one.

11. Inform the privileged users that they should send their jobs to the high-priority printer. All jobs sent to that printer will be processed before those sent to the other, low-priority printer.

STOP. You can log off of the Windows Server 2008 computer, or else remain logged on for subsequent exercises.

SCHEDULING PRINTER ACCESS

Sometimes, you might want to limit certain users' access to a printer to specific times of the day or night. For example, your organization might have a color laser printer that the company's graphic designers use during business hours, but which you permit other employees to use after 5:00 P.M. To do this, you associate multiple printers with a single print device, much as you did to set different printer priorities.

After creating two printers, both pointing to the same print device, you configure their scheduling using the following procedure.

 CONFIGURING A PRINTER'S SCHEDULE

GET READY. Log on to Windows Server 2008 using an account with the Manage Printer permission. When the logon process is completed, close the Initial Configuration Tasks window and any other windows that appear. In this exercise you will configure different permissions and availability for two separate printers: one called Designers to be made available to members of a "GraphicsDesign" group at all hours, and one called "AllUsers" to be made available to the EVERYONE special identity from 5 P.M. – 7 P.M., Monday through Friday. This exercise assumes that you have created a security group called "GraphicsDesign," either on the local computer or within the Active Directory domain as appropriate.

1. Click **Start**, and then click **Control Panel→Printers**. The Printers window appears.

2. Right-click the printer icon for the GraphicsDesign printer and then, from the context menu, select **Properties**. The Properties sheet for the GraphicsDesign printer appears.

3. Click the **Security** tab.

4. Add the GraphicsDesign security group and grant them the **Allow Print permission**.

5. Revoke the **Allow Print permission** from the Everyone special identity.

6. Click **OK** to close the Properties sheet.

7. Right-click **AllUsers printer** and then, from the context menu, select **Properties**. The Properties sheet for the AllUsers printer appears.

8. Click the **Advanced** tab.

9. Select the **Available from** radio button and then, in the two spin boxes provided, select the range of hours you want the printer to be available to all users. Notice that you do not need to modify the security settings for the AllUsers printer as this printer is available to the Everyone special identity; you are merely restricting the hours during which the printer is available to the Everyone group.

10. Click **OK** to close the Properties sheet.

STOP. You can log off of the Windows Server 2008 computer, or stay logged on for subsequent exercises.

CREATING A PRINTER POOL

As mentioned earlier, a printer pool is an arrangement that increases the production capability of a single printer by connecting it to multiple print devices. When you create a printer pool, the print server sends each incoming job to the first print device it finds that is not busy. This effectively distributes the jobs among the available print devices, providing users with more rapid service.

To create a printer pool, you must have at least two identical print devices, or at least print devices that use the same printer driver. The print devices must be in the same location, because there is no way to tell which print device will process a given document. You must also connect all of the print devices in the pool to the same print server. If the print server is a Windows Server 2008 computer, you can connect the print devices to any viable ports.

To configure a printer pool, use the following procedure.

 CREATE A PRINTER POOL

GET READY. Log on to Windows Server 2008 using an account with the Manage Printer permission. When the logon process is completed, close the Initial Configuration Tasks window and any other windows that appear.

1. Click **Start**, and then click **Control Panel→Printers**. The Printers window appears.

2. Right-click one of the printer icons and then, from the context menu, select **Properties**. The Properties sheet for the printer appears.

3. Click the **Ports** tab, and then select all of the ports to which the print devices are connected.

4. Select the **Enable printer pooling** checkbox, and then click **OK**.

STOP. You can log off of the Windows Server 2008 computer, or stay logged on for subsequent exercises.

■ Using the Print Services Role

THE BOTTOM LINE

All of the printer sharing and management capabilities discussed in the previous sections are available on any Windows Server 2008 computer in its default installation configuration. However, installing the Print Services role on the computer provides additional tools that are particularly useful to administrators involved with network printing on an enterprise scale.

When you install the Print Services role using Server Manager's Add Roles Wizard, a Role Services page appears, as shown in Figure 7-12, enabling you to select from the options listed in Table 7-3.

Figure 7-12

The Select Role Services page for the Print Services role

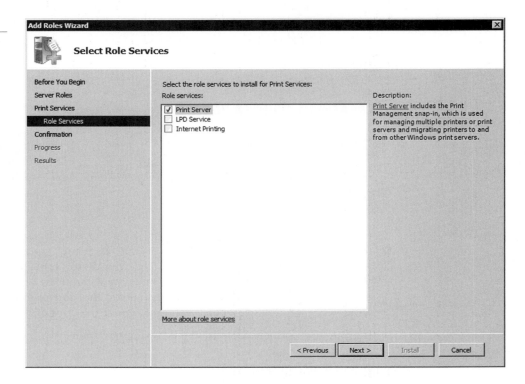

Table 7-3

Role Service Selection for the Print Services Role

ROLE SERVICE	WIZARD PAGES ADDED	SYSTEM SERVICES INSTALLED	DESCRIPTION
Print Server	[None]	Print Spooler (Spooler)	• Installs the Print Management console for Microsoft Management Console (MMC), which enables administrators to deploy, monitor, and manage printers throughout the enterprise. • This is the only role service that is required when you add the Print Services role.
LPD Service	[None]	TCP/IP Print Server (LPDSVC)	• Enables UNIX clients running the LPR (line printer remote) program to send their print jobs to Windows printers.
Internet Printing	[None]	• World Wide Web Publishing Service (w3svc) • IIS Admin Service (iisadmin)	• Creates a Web site that enables users on the Internet to send print jobs to shared Windows printers.

To install the Internet Printing role service, you must also install the Web Server (IIS) role, with certain specific role services, as well as the Windows Process Activation Service feature. The Add Roles Wizard enforces these dependencies by displaying an *Add role services and features required for Internet Printing?* message box, as shown in Figure 7-13, when you select the Internet Printing role service. Clicking *Add Required Role Services* causes the wizard to select the exact role services within Web Server (IIS) role that the Internet Printing service needs.

Figure 7-13

The Add role services and features required for Internet Printing? message box

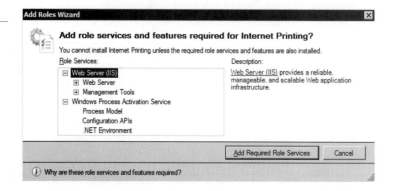

As always, Windows Server 2008 adds a new node to the Server Manager console when you install a role. The Print Services node contains a filtered view of print-related event log entries, a status display for the role-related system services and role services, and suggestions for recommended configuration tasks and best practices, as shown in Figure 7-14.

Figure 7-14

The Print Services node in Server Manager

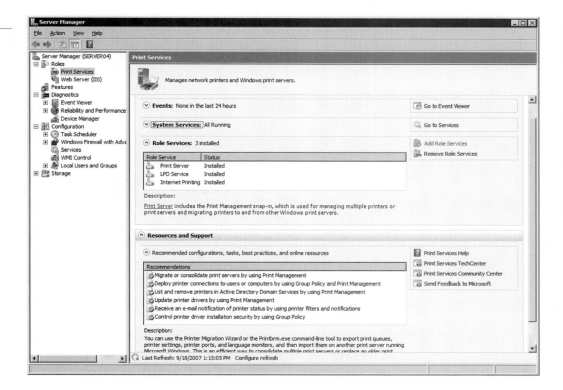

Using the Print Management Console

The Print Management snap-in for MMC is an administrative tool that consolidates the controls for the printing components throughout the enterprise into a single console. With this tool, you can access the print queues and Properties sheets for all of the network printers in the enterprise, deploy printers to client computers using Group Policy, and create custom views that simplify the process of detecting print devices that need attention due to errors or depleted consumables.

Windows Server 2008 installs the Print Management console when you add the Print Services role to the computer. You can also install the console without the role by adding the Print Services Tools feature, found under Remote Server Administration Tools→Role Administration Tools in Server Manager.

When you launch the Print Management console, the default display, shown in Figure 7-15, includes the following three nodes in the scope (left) pane:

Figure 7-15

The Print Management console

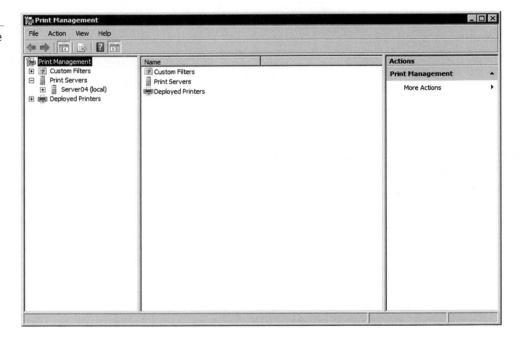

- *Custom Filters*—Contains composite views of all the printers hosted by the print servers listed in the console, regulated by customizable filters.
- Print Servers—Lists all of the print servers you have added to the console, and all of the drivers, forms, ports, and printers for each print server.
- Deployed Printers—Lists all of the printers you have deployed with Group Policy using the console.

The following sections demonstrate some of the administration tasks you can perform with the Print Management console.

Adding Print Servers

By default, the Print Management console displays only the local machine in its list of print servers. Each print server listed has four nodes beneath it, as shown in Figure 7-16, listing the drivers, forms, ports, and printers associated with that server.

Figure 7-16

A print server display in the Print Management console

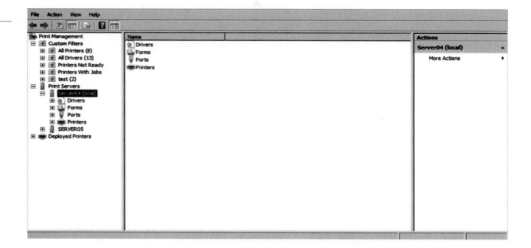

To manage other print servers and their printers, you must add them to the console, using the following procedure.

 ADD A PRINT SERVER

GET READY. Log on to Windows Server 2008 using a domain account with Administrator privileges. When the logon process is completed, close the Initial Configuration Tasks window and any other windows that appear. In this exercise you will add the Print Server Role and then add a print server. This exercise assumes that there is another server available on your network that is also running a print server, and that network discovery has been enabled on your network. If you do not have a second server available, you will not be able to complete Steps 5–7.

1. If Server Manager does not open automatically, click **Start**, and then click **Server Manager**. In the left-hand pane, click **Roles**.

2. In the right-hand pane, click **Add roles**. Click **Next** to bypass the initial Welcome screen.

3. The Select Server Roles screen appears. Place a checkmark next to **Print Services**. Click **Next** twice to continue.

4. The Select Role Services screen appears. Accept the default selection and click **Next**.

5. Click **Install** to install the Print Services server role. When the installation completes, click **Close**.

6. Click **Start**, and then click **Administrative Tools→Print Management**. The Print Management console appears.

7. Right-click the **Print Servers** node and, from the context menu, click **Add/Remove Servers**. The Add/Remove Servers dialog box appears, as shown in Figure 7-17.

Figure 7-17

The Add/Remove Servers dialog box

8. In the Specify Print Server box, click **Browse**. The Select Print Server dialog box appears, as shown in Figure 7-18.

Figure 7-18

The Select Print Server dialog box

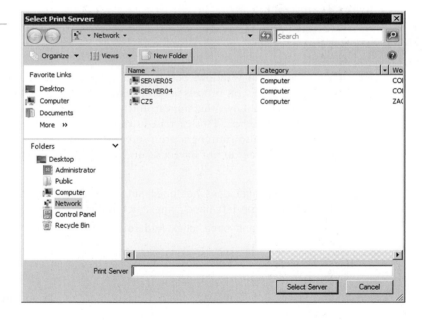

9. Select the print server you want to add to the console and click **Select Server**. The server you selected appears in the Add Server text box on the Add/Remove servers dialog box.

10. Click **Add to List**. The server you selected appears in the Print Servers list.

11. Click **OK**. The server appears under the Print Servers node.

STOP. You can log off of the Windows Server 2008 computer, or else remain logged on for subsequent exercises.

Viewing Printers

One of the major problems for printing administrators on large enterprise networks is keeping track of dozens or hundreds of print devices, all in frequent use, and all needing attention on a regular basis. Whether the maintenance required is a major repair, replenishing ink or toner, or just filling the paper trays, print devices will not get the attention they need until an administrator is aware of the problem.

The Print Management console provides a multitude of ways to view the printing components associated with the print servers on the network. To create views, the console takes the complete list of printers and applies various filters to it, to select which printers to display. Under the Custom Filters node, there are four default filters, as follows:

- All Printers—Contains a list of all the printers hosted by all of the print servers added to the console.
- All Drivers—Contains a list of all the printer drivers installed on all of the print servers added to the console.
- Printers Not Ready—Contains a list of all printers that are not reporting a Ready status.
- Printers With Jobs—Contains a list of all the printers that currently have jobs waiting in the print queue.

Views such as Printer Not Ready are a useful way for administrators to determine what printers need attention, without having to browse individual print servers or search through a long list of every printer on the network. In addition to these defaults, you can create your own custom filters with the following procedure.

 CREATE A CUSTOM FILTER

GET READY. Log on to Windows Server 2008 using a domain account with Administrator privileges. When the logon process is completed, close the Initial Configuration Tasks window and any other windows that appear.

1. Click **Start**, and then click **Administrative Tools→Print Management**. The Print Management console appears.
2. Right-click the **Custom Filters** node and, from the context menu, select **Add New Printer Filter**. The New Printer Filter Wizard appears, as shown in Figure 7-19.

Figure 7-19

The New Printer Filter Wizard

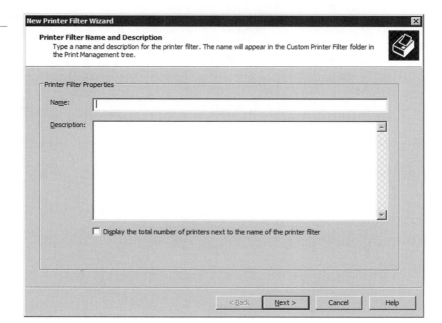

3. In the Name text box, key a name for the filter, and optionally, key a description for the filter in the Description text box. If you want the number of printers in the filtered list to appear next to the filter name, select the **Display the total number of filters next to the name of the printer filter** checkbox. Then click **Next**. The Define a printer filter page appears, as shown in Figure 7-20.

Figure 7-20

The Define a printer filter page

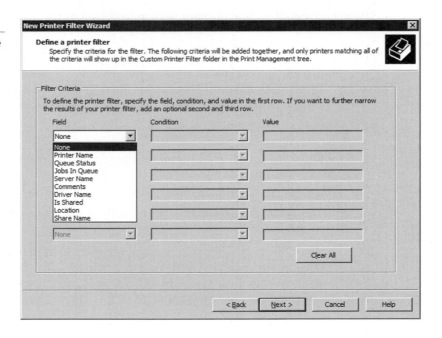

4. In the topmost row of boxes, select values for the **Field**, Condition, and Value fields. Then, select values for additional rows of boxes, if desired. Then click **Next**. The Set Notifications page appears, as shown in Figure 7-21.

Figure 7-21

The Set Notifications page

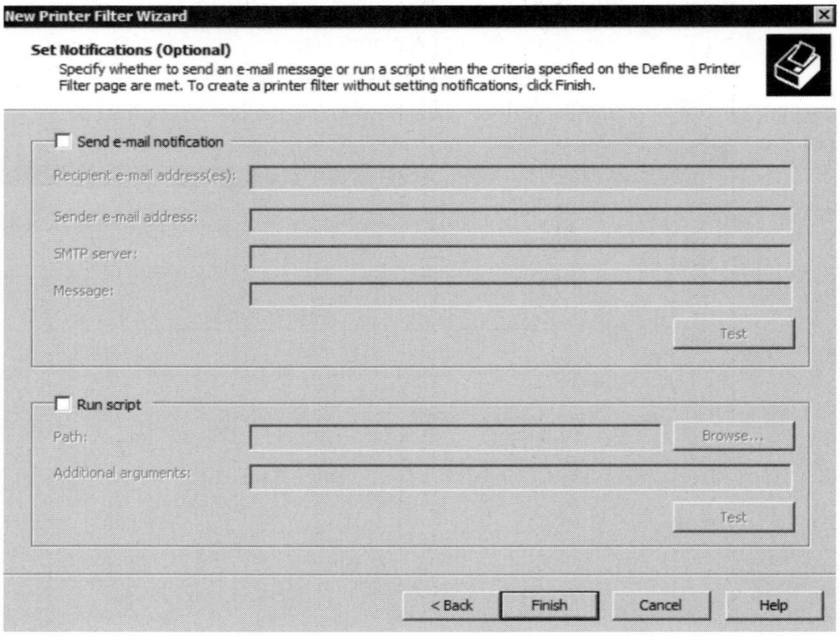

5. Select the **Send e-mail notification** checkbox to send a message to a specific person when there are printers meeting the criteria you specified on the Define a printer filter page. Use the text boxes provided to specify the sender's and recipient's e-mail addresses, the Simple Mail Transfer Protocol (SMTP) server that will send the message, and the text of the message itself.

6. Select the **Run script** checkbox to execute a particular script file when there are printers meeting the criteria you specified on the Define a printer filter page. Use the text boxes provided to specify the path to the script and any additional arguments you want the system to pass to the script when running it.

7. Click **Finish**. The new filter appears under the Custom Filters node.

STOP. You can log off of the Windows Server 2008 computer, or else remain logged on for subsequent exercises.

When creating filters, each entry in the Field drop-down list has its own collection of possible entries for the Condition drop-down list, and each Condition entry has its own possible entries for the Value setting. There are, therefore, many thousands of possible filter combinations.

For example, when you select Queue Status in the Field list, the Condition drop-down list presents two options: *is exactly* and *is not exactly*. After you select one of these Condition settings, you choose from the Value list, which displays all of the possible queue status messages that the print server can report, as shown in Figure 7-22.

Figure 7-22

Filter status values

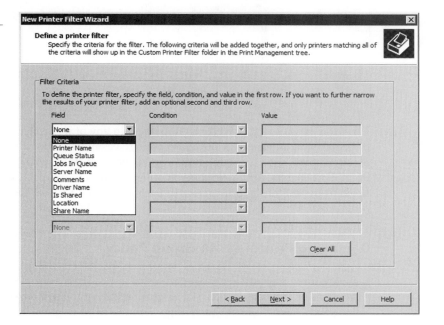

If you create a filter with the settings Queue Status, is exactly, and Error, the filter will display all of the printers that are currently reporting an error condition. A filter like this can be a useful tool for detecting printers reporting one specific condition, but there are many different status messages that indicate a print device stoppage. For the busy printer administrator, a better combination might be a filter with the settings Queue Status, is not exactly, and Ready. This way, the filter will display all of the printers suffering from abnormal conditions. These are the printers that need administrative attention.

Managing Printers and Print Servers

Once you have used filtered views to isolate the printers you want to examine, selecting a printer displays its status, the number of jobs currently in its print queue, and the name of the print server hosting it. If you right-click the filter in the scope pane and, from the context menu, select Show Extended View, an additional pane appears containing the contents of the selected printer's queue, as shown in Figure 7-23. You can manipulate the queued jobs just as you would from the print queue window on the print server console.

Figure 7-23

The Print Management console's extended view

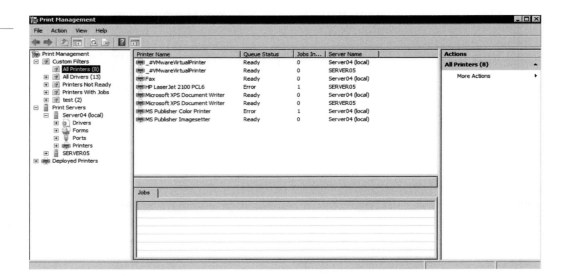

The Print Management console also enables administrators to access the configuration interface for any printer or print server appearing in any of its displays. Right-clicking a printer or print server anywhere in the console interface, and selecting Properties from the context menu, displays the exact same Properties sheet you would see on the print server computer itself. This enables administrators to configure printers and print servers without having to travel to the site of the print server or even establish a Remote Desktop connection to the print server.

Deploying Printers with Group Policy

Configuring a print client to access a shared printer is a simple matter of browsing the network or the Active Directory tree and selecting the printer you want the client to use. However, when you have to configure hundreds or thousands of print clients, the task becomes more complicated. One way to simplify the process of deploying printers to large numbers of clients is to use Active Directory.

Listing printers in the Active Directory database enables users and administrators to search for printers by name, location, or model (as long as you populate the Location and Model fields in the printer object). To create a printer object in the Active Directory database, you can either select the List in the directory checkbox while sharing the printer, or right-click a printer in the Print Management console and, from the context menu, select List in Directory.

To use Active Directory to deploy printers to clients, you must configure the appropriate policies in a Group Policy Object (GPO). You can link a GPO to any domain, site, or organizational unit (OU) in the Active Directory tree. When you configure a GPO to deploy a printer, all of the users or computers in that domain, site, or OU will receive the printer connection when they log on.

To deploy printers with Group Policy, use the following procedure. (The following exercise assumes that you are working in an Active Directory environment.)

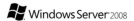 **DEPLOY PRINTERS WITH GROUP POLICY**

GET READY. Log on to Windows Server 2008 using a domain account with Administrator privileges. When the logon process is completed, close the Initial Configuration Tasks window and any other windows that appear.

1. Click **Start**, and then click **Administrative Tools→Print Management**. The Print Management console appears.

2. Right-click a printer in the console's scope pane and, from the context menu, select **Deploy with Group Policy**. The Deploy with Group Policy dialog box appears, as shown in Figure 7-24.

Figure 7-24

The Deploy with Group Policy dialog box

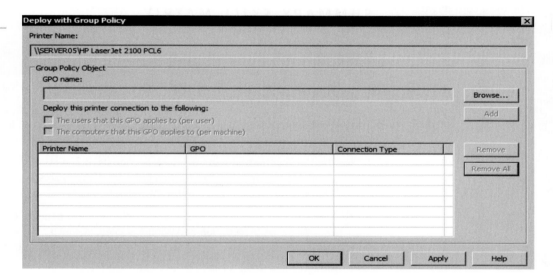

3. Click **Browse**. The Browse for a Group Policy Object dialog box appears, as shown in Figure 7-25.

Figure 7-25

The Browse for a Group Policy Object dialog box

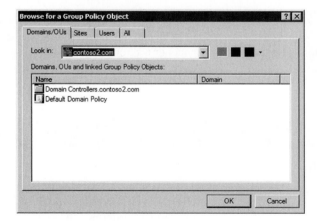

4. Select the group policy object you want to use to deploy the printer and click **OK**. The GPO you selected appears in the GPO Name field.

5. Select the appropriate checkbox to select whether to deploy the printer to the users associated with the GPO, the computers, or both. Then click **Add**. The new printer/GPO associations appear in the table.

Deploying the printer to the users means that all of the users associated with the GPO will receive the printer connection, no matter what computer they use to log on. Deploying the printer to the computers means that all of the computers associated with the GPO will receive the printer connection, no matter which users log on to them.

6. Click **OK**. A Print Management message box appears, informing you that the operation has succeeded.

7. Click **OK**, then click **OK** again to close the Deploy with Group Policy dialog box.

STOP. Close any open windows and log off of the Windows Server 2008 computer.

The next time the Windows Server 2008 or Windows Vista users and/or computers associated with the GPO refresh their policies or restart, they will receive the new settings, and the printer will appear in the Printers control panel.

SUMMARY SKILL MATRIX

IN THIS LESSON YOU LEARNED:

- Printing in Microsoft Windows typically involves the following four components: print device, printer, print server, and print driver.

- The printer driver enables you to configure the print job to use the various capabilities of the print device.

- The simplest form of print architecture consists of one print device connected to one computer, known a locally-attached print device. You can share this printer (and the print device) with other users on the same network.

- XML Paper Specification (XPS) is a new, platform-independent document format included with Windows Server 2008 and Windows Vista, in which print job files use a single XPS format for their entire journey to the print device, rather than being converted first to EMS and then later to PCL.

- With network-attached print devices, the primary deployment decision that the administrator must make is to decide which computer will function as the print server.

- Printer permissions are much simpler than NTFS permissions; they basically dictate whether users are allowed to merely use the printer, manage documents submitted to the printer, or manage the properties of the printer itself.

- The Print Management snap-in for MMC is an administrative tool that consolidates the controls for the printing components throughout the enterprise into a single console.

■ Knowledge Assessment

Fill in the Blank

Complete the following sentences by writing the correct word or words in the blanks provided.

1. A(n) _____ is the software interface through which a computer communicates with a print device.

2. When you connect a single print server to multiple print devices, you create what is called a(n) _____.

3. By default, all printers assign the Allow Print permission to the _____ special identity, which enables all users to access the printer and manage their own documents.

4. Users with the _____ permission can go beyond just manipulating queued documents; they can reconfigure the printer itself.

5. The _____ is the default print format used by the Windows 2000, Windows XP, and Windows Server 2003 operating systems.

6. A(n) _____ is a device driver that converts the print jobs generated by applications into an appropriate string of commands for a specific print device.

7. The _____ allows clients to print documents using HTTP traffic over an intranet or the World Wide Web.

8. Users with the _____ permission to a printer have the ability to pause, resume, restart, and cancel their own documents, but not documents created by any other user.

9. A(n) _____ print architecture consists of one print device connected to one computer.

10. _____ such as Printer Not Ready are a useful way for administrators to determine what printers need attention throughout a Windows Server 2008 network.

Multiple Choice

Select all answers that apply for the following questions.

1. Which printer permission allows users to pause, resume, restart, and cancel all users' documents and to control job settings for all documents?
   a. Print
   b. Manage Documents
   c. Manage Printers
   d. Full Control

2. What document format is a new, platform-independent format included with Windows Vista and Windows Server 2008?
   a. XML Paper Specification (XPS)
   b. Rich Text Format (RTF)
   c. Extensible Markup Language (XML)
   d. Directory Services Markup Language (DSML)

3. What kind of device receives print jobs from clients and sends them to either locally-attached or network-attached printer devices?
   a. Print device
   b. Print queue
   c. Print server
   d. Print driver

4. What kind of print device is connected to a TCP/IP network, either directly or through another computer?
   a. Print server
   b. Local print device
   c. Network-attached print device
   d. Print queue

5. What can you create to connect a single print server to multiple print devices?
   a. Print server
   b. Print queue
   c. Network printer
   d. Printer pool

6. What permission allows a user to share a printer, delete a printer, and change a printer's properties?
   a. Print
   b. Manage Documents
   c. Manage Printers
   d. Read Printers

7. What kind of printer is directly attached to a single computer, regardless of the interface it uses to connect?
   a. Network-attached printer
   b. Local printer
   c. Serial printer
   d. Parallel printer

8. What protocol allows users to print documents through an IIS server?
   a. HTTP
   b. HTTPS
   c. FireWire
   d. IPP

9. What describes the actual hardware that produces hard copy documents on paper or other print media?
   - **a.** Print queue
   - **b.** Print device
   - **c.** Print server
   - **d.** Printer pool

10. What permission allows users to pause, manage, and cancel only those printer documents that they have created?
    - **a.** Manage Printers
    - **b.** Manage Documents
    - **c.** Print
    - **d.** Full Control

■ Case Scenarios

Scenario 7-1: Configuring Windows Print Services

You are a desktop support technician for a law firm with a group of ten legal secretaries who provide administrative support to the attorneys. All of the secretaries use a single, shared, high-speed laser printer that is connected to a dedicated Windows Server 2008 print server. The secretaries print multiple copies of large documents on a regular basis, and although the laser printer is fast, it is kept running almost constantly. Sometimes the secretaries have to wait 20 minutes or more after submitting a print job for their documents to reach the top of the queue. The office manager has offered to purchase additional printers for the department. However, the secretaries are accustomed to simply clicking the Print button, and don't like the idea of having to examine multiple print queues to determine which one has the fewest jobs before submitting a document. What can you do to provide the department with a printing solution that will enable the secretaries to utilize additional printers most efficiently?

Maintaining and Updating Windows Server 2008

OBJECTIVE DOMAIN MATRIX

TECHNOLOGY SKILL	OBJECTIVE DOMAIN	OBJECTIVE DOMAIN NUMBER
Using the Performance Monitor	Capture performance data	5.2
Using the Windows Event Viewer	Monitor event logs	5.3
Using Network Monitor to Gather Network Data	Gather network data	5.4
Configuring Windows Server Update Services (WSUS)	Configure Windows Server Update Services (WSUS) server settings	5.1

KEY TERMS

Administrative Events
Automatic Updates
Background Intelligent Transfer
   Service (BITS)
Capture Filter
collector initiated
configuration information
Content Synchronization Service
Data Collector Set
Display Filter
Event trace data

Log on as a batch user
perfmon
performance counters
Performance Log Users
Performance Monitor
Performance Monitor Users
promiscuous mode
Reliability and Performance
   Monitor
Reliability Monitor
Resource View

source computer initiated
subscriptions
Windows Event Collector
   Service
Windows Server Update
   Services (WSUS)
WS-Management protocol

Lucerne Publishing is a global publishing firm with offices in North America, Europe, and India. Over the past several weeks, the IT staff at Lucerne Publishing has designed and implemented a Microsoft Windows Server 2008 network that offers numerous networking services to clients, as well as file and printer sharing capabilities. To maintain the Windows Server 2008 network, Lucerne Publishing needs to develop and implement an ongoing monitoring scheme to ensure that the new environment remains available for all users, workstations, and servers. Finally, Lucerne Publishing needs to develop an automated means of installing security updates and patches to the numerous workstations and servers deployed throughout the world.

In this lesson we will discuss the process of monitoring and updating a Windows Server 2008 infrastructure. This includes monitoring server performance using the new Reliability and Performance Monitor as well as the Windows Event Viewer and Network Monitor. We will also discuss the Windows Server Update Services (WSUS) service, which is a free download from the Microsoft Web site that allows administrators to centrally manage the approval and installation of updates on a Windows network.

■ Monitoring a Windows Server 2008 Network

THE BOTTOM LINE

Simply stated, there are two approaches to maintaining your network: the reactive approach and the proactive approach. After implementation of your network design is complete and you have verified that your network works properly, the reactive approach means that you will "wait and see" what problems arise. A proactive approach doesn't wait for problems to arise. A proactive approach to network management is preventative and uses tools such as the Performance and Reliability Monitor, the Event Viewer, and Network Monitor utilities. Proactive system administrators use these tools to help spot potential and actual networking issues without wasting time guessing what the problems might be because they lack historical data. They do this by systematically monitoring, logging, and analyzing the network's data.

There are three tools that can help you proactively troubleshoot network problems. First, you explore the Reliability and Performance Monitor (formerly called the Performance console), which provides an in-depth look into system performance measurement. Next you'll examine some of the new capabilities that are present in the Windows Server 2008 Event Viewer. Finally, you explore some of the advanced network traffic capture and analysis features found in Network Monitor.

Using the Reliability and Performance Monitor

The **Reliability and Performance Monitor** is a tool located within the Administrative Tools folder that combines features that had previously been spread across a number of tools: Performance Logs and Alerts, Server Performance Advisor, and System Monitor. The Reliability and Performance Monitor in Windows Server 2008 allows you to collect real-time information on your local computer or from a specific computer to which you have permissions. This information can be viewed in a number of different formats that include line charts and histograms. The reports can be saved or printed for documentation purposes. You can also customize the parameters that you want to track and store them in an MMC snap-in so that they can be used on other computers within your network. Figure 8-1 shows the Reliability and Performance Monitor.

Before you can effectively use the Reliability and Performance Monitor, you need to understand how to configure it so that you can obtain the desired information. The Reliability and Performance Monitor collects three types of information to monitor the performance of a Windows Server 2008 computer:

- **Performance counters**—These are the specific processes or events that you want to track. New performance counters are exposed within the Reliability and Performance Monitor as you add additional roles and services to a particular server. For example, within the DNS performance object, the Dynamic updates received per second counter will monitor the number of dynamic updates that were received by a particular server; these counters are visible only on servers that are running the DNS server role.

- **Event trace data**—This data is collected over time to provide a real-time view into the behavior and performance of the server operating systems and any applications that it is running.

- *Configuration information*—The Reliability and Performance monitor can query the Windows Registry for specific configuration data, either once or over a set period of time, to determine how a server is configured and whether changes to that configuration are affecting its performance.

Figure 8-1

Viewing the Reliability and Performance Monitor

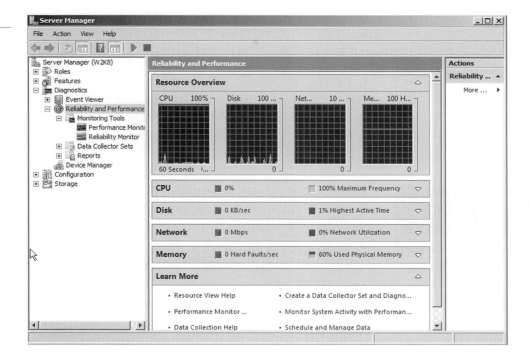

You can access the Reliability and Performance Monitor from the Server Manager console, or by keying *perfmon* from the Run line or the command prompt. Once this tool has launched, you can choose from one of three views:

- *Resource View*—This is the default view of the Reliability and Performance Monitor as shown in Figure 8-1. This view provides a quick overview of the four major performance components of a Windows server: CPU, Disk, Network, and Memory. You can drill down to a more detailed view of any of these four items by clicking the relevant item. For example, clicking CPU will provide a view similar to the Task Manager as shown in Figure 8-2, showing the executables that are currently running and the average CPU time being used by each.

Figure 8-2

The Resource View of the Reliability and Performance Monitor

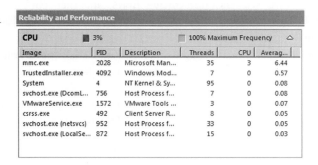

- *Performance Monitor*—This view provides a visual display of performance counters, either in real-time or as a way to view historical data that you captured previously. After you have determined the counters you want to monitor, you can view information about these counters in one of the following formats: Line graph type, Histogram bar graph type, or a Report graph type.

- *Reliability Monitor*—This view provides information about system events that can affect a server's stability, including software installation and uninstallation, as well as any application, operating system or hardware failures that have occurred over a particular time period.

USING THE PERFORMANCE MONITOR

Probably the most frequently used view within the Reliability and Performance Monitor is the Performance Monitor. One of the simplest methods is to open the Start menu, key perfmon.exe, and then click OK. Performance Monitor provides detailed information necessary for in-depth analysis, logging capabilities, and alerts, which are useful for early warnings of possible system issues.

CERTIFICATION READY?
Capture performance data

5.2

When you are ready to begin adding performance counters to be monitored, some of the performance objects and counters that are installed by default in Windows Server 2008 include the following:

- Browser
    - Announcements Domains/sec—the rate at which a domain has announced itself to the network
    - Election Packets/sec—the rate at which browser election packets have been received by the local computer
- Memory
    - Available bytes—the amount of physical memory available for allocation to a particular process
    - Committed Bytes—the amount of committed virtual memory
- Processor
    - % Processor Time—the amount of time the processor spends executing a non-idle thread

➔ USE THE PERFORMANCE MONITOR

GET READY. To perform these steps, log onto the server using an account with administrative credentials.

1. Click **Start**, click **Administrative Tools**, and then click **Reliability and Monitoring Tools Performance Monitor**. Drill down to **Monitoring Tools** and click **Performance Monitor**.

2. From the Performance Monitoring console, click the **green plus sign (+)** on the menu bar. The Add Counters dialog box opens.

3. In the Add Counters dialog box, select the computer from which you want to obtain data. If you select Use Local Computer Counters, data is collected from the local computer. If you choose Select Counters From Computer, you can use an IP address or the Universal Naming Convention (UNC) name of the computer from which you want to collect data, like \\server1.adatum.com. Figure 8-3 shows the Add Counters dialog box with the DNS object selected, showing the various counters you can add.

Figure 8-3

Adding a performance counter

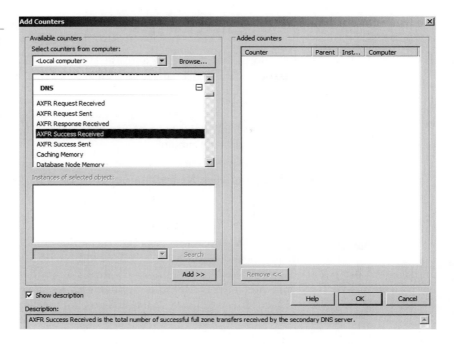

4. In the Performance Object list, select the performance object you want to monitor. For example, to monitor Active Directory, select the Directory Services collection.

5. Select the counters you want to monitor. If you want to monitor all counters, select the **All Instances** button from the Instances of Select Object dialog. If you want to monitor only particular counters, select the appropriate instance; you can select multiple counters by holding the **Ctrl** key and clicking the counters. For most Directory Services counters, for example, the only instance available will be the NTDS instance. For other types of counters, exercise caution when using the "All Instances" selection, as it can load a significant number of counters and make the display difficult to read.

6. Click the **Add** button.

7. When you are finished adding counters, click **OK**. The chosen counters are displayed in the lower part of the Reliability and Performance Monitor. Each counter is represented by a different color.

8. On the toolbar, you can change the display output to reflect a graph, histogram, or report display. It is easiest to use a graph format if you are monitoring performance over extended periods of time. Reports and histograms reflect only the most recent values and averages and might not reflect the information you need for long-term reporting.

PAUSE. Leave the Reliability and Performance Monitor open for the next exercise.

WORKING WITH DATA COLLECTOR SETS

One of the significant changes introduced in Windows Server 2008 performance monitoring is the *Data Collector Set*. Rather than manually adding individual performance counters anytime you want to monitor performance on a 2008 server, Data Collector Sets allow you to organize a set of performance counters, event traces, and system configuration data into a single "object" that you can reuse on one or more Windows Server 2008 servers. You can view the counters associated with Data Collector Sets in Performance Monitor view, use them to generate alert actions when particular performance thresholds are reached, and integrate them with the Windows Task Scheduler to collect performance data at specific times. There are three built-in Data Collector Sets within Windows Server 2008—LAN Diagnostics, System Diagnostics, and System Performance—or you can create your own custom sets. You also have the ability to create *Data Collector Set templates* that are based on the XML file format, thus allowing you to distribute templates across multiple servers for use by other administrators.

WORK WITH DATA COLLECTOR SETS

GET READY. To perform these steps, log onto the Windows Server 2008 server using an account with administrative credentials, or as a member of the Performance Log Users group (described in the next section).

1. Log onto the Windows Server 2008 computer. Open the Reliability and Performance Monitor from the left-hand pane of Server Manager, or by keying **perfmon** from the Run line or a command prompt.

2. In the left-hand pane, click the plus sign next to **Data Collector Sets**. Right-click **User Defined** and click **New→Data Collector Set**. You will see the screen shown in Figure 8-4.

Figure 8-4

Creating a new Data Collector Set

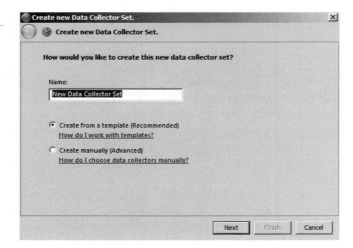

3. In the Name field, enter **Sample Data Collector Set**. Ensure that the *Create from a template* (*Recommended*) radio button is selected, and then click **Next.** You will see the screen shown in Figure 8-5.

Figure 8-5

Selecting a Data Collector Set template

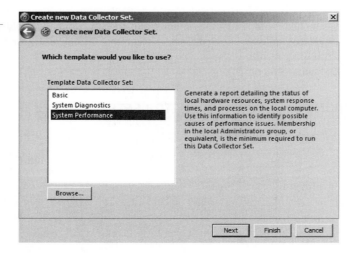

4. Ensure that the **System Performance** template is selected, and then click **Next**.

5. On the *Where would you like the data to be saved?* screen, accept the default directory location and then click **Next**. You will see the screen shown in Figure 8-6.

Figure 8-6

Confirming your selections

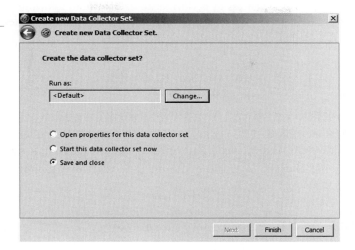

6. Select the **Save and close** radio button, and then click **Finish**. You will return to the Reliability and Performance Monitor screen, where you will see that the Data Collector Set you just created has a status of Stopped.

7. Right-click the **Data Collector Set** and click **Start**. You will see that the status in the right-hand pane changes to Running. After approximately one minute, the status will change to Compiling, and then to Stopped.

8. To view the performance data that was collected, navigate to **Reports→User Defined→Sample Data Collector Set**. You will see a report that was created by the Data Collector Set that ran in Step 7, similar to the one shown in Figure 8-7.

Figure 8-7

Viewing a report of performance data

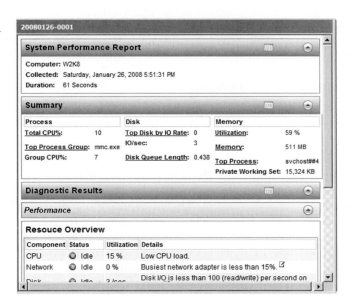

STOP. Close the Reliability and Performance Monitor.

SECURING ACCESS TO PERFORMANCE DATA

> A common request from network administrators in previous versions of Windows is the ability to delegate access to performance data without allowing full administrative rights to a particular server. To this end, Windows Server 2008 includes a number of built-in group objects that grant limited access to performance data.

Members of the built-in Users group on a Windows Server 2008 computer have very limited access to performance data, which includes the following:

- Members of the Users group can view previously–created log files to view historical data within the Performance Monitor console, but cannot view real-time data
- Members of the Users group can use the Reliability Monitor, but not the Resource view
- Members of the Users group are not able to create or modify Data Collector Sets

Members of the *Performance Monitor Users* group, by default, are delegated the following additional abilities to view performance data:

- Members of Performance Monitor Users can view both real-time and historical data within the Performance Monitor console, and can use the Reliability Monitor
- Members of Performance Monitor Users cannot create or modify Data Collector Sets or use the Resource View

CERTIFICATION READY?
Monitor event logs
5.3

Members of the *Performance Log Users* group have all of the rights available to normal Users and Performance Monitor Users. In addition, Performance Log Users also have the ability to create and modify Data Collector Sets, but only after an administrator has assigned this group the *Log on as a batch user* user right on the server or servers in question.

Using the Windows Event Viewer

> Windows Server 2008 uses the Windows Event Viewer to record system events that take place, such as security, application, and role-specific events. Active Directory–related events are recorded in the Directory Service log. The Directory Service log is created when Active Directory is installed. It logs informational events such as service start and stop messages, errors, and warnings. This log should be the first place you look when you suspect a problem with Active Directory.

Figure 8-8 shows the default view of the Event Viewer on a Windows Server 2008 computer, which is accessible from Server Manager by drilling down to the Diagnostics node or by selecting Event Viewer from the Administrative Tools folder on the Start menu. Since Event Viewer shows logs for both informational messages and error messages, it is important to monitor for events that can provide indications of overall system health. In the type field of any of the log files in Event Viewer, you should monitor and filter on events that indicate a warning or stop error. A warning is indicated by a yellow triangle with an exclamation mark, and a stop error is indicated by a red circle with an X on it. The event details will provide additional information that pertains to possible reasons for the entry in addition to resources that can provide possible solutions.

Figure 8-8

Viewing the Windows Event Viewer

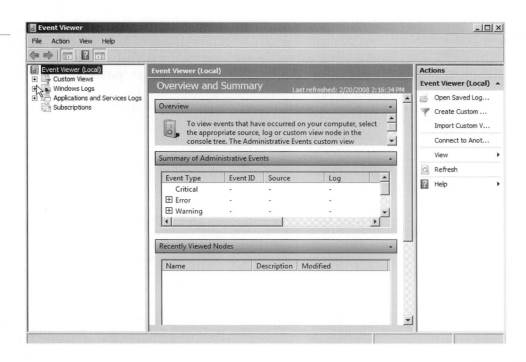

When you drill down into the Event Viewer node, you will see the following items:

- *Custom Views* — This is a new feature in the Windows Server 2008 Event Viewer, which allows you to create custom views of events that are recorded. By default, a single custom view is created on each Windows Server 2008 computer called ***Administrative Events***, which collects Critical, Error, and Warning events from all logs on the server. You can create any number of custom logs of your own; for example, you could create a Custom View on an Active Directory domain controller that displays only Critical errors from the DNS and Directory Services log. This folder also contains custom views that are associated with any installed server roles, such as DHCP server, DNS server, Active Directory Domain Services, etc.

- *Windows Logs*—this is the traditional view of the Windows Event Viewer, which sorts events into the following logs:

  - *Application Log*—records events associated with software that is installed on the server.

  - *Security Log*—Records events associated with successful or failed access to secured resources on the server. Windows Server 2008 will record entries to the Security log based on whatever auditing configuration has been set up for the server in question. It's also important to note that, in a default installation, only Administrators have access to the Security log on a Windows Server 2008 computer.

  - *Setup Log*—New to Windows Server 2008, this log records events associated with server installation, adding and removing server roles, installing applications, etc.

  - *System Log*—Records information associated with operating system events such as server restarts, issues with services, etc.

  - *Forwarded Events*—Also new to Windows Server 2008, this log records events that were forwarded to the Event Viewer on this server.

- *Applications and Services*—This provides various collections of Event Viewer entries associated with server hardware, Internet Explorer, and other Windows-based applications and components.

Another new feature of Windows Server 2008 Event Viewer is the ***Windows Event Collector Service***, which allows you to configure a single server as a repository of Event Viewer information for multiple computers. The Event Collector Service creates and manages ***subscriptions*** to one or more remote computers; these subscriptions collect events that match the criteria of an event filter that you define. The Event Collector service uses the ***WS-Management protocol*** to communicate with remote computers and transfer event log information from an event source to the local event log service. Subscriptions can be either ***collector initiated***, where the destination computer polls the source computers to pull the relevant information, or ***source computer initiated***, in which each source computer must be configured to push the relevant information to the server that has been configured as the repository.

Using Network Monitor to Gather Network Data

If you receive reports that a Windows Server 2008 computer is not responding fast enough, you might want to isolate the view of the network traffic that is being sent to or from that server. You may also need to view network traffic to determine if a client application is faulting, or to determine if a malicious user or virus is attempting to access the computer over the network. As of this writing, Windows Server 2008 does not include a built-in network monitor, but you can download and install the latest version of Network Monitor from the Microsoft Web site. This free download will allow you to view network traffic that is being sent to and from the network interface cards on a particular Windows Server 2008 computer. You can view network captures in real-time, or save the information to a file to be analyzed later.

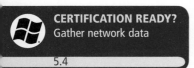

CERTIFICATION READY?
Gather network data

5.4

The version of Network Monitor that can be downloaded from the Microsoft Web site is a powerful tool; however, a more powerful version of the Network Monitor tool is available in Microsoft Systems Management Server and System Center Operations Manager (SCOM). The two main differences between these two versions of Network Monitor are:

- The version of Network Monitor that is built into Windows Server 2008 can capture only traffic sent to or from its own network interface; whereas the enhanced version of Network Monitor runs in ***promiscuous mode***, which means it can capture 100 percent of the network traffic available to the network interface.

- The enhanced version of Network Monitor enables you to see where other instances of Network Monitor are running. This information is useful when you set up multiple monitoring stations across your network and then use a central monitoring point to collect the data. Because sensitive data can be captured and examined using this tool, knowing who uses a version of the tool in promiscuous mode helps to maintain a secure network environment.

When you first launch Network Monitor, you will see the screen shown in Figure 8-9. You can press F10 to begin capturing network traffic, and F11 to end the capture. Figure 8-9 shows a typical network traffic capture, which allows you to browse the contents of individual data packets.

Figure 8-9

Viewing a typical network capture

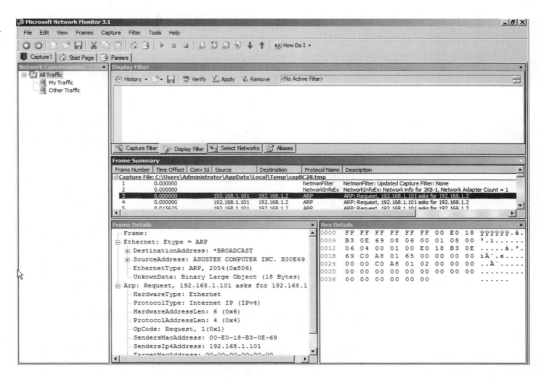

You can configure two types of filters within Network Monitor; there are a number of pre-configured filters, or you can create one or more to meet a specific requirement:

- **Capture Filter**—This will capture only the specific network traffic that you specify
- **Display Filter**—This will display only specific types of traffic, allowing you to view a subset of traffic that was captured

For an example of using Network Monitor to view network traffic, complete the following exercise.

USE NETWORK MONITOR TO GATHER NETWORK DATA

GET READY. This exercise assumes that you are logged onto a Windows Server 2008 computer using administrative credentials.

1. Download and install the latest version of Network Monitor (Network Monitor 3.1 at the time of this writing) from the Microsoft Web site, or use the installation file provided by your instructor.

2. Open the Network Monitor application from the Administrative Tools folder. In the Capture Network Traffic section, place a checkmark next to **Enable conversations (consumes more memory)**. Click **Create a new capture tab....**

3. Click **Capture→Start (F10)** to begin a network capture. To create some sample traffic to view, browse to a resource on your test network or open the Microsoft Web page in Internet Explorer.

4. Click **Capture→Stop (F11)** to stop the network capture.

5. To view only broadcast traffic, click **Filter→Display Filter→Load Filter→Standard Filters→Broadcasts**. Notice that the Display Filter screen changes as shown in Figure 8-10.

Figure 8-10

Viewing display filters

6. Click **Apply Filter** to apply the display filter to the network traffic that you have captured. Browse the results in the Frame Summary and Frame Details sections of the Network Monitor screen.

STOP. Close the Network Monitor application.

■ Configuring Windows Server Update Services (WSUS)

THE BOTTOM LINE

Traditionally, system administrators and users kept systems up-to-date by frequently checking the Microsoft Windows Update Web site or the Microsoft Security Web site for software updates. Administrators manually downloaded available updates, tested the updates in their environment, and then distributed the updates manually or with traditional software distribution tools. In a less favorable scenario, users on a corporate network were left to select, download, and install their own updates. These scenarios resulted in difficult processes for the system administrator and a potentially unreliable, insecure system for the user. To improve the manageability of this process, Microsoft introduced *Windows Server Update Services (WSUS)*, a Web-based tool for managing and distributing software updates that resolve known security vulnerabilities or otherwise improve performance of the Microsoft Windows XP, Windows Vista, Microsoft Windows Server 2003, and Windows Server 2008 operating systems. The latest version of WSUS (WSUS 3.0 with Service Pack 1 at the time of this writing) is a free download from the Microsoft Web site that can be installed on a Windows Server 2008 computer.

CERTIFICATION READY?
Configuring Windows
Server Update Services
(WSUS) server settings
5.1

Updates that can be deployed via WSUS can include security fixes, critical updates, and critical drivers. These updates resolve known security vulnerabilities and stability issues in the Windows XP, Windows Vista, and Windows Server 2003 and Windows Server 2008 operating systems.

The following are categories for the Windows operating system updates:

- Critical updates—Security fixes and other important updates that keep computers current and networks secure. A computer that is missing one or more critical updates should be considered a security risk, unstable, or both.
- Recommended downloads—The latest Windows and Microsoft Internet Explorer service packs and other important updates.
- Windows tools—Utilities and other tools that are provided to enhance performance, facilitate upgrades, and ease the burden on system administrators.
- Internet and multimedia updates—Includes Internet Explorer upgrades and patches, upgrades to Microsoft Windows Media Player, and similar updates.
- Additional Windows downloads—Updates for desktop settings and other Windows operating system features.
- Multilanguage features—Menus and dialog boxes, language support, and Input Method Editors for a variety of languages.
- Documentation—Deployment guides and other software-related documents are also available.

WSUS is a free product that provides a means of aggregating, testing, deploying, and providing notification of updates to client computers in your organization. WSUS can be deployed as a single server or as multiple servers to provide greater testing capabilities and load balancing.

Dynamic notification of updates to Windows client computers does not require that client computers have Internet access. WSUS extends current Microsoft Windows Update technologies and provides a solution to the previously discussed problem of managing and distributing critical Windows updates.

The WSUS solution comprises the following components:

- A content synchronization service — A server-side component on your organization's intranet that retrieves the latest critical updates from the Windows Update Web site. As new updates are added to Windows Update, the WSUS server automatically downloads and stores them based on an administrator-defined schedule, or the administrator can manually download them.

- An internal Windows Update server — This user-friendly server acts as the virtual Windows Update server for client computers. It contains the synchronization service and administrative tools for managing updates. It uses Hypertext Transfer Protocol (HTTP) to service requests for approved updates by the client computers that are connected to it. This server can also host critical updates (an example of a critical update is a security patch necessary to close a known vulnerability in the operating system) downloaded from the synchronization service and refer client computers to those updates.

- Automatic Updates on computers (desktops or servers) — A Windows feature that can be set up to automatically check for updates that are published on Windows Update or a WSUS server. WSUS uses this Windows feature to publish administrator-approved updates on an intranet. You can configure the Windows operating system to install updates on a schedule.

Administrators can test and approve updates from the public Windows Update site before deploying them on the corporate intranet. Deployment of these updates can take place as updates become available, or on a schedule that the administrator creates. If multiple servers run WSUS, the administrator controls which clients access particular servers that run WSUS. Administrators enable this level of control through Group Policy settings on computers that reside in an Active Directory environment, or by configuring individual registry keys on standalone computers.

WSUS is designed to quickly deliver critical updates for computers that run Windows 2000 and later operating systems inside your corporate firewall. It is not intended to serve as a replacement to your enterprise software-distribution solution, such as Microsoft Systems Management Server (SMS), System Center Configuration Manager (SCCM), or Group Policy–based software distribution. Many customers today use solutions such as SMS for complete software management, including responding to security and virus issues. SMS customers should continue using these solutions. In addition to providing administrative controls that are critical for medium-sized and large organizations, advanced solutions such as SMS provide the capability to deploy all software throughout an enterprise. WSUS is a focused solution; organizations that do not already have patch management solutions in place but that desire to more closely manage the update process should use this solution.

Understanding Windows Update and Automatic Updates

Windows Update and Automatic Updates are two separate components designed to work together to keep Windows operating systems updated and secure. The following sections discuss each of these components.

Windows Update is a Microsoft Web site that works with Automatic Updates to provide timely, critical, and noncritical system updates. Updates include security patches, updated drivers, and other recommended files. Windows Update scans your system to determine which updates your system is missing and provides a list of available downloads. Windows Update also maintains a history of the files you have downloaded.

In addition to downloads for your own system, the *Windows Update Catalog* provides updates for other systems that you may administer. Windows Update Catalog is a Web site that lists hardware and software designed for use with Windows Vista, Windows XP, Microsoft Windows 2000 Server products, and products in the Windows Server 2003 and Windows Server 2008 family. You can use this site to help you decide whether to purchase a particular

TAKE NOTE *

Although using Windows Update and Windows Update Catalog is helpful, it is still a manual process that does not scale well to hundreds or thousands of computers.

device or program and to evaluate whether a particular computer would support an upgraded operating system, as well as to help you make similar decisions about hardware and software.

Automatic Updates enables you to obtain critical software updates by automatically interacting with the Windows Update Web site. Automatic Updates can inform you when Windows updates are available and enable you to specify how and when you want to update Windows operating systems. These updates can include everything from critical updates to enhancements. Automatic Updates includes a range of options for how to update Windows operating systems. For example, you can set Windows to automatically download and install updates on a schedule that you specify. Or you can choose to have Windows notify you whenever it finds updates available for your computer. Windows can then download the update using the Background Intelligent Transfer Service (BITS) while you continue to work uninterrupted. After the download is complete, a balloon message and an icon appear in the notification area to alert you that the updates are ready to be installed. When you click the icon or message, Automatic Updates quickly guides you through the installation process. Depending on the type of update and the configuration of your system, you might have to restart your computer after certain components are installed.

Installing a Windows Server Update Services (WSUS) Server

Automatic Updates has been enhanced to support WSUS. This enhancement adds the following features when used in conjunction with a WSUS server:

- Approved content download from a WSUS server
- Scheduled content download and installation
- The ability to configure all Automatic Updates options by using Group Policy Object Editor or by editing the registry
- Support for systems without a local administrator logged on

In prior versions of WSUS, all administration of the service took place through an administrative Web site; in WSUS 3.0 and later, this administration now takes place through an MMC snap-in installed on the WSUS server or on a remote computer. This allows for significantly improved management functionality, including the ability to sort on various configuration elements, create custom views of the WSUS infrastructure, and to use the right-click menu to perform administrative tasks. WSUS 3.0 and later also includes improved reporting capabilities, as well as improved logging to the Windows Event Viewer.

WSUS has three main components:

- Windows Update Synchronization Service, which downloads content to your server that runs SUS
- A Web site hosted on a IIS server that services update requests from Automatic Updates clients
- A WSUS MMC Administration console

WSUS 3.0 and later has the following software and hardware requirements:

- A server running the Internet Information Service (IIS) server role, including the following components:
  - Windows Authentication
  - ASP.NET
  - 6.0 Management Compatibility
  - IIS Metabase Compatibility
- Microsoft Report Viewer Redistributable 2005
- Microsoft SQL Server 2005 Service Pack 1

- A minimum of 1 GB of free space on the system partition
- 20GB minimum free space on the volume used to store WSUS downloaded content
- 2GB free space on the volume where WSUS stores the Windows Internal Database

The WSUS server performs two primary functions:

- Synchronizing content with the public Windows Update site
- Approving content for distribution to your organization

Both functions are performed using the WSUS Administration MMC console. Synchronization can be scheduled or executed immediately. When packages have been downloaded, the system administrator selects packages to release to clients and clicks Approve. Clients are configured to use specific WSUS distribution points to retrieve approved packages.

 INSTALL A WINDOWS SERVER UPDATE SERVICES (WSUS) SERVER

GET READY. To perform this exercise, you must have the WSUS installation software available as well as the installation file for the Microsoft Report Viewer 2005 Redistributable package. You must also be logged onto the Windows Server 2008 computer with administrative privileges.

1. Open the Server Manager console. Drill down to **Roles**, then click **Add Roles**. Click **Next** to bypass the initial Welcome screen.
2. Place a checkmark next to **Web Server (IIS)** as shown in Figure 8-11. When prompted, click **Add Required Features**.

Figure 8-11

Adding the Web Server role

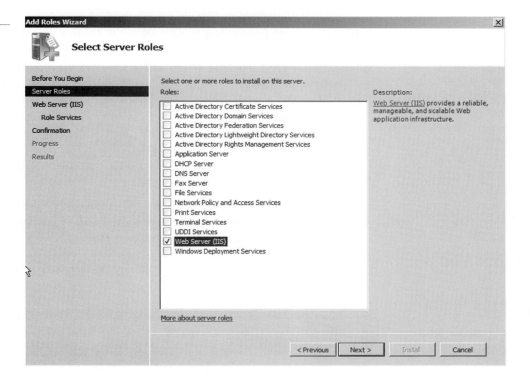

3. On the Select Role Services screen, place a checkmark next to **ASP.NET, Windows Authentication,** and **IIS 6 Metabase Compatibility;** click **Add Required Features** again when prompted.
4. Click **Next** twice, and then click **Install.** Click **Close** when the IIS installation completes.
5. Drill down to **Features,** then click **Add Features.** Place a checkmark next to **Windows Internal Database.** Click **Yes** to confirm. Click **Yes** and then **Install.** Click **Close** when the Windows Internal Database installation completes.

6. Double-click the **Microsoft Report Viewer 2005 Redistributable installation file** that you downloaded from the Microsoft Web site or that was provided by your instructor. Follow the installation prompts to install the Report Viewer.

7. Double-click the **WSUS installation file** that you downloaded from the Microsoft Web site or that was provided by your instructor.

8. Click **Next** to bypass the initial Welcome screen.

9. The Installation Mode screen appears. Select the **Full server installation including Administration Console** radio button. Click **Next**.

10. On the License Agreement screen, click **I accept the terms of the License agreement** and click **Next**.

11. On the Select Update Source screen shown, accept the default value of **Synchronize from Microsoft Update** and then click **Next**.

12. On the Database Options screen, accept the default values and then click **Next** twice.

13. On the Web Site Selection screen, accept the default values and then click **Next** twice.

14. Click **Finish** to install the WSUS files. The Windows Server Update Services Configuration Wizard appears. Click **Next** twice to bypass the initial Welcome screens.

15. The Choose Upstream Server screen appears. Ensure that the **Synchronize from Microsoft Updates** radio button is selected and then click **Next**.

16. The Specify Proxy Server screen appears. Enter any proxy information that is appropriate to your specific environment, if necessary, and then click **Next**.

17. Click **Start Connecting** to save your synchronization settings. Click **Next** again when the settings have saved. This may take several minutes.

18. The Choose Languages screen appears. Select the **Download updates only in these languages:** radio button, and place a checkmark next to the appropriate language for your region. Click **Next** to continue.

19. The Choose Products screen appears. To save disk space and synchronization time, de-select the **Windows** and **Office** checkboxes, and place a checkmark next to **Windows Server 2003**. Click **Next**.

20. The Choose Classifications screen appears. Accept the default values and click **Next**.

21. The Set Sync Schedule screen appears. Accept the default values and click **Next**.

22. The Finished screen appears. Remove the checkmark next to **Begin initial synchronization** and click **Next**, and then **Finish**.

After a pause, the Update Services MMC console appears, as shown in Figure 8-12.

Figure 8-12

Viewing the Update Services MMC Snap-In

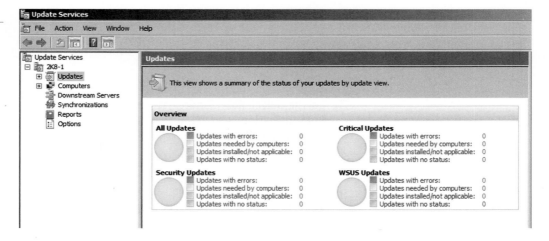

CLOSE. You have now installed the WSUS server software and performed an initial synchronization from the Windows Update server.

CONFIGURING WSUS DISTRIBUTION POINTS

A server that runs WSUS can be synchronized from the public Windows Update servers, from another server running WSUS, or from a manually configured content distribution point. WSUS servers can download and store content locally, or they can use the content on the Windows Update Web site.

In Figure 8-13, Server A and Server B both run WSUS. Server A synchronizes content over the Internet from the public Windows Update servers. Server A is a parent server; that is, a server configured to store content locally. Server B is also configured to store content locally; however, rather than synchronizing with the Windows Update site, it is configured to synchronize content from Server A. Server B is therefore a child server of Server A.

Figure 8-13

Viewing a distributed WSUS infrastructure

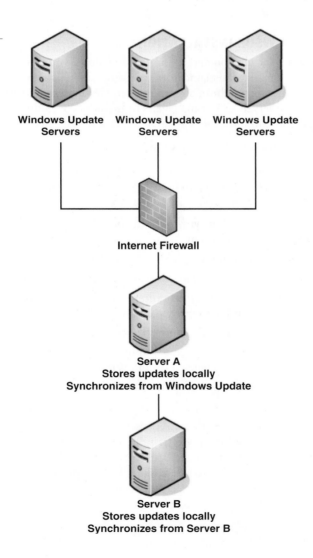

Windows Update Servers   Windows Update Servers   Windows Update Servers

Internet Firewall

Server A
Stores updates locally
Synchronizes from Windows Update

Server B
Stores updates locally
Synchronizes from Server B

Synchronizing from another server that runs WSUS, or a manually configured content distribution point, is useful in the following scenarios:

- You have multiple servers running WSUS in your organization and you do not want all of the servers to access the Internet to synchronize content.
- You have sites that do not have Internet access.
- You want to have the ability to test content in a test environment and push the content to your production environment.
- You want to provide redundancy in case of server failure.

When you install WSUS, a content distribution point is automatically created on that server. When you synchronize the server, its content is updated from the Windows Update download servers. The content distribution point is a virtual directory in IIS named Content. A virtual directory is a friendly name, or alias, either for a physical directory on your server hard drive that does not reside in the home directory or for the home directory on another computer. Because an alias is usually shorter than the path of the physical directory, it is more convenient for users to type. Downloaded content is stored in the physical location that is specified in the virtual directory (by default, C:/WSUS/WSUSContent) unless you choose to maintain content on *Microsoft.com*; in this case, the content distribution point is empty.

MANAGING A WSUS INSTALLATION

After completing installation and the initial download, you must manage both the server and the client. Server management includes reviewing and changing configuration options, automatically or manually synchronizing the server, viewing the update status, and backing up and restoring the server. Client management includes controlling download and installation behavior and configuration for Active Directory and non–Active Directory environments.

The five main administrative tasks for WSUS are these:

- Initial server configuration and post-installation
- Synchronization (manual and automatic) of content between the public Windows Update service and the server that runs WSUS
- Selection and approval of synchronized content to be published to computers that run the Automatic Updates client
- Backing up and restoring the WSUS server
- Monitoring server status and logs Initial server configuration options include the following:
    - Choice of whether the update files are hosted on the Internet Windows Update service or locally on your server that runs WSUS.
    - Proxy server information for the server to access the Internet.
    - Options for handling previously approved content. This is important if previously approved content is changed on the Windows Update service.
    - The list of client languages you would like to support.

One of the chief purposes of deploying a WSUS server is to control which updates clients receive and when they receive them. As described earlier, part of this distribution process approves each update. Although you can configure SUS to automatically approve every update that is downloaded from the Windows Update Web site, this is not recommended. The recommended practice is to test updates before approving and distributing them throughout your organization. In fact, the recommended best practice for deploying software updates includes the following four phases:

1. Assess how many servers and clients will require updating by the WSUS process, and what kind of WSUS infrastructure is needed to support this update process.
2. Identify the updates that are available, and determine which of the available updates are applicable to your environment.

3. Evaluate and plan to test updates in a controlled environment before releasing them to your entire client base en masse.

4. Deploy updates after you have tested them, by approving and scheduling the updates, and to then review the process after the deployment is complete.

In the following exercise, you will synchronize a WSUS server with the Windows Update Web site, create different groups of target computers, and approve and decline various updates to learn how to use the WSUS management interface.

➔ MANAGE A WSUS INSTALLATION

GET READY. This exercise assumes that you have installed WSUS and performed the WSUS Configuration Wizard as described previously in this section.

1. Log onto the WSUS server using administrative credentials. Launch the Update Services MMC console.

2. Drill down to **Update Services→Server Name>→Synchronizations**.

3. Right-click **Synchronizations** and click **Synchronize Now**. You can watch the progress of the synchronization in the main pane of the Update Services MMC console.

4. To approve or decline updates, navigate to **Update Services→>Server Name>→ Updates→All Updates**.

STOP. You can log off of the Windows Server 2008 computer, or else remain logged on for subsequent exercises.

MANAGING WSUS CLIENTS

To use the WSUS software, client computers must be running the updated Automatic Updates client. A newer version of the Automatic Updates client is necessary for some machines running Windows 2000 and Windows XP to use WSUS. You must install Automatic Updates only on computers running Windows 2000 with Service Pack 2 (or earlier) or Windows XP without Service Pack 1. Computers running Windows Server 2003, Windows Vista, and Windows Server 2008 need not download the newer version.

After you have installed the newer client, if necessary, you must configure Automatic Updates and specify the download behavior. There are several ways to configure Automatic Updates:

- By using a wizard that is automatically displayed 24 hours after Automatic Updates is initially installed.
- By using the Automatic Updates Configuration properties page in the Control Panel. You can also display this page by displaying the System properties.
- By using Group Policy Objects in an Active Directory environment.
- By configuring registry entries.

After you have determined how you will configure Automatic Updates, you can control how updates are downloaded and installed. Specifically, you can choose from the following:

- To be notified before updates are downloaded and again before the downloaded updates are installed
- For updates to be downloaded automatically and for the administrative user to be notified before updates are installed
- For updates to be downloaded automatically and installed based on the specified schedule

TAKE NOTE*

As with any infrastructure server, you should back up the WSUS server using the Windows Server Backup utility. Over time, a large number of updates will be downloaded, tested, approved, or deferred. A system failure that does not have a backup in place results in many lost hours of work.

Automatic Updates downloads updates based on the configuration options that the administrative user selected. It uses the **Background Intelligent Transfer Service (BITS)** to perform the download using idle network bandwidth. If Automatic Updates is configured to notify the user of updates that are ready to install, it checks to see whether a user with administrative privileges is logged on to the computer. If so, the user is notified. If not, the computer defers notification until a user with privileges logs on, so that Automatic Updates displays the available updates to install when a logged-on administrator clicks the balloon or notification area icon. The administrative user must then click the Install button to allow the installation to proceed. If the update requires a restart of the computer to complete the installation, a message is displayed that states that a restart is required. Until the system is restarted, Automatic Updates defers detection of additional updates.

Windows Server 2008 includes Group Policy settings that can be used to configure WSUS settings for Active Directory clients running Windows 2000 Service Pack 3 or later. These settings can be loaded into Group Policy Object Editor for deployment. If you configure clients by using Group Policy, the Group Policy settings override user-defined settings; the ability to configure Automatic Updates options on the client is disabled. The Configure Automatic Updates Group Policy setting (which can be accessed by opening the Group Policy Object Editor in Computer Configuration\Settings\Administrative Templates\Windows Components\Windows Update, then double-clicking Configure Automatic Updates in the details pane) specifies whether this computer receives security updates and other important downloads through Automatic Updates (see Figure 8-14).

When enabled, the Configure Automatic Updates policy also specifies the download and installation behavior, which can be one of the following three options:

- Notify For Download And Notify For Install—This option notifies a logged-on user with administrative privileges before the download and before the update installation.
- Auto Download And Notify For Install—This option automatically begins downloading updates and then notifies a logged-on administrative user before installing the updates.
- Auto Download And Schedule The Install—Typically, if Automatic Updates is configured to perform a scheduled installation, the recurring scheduled installation day and time are also set.

If the Configure Automatic Updates policy is disabled, Automatic Updates does not perform any system updating, and you must go to the Windows Update site to download and manually install any available updates.

When working with Group Policy, you can also configure the *Specify Intranet Microsoft Update Service Location* setting in the Computer Configuration\Policies\Administrative Templates\Windows Components\Windows Update section of the Group Policy Editor. You must set both of the following values to configure this policy setting (see Figure 8-14):

- Set The Intranet Update Service For Detecting Updates
- Set The Intranet Statistics Server

The expected value for each of these settings is a URL (such as http://computer*xx*), and both settings can point to the same server. If you specify a server running WSUS and specify a Web server for collecting statistics, computers running Automatic Updates send success or failure information about the download and installation status to the Web server's log files.

Figure 8-14

Configuring WSUS clients using
Active Directory Group Policy

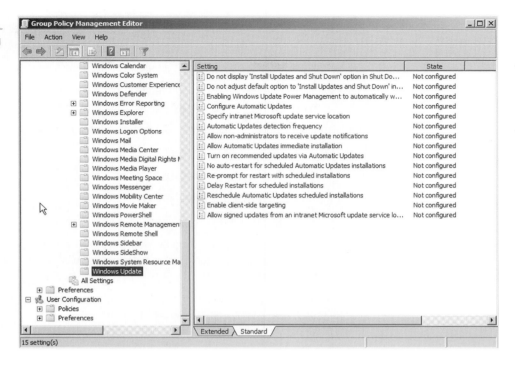

Another option to configure is the *Reschedule Automatic Updates Scheduled Installations GPO*
option. The purpose of this setting is to specify how much time (in minutes) to wait before
proceeding with a previously missed scheduled installation. The waiting period begins after
system startup. For this policy to be effective, the Configure Automatic Updates policy must be
enabled. Additionally, you can configure the *No Auto-Restart For Scheduled Automatic Updates
Installations*, which specifies that to complete a scheduled installation, Automatic Updates waits
for a user to restart the computer rather than causing the computer to restart automatically.
If this policy is set to Enabled, Automatic Updates does not restart a computer automatically,
though, depending on the type of update, you might still be asked to restart the computer.
As mentioned previously, Automatic Updates cannot detect future updates until the restart
occurs. If this policy is Disabled or Not Configured, Automatic Updates notifies the user that
the computer will automatically restart in five minutes to complete the installation. This policy
also requires that the Configure Automatic Updates policy be enabled.

SUMMARY SKILL MATRIX

IN THIS LESSON YOU LEARNED:

- When monitoring the health of Windows Server 2008, you can examine the Window
  Event Viewer to obtain information. By default, it logs informational events, such as service start and stop messages, errors, and warnings. Additional diagnostic logging can be
  achieved by modifying the registry.

- Reliability and Performance Monitor in Windows Server 2008 allows you to collect real-
  time information on your local computer or from a specific computer to which you have
  permissions. This information can be viewed in a number of different formats that include
  charts, graphs, and histograms.

- Reliability and Performance Monitor uses performance objects, or categories, and performance counters to organize performance information. Performance counters are the
  specific processes to monitor. Many counters are available.

- WSUS is a tool used to manage and distribute software updates that fix known security vulnerabilities or otherwise improve the performance of Microsoft operating systems.

- Updates can include items such as security fixes, critical updates, and critical drivers.

- Windows Update is a Microsoft Web site that works with Automatic Updates to provide timely critical and noncritical system updates.

- Automatic Updates enables you to automatically interact with the Windows Update Web site.

- WSUS has three main components:

  - A content synchronization service

  - An internal Windows Update server

  - Automatic Updates on computers (desktops or servers)

- WSUS server management includes reviewing and changing configuration options, automatically or manually synchronizing the server, viewing update status, and backing up and restoring the server.

- You can configure Automatic Updates through the Automatic Updates configuration page, Group Policy, and by configuring registry entries.

■ Knowledge Assessment

Matching

Match the following definitions with the appropriate term.

    a. Administrative Events
    b. Application Log
    c. Background Intelligent Transfer Service (BITS)
    d. Capture Filter
    e. collector initiated
    f. Data Collector Set
    g. Event trace data
    h. Log on as a batch user
    i. perfmon
    j. promiscuous mode

_____ **1.** This controls what types of traffic will be recorded by Network Monitor when you press F10.

_____ **2.** This right must be granted to Performance Log Users to allow them to create and manage Data Collector Sets.

_____ **3.** This custom view in the Event Viewer collects Critical, Error, and Warning events from all logs on a particular server.

_____ **4.** This capture mode enables Network Monitor to listen to all traffic that is being passed on a particular network segment.

_____ **5.** This service is used by WSUS to optimize network traffic while downloading updates.

_____ **6.** This type of forwarded event is initiated by the server acting as the event repository.

_____ **7.** This is the command-line method of launching the Performance Monitor MMC snap-in.

_____ **8.** This log provides a view of events related to software that has been installed on a Windows server computer.

_____ **9.** This is collected to provide a real-time view into the behavior and performance of a server and its applications.

_____**10.** This allows you to organize a set of performance counters, event traces, and system configuration data into a single reusable configuration item.

Multiple Choice

Select all answers that apply for the following questions.

1. This feature will automatically check for software updates that are published on a WSUS server.
   a. Windows Update
   b. Automatic Updates
   c. Windows Catalo
   d. Automatic Patching

2. This view of the Windows Event Viewer allows you to configure a Windows Server 2008 computer to act as a repository for Event Viewer entries from one or more remote computers.
   a. WSUS
   b. Windows Catalog
   c. Network Monitor
   d. Forwarded Events

3. The following user group can view both real-time and historical data within the Performance Monitor console, but cannot create or modify Data Collector Sets:
   a. Performance Monitor Users
   b. Performance Log Users
   c. Power Users
   d. Users

4. In order to collect events from remote computers that match the criteria of one or more event filters that you define, you will create one or more of the following:
   a. Custom View
   b. Subscription
   c. Forwarded Event
   d. Event Viewer

5. What protocol does the Windows Event Viewer use to configure event forwarding?
   a. ARP
   b. RPC over IP
   c. WS-DirectoryServices
   d. WS-Management

6. This is a new Event Log in Windows Server 2008, used to capture information regarding operating system and application installations and un-installations.
   a. Application Log
   b. System Log
   c. Setup Log
   d. Administrative Events

7. The following service allows you to configure a single server as a repository of Event Viewer information for multiple computers:
   a. Windows Server Update Service
   b. Windows Event Collector Service
   c. Windows Event Viewer
   d. Windows Event Forwarder

8. The following allows you to display only those packets matching a particular set of criterion among a larger set of packets that have been captured by Network Monitor:
   a. Capture Filter
   b. Event Filter
   c. Custom View
   d. Display Filter

9. The following user group can view both real-time and historical data within the Performance Monitor console, and can also create and modify Data Collector Sets:
   a. Performance Monitor Users
   b. Performance Log Users
   c. Power Users
   d. Users

10. The following is a server-side component within WSUS that retrieves the latest critical updates from the Windows Update Web site:
   a. Content Synchronization Service
   b. Microsoft Update
   c. Performance Monitor
   d. Event Forwarder

■ Case Scenarios

Scenario 8-1: Using Network Monitor

You have recently taken over the administration of a small Windows Server 2008 network. Your predecessor did not leave any documentation concerning the software and services that are in use on the network, so you decide to use Network Monitor to determine what kind of network traffic is being passed to and from a particular Windows Server 2008 server. Using the built-in capture and display filters in Network Monitor, name five of the filters that you can apply and provide the command used to create each of them.

Scenario 8-2: Stage and Test WSUS Updates

You are deploying WSUS in your organization. Several workstations in your organization run a non-Microsoft application that was negatively impacted in the past after downloading certain updates. As a result, many of the users of that application have disabled the update feature and are reluctant to participate in the SUS server deployment. How should you design your deployment plan so that you can stage and test updates before distributing them to the rest of the organization?

Securing Data Transmission and Authentication

OBJECTIVE DOMAIN MATRIX

TECHNOLOGY SKILL	OBJECTIVE DOMAIN	OBJECTIVE DOMAIN NUMBER
Securing Network Traffic with IPSec	Configure IPSec	1.4
Configuring Network Authentication	Configure network authentication	3.3
Configuring the Windows Firewall	Configure firewall settings	3.5

KEY TERMS

Authentication exemption
Authentication Header
   (AH)
authentication method
checksum
Connection Security Rules
cookie
default response rule
dynamic rekeying

Encapsulating Security Payload
   (ESP)
exceptions
identity spoofing
IPSec
Isolation
LM Authentication
mirrored
NTLM Authentication

NTLMv2 Authentication
packet sniffer
quick mode negotiation
Server-to-server
scopes
transport mode
Tunnel
tunnel mode

Contoso Pharmaceuticals Ltd. is a medical research company with offices in Chicago, Illinois; New York, New York; and Perth, Australia. Because of the sensitive nature of the data being transmitted by the Contoso research department, management has expressed a concern that information must be protected against any kind of computer-based eavesdropping as research data is shared between offices. In order to protect this sensitive data, the Contoso IT department has been charged with creating a plan to protect network data transmissions.

In this lesson, we will discuss the technologies available in Windows Server 2008 to secure the transmission of network traffic. We will begin with an overview of Internet Protocol Security (IPSec), which can be used to provide authentication and/or encryption of traffic being sent over a Windows network. We will then discuss the use of the Windows Firewall to control inbound and outbound traffic.

■ Securing Network Traffic with IPSec

THE BOTTOM LINE

Whether you have a public presence on the Internet or maintain a private network, securing your data is a core requirement. Much attention is placed on perimeter security and preventing attacks from outside the network. Much less attention is focused on attacks within the network, where an attack is more likely to occur. A solid security strategy employs many layers of coordinated security. Organizations deploy measures to secure the network perimeter and secure access to resources by instituting authentication and access control; however, securing the actual Internet Protocol (IP) packets and their contents is often overlooked. This section focuses on securing IP traffic by using IPSec. We discuss the purpose and features of IPSec, how to define and deploy IPSec policies, and we introduce how to implement IPSec using certificates. After we explain the purpose of IPSec and how to deploy it, we then explain how to manage and monitor IPSec using tools such as the Resultant Set of Policy (RSoP) wizard, Event Viewer, and netsh.

CERTIFICATION READY?
Configure IPSec

1.4

Within the TCP/IP protocol suite, recall that the two transport layer protocols are the Transmission Control Protocol (TCP) and the User Datagram Protocol (UDP). Both TCP and UDP contain a *checksum* in the header of each packet, that is, a mathematical value that is used to provide an integrity check for the packet in question. If the data is corrupted while in transit, this checksum will alert the receiver of the problem and the packet will be dropped by the receiving computer. However, because this checksum algorithm is well known, a malicious user can intercept an IP packet, view and modify its contents, recompute the checksums, and then forward the packet to its destination without the knowledge of either the receiver or sender. Because of the limited functionality of the TCP and UDP checksums, the destination node is not aware and cannot detect that the packet was modified.

Historically, network applications that required security were forced to provide it for themselves, leading to a variety of autonomous and incompatible security standards that decreased the ability of hosts from different organizations to communicate with one another. To address this, the *IPSec* suite of protocols was introduced to provide a series of cryptographic algorithms that can be used to provide security for all TCP/IP hosts at the Internet layer, regardless of the actual application that is sending or receiving data. With IPSec, a single security standard can be used across multiple heterogeneous networks, and individual applications need not be modified to use it.

IPSec has two principle goals:

- To protect the contents of IP packets
- To provide a defense against network attacks through packet filtering and the enforcement of trusted communication

Both goals are met through the use of cryptography-based protection services, security protocols, and dynamic key management. This foundation provides both the strength and flexibility to protect communications between private network computers, domains, sites (including remote sites), extranets, and dial-up clients. It can even be used to block receipt or transmission of specific traffic types.

IPSec has a number of features that can significantly reduce or prevent the following attacks:

- *Packet sniffing*—A packet sniffing attack is one in which an application or device (called a **packet sniffer**) monitors and reads network packets as they traverse a wired or wireless network. If the packets being sniffed are not encrypted, that is, if they are being transmitted as clear-text, a packet sniffer can provide a full view of the data contents or *payload* that is

contained inside the packet, thus compromising the confidentiality of the data. (Network Monitor, discussed in the previous lesson, is an example of a packet sniffer.) IPSec includes mechanisms that provide data confidentiality by encrypting the payload of IP packets.

- *Data modification*—An attacker can modify a network packet that is in transit over a network and send counterfeit data, which might prevent the receiver from receiving the correct information or might allow the attacker to obtain additional, possibly secure, information. IPSec uses cryptography-based keys that are shared only by the sending and receiving computers to create a *cryptographic checksum* for each IP packet that is secured using IPSec to protect the integrity of the data. Any modification to the packet data alters this checksum, which indicates to the receiving computer that the packet was modified in transit.

- **Identity spoofing** — An attacker can falsify or "spoof" the identity of either the sending or receiving computer by using special programs to construct IP packets that appear to originate from valid addresses inside of a trusted network. IPSec allows the exchange and verification of identities without exposing that information to interpretation by an attacker. This process, called *mutual authentication,* is used to establish trust between the communicating systems, after which only trusted systems can communicate with each other. After identities are established, IPSec uses cryptography-based keys, shared only by the sending and receiving computers, to create a cryptographic checksum for each IP packet. The cryptographic checksum ensures that only the computers that have knowledge of the keys can send each packet.

- *Man-in-the-middle attacks*—In this type of attack, someone between the two communicating computers is actively monitoring, capturing, and controlling the data transparently (for example, the attacker might be intercepting data between a sending and receiving computer to steal information, potentially by sending a copy of each packet to another server that is controlled by the attacker). IPSec protects against man-in-the-middle-attacks through a combination of mutual authentication and the use of shared cryptography-based keys to confirm the integrity of each packet as well as the identity of the sending and receiving computers.

- *Denial of service attacks (DoS)*—This type of attack prevents the normal use of computers or network resources. Flooding e-mail accounts with unsolicited messages is an example of a DoS attack. IPSec uses IP packet filtering methodology as the basis for determining whether communication is allowed, secured, or blocked. This determination is based on the IP address ranges, IP protocols, or even specific TCP and UDP ports.

Understanding IPSec

Before we can discuss how IPSec works and review the steps for IPSec configuration, you must understand some of the features, terminology, and components of the IPSec framework. IPSec is an architectural framework that provides cryptographic security services for IP packets. IPSec is an *end-to-end* security technology. This means that the only nodes aware of the presence of IPSec are the two hosts using IPSec that communicate with each other. Intermediate routers have neither knowledge of the security relationship nor any "need to know," and they forward the IP packets as they would any others. Each computer handles security at its respective end with the assumption that the medium over which the communication takes place is not secure.

IPSec can be deployed to protect data transmissions in the following scenarios:

- Local Area Network (LAN)—Client/server and peer-to-peer LANs
- Wide area network (WAN)—Router-to-router and gateway-to-gateway WANs
- Remote access—Dial-up clients and Internet access from private networks

Typically, both sides require a shared IPSec configuration, which is called an *IPSec policy,* to establish security settings that will allow two systems to agree on how to transmit secured traffic between them. The Microsoft Windows 2000, Windows XP, Windows Vista, Windows Server 2003, and Windows Server 2008 implementations of IPSec are based on industry standards developed by the Internet Engineering Task Force (IETF) IPSec working group.

IPSec has many security features designed to meet the goals of protecting IP packets and defend against attacks through filtering and trusted communication. Some of these security features include the following:

- Automatic security associations—IPSec uses the *Internet Security Association and Key Management Protocol (ISAKMP)* protocol to dynamically negotiate a mutual set of security requirements between two hosts that are attempting to communicate with each other. These two hosts do not require identical policies; they require only a policy that is configured with sufficient negotiation options to establish a common set of requirements, called a *security association,* to allow for communication. (We will discuss security associations in more detail in a subsequent section.)

- IP packet filtering—This filtering process allows or blocks communications specifying source or destination addresses, address ranges, protocols, or even specific TCP or UDP ports. For example, you could configure an IPSec packet filter to allow only inbound traffic to a particular destination computer on TCP port 25, or allow only outbound traffic from a range of source computers if that traffic is sent to a particular destination.

- Network layer security—IPSec exists at the Network Layer of the OSI, providing automatic, transparent security for all applications residing at the higher Transport, Session, Presentation, and Application layers.

- Peer authentication—IPSec verifies the identity of the peer computer before any data is sent. IPSec peer authentication for Windows Server 2008 can be based on pre-shared keys, public keys (such as X.509 certificates), or the Kerberos protocol when integrated with Active Directory.

- Data origin authentication—Data origin authentication prevents a malicious user from intercepting packets and posing as the sender, using the identity spoofing attack discussed earlier. Each TCP/IP packet protected with IPSec contains a cryptographic checksum in the form of a keyed hash. The cryptographic checksum is also known as an *Integrity Check Value (ICV)* or *hash-based message authentication code (HMAC)*. A *hash* is a one-way cryptographic algorithm that takes an input message of arbitrary length and produces a fixed-length digest. A *keyed hash* includes the secret key in its calculation. The cryptographic checksum ensures that only a computer with knowledge of the shared secret key sent the packet. A malicious user masquerading as the sender cannot calculate a correct cryptographic checksum, and if the cryptographic checksum fails, the receiving peer discards the packet.

- Data integrity—By including the cryptographic checksum, IPSec protects the data transfer process from unauthorized, undetected modification during transit, ensuring that the information that is received is the same as the information that was sent. A malicious user who modifies the packet contents must also properly update the cryptographic checksum, which is virtually impossible without knowledge of the shared key.

- Data confidentiality—Even if an IPSec-encrypted packet is intercepted and viewed, the interceptor can view only the encrypted data. Without knowledge of the secret key used to encrypt the data, the original data remains hidden. Because the secret key is shared between the sender and the receiver, data confidentiality ensures that the data can be decrypted and disclosed only by the intended receiver.

- Anti-replay—By using a sequence number on each protected packet sent between IPSec peers, a data exchange between IPSec peers is protected against *replay,* in which network traffic is captured by a packet sniffer and then re-inserted onto the network at a later time to establish a security relationship or gain unauthorized access to information or resources.

- Key management—Data origin authentication, data integrity, and data confidentiality depend on the shared knowledge of a secret key. If the key is compromised, the communication is no longer secure. To keep malicious users from determining the key through any method except brute force (trying all possible key combinations until the key is discovered), IPSec provides a secure way to exchange key information to derive a secret shared key and to periodically change the keys used for secure communications.

TAKE NOTE *

Windows computers must be a member of an Active Directory domain to authenticate using Kerberos.

You can configure IPSec to use one of two modes: transport mode or tunnel mode:

- ***Transport mode***—Use transport mode when you require packet filtering and when you require end-to-end security. Both hosts must support IPSec using the same authentication protocols and must have compatible IPSec filters.

- ***Tunnel mode***—Use tunnel mode for site-to-site communications that cross the Internet (or other public networks). Tunnel mode provides gateway-to-gateway protection.

The IPSec protocol suite provides security using a combination of individual protocols, including the *Authentication Header (AH)* protocol and the *Encapsulating Security Payload (ESP)* protocol. These protocols work independently or in tandem, depending on the need for confidentiality and authentication:

- The ***Authentication Header (AH)*** protocol provides authentication, integrity, and anti-replay for the entire packet (both the IP header and the data payload carried in the packet). It does not provide confidentiality, which means that it does not encrypt the data. The data is readable, but protected from modification. AH uses keyed hash algorithms to sign the packet for integrity.

- The ***Encapsulating Security Payload (ESP)*** protocol provides confidentiality (in addition to authentication, integrity, and anti-replay) for the IP payload. ESP in transport mode does not sign the entire packet; only the IP payload (not the IP header) is protected. ESP can be used alone or in combination with AH. For example, when used in combination with AH, the IP payload sent from COMPUTERA to COMPUTERB is encrypted and signed for integrity. Upon receipt, after the integrity verification process is complete, the data payload in the packet is decrypted. The receiver can be certain of who sent the data, that the data is unmodified, and that no one else was able to read it.

To further control the behavior of IPSec, Windows Server 2008 supports a number of different encryption algorithms and integrity algorithms that can be implemented to allow interoperability with different types of networked computers. Table 9-1 lists the available encryption and integrity algorithms, and the characteristics of each one:

Table 9-1

Encryption and Integrity Algorithms in Windows Server 2008 IPSec

ALGORITHM	USED FOR (ENCRYPTION OR INTEGRITY)	CHARACTERISTICS
AES-256	Encryption	Offers the strongest level of security with the highest resource usage on the host. Compatible only with Windows Vista and Windows Server 2008.
AES-192	Encryption	Somewhat less secure than AES-256, medium resource usage on the host. Compatible only with Windows Vista and Windows Server 2008.
AES-128	Encryption	Default IPSec encryption algorithm in Windows Server 2008. Compatible only with Windows Vista and Windows Server 2008.
3DES	Encryption	Used for backward compatibility while still providing an acceptable level of encryption.
DES	Encryption	Used for backward compatibility only; its use is not recommended.
SHA1	Integrity	Stronger choice of integrity algorithm, higher resource usage on the host.
MD5	Integrity	Used for backward compatibility only; its use is not recommended.

UNDERSTANDING IPSEC SECURITY ASSOCIATIONS (SAS)

A security association (SA) is the combination of security services, protection mechanisms, and cryptographic keys mutually agreed to by communicating peers. The SA contains the information needed to determine how the traffic is to be secured (the security services and protection mechanisms) and with which secret keys (cryptographic keys). Two types of SAs are created when IPSec peers communicate securely: the *ISAKMP SA* and the *IPSec SA*.

The ISAKMP SA, also known as the *main mode SA*, is used to protect IPSec security negotiations. The ISAKMP SA is created by negotiating the *cipher suite* (a collection of cryptographic algorithms used to encrypt data) used for protecting future ISAKMP traffic, exchanging key generation material, and then identifying and authenticating each IPSec peer. When the ISAKMP SA is complete, all future SA negotiations for both types of SAs are protected. This is an aspect of secure communications known as *protected cipher suite negotiation*. Not only is the data protected, but the determination of the protection algorithms negotiated by the IPSec peers is also protected. To break IPSec protection, a malicious user must first determine the cipher suite protecting the data, which represents another barrier. For IPSec, the only exception to complete protected cipher suite negotiation is the negotiation of the cipher suite of the initial ISAKMP SA, which is sent as plaintext.

The IPSec SA, also known as the *quick mode SA*, is used to protect data sent between the IPSec peers. The IPSec SA cipher suite negotiation is protected by the ISAKMP SA, so that no information about the type of traffic or the protection mechanisms is sent as plaintext. For a pair of IPSec peers, two IPSec SAs always exist for each protocol in use: one that is negotiated for inbound traffic, and one for outbound traffic. The inbound SA for one IPSec peer is the outbound SA for the other.

For each IPSec session that is established between two hosts, the IPSec peers must track the usage of three different SAs:

- the ISAKMP SA
- the inbound IPSec SA
- the outbound IPSec SA

To identify a specific SA for tracking purposes, a 32-bit number known as the *Security Parameters Index (SPI)* is used. The SPI, which is stored as a field in the IPSec headers, indicates which SA the destination should use, and is sent with every packet. The responder is responsible for providing a unique SPI for each protocol.

UNDERSTANDING THE INTERNET KEY EXCHANGE (IKE)

The *Internet Key Exchange (IKE)* is a standard that defines a mechanism to establish SAs. IKE combines ISAKMP and the *Oakley Key Determination Protocol,* a protocol that is based on the *Diffie-Hellman key exchange algorithm,* to generate secret key material. The Diffie-Hellman key exchange algorithm allows two peers to determine a secret key by exchanging unencrypted values over a public network. In order to perform this task, the Diffie-Hellman key exchange process derives a secret key known only to the two peers by exchanging two numbers over a public network. A malicious user who intercepts the key exchange packets can view the numbers, but cannot perform the same calculation as the negotiating peers in order to derive the shared secret key.

The Diffie-Hellman key exchange process does not prevent a man-in-the-middle attack, in which a malicious user between the negotiating peers performs two Diffie-Hellman exchanges, one with each peer. When both exchanges are complete, the malicious user has the secret keys to communicate with both peers. To prevent such an attack, Windows Server

TAKE NOTE*

The node that initiates an IPSec session is known as the *initiator*. The node that responds to a request to perform IPSec protection is known as the *responder*. The initiator chooses the ISAKMP SA SPI, and each IPSec peer chooses the IPSec SA SPIs for its outbound traffic.

2008 IPSec performs an immediate authentication after the Diffie-Hellman key exchange is complete. If the IPSec peer cannot perform a valid authentication, the security negotiation is abandoned before any data is sent.

Windows Server 2008 IPSec also supports ***dynamic rekeying,*** which is the determination of new keying material through a new Diffie-Hellman exchange on a regular basis. Dynamic rekeying is based on an elapsed time, 480 minutes or 8 hours by default, or the number of data sessions created with the same set of keying material (by default, this number is unlimited).

For more information about the IKE negotiation process, see RFC 2409, "The Internet Key Exchange (IKE)," at *http://www.ietf.org.*

Understanding IPSec Policies

IPSec policies are the security rules that define the desired security level, hashing algorithm, encryption algorithm, and key length. These rules also define the addresses, protocols, DNS names, subnets, or connection types to which these security settings will apply. IPSec policies can be configured to meet the security requirements of a user, group, application, domain, site, or for an entire enterprise network. Windows Server 2008 has integrated management of IPSec into the Windows Firewall with Advanced Security MMC snap-in.

To better understand the capabilities of a policy, you must also understand the components of a policy. The components of an IPSec policy are as follows:

- *Tunnel setting*—The IP address of the tunnel endpoint (if you are configuring IPSec tunneling to protect the packet destination).
- *Network type*—The type of connection affected by the IPSec policy: all network connections, LAN, or remote access.
- *IP filter*—A subset of network traffic based on IP address, port, and transport protocol. It informs IPSec which outbound and inbound traffic should be secured. An IP Filter can be ***mirrored,*** meaning that traffic that is defined in one direction will also be defined in the opposite direction. For example, a mirrored IP filter might include both inbound and outbound traffic on TCP port 80 for a particular host. An IP filter consists of the following components:
  a. Source address—The source address that this filter defines. This can be configured as one of the following:
      i. My IP Address
      ii. Any IP Address
      iii. A Specific DNS Name
      iv. A Specific IP Address or Subnet
      v. DNS Servers (all configured DNS servers for a particular host)
      vi. WINS Servers (all configured WINS servers for a particular host)
      vii. DHCP Server (the DHCP server that a particular host obtained its IP address from
      viii. Default Gateway (the default gateway configured on a particular host)
  b. Destination address—The destination address that this filter defines. This can be configured using the same choices as the Source address: selection.
  c. IP Protocol Type—The transport layer protocol that this filter defines. This can be configured as any one of the following:
      i. Any
      ii. EGP
      iii. HMP

iv. ICMP

v. Other

vi. RAW

vii. RDP

viii. RVD

ix. TCP

x. UDP

xi. XNS-IDP

d. IP Protocol Port—If TCP or UDP is the selected IP Protocol Type, this indicates the TCP or UDP port number that the IP Filter applies to. This can be configured as any one of the following:

i. From Any Port—Specifies all ports as a source TCP or UDP port.

ii. From A Specific Port—Specifies a single TCP or UDP source port.

iii. To Any Port—Specifies all ports as a destination TCP or UDP port.

iv. To A Specific Port—Specifies a single TCP or UDP destination port.

• *IP filter list*—The concatenation of one or more IP filters, which define a range of network traffic.

• *Filter action*—How IPSec should secure network traffic. Predefined filter actions include the following: Permit, Request Security (Optional), and Require Security.

• ***Authentication method***—One of the security algorithms and types used for authentication and key exchange, as shown in Figure 9-1:

Figure 9-1

Viewing IPSec authentication methods

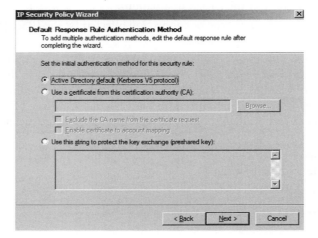

a. *Kerberos v5 protocol*—This is the default authentication method used by IPSec policies deployed within an Active Directory domain; this authentication method can *only* be used in an Active Directory environment.

b. *PKI Certificate from a Certification Authority (CA)*—This authentication method uses PKI certificates from a trusted Certification Authority, which provides the ability to deploy IPSec securely in a non-Active Directory environment. When using this authentication method, you can include one or both of the following optional settings:

i. Exclude the CA name from the certificate request—You can use this setting to increase the security of PKI certificate requests so that they do not expose information about your internal CAs on a public network.

ii. Enable certificate to account mapping—This allows IPSec to map a computer's PKI certificate to a computer account within Active Directory; for example, use this to perform certificate to account mapping for a workgroup-joined computer that needs to secure communications with computers in a remote Active Directory domain.

c. Pre-shared key—This is the least secure authentication method for IPSec; it uses a pre-configured text string to secure communications between hosts. This authentication method should only be used if no other alternative exists.

CREATING IPSEC POLICIES

In previous versions of Windows Server (Windows 2000 Server and Windows Server 2003), IPSec policies were created and maintained using the IP Security Policy MMC snap-in. This snap-in is still present in Windows Server 2008 to allow you to create IPSec policies that can be applied to Windows 2000, Windows XP, and Windows Server 2003 computers. If you are supporting Windows Server 2008 and Windows Vista computers exclusively, however, you can use the new Windows Firewall with Advanced Security MMC snap-in to create and manage IPSec Policies, which are now called *Connection Security Rules*.

WARNING Previous versions of Windows supported a *default response rule* in IPSec, which was activated by default for all policies. This rule was used to ensure that the computer responds to requests for secure communication. If an active policy did not have a rule defined for a computer that requests secure communication, the default response rule was applied and security was negotiated. For example, when COMPUTERA communicated securely with COMPUTERB, and COMPUTERB did not have an inbound filter defined for COMPUTERA, the default response rule was used. The default response rule is no longer used by Windows Vista and Windows Server 2008, but can still be configured for backwards compatibility.

In this section, we will first focus on creating an IPSec policy for Windows 2000, Windows XP, and Windows Server 2003 computers using the IP Security Policies MMC snap-in. After that, we will cover the steps to create a new Connection Security Rule within the Windows Server 2008 Windows Firewall with Advanced Security MMC snap-in.

When you add the IP Security Policy Management snap-in to an MMC console, you have four options for managing IPSec policies:

- Local Computer—Use this option to manage IP Security Policies on the computer on which the console is running.
- The Active Directory Domain Of Which This Computer Is A Member—Use this option when you want to manage policies that apply to the entire local Active Directory domain.
- Another Active Directory Domain (Use The Full DNS Name Of IP Address)—Use this option when you want to manage policies that apply to a remote Active Directory domain.
- Another Computer—Use this option to manage the policies stored locally on another computer.

IPSec policies are hierarchical in nature, and are organized as follows:

- Each IPSec policy consists of one or more IP Security Rules.
- Each IP Security Rule includes a single IP Security Action that is applied to one or more IP Filter Lists.
- Each IP Filter List contains one or more IP Filters.

TAKE NOTE *

Only one IPSec policy can be active on any one computer at a given time. If you wish to assign a new IPSec policy to a particular computer, you must first un-assign the existing IPSec policy.

All of these components are modular, which means that a single IP filter list can be configured within one or more IP Security Rules, and an IP Security Rule can be configured as a part of one or more IPSec policies. Once an IPSec policy has been created, it must be *assigned* to a single computer or a group of computers before it will take effect.

If you have never worked with IPSec policies before, the number of different wizards and configuration screens can be confusing at first. The high-level tasks involved in creating your first IPSec policy are as follows:

1. Select the option to create a new IPSec policy. This will prompt you to launch the IP Security Rule wizard.

   a. Select the option to create a new IP Security Rule. This will prompt you to create a new IP Filter List.

   i. Select the option to create a new IP Filter List.

   ii. Select the option to create a new IP Filter. This will prompt you to launch the New IP Filter Wizard. Once you have created one or more IP Filters, you can finish creating the IP Filter List.

iii. Once you have created one or more IP Filter Lists, select the option to create one or more Filter Actions. This will launch the IP Security Filter Action Wizard.

iv. Once you have created one or more IP Security Filter Actions, you can complete the IP Security Rule Wizard.

b. Once you have created one or more IP Security Rules, you can complete the IPSec Policy Wizard.

2. Once you have completed the IPSec Policy Wizard, you can assign your new IPSec policy to a single computer or a group of computers.

 CREATE AN IP SECURITY POLICY USING THE IP SECURITY POLICIES MMC SNAP-IN

GET READY. This exercise assumes that you are logged onto a Windows Server 2008 computer in a workgroup configuration, and that you are logged in using local Administrator credentials.

1. Create a blank MMC console by clicking the **Start** button, keying **mmc**, and clicking **OK**.

2. Click **File→Add/Remove Snap-in**. The Add or Remove Snap-ins screen will appear.

3. In the Available Snap-ins column, select **IP Security Policy Management** and click **Add**. The Select Computer or Domain screen will appear.

4. Ensure that the **Local computer** radio button is selected. Click **Finish** and then **OK** to create the MMC snap-in. You will see a screen similar to that shown in Figure 9-2.

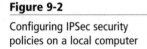

Figure 9-2

Configuring IPSec security policies on a local computer

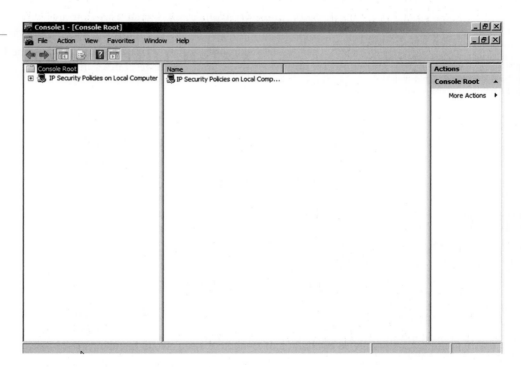

5. Right-click **IP Security Policies on Local Computer** and click **Create IP Security Policy**.... Click **Next** to bypass the initial Welcome screen. The IP Security Policy Name screen will appear.

6. In the Name: text box, enter **Sample IPSec Policy**. Click **Next** to continue. The Requests for Secure Communication screen will appear. On this screen you would enable the Default Response Rule for backwards compatibility. Place a checkmark

next to **Activate the default response rule (earlier versions of Windows only)** and click **Next**. The Default Response Rule Authentication Method screen appears.

7. Select the **Use this string to protect the key exchange (pre-shared key)** radio button. In the pre-shared key text box, enter the following string: **1234567890**. Click **Next** to continue. You will see the screen shown in Figure 9-3.

Figure 9-3

Configuring shared key authentication methods

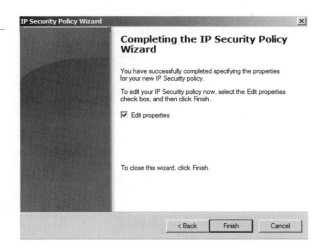

⚠️ **WARNING** On a production network, you should not configure IPSec to use a pre-shared key; this is being done for demonstration purposes only.

8. Ensure that there is a checkmark next to **Edit properties**, and then click **Finish**. The Sample IPSec Policy Properties screen appears, as shown in Figure 9-4.

Figure 9-4

Viewing the properties of an IPSec rule

9. As you can see, the default response rule has already been created. To create a new IP Security Rule, click **Add** to launch the New IP Security Rule Wizard. Click **Next** to bypass the initial Welcome screen.

10. The Tunnel Endpoint screen appears. Accept the default selection and then click **Next**.

11. The Network Type screen appears. Accept the default selection and then click **Next**.

12. The IP Filter List screen appears. As you can see, there are no IP Filter Lists configured, so you must now create one. Click **Add**. You will see the screen shown in Figure 9-5.

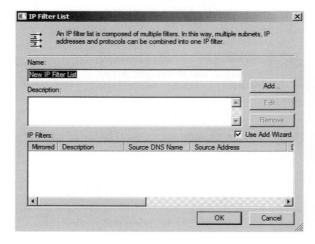

13. In the Name: text box, enter **Sample IP Filter List**. As you can see, there are no IP Filter Lists configured, so you must now create one. Click **Add** to launch the New IP Filter Wizard. Click **Next** to bypass the initial Welcome screen.

14. The IP Filter Description and Mirrored property screen appears. Click **Next** to accept the default values.

15. The IP Traffic Source screen appears. Select the **My IP Address** option from the Source address: dropdown box. Click **Next**.

16. The IP Traffic Destination screen appears. Select the **Any IP Address** option from the Destination address: dropdown box. Click **Next**.

17. The IP Protocol Type screen appears. Select the **TCP** option from the Select a protocol type: dropdown box. Click **Next**.

18. The IP Protocol Port screen appears. Select the **From any port** and **To any port** radio buttons. Click **Next**.

19. The Completing the IP Filter Wizard screen appears. Click **Finish**.

20. You are now returned to the IP Filter List screen, as shown in Figure 9-6. Click **OK** to create the new IP Filter List.

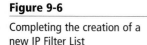

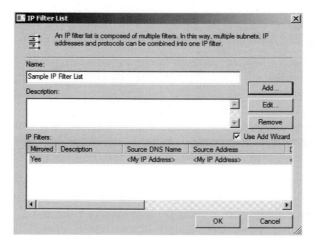

21. You are now returned to the IP Security Rule Wizard, screen as shown in Figure 9-7. Select the **Sample IP Filter List** radio button, and then click **Next**.

Figure 9-7

Configuring an IP Security Rule

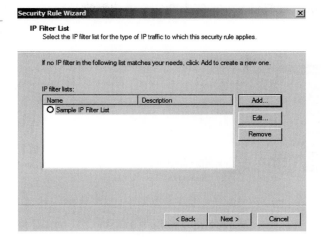

22. The Filter Action screen appears. As you can see, there are no Filter Actions configured, so you must now create one. Click **Add** to launch the New Filter Action Wizard. Click **Next** to bypass the initial Welcome screen.

23. The Filter Action Name screen appears. Enter **Sample Filter Action** in the Name: screen and then click **Next**.

24. The Filter Actions General Options screen appears, as shown in Figure 9-8. Select the **Permit** radio button. Click **Next** and then **Finish** to create the new Filter Action.

Figure 9-8

Creating an IP Filter Action

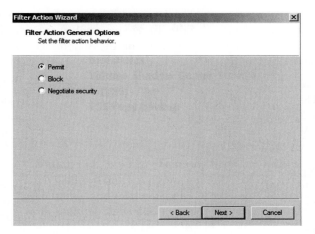

TAKE NOTE*

If you select the "Negotiate Security" option, you will be presented with a number of additional configuration screens. We will explore these in the 70-642 Lab Manual corresponding to this lesson.

25. You will be returned to the Security Rule Wizard. Select the Sample Filter Action that you just created and then click **Next**.

26. Click **Finish**. You will be returned to the Sample IPSec Policy properties screen shown in Figure 9-9. Click **OK** to save your changes to the Sample IPSec Policy.

Figure 9-9

Completing the creation of an IPSec policy

27. To assign this policy, right-click **Sample IPSec Policy** and click **Assign**. To remove this policy, right-click **Sample IPSec Policy** and click Un-Assign.

STOP. To modify an existing policy or any of its components, drill down to the item that you want to modify and then click **Edit**. To remove a policy or any of its components, drill down to the item that you want to remove, and on the Action menu, click **Delete**. Close the MMC window before continuing.

In the previous exercise, you created an IPSec policy using the IP Security Policies MMC snap-in. Use this snap-in to configure IPSec policies that require down-level compatibility to Windows 2000, Windows XP, and Windows Server 2003 computers. To create a policy on a Windows Vista/Windows Server 2008 network, follow the steps in the next exercise to create a Connection Security Rule.

The driving factor behind combining administration of the Windows Firewall with IPSec policies is to streamline network administration on a Windows Server 2008 computer. In Windows Server 2003, it was possible to configure duplicate or even contradictory settings between IPSec and the Windows Firewall (where the Windows Firewall was allowing a particular type of inbound traffic but IPSec was blocking it, for example), which made for extremely difficult troubleshooting scenarios. In addition, in Windows Server 2003, Windows Firewall and IPSec each possessed certain functionality that the other did not, and integrating the two often proved challenging: IPSec filters could control outbound traffic while the Windows Firewall could not, and the Windows Firewall could control traffic on the basis of a specific .exe file while IPSec could not.

The Windows Firewall with Advanced Security allows you to configure a number of default settings for any IPSec rules that you configure. You can configure IPSec defaults in areas listed in Table 9-2.

Table 9-2

Default IPSec Settings for the Windows Firewall with Advanced Security

SETTINGS	VALUE
Data Integrity	
Key lifetime (minutes)	480
Key lifetime (sessions)	0 (re-keys will be determined only by the key lifetime in minutes)
Key exchange algorithm	Diffie-Hellman Group 2
Security methods (integrity)	SHA1
Security methods (encryption)	AES-128 (primary)/3-DES (secondary)
Data Integrity	
Protocol	ESP (primary)/AH (secondary)
Data integrity	SHA1
Key lifetimes	60 minutes/100,000 kb transmitted
Data Encryption	
Protocol	ESP
Data Integrity	SHA1
Data Encryption	AES-128 (primary)/3-DES (secondary)
Key lifetimes	60 minutes/100,000 kb transmitted
Authentication	
Authentication method	Kerberos v5

Windows Server 2008 comes with four pre-configured Connection Security Rule templates, or you can create a completely customized set of security rules. We will discuss each of these in turn, including the configuration elements contained within each one.

The first type of Connection Security Rule is the *Isolation* rule. This allows you to restrict inbound and outbound connections based on certain sets of criteria, such as membership in a particular Active Directory domain. Creating an Isolation rule requires the following configuration choices:

- Inbound vs. outbound authentication requirements—You can configure any one of the following:
  a. Request authentication for inbound and outbound connections
  b. Require authentication for inbound connections and request authentication for outbound connections
  c. Require authentication for both inbound and outbound connections
- Authentication method—You can choose any one of the following:
  a. Default—uses the default IPSec setting
  b. Computer and user (Kerberos v5)—authorizes both the computer and user account
  c. Computer (Kerberos 5)—authorizes connections based only on the computer account
  d. Computer certificate—uses PKI certificates to authorize connections
  e. Advanced—here you can configure custom authentication methods

- Profile—This is a new feature of the Windows Firewall in Windows Vista and Windows Server 2008 that allows you to designate a particular network connection to receive a particular set of configuration settings, based on how you have defined the "trustworthiness" of the connection. You can choose any or all of the following:
  a. Domain—applies when the computer is connected to an Active Directory domain
  b. Private—applies when the computer is connected to a private network, such as a home network or other trusted location
  c. Public—applies when the computer is connected to a public network, like an Internet café or the wireless network in an airport
- Name—A name and description of the Connection Security Rule.

The second type of Connection Security Rule is the **_Authentication exemption_** rule. As the name implies, this allows you to specify one or more computers that do not need to be authenticated in order to pass traffic; for example, defining a DHCP server that should not have an Isolation connection security rule apply to it. Creating an Authentication exemption rule requires the following configuration choices:

- Exempt computers—You can choose from one of the following:
  a. This IP address or subnet—If you are specifying a particular subnet, this is expressed in CIDR notation, such as 192.168.2.0/24 for the 192.168.2.0 Class C address range.
  b. This IP address range—This allows you to specify a range of IP addresses that cannot be expressed in CIDR notation, such as 192.168.2.1 through 192.168.2.15.
  c. Predefined set of computers—This can include any of the following selections; the computers included in these sets will update automatically as the computer's IP address information changes:
    i. Default gateway
    ii. WINS servers
    iii. DNS servers
    iv. Local subnet
- Profile—Just like the Isolation rule, this can be one or more of the following:
  a. Domain
  b. Public
  c. Private
- Name—A name and description of the Connection Security Rule.

The third pre-built Connection Security Rule is the **_Server-to-server_** rule. As you might guess, this Connection Security Rule secures traffic between two servers or two groups of servers. Creating a Server-to-server rule requires the following configuration choices:

- Endpoints—You must define the server(s) or device(s) that make up Endpoint 1 and Endpoint 2. The computer(s) in each endpoint can consist of the following:
  a. Any IP address.
  b. This IP address or subnet.
  c. This IP address range.
  d. Predefined set of computers:
    i. Default gateway
    ii. WINS servers
    iii. DNS servers
    iv. Local subnet

TAKE NOTE * You can also customize whether a Server-to-server rule should apply to all network interfaces in each endpoint, or to LAN connections only, remote access connections only, or wireless connections only.

- Authentication requirements—Just like when configuring an Isolation rule, you can configure any one of the following:
    a. Request authentication for inbound and outbound connections
    b. Require authentication for inbound connections and request authentication for outbound connections
    c. Require authentication for both inbound and outbound connections
- Authentication method—This is similar to configuring an Isolation rule; select one of the following authentication methods:
    a. Computer certificate—here you will select the Certification Authority that this rule should trust
    b. Pre-shared key—this is the least secure authentication method for IPSec; it uses a preconfigured text string to secure communications between hosts and should be used only if no other alternative exists
    c. Advanced—here you can configure a custom authentication method
- Profile—Just like the first two rule types, this can be one or more of the following:
    a. Domain
    b. Public
    c. Private
- Name—A name and description of the Connection Security Rule.

The fourth and final pre-configured Connection Security Rule that you can configure is a ***Tunnel***. This is similar to the Server-to-server rule, but it will secure traffic only between two tunnel endpoints, not between the actual hosts that will be sending and receiving secured traffic. Creating a Tunnel rule requires the following configuration choices:

- Endpoint computers—Just like the Server-to-server rule, you must define the server(s) or device(s) that make up Endpoint 1 and Endpoint 2.
- Local tunnel computer—The IP address of the gateway that is closest to Endpoint 1.
- Remote tunnel computer—The IP address of the gateway that is closest to Endpoint 2.
- Authentication method—This is again similar to configuring an Isolation rule; select one of the following authentication methods:
    a. Computer certificate—Here you will select the Certification Authority that this rule should trust.
    b. Pre-shared key—This is the least secure authentication method for IPSec; it uses a pre-configured text string to secure communications between hosts and should be used only if no other alternative exists.
    c. Advanced—Here you can configure a custom authentication method.
- Profile—Like all other rule types, this can be one or more of the following:
    a. Domain
    b. Public
    c. Private
- Name—A name and description of the Connection Security Rule.

As you can see, there are numerous options when creating a Connection Security Rule in Windows Server 2008. In the following exercise, we will walk through the creation of an Isolation rule and an Authentication exemption rule.

 CREATE A CONNECTION SECURITY RULE IN THE WINDOWS FIREWALL WITH ADVANCED SECURITY MMC SNAP-IN

GET READY. This exercise assumes that you are logged onto a Windows Server 2008 computer in a workgroup configuration, and that you are logged in using local Administrator credentials.

PART A—Configure an Isolation Rule

1. Click the Start button, click **Administrative Tools**, and then click **Windows Firewall with Advanced Security**. You will see the screen shown in Figure 9-10.

Figure 9-10

Viewing the Windows Firewall with Advanced Security MMC Snap-In

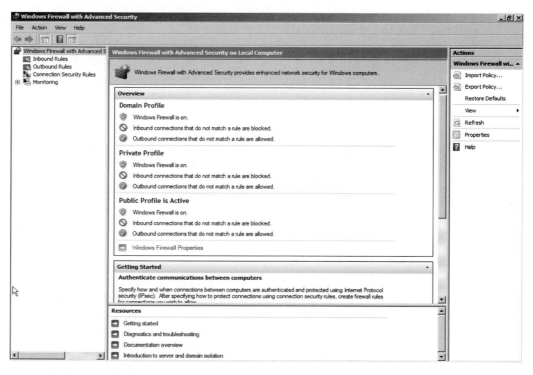

2. Drill down to Connection Security Rules in the left-hand pane. Right-click **Connection Security Rules** and click **New Rule. . . .** You will see the screen shown in Figure 9-11.

Figure 9-11

Creating a Connection Security Rule

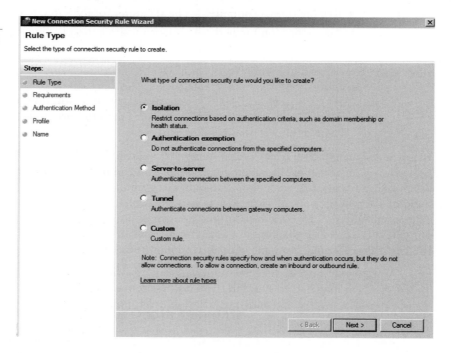

3. On the Rule Type screen, select the **Isolation** radio button and then click **Next**.

4. The Requirements screen appears. Select the **Request authentication for inbound and outbound connections** radio button, and then click **Next**.

5. The Authentication Method screen appears. Select the **Computer (Kerberos v5)** radio button and then click **Next**.

6. The Profile screen appears. Remove the checkboxes next to **Public and Private** and then click **Next**.

7. The Name screen appears. Enter **Domain Isolation** in the Name field, and then click **Finish**.

PART B—Configure an Authentication Exemption Rule

1. Right-click **Connection Security Rules** and click **New Rule. . . .**

2. The Rule Type screen appears. Select the **Authentication exemption** radio button and then click Next.

3. The Exempt Computers screen appears. Click **Add**. You will see the screen shown in Figure 9-12.

Figure 9-12

Creating an Authentication exemption rule

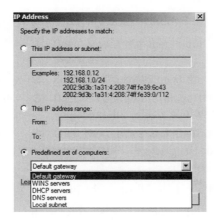

4. Select the **Predefined set of computers** radio button. Select **DNS Servers** from the dropdown box. Click **OK** and then click **Next**.

5. The Profile screen appears. Remove the checkboxes next to **Public and Private** and then click **Next**.

6. The Name screen appears. Enter **Domain Isolation Exemption** in the Name field, and then click **Finish**. You can see the finished result in Figure 9-13.

Figure 9-13

Viewing configured Connection Security Rules

STOP. Before continuing, remove both Connection Security Rules that you just created by right-clicking each item and clicking **Delete.**

INTRODUCING THE IPSEC DRIVER

The IPSec driver receives the active IP filter list from the IPSec Policy Agent. The Policy Agent then checks for a match of every inbound and outbound packet against the filters in the list. The IPSec driver stores all current quick mode SAs in a database. The IPSec driver uses the SPI field to match the correct SA with the correct packet. When an outbound IP packet matches the IP filter list with an action to negotiate security, the IPSec driver queues the packet, and then the IKE process begins negotiating security with the destination IP address of that packet.

After a successful negotiation is completed, the IPSec driver on the sending computer performs the following actions:

1. The IPSec driver receives the SA that contains the session key from the IKE process.
2. The IPSec driver locates the outbound SA in its database and then inserts the SPI from the SA into the header.
3. The IPSec driver signs the packets and encrypts them if confidentiality is required.
4. The IPSec driver sends the packets to the IP layer to be forwarded to the destination computer.

If the negotiation fails, the IPSec driver discards the packet.

When an IPSec-secured inbound packet matches a filter in the IP filter list, the IPSec driver performs the following actions:

1. The IPSec driver receives the session key, SA, and SPI from the IKE process.
2. The IPSec driver locates the inbound SA in its database using the destination address and SPI.
3. The IPSec driver checks the signature and, if required, decrypts the packets.
4. The IPSec driver searches the IP packets for a matching filter in the filter list to ensure that no traffic, other than what was agreed upon during the negotiation, is received.
5. The IPSec driver sends packets to the TCP/IP driver to pass to the receiving application.

When an unsecured IP packet is received, the IPSec driver searches for a matching filter in the filter list. If a match occurs and the filter action for that filter either requires IP Security or blocks the packet, the packet is discarded.

UNDERSTANDING THE SECURITY NEGOTIATION PROCESS

IPSec processing can be divided into two types of negotiation: main mode negotiation and quick mode negotiation. In this section, we will describe both negotiation processes in detail.

Let's look at a high-level overview of the overall security negotiation process between two computers, COMPUTERA and COMPUTERB:

1. COMPUTERA requests secured communications with COMPUTERB.
2. Main mode negotiations begin and are completed for the master key and the IKE SA—see the remainder of this section for further detail.
3. Quick mode negotiation of an SA pair (inbound and outbound) for each host is completed.
4. The application packets from COMPUTERA are passed by the TCP/IP driver to the IPSec driver.

5. The IPSec driver formats and cryptographically processes the packets and then sends them to COMPUTERB using the outbound SA.

6. Secure packets cross the network.

7. The IPSec driver on COMPUTERB cryptographically processes the packets arriving on the inbound SA, formats them as normal IP packets, and then passes them to the TCP/IP driver.

8. The TCP/IP driver passes the packets to the application on COMPUTERB.

Now let's look at each negotiation process in more detail.

Oakley *main mode negotiation* is used to determine encryption key material and security protection for use in protecting subsequent main mode or quick mode communications, as follows:

1. A communication packet is sent from COMPUTERA to COMPUTERB.

2. The IPSec driver on COMPUTERA checks its outbound IP filter lists and concludes that the packets match a filter, and that the filter action is "Negotiate Security," meaning that the packets must be secured.

3. The IPSec driver begins the IKE negotiation process.

4. COMPUTERA checks its policy for the main mode settings (authentication, Diffie-Hellman group, encryption, and integrity) to propose to COMPUTERB.

5. COMPUTERA sends the first IKE message using UDP source port 500 and destination port 500.

6. COMPUTERB receives the IKE main mode message that requests secure negotiation and then uses the source IP address and destination IP address of the packet to look up its own IKE filter. The IKE filter provides the security requirements for communications from Host A.

7. If the security settings proposed by COMPUTERA are acceptable to COMPUTERB, negotiation of the main mode or IKE SA begins.

8. Both computers negotiate options, exchange identities and authenticate them, and generate a master key. The IKE SA is established.

In summary, main mode negotiation creates the ISAKMP SA. The initiator and responder exchange a series of ISAKMP messages to negotiate the cipher suite for the ISAKMP SA (in plaintext), exchange key determination material (in plaintext), and finally identify and authenticate each other (in encrypted text).

When main mode negotiation is complete, each IPSec peer has selected a specific set of cryptographic algorithms for securing main mode and quick mode messages, has exchanged key information to derive a shared secret key, and has performed authentication. Before secure data is sent, a ***quick mode negotiation*** must occur to determine the type of traffic to be secured and how it will be secured. A quick mode negotiation is also done when a quick mode SA expires.

Quick mode messages are ISAKMP messages that are encrypted using the ISAKMP SA. As noted previously, the result of a quick mode negotiation is two IPSec SAs: one for inbound traffic and one for outbound traffic. The process is as follows:

1. COMPUTERA performs an IKE mode policy lookup to determine the full policy.

2. COMPUTERA proposes its options (cryptographic, as well as frequency of key changes, and so on) and filters to Host B.

3. COMPUTERB does its own IKE mode policy lookup. If it finds a match with the one proposed by COMPUTERA, it completes the quick mode negotiation to create a pair of IPSec SAs.

4. One SA is outbound and the other one is inbound. Each SA is identified by an SPI, and the SPI is part of the header of each packet sent. COMPUTERA's IPSec driver uses the outbound SA and signs and, if specified, encrypts the packets. If hardware

offload of IPSec cryptographic functions is supported by the network card, the IPSec driver just formats the packets; otherwise, it formats and cryptographically processes the packets.

5. The IPSec driver passes the packets to the network adapter driver.

6. The network adapter driver puts the network traffic onto the physical network media.

7. The network adapter at COMPUTERB receives the (encrypted) packets from the network.

8. The SPI is used to find the corresponding SA. (This SA has the associated cryptographic key necessary to decrypt and process the packets.)

9. If the network adapter is specifically designed to perform encryption and therefore can decrypt the packets, it will do so. It passes the packets to the IPSec driver.

10. COMPUTERB's IPSec driver uses the inbound SA to retrieve the keys and processes the packets if necessary.

11. The IPSec driver converts the packets back to normal IP packet format and passes them to the TCP/IP driver, which in turn passes them to the receiving application.

12. IPSec SAs continue processing packets. SAs are refreshed by IKE quick mode negotiation for as long as the application sends and receives data. When the SAs become idle, they are deleted.

Unlike quick mode negotiations, IKE main mode negotiations are not deleted when traffic is idle. IKE main mode has a default lifetime of 8 hours, but this number is configurable from 5 minutes to a maximum of 48 hours. Within the configured time frame, any new network communications between COMPUTERA and COMPUTERB will trigger only a new quick mode negotiation. If IKE main mode expires, a new IKE mode is negotiated as described above.

INTRODUCING THE IPSEC POLICY AGENT SERVICE

The purpose of the *IPSec Policy Agent* is to retrieve information about IPSec policies and to pass this information to other IPSec components that require it in order to perform security functions. The IPSec Policy Agent is a service that resides on each computer running a Windows Server 2008 operating system, appearing as IPSec Services in the list of system services in the Services console.

The IPSec Policy Agent has several responsibilities within the operating system, including the following:

• Retrieves the appropriate IPSec policy (if one has been assigned) from Active Directory if the computer is a domain member; or it retrieves the IPSec policy from the local registry if the computer is not a member of a domain.

• Polls for changes in policy configuration.

• Sends the assigned IPSec policy information to the IPSec driver.

• If the computer is a member of a domain, policy retrieval occurs when the system starts, at the interval specified in the IPSec policy, and at the default Group Policy refresh interval. You can also manually poll Active Directory for policies that use the gpupdate /target:computer command.

The following are additional aspects of IPSec policy behavior for a computer that is a member of an Active Directory domain:

• If IPSec policy information is centrally configured for computers that are domain members, the IPSec policy information is stored in Active Directory and cached in the local registry of the computer to which it applies.

• If the computer is temporarily not connected to the domain and policy is cached, new policy information for that computer replaces old, cached information when the computer reconnects to the domain.

- If the computer is a stand-alone computer or a member of a domain that is not using Active Directory for policy storage, IPSec policy is stored in the local registry.
- If there are no IPSec policies in Active Directory or the registry when the IPSec Policy Agent starts automatically at system start time, or if the IPSec Policy Agent cannot connect to Active Directory, the IPSec Policy Agent waits for the policy to be assigned or activated.

Deploying IPSec

> IPSec policies can be deployed using local policies, Active Directory, or both. Each method has its advantages and disadvantages.

Only one local Group Policy Object (GPO), often referred to as the *local computer policy*, is stored on a local computer. When using this local GPO, you can store Group Policy settings on individual computers regardless of whether they are members of an Active Directory domain. On a network without an Active Directory domain (a network that lacks a Windows 2000, Windows Server 2003, or Windows Server 2008 domain controller), the local GPO settings determine IPSec behavior because they are not overwritten by other GPOs. The local GPO can be overwritten by GPOs associated with sites, domains, or organizational units (OUs) in an Active Directory environment.

You should use the local policy in the following two scenarios:

- You have no Active Directory infrastructure in place, or you have a very small number of computers that need to use IPSec.
- You do not want to centralize the organization's IPSec strategy.

Permanent IPSec polices are known as *persistent policies*. You can configure persistent policies to extend existing Active Directory–based or local IPSec policies, override Active Directory–based or local IPSec policies, and enhance security during computer startup. Persistent policies enhance security by providing a secure transition from computer startup to Active Directory–based IPSec policy enforcement. Persistent policies, if configured, are stored in the local registry. You can update a persistent policy at any time, as long as the IPSec service is running. However, changes in persistent policy are not active immediately. You must restart the IPSec service to load the new persistent policy settings.

The settings of a local IPSec policy are added to the persistent policy if a persistent policy has been configured. If an Active Directory–based IPSec policy is assigned and the computer is connected to an Active Directory domain, the settings of the Active Directory–based policy are applied instead. If you have configured Active Directory–based policies, you can use a persistent policy as a tool to require that traffic to Active Directory always be secured by IPSec, including the retrieval of Active Directory–based IPSec policies. When an Active Directory–based or local policy is applied, those policy settings are added to the persistent policy settings.

To deploy IPSec policies using Active Directory, you can assign IPSec policies to the target GPO of a site, domain, or OU. Assign the policies to a GPO that propagates to all computer accounts affected by that GPO. You can use the IP Security Policy Management console or the netsh command-line utility to manage an Active Directory–based policy.

An Active Directory–based policy overrides any local IPSec policy that is assigned and adds to the persistent IPSec policy that has already been applied by the IPSec Policy Agent, if a persistent policy has been configured. If there is a conflict between a persistent IPSec policy and either a domain or local policy, the persistent policy settings prevail.

When assigning an IPSec policy in Active Directory, consider the following:

- You can assign the list of all IPSec policies at any level in the Active Directory hierarchy. However, only a single IPSec policy can be assigned at a specific level in Active Directory.

X REF

See the "Managing and Monitoring IPSec" section later in this lesson for more information about the netsh command.

- An OU inherits the policy of its parent OU unless policy inheritance is explicitly blocked or policy is explicitly assigned.
- IPSec policies from different OUs are never merged.
- An IPSec policy that is assigned to an OU in Active Directory takes precedence over a domain-level policy for members of that OU.
- An IPSec policy that is assigned to the lowest-level OU in the domain hierarchy overrides an IPSec policy that is assigned to a higher-level OU for member computers of that OU.

TAKE NOTE*

You can use the mnemonic "LSDOU" to remember the order in which IPSec policies are applied: first local policies, then site-linked policies, followed by domain-linked policies, then OU policies—first parent OUs followed by child OUs. You can learn more about Group Policy Object application in the MOAC textbook *Planning, Implementing, and Maintaining Windows Server Active Directory Infrastructure* (70–640).

- The highest possible level of the Active Directory hierarchy should be used to assign policies to reduce the amount of configuration and administration required.

You should use Active Directory to deploy policies if your enterprise meets the following criteria:

- An Active Directory infrastructure is in place.
- You use a substantial number of computers that must be grouped for IPSec assignment.
- You want to centralize the organization's IPSec strategy.

You can deploy IPSec in an environment in which you have computers that are members of a domain and that receive their IPSec policy through an Active Directory group policy, in addition to computers that are not members of a domain and that receive their IPSec policy through a local group policy. Regardless of how the IPSec policies are received, two computers that must communicate with each other can negotiate with each other using the rules defined in their IPSec policies.

When deploying IPSec policies via GPO, there are three built-in IPSec policies that are present by default; these are a holdover from the IPSec policies that are supported by Windows 2000 Server, Windows Server 2003, and Windows XP:

- Use the *Client (Respond Only)* policy on computers that normally do not send secured data. This policy does not initiate secure communications. If security is requested by a server, the client responds and secures only the requested protocol and port traffic with that server.
- The *Server (Request Security)* policy can be used on any computer—client or server—that needs to initiate secure communications. Unlike the Client policy, the Server policy attempts to protect all outbound transmissions. Unsecured, inbound transmissions are accepted; however, they are not resolved until IPSec requests security from the sender for all subsequent transmissions. This policy requires the Kerberos security protocol.
- The strictest of the predefined policies, the *Secure Server (Require Security)* policy, does not send or accept unsecured transmissions. Clients attempting to communicate with a secure server must use at least the Server predefined policy or an equivalent. Like the Server policy, the Secure Server policy uses Kerberos authentication.

In addition, you can also use Group Policy to configure Connection Security Rules for your Windows Server 2008 and Windows Vista clients. Figure 9-14 illustrates the IPSec Policies node of the Group Policy Object; Figure 9-15 shows the Windows Firewall with Advanced Security node.

Figure 9-14

Viewing the IPSec Policies node of a Group Policy Object

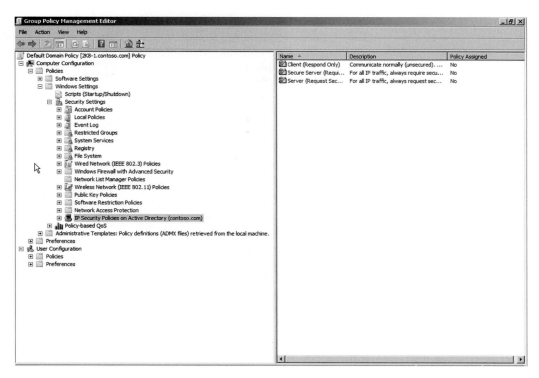

Figure 9-15

Viewing the Windows Firewall with Advanced Security node of a Group Policy Object

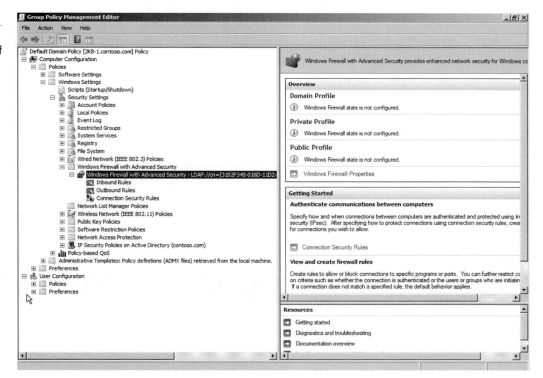

Managing and Monitoring IPSec

Windows Server 2008 provides several tools you can use to manage and monitor IPSec, including the IP Security Monitor, RSoP, Event Viewer, and the netsh command-line utility. In addition, the new Windows Firewall with Advanced Security MMC snap-in provides additional monitoring of Connection Security Rules and IPSec Security Associations. In this section, we will examine each of these tools in turn.

In Windows 2000, IP Security Monitor is implemented as an executable program (Ipsecmon). In Windows XP, Windows Server 2003, and Windows Server 2008, IP Security Monitor is implemented as a Microsoft Management Console (MMC) snap-in and includes enhancements that allow you to do the following:

- Monitor IPSec information for your local computer and for remote computers.
- View details about active IPSec policies including the name, description, date last modified, store, path, OU, and Group Policy Object name.
- View main mode and quick mode generic filters and specific filters.
- View main mode and quick mode statistics. (For information about the statistics displayed in IP Security Monitor, see Main Mode and Quick Mode statistics in IP Security Monitor.)
- View main mode and quick mode security associations.
- View main mode IKE policies.
- View quick mode negotiation policies.
- Customize refresh rates, and use DNS name resolution for filter and SA output.
- Search for specific main mode or quick mode filters that match any source or destination IP address, a source or destination IP address on your local computer, or a specific source or destination IP address.

Information that you can obtain from the IP Security Monitor MMC snap-in includes the following:

- The name of the active IPSec policy
- Details about the active IPSec policy
- Quick mode statistics
- Main mode statistics
- Information about active SAs

Viewing IPSec statistics in IP Security Monitor is simply a matter of expanding the server node, expanding the main mode node or the quick mode node, and then selecting the Statistics node. Understanding what each statistic means is more difficult. Table 9-3 describes the most common main mode statistics. (Table 9-4 describes the most common quick mode statistics.) In Table 9-3, several statistics appear to be related to quick mode. They are related, but they are initialized during the main mode IKE negotiation process, hence their inclusion as part of the main mode statistics table.

Table 9-3

IPSec Main Mode Statistics

STATISTIC	DESCRIPTION
Active Acquire	Number of pending requests for IKE negotiation for SAs between IPSec peers.
Active Receive	Number of IKE messages queued for processing.
Acquire Failures	Number of failed outbound requests that occurred to establish the SA since the IPSec service started.
Receive Failures	Number of errors found in the IKE messages received since the IPSec service last started.
Send Failures	Number of errors that occurred when sending IKE since the IPSec service last started.
Acquire Heap Size	Number of successive outbound requests to establish SAs.
Receive Heap Size	Number of IKE messages in IKE receive buffers.

(continued)

Table 9-3 *(continued)*

STATISTIC	DESCRIPTION
Authentication Failures	Number of authentication failures that occurred since the IPSec service last started. If you cannot make an IPSec connection, check to see whether authentication failures increase during an attempt. If they do increase, authentication is the issue. Check to see that shared secrets match, peers are members of the domain, and certificates are correct.
Negotiation Failures	Number of main mode negotiation failures since the IPSec service last started. Attempt to communicate and see whether negotiation failures increase. If they do increase, check the authentication and security method settings for unmatched or incorrect configuration.
Invalid Cookies Received	The total number of cookies that could not be matched with an active main mode SA since the IPSec service was last started. A *cookie* is a value contained in a received IKE message that is used to help identify the corresponding main mode SA.
Total Acquire	The total number of requests that have been submitted to IKE since the IPSec service was last started to establish an SA. This number includes acquires that result in soft SAs.
Total Get SPI	The total number of requests that have been submitted by IKE to the IPSec driver to obtain a unique SPI since the IPSec service was last started. The SPI matches inbound packets with SAs.
Key Additions	The total number of outbound quick mode SAs that have been added by IKE to the IPSec driver since the IPSec service was last started.
Key Updates	The total number of inbound quick mode SAs that have been added by IKE to the IPSec driver since the IPSec service was last started.
Get SPI Failures	The total number of failed requests that have been submitted by IKE to the IPSec driver to obtain a unique SPI since the IPSec service was last started.
Key Addition Failures	The total number of failed outbound quick mode SA addition requests that have been submitted by IKE to the IPSec driver since the IPSec service was last started.
Key Update Failures	The total number of failed inbound quick mode SA addition requests that have been submitted by IKE to the IPSec driver since the IPSec service was last started.
ISADB List Size	The number of main mode state entries. This number includes successfully negotiated main modes, main mode negotiations in progress, and main mode negotiations that failed or expired and have not yet been deleted.
Connection List Size	The number of quick mode negotiations that are in progress.
IKE Main Mode	The total number of successful SAs that have been created during main mode negotiations since the IPSec service was last started.
IKE Quick Mode	The total number of successful SAs that have been created during quick mode negotiations since the IPSec service was last started.
Soft Associations	The total number of SAs formed with computers that have not responded to main mode negotiation attempts since the IPSec service was last started. Although these computers did not respond to main mode negotiation attempts, IPSec policy allowed communications with the computers. Soft SAs are not secured by IPSec.
Invalid Packets Received	The total number of invalid IKE messages that have been received since the IPSec service was last started. This number includes IKE messages with invalid header fields, incorrect payload lengths, and incorrect values for the responder cookie. Invalid IKE messages are commonly caused by retransmitted IKE messages or an unmatched preshared key between the IPSec peers.

Table 9-4 describes the most common quick mode statistics.

Table 9-4

IPSec Common Quick Mode Statistics

STATISTIC	DESCRIPTION
Active Security Association	Number of quick mode SAs.
Offloaded Security Associations	Number of quick mode SAs offloaded to hardware. Some network adapters process cryptography data themselves to increase overall performance.
Pending Key Operations	Number of key exchange operations in progress.
Key Additions	Number of keys for quick mode SAs successfully added since the computer started.
Key Deletions	Number of keys for quick mode SAs successfully deleted since computer started.
Rekeys	Number of successful rekey operations for quick mode.
Active Tunnels	Number of active tunnels.
Bad SPI Packets	Number of packets with incorrect SPI since the computer was last started. The SPI might have expired and an old packet just arrived. This will likely be larger if rekeying is frequent and there is a large number of SAs. Might indicate a spoofing attack.
Packets Not Decrypted	Number of packets that could not be decrypted since the computer was last started. A packet might not be decrypted if it fails a validation check.
Packets Not Authenticated	Number of packets for which data could not be verified (for which the integrity hash verification failed) since the computer was last started. Increases in this number might indicate an IPSec packet spoofing or a modification attack or packet corruption by network devices.
Packets With Replay Detection	Number of packets containing an invalid sequence number since the computer was last started. Detection increases might mean network problems or a replay attack.
Confidential Bytes Sent	Number of bytes sent using the ESP protocol since the computer was last started.
Confidential Bytes Received	Number of bytes received using the ESP protocol (excluding nonencrypted ESP) since the computer was last started.
Authenticated Bytes Sent	Number of authenticated bytes sent using the AH protocol or the ESP protocol since the computer was last started.
Authenticated Bytes Received	Number of authenticated bytes received using the AH protocol or the ESP protocol since the computer was last started.
Transport Bytes Sent	Number of bytes sent using IPSec transport mode since the computer was last started.
Transport Bytes Received	Number of bytes received using IPSec transport mode since the computer was last started.
Bytes Sent In Tunnels	Number of bytes sent using the IPSec tunnel mode since the computer was last started.
Bytes Received In Tunnels	Number of bytes received using the IPSec tunnel mode since the computer was last started.
Offloaded Bytes Sent	Number of bytes sent using hardware offload since the computer was last started.
Offloaded Bytes Received	Number of bytes received using hardware offload since the computer was last started.

Resultant Set of Policy (RSoP) is another MMC snap-in that can be used to view IPSec policy configuration data. In addition to viewing the policies with the IP Security Monitor, you can use RSoP to determine the IPSec policies that are assigned but that are not applied to IPSec clients. The RSoP snap-in displays only detailed IPSec policy settings, not any information about active connections or security associations. It shows the filter rules, filter actions, authentication methods, tunnel endpoints, and the connection type for the policy that is applied.

You can also use the Windows Event Viewer (discussed in the previous lesson) to view the following IPSec-related events:

- IPSec Policy Agent events in the System log
- IPSec driver events in the System log
- IKE events in the System log
- IPSec policy change events in the System log

At the command line, netsh is a native Windows Server 2003 and Windows Server 2008 command-line tool that you can use to display or modify the local or remote network configuration of a computer running Windows Server 2003. You can run netsh from a batch file or from the command prompt. The netsh commands for IPSec can be used to configure IPSec policies only on computers running members of the Windows Server 2003 and Windows Server 2008 family.

To set the netsh IPSec context, type netsh at the command prompt and then press Enter, then key ipsec and press Enter. From here, you can enter the word static at the netsh IPSec prompt. Static mode allows you to create, modify, and assign policies without affecting the active IPSec policy. (You can also key dynamic to access dynamic mode, which allows you to display the active state and immediately implement changes to the active IPSec policy.) Dynamic netsh commands affect the service only when it runs. If it is stopped, dynamic policy settings are discarded. The full syntax of the netsh command can be obtained by typing netsh /? at the Windows command prompt.

> ⚠ **WARNING**
>
> If you must immediately initiate a change to IPSec processing, dynamic mode is very useful because commands issued in that mode are implemented immediately (except when a service must be stopped and restarted). However, dynamic mode is also a mixed blessing. If you make a mistake in dynamic mode, you do not have the opportunity to discover it before implementing the change; therefore, you could accidentally create an incorrect configuration without warning.

You can also use netsh to monitor the current IPSec session. Monitoring consists of either displaying policy information, obtaining diagnostics and logging IPSec information, or both. Any information you can find with the IP Security Monitor snap-in, you can find with netsh. To find out what the current IPSec policy is, use the Show command from either the static or dynamic menu context. If you choose to use the Show All command, a lot of information will be returned, as displayed in Figure 9-16 (note that this is only part of the information that would be displayed).

Because of the potentially large amount of available information, it is useful to view only a portion of the IPSec configuration information. Several Show commands are available to do this,

Figure 9-16

Viewing netsh results

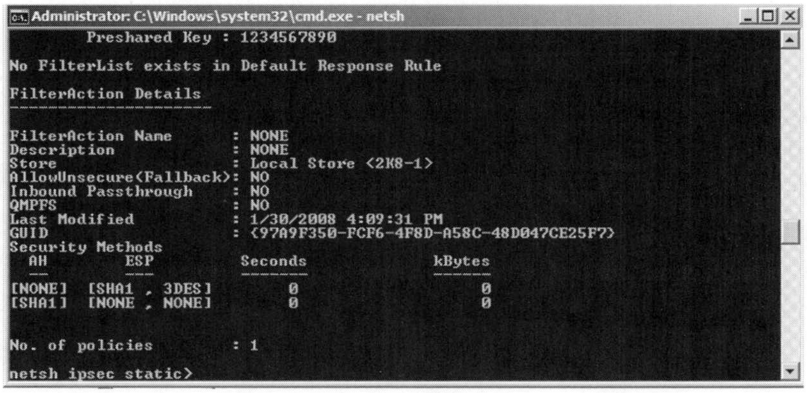

some of which are listed in Table 9-5. You can enter all of the commands from the netsh IPSec dynamic or the netsh IPSec static context or, with modification, from the command line.

Table 9-5

Netsh IPSec Static Show Commands

OPERATION	COMMAND
To display a specific filter list, use…	show filterlist name =filterlistname
To display the policy assigned to the specified GPO, use…	show gpoassignedpolicy name =name
To display a specific policy, use…	show policy name =policyname
To display a specific rule, use…	show rule name =rulename

One of the steps in diagnosing IPSec problems—or just establishing that the policy is working like you think it should—is to obtain information about the current policy. The Show commands described in Table 9-5 provide that information. The information that each command reveals identifies the settings in the policy. For example, the Show Filterlist command lists the information in the policies filter list.

Some examples of the Show command syntax are illustrated in Table 9-6. In Table 9-7, in the commands, the equal sign is part of the command and the bold words are replaced by a value as indicated.

Table 9-6

Descriptions of Show Command Syntax

COMMAND	DESCRIPTION
show config	Displays IPSec configuration and boot time behavior.
show mmsas	Displays information on the IPSec main mode SA. You can see the source and destination addresses. When used with the Resolvedns=yes switch, the names of the computers are also displayed.
show qmsas	Displays information about the IPSec quick mode SAs.
show stats	Displays the IKE main mode statistics, IPSec quick mode statistics, or both. The statistics are the same ones as those described in Table 9-4.

In addition to Show commands, you can use several dynamic mode netsh IPSec diagnostic commands to obtain diagnostic information, such as those listed in Table 9-7.

Table 9-7

Dynamic Mode Netsh IPSec Diagnostic Commands

COMMAND	DESCRIPTION
set config property=ipsecdiagnostics value=**value**	Can be set with a value of 0 to 7, which indicates the level of IPSec diagnostic logging. The default is 0, which means logging is disabled. The level 7 causes all logging to be performed. The computer must be restarted for logging to begin.

(continued)

Table 9-7 *(continued)*

COMMAND	DESCRIPTION
set config property=ipsecloginterval value=**value**	Indicates how frequently in seconds the IPSec events are sent to the system event log. The range of the value parameter is 60 to 86,400 with a default of 3600.
set config property=ikelogging value=**value**	Can be set with a value of 0 or 1 to determine whether IKE (Oakley) logging will occur. This command produces a log with a copious amount of information. You must understand the Requests for Comments (RFCs) at the expert level to completely understand the Oakley logs.
set config property=strongcrlcheck value=**value**	Determines whether certificate revocation list (CRL) checking is used. If the value is 0, CRL checking is disabled. If 1 is the value, certificate validation fails only if the certificate is revoked. Level 2 fails if any CRL check error occurs. A CRL check fails if the CRL cannot be located on the network. You can make other diagnostic efforts by modifying the current policy to reduce security. For example, if you change authentication to Shared Secret on both computers instead of Kerberos or Certificates, you eliminate the possibility that the problem is related to authentication

■ Configuring Network Authentication

THE BOTTOM LINE

In addition to securing network traffic with IPSec, another common issue is securing the network authentication process. The default authentication protocol in an Active Directory network is the Kerberos v5 protocol, but there are situations in which the *NT LAN Manager (NTLM)* authentication protocols come into play. NTLM is typically considered a legacy authentication protocol, but it is still required in numerous scenarios, such as when computers are configured in a workgroup configuration instead of an Active Directory domain, as well as when you have configured a trust relationship with a down-level network such as a Windows 2000 domain.

CERTIFICATION READY?
Configure Network Authentication
3.3

NTLM authentication has been in use on Windows networks since the very early days of Windows networking. Unfortunately, this means that there are many different "flavors" of NTLM authentication, some of which are far less secure than others. The available versions of NTLM authentication are:

- *LM Authentication* This is the weakest form of NTLM authentication, which has been in use since the earliest days of Windows networking with Windows NT and Windows 95 and 98. Passwords that are stored using LM authentication can be easily hacked by any malicious user who can obtain access to the LM-encrypted packets through the use of a network sniffer. LM Authentication is almost entirely deprecated in modern networks, and is disabled by default on Windows Server 2003 and later computers.

- *NTLM Authentication* This is the "middle of the road" form of NTLM authentication that was used to improve upon the security of LM Authentication.

- *NTLMv2 Authentication* This is the strongest form of NTLM authentication available. When NTLMv2 was first introduced, there were concerns surrounding the deployment of it as it was not supported by all available operating systems at the time: Windows 95 and Windows 98 clients required additional software to be installed before they could use NTLMv2 authentication. In modern networks running Windows 2000 and later operating systems, this should be a non-issue as NTLMv2 support is built in by default.

NTLM authentication settings are managed via Group Policy, either through a domain-based GPO in an Active Directory environment, or by using Local Group Policy Objects for workgroup or stand-alone computers.

NTLM authentication levels are controlled by the Computer Configuration→Policies →Windows Settings→Security Settings→Security Options→Network security: NTLM authentication levels security setting policy node shown in Figure 9-17. This GPO node allows you to select one of the following options:

Figure 9-17

Viewing NTLM Authentication settings

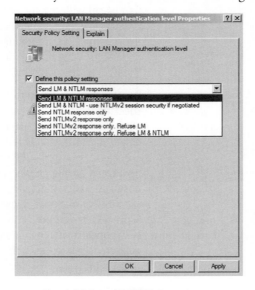

- Send LM and NTLM responses
- Send LM and NTLM—use NTLMv2 session security if negotiated
- Send NTLM response only
- Send NTLMv2 response only
- Send NTLMv2 response only—refuse LM
- Send NTLMv2 response only—refuse LM and NTLM

By allowing only the most stringent levels of NTLM authentication on your network, you can improve the overall communications security of Windows Server 2008 computers, whether in an Active Directory or a workgroup environment.

Once you have mandated the use of NTLM or NTLMv2 network authentication, you can also enable the *Do not store LAN Manager hash value on next password change.* (This setting is enabled by default in a Windows Server 2008 Active Directory domain.)

The Security Options category also includes options to configure authentication and communication security settings involving LDAP and SMB security, which are two other common protocols used on a Windows Server 2008 network. By using a domain-based GPO, you can further secure LDAP and SMB through the use of the following Group Policy settings:

- Domain controller: LDAP server signing requirements—Controls whether LDAP traffic between domain controllers and clients must be signed. This setting can be configured with a value of None or Require signing.
- Domain member: Digitally sign or encrypt or sign secure channel data (always)— Controls whether traffic between domain members and the domain controllers will be signed and encrypted at all times.
- Domain member: Digitally encrypt secure channel data (when client agrees)—Indicates that traffic between domain members and the domain controllers will be encrypted only if the client workstations are able to do so.
- Domain member: Digitally sign secure channel data (when client agrees)—Indicates that traffic between domain members and the domain controllers will be signed only if the client services are able to do so.

- Microsoft network client: Digitally sign communications (always)—Indicates that Server Message Block (SMB) signing will be enabled by the SMB signing component of the SMB client at all times.

- Microsoft network client: Digitally sign communications (if server agrees)—Indicates that SMB signing will be enabled by the SMB signing component of the SMB client only if the corresponding server service is able to do so.

- Microsoft network server: Digitally sign communications (always)—Indicates that SMB signing will be enabled by the SMB signing component of the SMB server at all times.

- Microsoft network server: Digitally sign communications (if server agrees)—Indicates that SMB signing will be enabled by the SMB signing component of the SMB server only if the corresponding client service is able to do so.

■ Configuring the Windows Firewall

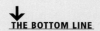

THE BOTTOM LINE

Beginning with Windows Server 2003 Service Pack 1, the Windows server operating system has included a built-in *stateful firewall* called the *Windows Firewall*. A stateful firewall is so named because it can track and maintain information based on the status of a particular connection; if a user from COMPUTERA connected to COMPUTERB's Web server, a stateful firewall can allow all network traffic that is related to that "conversation" between COMPUTERA and COMPUTERB. The Windows Firewall is enabled by default on all new installations of Windows Server 2008, and can be managed manually via the Windows Firewall Control Panel applet, the new Windows Firewall with Advanced Security MMC snap-in (discussed earlier), or via Group Policy Objects in an Active Directory environment. The default configuration of the Windows Firewall in Windows Server 2008 will block all unsolicited inbound traffic; that is, attempts to access the computer from a remote network host that has not been specifically authorized by the administrator of the local server.

CERTIFICATION READY?
Configure Firewall Settings

3.5

The most basic configurations of the Windows Firewall can be managed in the Windows Firewall Control Panel applet, which can be accessed from the Windows Control Panel or via the Server Manager MMC snap-in. The Windows Firewall applet is shown in Figure 9-18.

Figure 9-18

The Windows Firewall Control Panel applet

From the Windows Firewall Control Panel applet, you can manage the following configuration items:

- Turn the Windows Firewall on or off—Turning the Windows Firewall completely off is not recommended, as you are losing protection against unsolicited inbound traffic.
- Allow a program through the Windows Firewall—If you know that your Windows Server 2008 computer is being used by remote clients, you can configure **exceptions** to the Windows Firewall configuration that will allow certain types of inbound traffic.

By clicking the Turn the Windows Firewall on or off hyperlink, you will be taken to the screen shown in Figure 9-19. From here, you can configure the Windows Firewall in one of three states:

Figure 9-19

Configuring the Windows Firewall

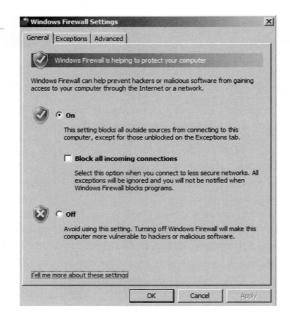

- On—This is the default configuration of the Windows Firewall. Any unsolicited inbound network traffic will be blocked, except for traffic that matches any exceptions you have defined.
- On, block all incoming connections—By placing a checkmark next to Block all incoming connections, you will force the Windows Firewall to block all incoming traffic, including blocking any traffic relating to exceptions you have created. You might select this option to temporarily disallow network traffic to all services on a Windows Server 2008 computer in order to troubleshoot a software issue, or if a virus or other piece of malware has infected remote machines on your network.
- Off—As stated above, this configuration is not recommended as you lose all network protection associated with the Windows Firewall.

From the Exception tab shown in Figure 9-20, you can create exceptions that will allow inbound traffic sent to specific services, .EXE files, or TCP or UDP port numbers. There are a number of pre-configured exceptions in the Windows Server 2008 Windows Firewall, listed here:

- BITS Peercaching—Allows Background Intelligent Transfer Service (BITS) clients in the same subnet to share files in their BITS cache.
- COM+ Network Access—Allows the remote activation of COM+ components.
- Core Networking—Allows basic ports required for basic IPv4 and IPv6 connectivity (enabled by default).
- Distributed Transaction Coordinator—Coordinates transactions that update transaction-related resources, such as databases and message tracking systems.

Figure 9-20

Viewing Windows Firewall
exceptions

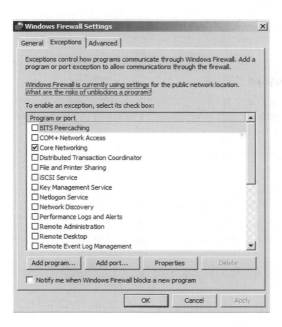

- File and Printer Sharing—Allows inbound access to file shares configured on the local computer.
- iSCSI Service—Allows access to iSCSI servers and devices for use by iSCSI Storage Area Networks.
- Key Management Service—Used for tracking license compliance of Microsoft products.
- Netlogon Service—Used to maintain a secure connection between Active Directory domain controllers and clients.
- Network Discovery—New to Windows Vista and Windows Server 2008, allows hosts to discover network services being offered by other computers on the network via Universal Plug and Play (UPnP) and other services related to publishing network services.
- Performance Logs and Alerts—Allows remote access to the Performance Logs and Alerts service.
- Remote Administration—Allows remote access to administration utilities such as the Computer Management MMC snap-in.
- Remote Desktop—Allows access to the Remote Desktop console, which runs on TCP port 3389 by default.
- Remote Event Log Management—Allows remote viewing and management of local event logs.
- Remote Scheduled Tasks Management—Allows remote viewing and management of the task scheduler on the local computer.
- Remote Service Management—Allows remote management of local services.
- Remote Volume Management—Allows remote management of local disks and volumes.
- Routing and Remote Access—Allows incoming RAS and VPN connections.
- Secure Socket Tunneling Protocol—Allows incoming connections using SSTP, a new feature that allows VPN connections over the secure SSL port of 443, also known as HTTPS.
- SNMP Trap—Allows traffic related to the SNMP Trap service to be received by the local computer.
- Windows Firewall Remote Management—New to Windows Server 2008, this allows the Windows Firewall on the local computer to be managed from a remote console.
- Windows Management Instrumentation (WMI)—Allows remote management of a Windows computer using a set of manageable and scriptable components and classes.

TAKE NOTE*

You will see that you cannot modify the properties of these built-in exceptions from this interface. These exceptions can only be modified using the Windows Firewall with Advanced Security MMC snap-in, discussed previously in the IPSec section as well as later in this section.

- Windows Remote Management—Allows remote management using the WS-Management protocol.
- Windows Security Configuration Wizard—Allows remote access to the Security Configuration Wizard.

Exceptions in the Windows Firewall can be configured to allow inbound traffic from one of the following ***scopes***; that is, the source IP address or range of addresses that inbound traffic will be permitted from:

- Any computer (including those on the Internet)—Allows incoming traffic from any source IP address.
- My network (subnet) only—Allows incoming traffic from a source IP address on the same network as the destination host, based on the IP address and subnet mask of the destination.
- A specific range of IP addresses—Allows incoming traffic from a source IP address range, based on CIDR notation, such as *192.168.1.0/24, 192.168.2.32/28,* etc.

TAKE NOTE* You do have the ability to modify the scope of the built-in exceptions.

In the following exercise, you will create a firewall exception for both an executable program, as well as for a TCP port.

CONFIGURE THE WINDOWS FIREWALL

GET READY. This assumes that you are signed onto a Windows Server 2008 computer with local Administrator privileges.

1. Click the **Start** button, then click **Control Panel**.
2. Double-click the **Windows Firewall** applet.
3. The Windows Firewall screen appears. Click **Allow a program through Windows Firewall**.
4. The Windows Firewall Settings screen appears. Click the **Exceptions** tab. You will see the screen that was shown in Figure 9-20.
5. Click the **Add program** button. The Add a Program screen appears.
6. Click **Internet Explorer** to create an exception to allow inbound connections to the iexplore.exe executable.
7. Click **OK.** You will see Internet Explorer added to the list of exceptions, with a checkmark next to it to indicate that it is enabled.
8. Click **Add port.** You will see the screen shown in Figure 9-21.

Figure 9-21

Configuring a port-based exception

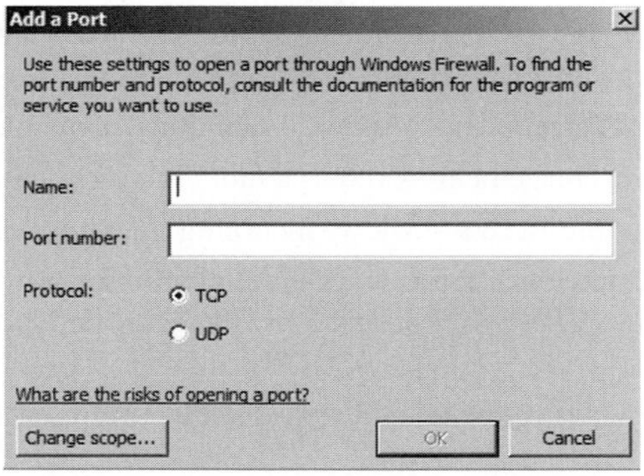

9. In the Name: field, enter **HTTP**. In the Port number: field, enter **80**. Select the **TCP** protocol, and then click **OK.**

PAUSE. Before continuing, highlight each exception that you created in this exercise and click **Delete**.

In the previous exercise, you created exceptions for the Windows Firewall in Windows Server 2008. Next we will examine the Windows Firewall with Advanced Security MMC snap-in, used to configure advanced settings within the Windows Firewall.

As we discussed in the IPSec section, the Windows Firewall with Advanced Security MMC snap-in is a new feature in Windows Vista and Windows Server 2008 that allows you to configure new features within the Windows Firewall, including:

- The ability to control both inbound and outbound connections—Previous versions of the Windows Firewall allowed you to control only inbound traffic.
- Integration with IPSec in the form of Connection Security Rules—In previous versions, IPSec and the Windows Firewall were configured completely separately, which could lead to unpredictable or difficult-to-troubleshoot behavior.
- Granular configuration and monitoring of built-in exceptions—In Windows Server 2003, it was not possible to modify or add to the ports used by built-in Windows Firewall exceptions.
- Network profiles—As we've discussed, Windows Server 2008 creates three default network profiles for which you can define default behaviors.

Figure 9-22 shows you the Inbound Connections view of the Windows Firewall with Advanced Security MMC snap-in; from this screen you can view and modify individual elements of pre-defined Windows Firewall exceptions as well as creating your own.

Figure 9-22

Viewing inbound exceptions in Windows Firewall with Advanced Security

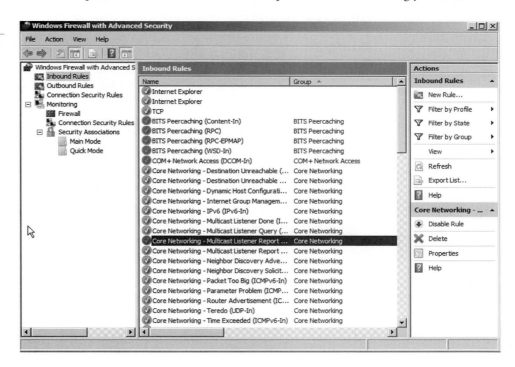

SUMMARY SKILL MATRIX

IN THIS LESSON YOU LEARNED:

- IPSec is the standard method of providing security services for IP packets.

- ESP protocol provides confidentiality (in addition to authentication, integrity, and anti-replay) for the IP payload, while the AH protocol provides authentication, integrity, and anti-replay for the entire packet.

- Two types of SAs are created when IPSec peers communicate securely: the ISAKMP SA and the IPSec SA.

- To negotiate SAs for sending secure traffic, IPSec uses IKE, a combination of ISAKMP and the Oakley Key Determination Protocol. ISAKMP messages contain many types of payloads to exchange information during SA negotiation.

- Main mode negotiation is used to establish the ISAKMP SA, which is used to protect future main mode and all quick mode negotiations.

- Quick mode negotiation is used to establish the IPSec SA to protect data.

- You can use netsh IPSec static mode to create and assign IPSec policies, add a persistent policy, and change other configuration features.

- You can use Active Directory Group Policy Objects or the Local Group Policy Object to configure NTLM authentication levels on a Windows Server 2008 computer.

- The Windows Firewall with Advanced Security MMC snap-in allows you to control inbound and outbound traffic on a Windows Server 2008 computer, as well as integrating Windows Firewall configuration with IPSec through the use of Connection Security Rules.

■ Knowledge Assessment

Fill in the Blank

Complete the following sentences by writing the correct word or words in the blanks provided.

1. The _____ was configured in Windows 2000, Windows Server 2003, and Windows XP IPSec policies to ensure that the computer responds to requests for secure communication.

2. A(n) _____ attack is one in which a malicious user masquerades as the legitimate sender or recipient of network traffic.

3. The strongest form of NT LAN Manager authentication is _____ .

4. IPSec _____ is used to provide end-to-end security, in which both hosts support IPSec using the same authentication protocols.

5. A(n) _____ connection security rule allows you to restrict inbound and outbound connections based on certain sets of criteria, such as membership in a particular Active Directory domain.

6. Microsoft Network Monitor is an example of a real-world _____ .

7. The Windows Firewall with Advanced Security MMC snap-in allows you to integrate IPSec into the Windows Firewall by configuring one or more _____ .

8. The default _____ for IPSec connections in an Active Directory environment is the Kerberos v5 protocol.

9. Each Windows Firewall exception can be configured with a specific _____ to control which computers the local computer will accept connections from.

10. A(n) _____ must occur before secure traffic can be sent, in order to determine the type of traffic to be secured and how it will be secured.

Multiple Choice

Select all answers that apply for the following questions.

1. This is used to provide gateway-to-gateway protection for site-to-site communications that cross the Internet (or other public networks).
   - a. Transport mode
   - b. Quick mode
   - c. Main mode
   - d. Tunnel mode

2. Windows Server 2003 supports the following feature, which is used to determine new keying material through a new Diffie-Hellman exchange on a regular basis:
   a. Dynamic rekeying
   b. Dynamic mode
   c. Dynamic association
   d. Dynamic policy

3. The following protocol provides confidentiality (in addition to authentication, integrity, and anti-replay) for the IP payload:
   a. Encapsulating Security Payload (ESP)
   b. Authentication header (AH)
   c. NTLMv2
   d. LM

4. This suite of protocols was introduced to provide a series of cryptographic algorithms that can be used to provide security for all TCP/IP hosts at the Internet layer, regardless of the actual application that is sending or receiving data.
   a. ESP
   b. IKE
   c. IPSec
   d. NTLM

5. The following is a value contained in a received IKE message that is used to help identify the corresponding main mode SA:
   a. Cookie
   b. Cache
   c. Exception
   d. ISAKMP

6. This Connection Security Rule allows you to specify one or more computers that do not need to be authenticated in order to pass traffic.
   a. Isolation
   b. Server-to-server
   c. Tunnel
   d. Authentication exemption

7. You can configure the Windows Firewall to allow one or more inbound connections based on any of the following that you configure:
   a. Exemption
   b. Isolation
   c. Exception
   d. Tunnel

8. An IP Filter in which traffic that is defined in one direction will also be defined in the opposite direction is said to be:
   a. Symmetrical
   b. Mirrored
   c. Asymmetrical
   d. Exempted

9. The following NTLM Authentication type is disabled by default in Windows Server 2003 and Windows Server 2008 servers; it should not be used in a production environment as it is weak and can be easily hacked by malicious users:
   a. NTLMv2 authentication
   b. NTLM authentication
   c. LM authentication
   d. Kerberos v5 authentication

10. This is a mathematical value that is used to provide an integrity check for a TCP or UDP packet.
    a. Checksum
    b. Header
    c. Hash
    d. Cipher Suite

■ Case Scenarios

Scenario 9-1: Securing Communications

You administer a Windows Server 2008 Active Directory domain. All client PCs are in a top-level OU called Clients, and all server PCs (apart from domain controllers) are in a top-level OU called Servers. The domain controllers are in their default OU. The Secure Server (Require Security) default IPSec policy has been assigned to all servers, including domain controllers. The Client (Respond Only) default IPSec policy has been assigned to all clients. All client PCs are Windows 2000 Professional hosts.

Management is concerned that the client computers in the Research department do not securely communicate with one another and with other clients. Only four such machines exist. On one of them, you create a custom policy that requires secure communications. You export it to a file and import it into the other three client machines in the Research department. You assign the policy on all four machines.

Next, you use the IP Security Monitor console on one of the machines and find that no SAs are set up between the Research department hosts or between these machines and clients in other departments. You capture traffic using Network Monitor and discover that unencrypted traffic is passing between the Research clients. What is the first step you should take to solve the problem?

    a. Change the authentication method on the custom policy to use a pre-shared key.

    b. Change the encryption algorithm from Triple DES (3DES) to Data Encryption Standard (DES).

    c. Create an OU containing the client computers that require IPSec security.

    d. Move the Research department computer accounts into the Servers OU.

Scenario 9-2: Troubleshooting IPSec

Your company does not use a domain structure; it uses workgroups. The Research workgroup has six clients running Windows XP Professional, four clients running Windows 2000 Professional, and two stand-alone servers running Windows Server 2008. Communication between hosts in this workgroup must be secure. A member of your support staff configures and assigns an IPSec security policy on all hosts in the Research workgroup. All hosts can ping each other by IP address, but the Research department staff cannot access files on the servers from their client PCs. You have enabled auditing of the success and failure of logon events on each server.

You log on to one of the servers using the local administrator account, you access the Security Settings node within Local Computer Policy, and you enable success and failure auditing for logon events. You open Event Viewer and locate a failure audit event 547 in the security log. The failure reason given is, "Failed to obtain Kerberos server credentials for the ISAKMP/ERROR_IPSEC_IKE service." What is a potential cause of the problem?

    a. The default response rule is not activated.

    b. Kerberos has been specified as the authentication method.

    c. The 3DES encryption algorithm has been specified, and it cannot be used on the clients running Windows 2000.

    d. The incorrect policy has been assigned.

Maintaining Network Health

OBJECTIVE DOMAIN MATRIX

TECHNOLOGY SKILL	OBJECTIVE DOMAIN	OBJECTIVE DOMAIN NUMBER
Understanding the Components of NAP	Configure Network Access Protection (NAP)	3.2

KEY TERMS

Certificate Practice Statement (CPS)

Certification Authority (CA)

Certification Authority Web Enrollment

Certificate Revocation List (CRL)

DHCP enforcement

enforcement point

enterprise CA

health certificate

Health Registration Authority (HRA)

intermediate CA

key archival

key recovery agents

NAP administration server

NAP Agent

Online Responder

private key

public key

public key cryptography

recovery agents

revocation configuration

root CA

shared secret key

Simple Certificate Enrollment Protocol (SCEP)

smart card

smart card reader

Statement of Health (SOH)

Statement of Health Response (SOHR)

System Health Agent (SHA)

System Statement of Health (SSOH)

System Statement of Health Response (SSOHR)

Lucerne Publishing has recently completed a deployment of the Active Directory Domain Services. Now that this is complete, management has expressed a desire to allow staff members to encrypt confidential data on the network such as files and e-mail messages. To enable this functionality, the network administrators at Lucerne Publishing will deploy a Public Key Infrastructure (PKI) using Microsoft's Active Directory Certificate Services (AD CS). In this lesson, you will receive an overview of the technology used by PKI, as well as the services and features offered through the AD CS server role. This will include a discussion of the terminology used in a PKI infrastructure, as well as how to design and deploy a PKI within a Windows Server 2008 environment.

In this lesson we will discuss two Windows Server 2008 services that can be used to secure user data and network traffic, as well as help administrators to establish and enforce policies regarding which computers can and cannot access resources on a Windows Server 2008 network. Active Directory Certificate Services is the Microsoft implementation of a Public Key Infrastructure (PKI) service, and Network Access Protection (NAP) is a new feature in

2008 that enables you to allow or restrict access to a Windows Server 2008 network using a number of different mechanisms and criteria.

■ Introducing Active Directory Certificate Services

THE BOTTOM LINE

The new Active Directory Certificate Services (AD CS) role in Windows Server 2008 is a component within Microsoft's larger Identity Lifecycle Management (ILM) strategy. ILM allows network administrators and owners to configure access rights for users during the users' entire lifecycle within an organization. This includes initially provisioning a user account, modifying access rights as a user's role changes within an organization, and finally deprovisioning a user account when the user's relationship with an organization is ended. The role of AD CS in ILM is to provide services for managing public key certificates that can be used by any security system that relies on a PKI for authentication or authorization.

Introducing the Public Key Infrastructure

Before you can deploy Certificate Services, it is important to understand how a PKI works, because the AD CS role in Windows Server 2008 allows you to deploy and manage your own PKI, as well as interoperate with PKI deployments in other environments. The ultimate purpose of a PKI is to provide assurances that, when you are communicating with an external entity (a reputable online retailer, for example) or an internal entity such as when sending secure e-mails within your organization, you can confirm that you are actually dealing with the entity that you *think* you are dealing with, rather than someone pretending to be that entity (such as a hacker pretending to be a reputable online retailer to steal credit card information.) While a full discussion of the mathematics and architecture of PKI is beyond the scope of this book, this lesson provides a high-level understanding of how PKI works, as well as the terminology that you need to know.

X REF

For an in-depth discussion of Public Key Infrastructure within Windows Server 2008, refer to *Windows Server 2008 PKI and Certificate Security,* by Brian Komar, from Microsoft Press.

In brief, PKI consists of a number of elements that allow two parties to communicate securely without any previous communication, through the use of a mathematical algorithm called ***public key cryptography***. Public key cryptography, as the name implies, stores a piece of information called a ***public key*** for each user/computer/etc. that is participating in a PKI. Each user/computer/etc. also possesses a ***private key***, a piece of information that is known only to the individual user or computer. By combining the (well-known and easily obtainable) public key with the (hidden and well-secured) private key, one entity (you, for example) can communicate with another entity (a secured Web site, for example) in a secure fashion without needing to exchange any sort of ***shared secret key*** beforehand. A shared secret key, as the name implies, is a secret piece of information that is shared between two parties prior to being able to communicate securely. While securing communications using a shared secret can often be more efficient due to the simpler mathematical algorithms involved, it is far less flexible and scalable to deploy than a PKI. Imagine, for example, if everyone on the Internet needed to create and exchange one of these secret keys when they wanted to buy something from a secured Web site; e-commerce as we know it would scarcely be as prolific as it has become over the past decade.

When working with a PKI, you will encounter the following common terms.

- ***Certification Authority (CA)***—This is an entity, such as a Windows Server 2008 server running the AD CS server role, that issues and manages digital certificates for use in a PKI, as well as public/private key pairs for users and computers who rely on the PKI to provide security services. Certificate authorities are *hierarchical,* which means that you can have many *subordinate* CAs within an organization that chain upwards to a single ***root CA*** that is authoritative for all Certificate Services within a given network. Many organizations will use a three-tiered hierarchy, where a single root CA will issue certificates to a number of ***intermediate CAs*** that are used to organize the PKI infrastructure.

TAKE NOTE *

In this three-tiered hierarchy, an intermediate CA is often referred to as a *subordinate CA,* while the third-tier CA that issues certificates to users and computers is called the *issuing CA.*

These second-tier CAs then issue certificates to third-tier CAs that will actually issue certificates to end users, servers, and workstations.

- **Digital certificate**—Sometimes just called a certificate, this digital document contains identifying information about a particular user, computer, service, and so on. The digital certificate contains the certificate holder's name and public key, the digital signature of the Certificate Authority that issued the certificate, as well as the certificate's expiration date.

- **Digital signature**—This electronic signature (created by a mathematical equation) proves the identity of the entity that has signed a particular document with the user's private key. The key to digital signatures is that the signatures are created by encrypting data with a private key, which only the user possesses, while they can be decrypted using the public key that is available to anyone with whom the user wishes to communicate securely. Much like when a person signs a paper document, when an entity signs a document electronically it is attesting to the fact that the document originated from the person or entity in question. In cases where a digital signature is used to sign something like an e-mail message, a digital signature will also indicate that the message is authentic and has not been tampered with since it left the sender's Outbox.

- **Certificate Practice Statement (CPS)**—This provides a detailed explanation of how a particular Certification Authority manages certificates and keys.

- **Certificate Revocation List (CRL)**—This list identifies certificates that have been revoked or terminated, and the corresponding user, computer, or service. Services that utilize PKI should reference the CRL to confirm that a particular certificate has not been revoked prior to its expiration date.

- **Certificate templates**—Templates used by a CA to simplify the administration and issuance of digital certificates. This is similar to how templates can be used in other applications such as office productivity suites or creating objects within Active Directory.

- **Smart cards**—Small physical devices, usually the size of a credit card or keychain fob, that have a digital certificate installed on them. By using a **smart card reader**, a physical device attached to a workstation, users can use a smart card to authenticate to an Active Directory domain, access a Web site, or authenticate to other secured resources.

- **Self-enrollment**—As the name suggests, this feature enables users to request their own PKI certificates, typically through a Web browser.

- **Autoenrollment**—A PKI feature supported by Windows Server 2003 and later, which allows users and computers to automatically enroll for certificates based on one or more certificate templates, as well as using Group Policy settings in Active Directory. Because this feature is supported only in Windows Server 2003 or later, certificate templates that are based on Windows 2000 will not allow autoenrollment to maintain backwards compatibility.

- **Recovery agents**—Configured within a CA to allow one or more users (typically administrators) in an Active Directory environment to recover private keys for users, computers, or services if their keys are lost. For example, if a user's hard drive crashes and the user has not backed up the private key, any information that the user has encrypted using the certificate will be inaccessible until a recovery agent retrieves the user's private key.

- **Key archival**—The process by which private keys in an Active Directory environment are maintained by the CA for retrieval by a recovery agent, if at all. Most commercial CAs do not allow key archival at all; if a customer loses a private key and has not taken a backup, the user simply needs to purchase a new certificate. In a Windows PKI implementation, users' private keys can be stored within Active Directory to simplify and automate both the enrollment and the retrieval process.

Within Windows Server 2008, the Active Directory Certificate Services server role consists of the following services and features:

- **Certification Authorities (CAs)**—As mentioned previously, CAs issue and manage PKI certificates to users, computers, and services on a network. CAs can exist in a hierarchical structure consisting of a root CA and one or more subordinate CAs beneath the root.

TAKE NOTE *
The AD CS in Windows Server 2008 implements Cryptography Next Generation (CNG), which provides an Application Programming Interface (API) that allows developers to create custom PKI-based applications.

- *Web enrollment*—This feature allows users to connect to a Windows Server 2008 CA through a Web browser to request certificates and obtain an up-to-date Certificate Revocation List.

- *Online Responder*—This service responds to requests from clients concerning the revocation status of a particular certificate, sending back a digitally signed response indicating the certificate's current status. The Online Responder is used in situations where a traditional CRL isn't an optimal solution. Instead, the Online Responder uses the Online Certificate Status Protocol (OCSP) to return certificate status information to the requester; as the name suggests, this protocol is used to respond to queries from clients who have requested data about the status of a PKI certificate that has been issued by a particular CA. OCSP transactions must be digitally signed, which can be enabled by using an OCSP Response Signing certificate template on any CA that will be used as an Online Responder. You can configure a single Online Responder to service certificate status requests, or you can deploy Responder arrays, multiple Online Responders that are linked together to process status requests.

- *Network Device Enrollment Service (NDES)*—This service allows devices, such as hardware-based routers and other network devices and appliances, to enroll for certificates within a Windows Server 2008 PKI that might not otherwise be able to do so. This service enrolls these devices for PKI certificates using the **Simple Certificate Enrollment Protocol (SCEP),** a network protocol that allows network devices to enroll for PKI certificates.

TAKE NOTE *

The NDES and Online Responder components of the AD CS role are available only in the Enterprise and Datacenter editions of Windows Server 2008.

When deploying a Windows-based PKI, two different types of CAs can be deployed:

- A *standalone CA* is not integrated with Active Directory, and relies on administrator intervention to respond to certificate requests. You can use a standalone CA as both a root and a subordinate CA in any PKI infrastructure. In many environments, the root CA in a PKI enterprise is taken offline for added security. To use this offline root functionality, the root CA must be a standalone CA.

- An *enterprise CA* integrates with an Active Directory domain, and it can use certificate templates to allow autoenrollment of digital certificates, as well as storing the certificates themselves within the Active Directory database. You can use an enterprise CA as both a root and a subordinate CA in any PKI infrastructure.

X REF

For more information on installing and configuring the Active Directory Domain Services (AD DS) server role, refer to the 70-640 MOAC exam guide.

Installing Active Directory Certificate Services

After you have developed an understanding of the underlying concepts behind a PKI, you are ready to begin configuring the AD CS server role. In this section, we will focus on installing a standalone CA.

TAKE NOTE *
While PKI services in Windows Server 2008 are branded as part of Active Directory (Active Directory Certificate Services), AD CS in Windows Server 2008 can be used to deploy PKI services either with or without the presence of an Active Directory environment.

⊙ INSTALL ACTIVE DIRECTORY CERTIFICATE SERVICES

GET READY. This exercise will install the AD CS server role on a standalone Windows Server 2008 server named CA.

1. Log onto the CA server as the local administrator or with a user account possessing administrative privileges.

2. If the Server Manager console does not appear automatically, click the **Start** button and select **Server Manage**r from the Start menu. Expand the Server Manager console to full-screen if necessary.

3. In the left pane, click the **Roles** node.

4. In the right pane, click **Add Role**. Click **Next** to bypass the initial welcome screen. The Select Server Roles screen is displayed.

5. Place a checkmark next to **Active Directory Certificate Services** and click **Next**. An informational screen is displayed, describing the AD Certificate Services role.

6. Read the information presented and click **Next**. The Select Role Services screen is displayed.

7. If it is not already present, place a checkmark next to **Certification Authority** and click **Next**. The Specify Setup Type screen is displayed as shown in Figure 10-1. Notice that the **Enterprise** option is not available; this is because the server is not a member of an Active Directory domain.

Figure 10-1

Selecting the CA Setup Type

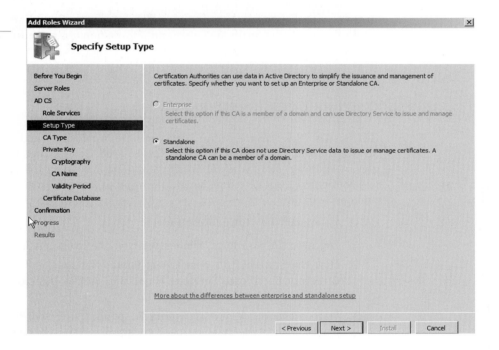

8. Confirm that the **Standalone** radio button is selected and then click **Next**. The Specify CA Type screen is displayed.

9. Confirm that the **Root CA** radio button is selected and click **Next**. The Set Up a Private Key screen is displayed.

10. Select the **Create a new private key** radio button and click **Next**. The Configure Cryptography for CA screen is displayed.

11. Accept the default values and click **Next**. The Configure CA Name screen is displayed.

12. Accept the default value of **CA-CA** and click **Next**. The Set Validity Period screen is displayed.

13. Accept the default value of 5 years and click **Next**. The Configure Certificate Database screen is displayed.

14. Accept the default values and click **Next**. The Confirm Installation Selections screen is displayed.

15. Verify that your selections are correct and click **Install.** After a few minutes, the Installation Results screen is displayed.

16. Click **Close** to complete the installation.

PAUSE. Remain logged onto the server to complete the next exercise.

In the previous exercise, you installed the Active Directory Certificate Services role onto a Windows Server 2008 computer. In the following section, you will configure your CA to support the Online Responder and perform other steps required to issue certificates for network clients.

Configuring Certificate Revocation

In Windows Server 2008, you can configure one or more Online Responders to make revocation information available for one or more CAs. To enable this, each individual CA must be configured with its own *revocation configuration* so that Online Responders can provide the correct information to clients using the OCSP. The Online Responder can be installed on any server running Windows Server 2008 Enterprise or Datacenter editions, while the certificate revocation information can come from any 2003, 2008, or even non-Microsoft CAs.

 CONFIGURE CERTIFICATE REVOCATION

GET READY. This exercise assumes that you have installed the Active Directory Certificate Services role on a standalone Windows Server 2008 server named CA, as described in the previous exercise. First, you will install the Online Responder role service, after which you will configure certificate templates and the appropriate settings to establish the CA's revocation configuration.

PART A—Install the Online Responder

1. Log onto CA as a local administrator on the local computer.

2. Click the **Start** button, then select **Server Manager.** Drill down to **Roles→Active Directory Certificate Services.** Right-click **Active Directory Certificate Services** and select **Add Role Services.**

3. Place a checkmark next to **Online Responder.** The Add Role Services screen is displayed, indicating that you need to install several IIS components to install the Online Responder.

4. Click **Add Required Role Services**, and then click **Next** to continue. The Introduction to Web Server (IIS) screen is displayed.

5. Read the informational message concerning the installation of the Web Server role and click **Next.** The Select Role Services screen is displayed.

6. Accept the default IIS features to install and click **Next.** The Confirm Installation Selections screen is displayed.

7. Click **Install** to install the Online Responder role service. The Installation Progress screen is displayed. After a few minutes, the installation will complete.

8. Click **Close** when prompted.

Part B—Establish a Revocation Configuration for the Certification Authority

1. In the left pane of Server Manager, navigate to **Roles→Active Directory Certificate Services→Online Responder: CA→Revocation Configuration.** (If the Online Responder node does not appear, close the Server Manager console and re-open it.)

2. Right-click **Revocation Configuration** and click **Add Revocation Configuration** as shown in Figure 10-2. The Getting Started with Adding a Revocation Configuration screen is displayed.

Figure 10-2

Adding a revocation configuration

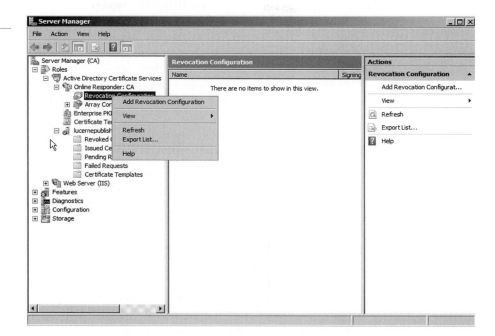

3. Read the information on the Getting Started screen and then click **Next**. The Name the Revocation Configuration screen is displayed.

4. Key **CA-REV** and click **Next**. The Select CA Certificate Location screen is displayed.

5. Select the **Select a certificate from the Local certificate store** radio button, and click **Next**. The Choose CA Certificate screen is displayed.

6. Click **Browse**. The Select Certification Authority screen is displayed.

7. Select the CA-CA certificate, and then click **OK**. Click **Next** to continue. The Select Signing Certificate screen is displayed as shown in Figure 10-3.

Figure 10-3

Selecting an OCSP Signing Certificate

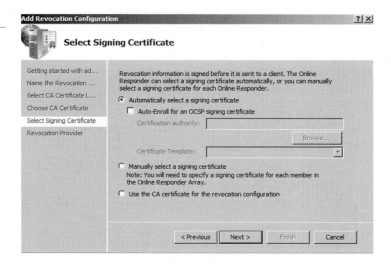

8. Select the **Use the CA certificate for the revocation configuration** radio button.

9. Click **Next** and then click **Finish** to configure the Revocation Configuration.

PAUSE. You can log out of the CA computer or remain logged in for subsequent exercises.

In the previous exercise, you configured a certificate revocation configuration for a Windows Server 2008 Certification Authority.

Managing Certificate Enrollments

Using a Windows Server 2008 CA, you can manage certificate enrollment in a number of ways depending on the needs of your organization. In this section, we will discuss the mechanisms that can be used to enroll various entities for PKI certificates, including users and workstations, as well as scenarios requiring specialized certificates such as those used by network devices and smart card enrollment agents.

In a Windows Server 2008 Active Directory environment, you can automate the distribution of PKI certificates using any combination of the following features:

- Certificate templates can be used to automate the deployment of PKI certificates by controlling the security settings associated with each template. The Security tab in the Certificate Templates snap-in allows an administrator to configure any of the following permissions on a certificate template:

  - The *Full Control ACL* allows a user to perform any action against a particular template; this should be reserved for CA administrators only.
  - The *Read ACL* allows users or computers to read a certificate template.
  - The *Write ACL* allows users or computers to modify a certificate template; this should also be reserved for CA administrators.
  - The *Enroll ACL* allows users or computers to manually request a certificate based on this template.
  - The *Autoenroll ACL* allows users or computers to be automatically issued certificates based on this template. For the Autoenroll permission to function, the Enroll permission must also be configured for the user, computer, or group in question. Additionally, you will need to configure an autoenrollment policy for your Active Directory domain using Group Policy.

- Group Policy can be used to establish autoenrollment settings for an Active Directory domain. Like other GPO settings, this is managed using the Group Policy Management MMC snap-in. The relevant settings to control PKI autoenrollment can be found in the User Configuration→Windows Settings→Security Settings→Public Key Policies or Computer Configuration→Windows Settings→Security Settings→Public Key Policies nodes. The Certificate Services Client–Autoenrollment node includes the following settings:

  - Enroll certificates automatically.
  - Do not enroll certificates automatically.
  - If you select the option to enroll certificates automatically, you can also select one or more of the following settings:
    - *Renew expired certificates, update pending certificates, and remove revoked certificates.*
    - *Update certificates that use certificate templates.*
    - *Expiry notification* to notify when a certificate has only a certain percentage of its lifetime remaining.

These topics are covered at length in the 70-640 MOAC exam guide.

In a non-Active Directory environment, clients can enroll manually for certificates using either of the following:

- The Certificate Request Wizard allows a user to manually create a certificate request file using the Certificates MMC snap-in; this wizard creates a request file that can be used by the Certification Authority MMC to generate a certificate based on the request.
- **Certification Authority Web Enrollment** allows users to manually request certificates using a Web interface, located by default at *https://<CA Name/certsrv* on a CA that is running the Certification Authority Web Enrollment role service.

Configuring CA Server Settings

You should be aware of a number of additional configuration settings before you begin the process of enrolling users and computers for PKI certificates. In this section, we will discuss configuring settings such as key archival and recovery, assigning administrative roles, and backing up and restoring the CA database.

CONFIGURING KEY ARCHIVAL AND RECOVERY

One of the challenges of managing PKI certificates in an enterprise environment is users losing the private keys associated with their certificates. This can happen for any number of reasons, such as a user stored a certificate on a laptop that is lost, stolen, or compromised by a virus; a workstation's operating system becomes corrupted and needs to be reinstalled from scratch and the user does not have a backup copy of his or her private key; and so on. This risk can be alleviated in an Active Directory environment by the use of key archival on one or more CAs, which will store an escrow copy of each certificate's private key on the CA in case it needs to be restored for any reason. This escrow copy of a private key can be restored by one or more *key recovery agents,* user accounts that are configured with a Key Recovery Agent certificate that allows them to perform this sensitive task.

You can configure a Windows Server 2008 CA to allow a single key recovery agent to recover a private key, or in especially high-security environments you can specify that multiple key recovery agents are required to perform this task. Key archival and recovery is not enabled by default on a Windows Server 2008 Certification Authority; it must be manually configured by an administrator. Only those certificates that are issued subsequent to enabling key archival will be protected by this feature; any certificates that were issued by a CA prior to configuring these settings will not be protected and will need to be re-issued by the CA.

MAINTAINING A WINDOWS SERVER 2008 CA

Like its predecessor, Windows Server 2003, Windows Server 2008 has an overall focus on least-privilege and role-based administration. In the Certificate Services role, this means multiple predefined roles can each perform a specific set of tasks. In this section, we will discuss each of the available Certification Authority roles, and the specific privileges held by each one. We will also cover the steps needed to back up and restore the Certificate Services database.

In Windows Server 2008, you can assign users to one or more of the following predefined security roles within Certificate Services:

- CA Administrator—This role is responsible for the overall management of a CA, including the ability to delegate all other roles to additional users and groups. CA Administrators have the following permissions within the Certificate Services role:
  - Configure policy and exit modules.
  - Start and stop the AD Certificate Services service.
  - Configure AD CS roles and CA extensions.
  - Define key recovery agents.
  - Configure certificate manager restrictions.
  - Delete one or more records in the CA database.
  - Modify Certificate Revocation List (CRL) publication schedules.
  - Read records and configuration information in the CA database.

- Certificate managers—Tasked with issuing and managing certificates, including approving certificate enrollment and revocation requests. Certificate managers have the following privileges:
  - Perform bulk deletions in the CA database.
  - Issue, approve, deny, revoke, reactivate, and renew certificates.
  - Recover archived keys.
  - Read records and configuration information in the CA database.
- Backup operators—Able to back up and restore the operating system files and folders, and possess the following permissions:
  - Backup and restore the System State, including CA information.
  - Start and stop the AD CS service.
  - Possess the system backup user right.
  - Read records and configuration information in the CA database.
- Auditors—Able to manage and read security logs on a computer running the AD CS role, and have the following operating system privileges:
  - Configure audit parameters.
  - Read audit logs.
  - Possess the system audit user right.
  - Read records and configuration information in the CA database.

TAKE NOTE *

Two additional CS-related tasks need to be performed by the local administrator of the server in question: installing a CA and renewing CA keys.

After you have assigned one or more users to the role of Backup Operator of a CA, you can back up and restore a CA using one of two methods:

- Using the Certification Authority snap-in (either standalone or via Server Manager), right-click the name of the CA and select All Tasks→Back up CA or All Tasks→Restore CA, depending on which task you need to perform.
- From the command line, use the certutil tool with the following syntax: certutil–backup <BackupDirectory> or certutil–restore <BackupDirectory>.

Certutil (certutil.exe) is an extremely flexible command-line utility for administering Active Directory Certificate Services. From a command prompt, key certutil /? for a full list of available command-line switches for this tool.

■ Introducing Network Access Protection (NAP)

One of the greatest challenges faced by administrators in securing corporate networks is in protecting corporate networks from "unhealthy" computers on the network. Because of the increased prevalence of high-speed Internet connectivity, home-based "virtual office" workers, and the VPN access to corporate resources that these require, it is no longer sufficient to simply deploy a perimeter firewall and rely on this device to protect your internal network resources; the notion of the network "perimeter" on a modern network is far less well-defined than in previous years. Because of this, maintaining a reliance solely on a perimeter firewall creates so-called "eggshell" security, in which a corporate network has a significantly hardened perimeter (the firewall), but the interior of the network is "soft" and easily compromised. Microsoft has released a number of technologies to help to address this, including the Windows Firewall to protect individual Windows workstations and servers, and IPSec to secure network traffic. However, prior to the release of Windows Server 2008, there was a significant gap in this protection: How can you prevent network clients that have been virus-infected, compromised, or that simply do not adhere to corporate configuration standards from accessing (and potentially damaging) critical network resources? Enforcing these requirements becomes even more difficult when the computers in question are not under direct administrator control, such as home computers or traveling laptops. The solution to this is Network Access Protection, or NAP.

CERTIFICATION READY?
Configure Network
Access Protection (NAP)

3.2

Network Access Protection is a solution that controls access to corporate network resources based on the identity of the computer attempting to connect to the resource, as well as the connecting computer's compliance with corporate policies and standards such as software update levels, Windows Firewall configurations, and the like.

If a connecting computer is out of compliance with standards that an administrator has defined, NAP can block access to critical resources and (depending on the configuration item that is out of compliance) can automatically remediate the situation. For example, if a user turns off his or her Windows Firewall and this violates the NAP access policies that you have defined, the NAP client software will attempt to automatically turn the Windows Firewall back on; if it fails, it will block access to network resources until the situation is resolved. NAP includes a number of built-in enforcement mechanisms, and includes a published Application Programming Interface (API) to allow third-party vendors to plug their own products into the NAP enforcement architecture. One common example of this is antivirus application vendors, many of whom have written plug-ins to allow NAP enforcement to be based on compliance with up-to-date antivirus signature files and the like.

Network Access Protection includes a number of built-in *enforcement methods*, which define the mechanisms that NAP can use:

> ⚠️ **WARNING** DHCP is the only NAP enforcement method that can be deployed in a non-Active Directory environment. DHCP enforcement is also the least secure enforcement method, as a user can simply configure their computer with a static IP configuration to bypass any DHCP enforcement method that is in place.

- **DHCP enforcement.** This enforcement method uses DHCP configuration information to ensure that NAP clients remain in compliance; if a NAP client is out of compliance, NAP will instruct the DHCP server to provide a DHCP configuration to the client that will limit its network access until the compliance issue is resolved.

- **Internet Protocol Security (IPSec) enforcement.** This enforcement method uses IPSec that has been secured by specially configured PKI certificates known as **health certificates**, which are issued to clients that meet defined compliance standards. If clients cannot provide the necessary health certificate, they will not be able to participate in IPSec-secured traffic.

- **VPN enforcement.** This enforcement method restricts the level of network access that a remote access client can obtain, based on the health information that the clients presents when the VPN connection is made. For example, you may define a NAP policy in which corporate laptops receive full network access upon creating a VPN connection, whereas clients connecting to VPN using their home computers will receive access only to a limited subset of corporate resources.

- **802.1X enforcement.** This enforcement method uses 802.1X-aware network access points, such as network switches or wireless access points, to restrict network access of noncompliant resources.

- **Terminal Services Gateway (TS Gateway) enforcement.** This enforcement method integrates with new Terminal Services functionality that is built into Windows Server 2008 that allows authorized remote users to connect to resources on an internal corporate or private network, from any Internet-connected device. NAP can restrict connection attempts by TS Gateway clients just as with other enforcement methods.

X REF

A full discussion of the new Terminal Services functionality can be found in the 70-643 MOAC exam guide *Configuring Windows Server 2008 Applications Platform*.

Windows Server 2008, Windows Vista, and Windows XP with Service Pack 3 all have a built-in NAP client, and third-party vendors can use the NAP API to write additional clients for additional operating systems such as Macintosh and Linux computers.

Understanding the Components of NAP

In order to deploy Network Access Protection, you will need to have an understanding of the components required to implement NAP, as well as the ways in which NAP can be used to enforce policy compliance on your network. In this section, we will discuss the main components of the NAP architecture, and the various enforcement mechanisms that can be deployed.

The overall architecture of NAP involves the following components:

- NAP client-side components

  - NAP *Enforcement Client (EC)* components—Each client contains an EC for each NAP enforcement mechanism. For example, the NAP client software includes a NAP EC for each built-in enforcement mechanism on the NAP server: DHCP, 802.1X, IPSec, and VPN.

  - One or more **System Health Agents (SHAs)**—This is a component that maintains information and reporting on one or more elements of the health of a NAP client: A client might have one SHA to manage and report on the health of a computer's anti-virus signatures, and another to report on the health of the client operating system's software update levels. For example, Windows Server 2008, Windows Vista, and Windows XP with Service Pack 3 all have a built-in Windows SHA that monitors the settings configured within the Windows Security Center. Third-party vendors can use the NAP API to write additional System Health Agents to plug into third-party products. To indicate the health status of a particular SHA, each SHA creates a **Statement of Health (SOH)** that it transmits to the NAP Agent, discussed below. Each SHA will generate a new Statement of Health (that is then passed onto the NAP Agent) whenever its status is updated; for example, an antivirus SHA will generate a new SOH if it detects that new antivirus signatures have been installed on the client, and the built-in Windows SHA will generate a new SOH if the Windows Firewall is turned on or off. In this way, System Health Agents provide continuous monitoring of system compliance, not just a one-time check when a client first attempts to access protected resources.

  - A client-side API for both the Enforcement Client and System Health Agent components—Allows third-party vendors to write their own ECs and SHAs.

  - The **NAP Agent**—Maintains information about the health of the NAP client computer and transmits information between the NAP Enforcement Clients and the System Health Agents. The NAP Agent combines the Statement of Health from each SHA into a single **System Statement of Health (SSOH)**, which it then passes to the Enforcement Clients. The Enforcement Clients then use this system SOH to request network access by passing the SSOH information on to the NAP server components, discussed next.

- NAP server-side components

  - NAP *Enforcement Server (ES)* components—As the name suggests, these components are analogous to the Enforcement Clients; one exists for each NAP enforcement method. A server that operates the NAP Enforcement Server components is referred to as a NAP **enforcement point**. Enforcement Servers receive information from the Enforcement Clients on each client, which is then consumed by other components of the NAP server-side architecture. Depending on the enforcement method in use, a NAP enforcement point can take a number of different forms, such as an 802.1X-capable Wireless Access Point for 802.1X enforcement, a Windows Server 2008 DHCP server for the DHCP enforcement method, or a **Health Registration Authority (HRA)** that can obtain health certificates from client computers when the IPSec enforcement method is used.

  - One or more *System Health Validators (SHVs)*—When the client NAP Agent transmits an SSOH to the NAP server components, the SHVs will return a **Statement of Health Response (SOHR)**, which will instruct the client-side SHA if any action is required to bring the client into compliance. For example, the SHV for a piece of antivirus software might prompt the client's antivirus software to initiate an antivirus definitions update of the locally-installed client software.

  - A NAP *health policy server*—Receives information from NAP enforcement points. The health policy server stores NAP health requirement policies and provides health state validation for NAP clients. When implementing NAP, the health policy server component is provided by a Windows Server 2008 server that is running the Network Policy Server (NPS) server role, which was introduced in Lesson 5.

- The **NAP administration server**—Manages the NAP server-side components already discussed by performing the following functions:
  - Obtains the SSOH for a NAP client from the relevant NAP Enforcement Service.
  - Distributes each Statement of Health within the System Statement of Health to the appropriate System Health Validator for analysis and further action, if needed.
  - Collects the Statement of Health Response from each SHV and passes the information on to the NPS service.
- The *NPS service* combines each Statement of Health Response into a **System Statement of Health Response (SSOHR)**. This combined response indicates whether the NAP client is compliant according to the policies defined by the NAP implementation, and passes the information back to the Enforcement Server component to respond accordingly. For example, if a DHCP client is not in compliance, the NPS service will instruct the DHCP ES (the DHCP server) to provide the NAP client with DHCP configuration information that will restrict its network access. As another example, if an 802.1X client has submitted a SSOH that indicates that the client is in compliance with configured NAP policies, the NPS service will instruct the 802.1X ES (the 802.1X-enabled wireless access point) to allow the client the requisite level of network access.
- *Health requirement servers*—Provide current health state information to NPS health policy servers. A common example of a health requirement server would be a management server for a corporate antivirus product, which would maintain information about the latest version of antivirus signature files that have been deployed on a corporate network.
- *Remediation servers*—An optional component that can be deployed to allow noncompliant client computers to achieve network compliance and gain network access. For example, you might deploy an antivirus update server and a WSUS server on a restricted network segment, and configure the NAP Enforcement Server to allow noncompliant servers to access that restricted network segment for the purpose of downloading the necessary signature files and updates to achieve compliance.

To understand how these components combine to allow or disallow client access, let's look at the following example: Contoso, Ltd., has configured a NAP infrastructure using the DHCP enforcement method. Because they wanted to introduce NAP gradually, the only currently enforced rule is that each client must have the Windows Firewall turned on in order to gain access to Contoso's network resources. A Contoso employee plugs their Windows Vista laptop called ENG-LAPTOP1, which has the Windows Firewall enabled, into the network jack at their desk, and the following takes place:

1. The built-in Windows System Health Agent (SHA) on ENG-LAPTOP1 creates a Statement of Health (SOH) indicating the health status of the Windows Firewall, i.e., that the Windows Firewall is turned on.
2. The SHA passes this Statement of Health to the NAP Agent on the client. Since there is only one SHA in use at the moment, the NAP Agent takes the information in this SOH and creates a System Statement of Health (SSOH), which it passes on to the NAP Enforcement Client (EC).
3. The Enforcement Client passes the SSOH onto the Enforcement Server (ES), which then passes the information onto the Administration Server.
4. The NAP Administration Server takes the individual Statements of Health contained within the System Statement of Health, and passes each SOH to the relevant System Health Validator (SHV).
5. The System Health Validator examines the SOH from ENG-LAPTOP1, and creates a Statement of Health Response (SOHR) indicating any action that needs to be taken in order for the client to become compliant. Since the Windows Firewall is enabled on ENG-LAPTOP1, no action is required.

6. Each SHV passes its SOHR back to the NAP Administration Server, which passes them on to the NPS Service.

7. The NPS Service combines each SOHR into a System Statement of Health Response (SSOHR), and then passes this SSOHR back to the Enforcement Server to respond accordingly. Since the SSOHR for ENG-LAPTOP1 indicates that it is in compliance with the standards defined for this NAP implementation, the DHCP Enforcement Server provides ENG-LAPTOP1 with an IP lease that grants network access.

Let's examine what would happen in this example if we added another System Health Validator. So in addition to the Windows Firewall being turned on, Contoso, Ltd., determines that a compliant client computer must have antivirus definitions that are no more than two weeks old. In this case, the Statement of Health created by the built-in Windows SHA is combined with the Statement of Health created by the antivirus vendor's SHA. Each SOH is then passed onto the respective System Health Validator, one that is built into Windows, and the other that was written by the antivirus vendor. If ENG-LAPTOP1 has been off of the corporate network for a number of weeks and does not have the appropriate antivirus signature, the SOHR from the antivirus SHV will indicate that ENG-LAPTOP1 is not in compliance, and this information will be placed into the SSOHR that is passed back to the Enforcement Server. When the Enforcement Server sees that one of the SOHRs it received indicates that this client is out of compliance, it will respond accordingly, potentially refusing to provide network access. Notice that in this second example, ENG-LAPTOP1 is considered out of compliance even though the Windows Firewall is turned on; information from the antivirus vendor SHA renders the computer out of compliance even though the built-in Windows SHA was in compliance. In this way, the Enforcement Server uses a "pass-fail" mechanism to determine compliance: if a client fails even a single compliance check, the client as a whole is considered out of compliance and the ES responds accordingly.

In the case of the built-in Windows Security Health Validator, NAP can perform autoremediation if it detects that the client is out of compliance. If the Windows Firewall on ENG-LAPTOP1 had been turned off, for example, the SOHR from the System Health Validator would have prompted the NAP client to automatically turn the client's Windows Firewall on; in many cases, the end user might not even realize that this has occurred.

Depending on the configuration item that is being monitored for compliance, autoremediation may or may not be possible. In the case of the antivirus signatures in our second example, the antivirus vendor's software might be configured to direct clients to a remediation server to update their antivirus signatures in order to gain or regain network access. In this case, you might configure a "quarantined" network segment that noncompliant computers can have access to, and place one or more remediation servers on this segment to allow these computers to download antivirus signatures, Windows updates, and the like. You can use this quarantine functionality to protect your critical network resources without denying access to noncompliant computers outright, thus allowing the users of these computers to self-remediate rather than needing to contact a corporate help desk for assistance.

Deploying Network Access Protection

Once you have developed an understanding of the components of NAP, you can take steps to deploy it in your Windows environment to provide health enforcement for servers and clients. Your first decision point is to determine which enforcement method or methods you will use to provide NAP health enforcement. As we've discussed, you can deploy one or multiple enforcement methods depending on how your environment is configured. In this section we will discuss deploying NAP using the DHCP enforcement method, as this method does not require an Active Directory infrastructure.

 REF

For a full discussion of deploying NAP in a production environment, using DHCP and other enforcement methods, refer to *Windows Server 2008 Networking and Network Access Protection (NAP)* from Microsoft Press.

In order to deploy the DHCP enforcement mechanism within Network Access Protection, you must first deploy a DHCP server running Windows Server 2008. Installing and configuring DHCP was discussed in Lesson 3. As a review, the following exercise will install and configure a DHCP scope on a Windows Server 2008 computer.

 INSTALL AND CONFIGURE A DHCP SERVER IN WINDOWS SERVER 2008

GET READY. This exercise assumes that you have installed Windows Server 2008 in a work-group configuration with a static IP address, and that you are logged onto the server using administrative credentials.

1. If Server Manager does not appear automatically, click the **Start** button and then click **Server Manager**. In the left-hand pane, click the plus sign next to **Roles**.

2. In the right-hand pane, click **Add Role**. Click **Next** to bypass the initial Welcome screen. The Select Server Roles screen appears.

3. Place a checkmark next to **DHCP Server** and click **Next**. The Introduction to DHCP Server screen appears. Click **Next** again.

4. The Select Network Connection Bindings screen appears. Click **Next** three times to continue.

5. The Add or Edit DHCP Scopes screen appears. Click **Add**. The Add Scope window appears.

6. Enter the following information to create a new DHCP scope and then click **OK**.
    Scope Name
    Starting IP Address
    Ending IP Address
    Subnet Mask
    Default gateway (optional)
    Subnet Type (Wired – 6 day lease time, or Wireless – 8 hour lease time.)

7. Click **Next** three times and then **Install** to create the DHCP scope.

PAUSE. Click **Close** when the installation of the DHCP Server role has completed. Remain logged onto the server for the following exercise.

In the previous exercise, you installed the DHCP Server role on a Windows Server 2008 computer. In the next exercise, you will install the Network Policy Server role to allow the server to function as both a NAP health policy server as well as a NAP enforcement server.

 INSTALL THE NETWORK POLICY SERVER ROLE

GET READY. This exercise assumes that you have completed the previous exercises, and that you are logged onto the Windows Server 2008 computer with administrative privileges.

1. If Server Manager does not appear automatically, click the **Start** button and then click **Server Manager**. In the left-hand pane, click the plus sign next to **Roles**.

2. In the right-hand pane, click **Add Role**. Click **Next** to bypass the initial Welcome screen. The Select Server Roles screen appears.

3. Place a checkmark next to **Network Policy** and **Access Services**. Click **Next** twice to continue. The Select Role Services screen appears.

4. Place a checkmark next to **Network Policy Server**. Click **Next** and then **Install** to add the NPS role service.

5. Click **Close** when the Add Role wizard completes.

6. To configure the server to perform NAP enforcement, click **Start→Administrative Tools→Network Policy Server**. You will see the Getting Started screen shown in Figure 10-4.

Figure 10-4

Getting Started screen for installing NPS

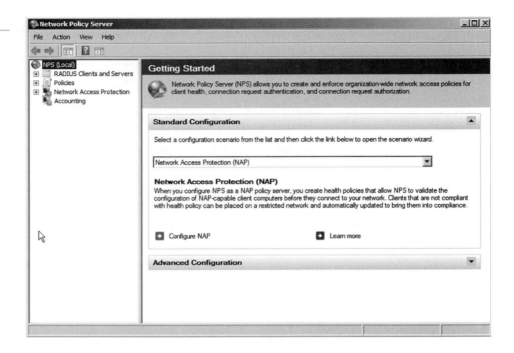

7. Click **Configure NAP**. You will see the Select Network Connection Method Used for NAP screen. In the Network Connection dropdown box, select **Dynamic Host Configuration Protocol (DHCP)**. In the Policy Name text box, accept the default selection of **NAP DHCP**. Your screen will resemble the one shown in Figure 10-5. Click **Next** twice to continue.

Figure 10-5

Selecting the network connection method

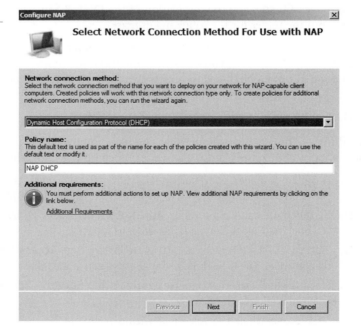

8. The Specify DHCP Scopes screen appears. Click **Add**, and enter the name of the DHCP scope that you created in the previous exercise. Click **Next** three times to continue.

9. The Define NAP Health Policy screen appears, as shown in Figure 10-6. From here you can define the following options:

Enable Auto-Remediation of Client Computers. This option is selected by default.

Allow/Deny Full Access to NAP-Ineligible Client Computers. The Deny option is selected by default.

Figure 10-6

The Define NAP Health Policy screen

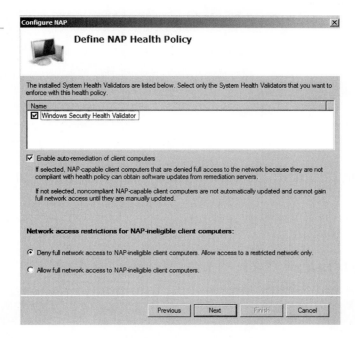

10. Click **Next** and then **Finish** to complete the initial configuration of NAP.

11. To customize the configuration of NAP, drill down to **Network Access Protection→System Health Validators** in the left-hand pane of the NPS console. In the right-hand pane, double-click the **Windows Security Health Validator**. Click **Configure**. You will see the screen shown in Figure 10-7. From here you can configure which components of the Windows Security Health Validator will be used to determine client health, including:

- Windows Firewall enabled
- Antivirus application enabled
- Antivirus definitions up-to-date
- Anti-spyware application enabled (Not available in the Windows XP NAP Agent)
- Anti-spyware definitions up-to-date (Not available in the Windows XP NAP Agent)
- Automatic Updates enabled
- Windows software updates, based on either the Microsoft Web site or an internal WSUS server

Figure 10-7

Defining a Windows Security
Health Validator policy

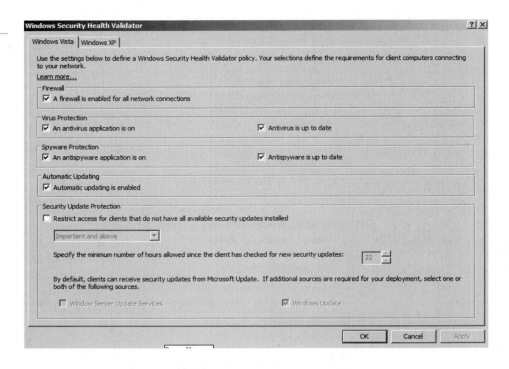

STOP. Close the Network Policy Server MMC console and log off of the Windows Server 2008 computer.

In the previous exercise, you installed and configured a Network Access Protection enforcement server.

SUMMARY SKILL MATRIX

IN THIS LESSON YOU LEARNED:

- The Active Directory Certificate Services (AD CS) role in Windows Server 2008 is a component within Microsoft's larger Identity Lifecycle Management (ILM) strategy. The role of AD CS in ILM is to provide services for managing a Windows Public Key Infrastructure (PKI) for authentication and authorization of users and devices.

- A PKI allows two parties to communicate securely without ever having communicated with one another before any previous communication, through the use of a mathematical algorithm called public key cryptography.

- PKI certificates are managed through Certificate Authorities that are hierarchical, which means that you can have many subordinate CAs within an organization that chain upwards to a single root CA.

- A Certificate Revocation List (CRL) identifies certificates that have been revoked or terminated.

- Web enrollment allows users to connect to a Windows Server 2008 CA through a Web browser to request certificates and obtain an up-to-date Certificate Revocation List.

- The Network Device Enrollment Service (NDES) allows network devices to enroll for certificates within a Windows Server 2008 PKI using the Simple Certificate Enrollment Protocol (SCEP).

- When deploying a Windows-based PKI, two different types of CAs can be deployed: enterprise CAs and standalone CAs. A standalone CA is not integrated with Active Directory, and relies on administrator intervention to respond to certificate requests.

- An enterprise CA integrates with Active Directory. It can use certificate templates as well as Group Policy Objects to allow for autoenrollment of digital certificates, as well as storing digital certificates within the Active Directory database for easy retrieval by users and devices.

- Network Access Protection (NAP) is a policy enforcement mechanism that is used to allow or reject access to Windows network resources on the basis of policy decisions, such as whether the Windows Firewall is turned on or if antivirus signatures are up-to-date.

- NAP can be configured with one of four built-in enforcement mechanisms: DHCP, 802.1X, IPSec, and VPN.

- The NAP client includes one or more System Health Agents (SHAs), which map to System Health Validators (SHVs) within the NAP server architecture.

■ Knowledge Assessment

Fill in the Blank

Complete the following sentences by writing the correct word or words in the blanks provided.

1. A(n) _____ is a CA that integrates with Active Directory and allows for autoenrollment of user and computer certificates through the use of Group Policy and certificate templates.

2. The top-level CA in any PKI hierarchy is the _____.

3. One alternative to using public key cryptography is by using a(n) _____.

4. Each PKI certificate consists of a public key that is widely known, and a(n) _____ that is known only to the user or computer who holds the certificate.

5. Users can request certificates via the Web using the _____ service.

6. A(n) _____ obtains PKI health certificates from client computers when the IPSec NAP enforcement method is used.

7. The _____ method is the only NAP enforcement agent that can be deployed in the absence of an Active Directory domain.

8. _____ provide continuous monitoring of system compliance on all NAP clients.

9. The _____ distributes Statement of Health information to the appropriate System Health Validators.

10. Each System Health Agent provides a _____ regarding its health status.

Multiple Choice

Select all answers that apply for the following questions.

1. Each server that functions as a CA must be configured with a(n):
   a. Revocation configuration
   b. Key Recovery Agent
   c. User template
   d. Online Responder

2. An organization can have one or more of these to distribute the load of issuing certificates in a geographically dispersed organization:
   a. Root CA
   b. Enterprise CA
   c. Standalone CA
   d. Intermediate CA

3. In order to authenticate using a smart card that has been configured for their use, a user must have the following installed at their workstation:
   a. smart card enrollment station
   b. Online Responder
   c. smart card reader
   d. smart card enrollment agent

4. Which component of Active Directory Certificate Services uses the Online Certificate Status Protocol to respond to client requests?
   - **a.** NDES
   - **b.** Online Responder
   - **c.** Certificate Revocation List
   - **d.** Subordinate CA

5. The IPSec NAP Enforcement method relies on this type of PKI certificate to perform its enforcements.
   - **a.** OCSP certificate
   - **b.** recovery certificate
   - **c.** NAP certificate
   - **d.** health certificate

6. A server that operates the NAP Enforcement Server components is referred to as a(n):
   - **a.** enforcement agent
   - **b.** enforcement point
   - **c.** enforcement service
   - **d.** enforcement mark

7. The Network Device Enrollment Service (NDES) uses the following protocol to enroll network devices for PKI certificates:
   - **a.** Certificate Revocation Protocol
   - **b.** Online Certificate Status Protocol
   - **c.** Simple Certificate Enrollment Protocol
   - **d.** Certificate Issuance Protocol

8. Statements of Health from each SHA are combined to create a:
   - **a.** System Statement of Health
   - **b.** Statement of Health Response
   - **c.** Overall Statement of Health
   - **d.** System Statement of Health Response

9. The following NAP component transmits information between the NAP Enforcement Clients and the System Health Agents:
   - **a.** NAP Client
   - **b.** NAP Service
   - **c.** NAP Enforcement Service
   - **d.** NAP Agent

10. This provides a detailed explanation of how a particular Certification Authority manages certificates and keys.
    - **a.** Certificate Revocation List
    - **b.** Key Management Service
    - **c.** Certificate Practice Statement
    - **d.** Revocation Configuration

■ Case Scenarios

Scenario 10-1: Consulting for Contoso, Ltd.

You are a computer consultant for Kevin Browne, the Chief Security Officer of Contoso, Ltd. Contoso, Ltd. has a single Active Directory domain structure with the domain *contoso.com*. Contoso, Ltd. has research contracts with numerous pharmaceutical companies worldwide, with 50 locations in 12 countries. Some Contoso offices have full T1 or T3 connectivity back to the corporate headquarters office in Chicago, IL; other offices, however, connect via slow and sometimes heavily utilized satellite links. All Contoso servers are running Windows Server 2008, and all Contoso workstations are running Windows XP Professional or Windows Vista Enterprise.

Given the sensitive nature of the data that Contoso's researchers work with on a daily basis, the CSO of Contoso wants to implement the ability for researchers to encrypt their files and e-mail messages against tampering by any outsiders. Since some of the work being done requires Contoso to conform to government security standards in many countries, Kevin wishes to deploy this capability in the most secure manner possible. However, he is concerned with adding additional traffic to the already overburdened WAN links at some locations, as this would adversely affect the researchers' ability to perform their research.

Based on this information, answer the following questions regarding the recommendations that you would make to Contoso, Ltd.

1. In order to minimize the burden on Contoso Ltd's WAN links, how would you recommend deploying Certificate Authority computers within their environment?

2. The Contoso, Ltd. CSO has read about the security benefits of deploying an offline root CA. In order to use this feature, how must you design the Contoso, Ltd. PKI infrastructure?

Maintaining Windows Server 2008 File Services

OBJECTIVE DOMAIN MATRIX

Technology Skill	Objective Domain	Objective Domain Number
Configuring Shadow Copies of Shared Folders	Configure shadow copy services	4.3
Configuring Disk Quotas	Manage disk quotas	4.5
Backing Up Windows Server 2008	Configure backup and restore	4.4

KEY TERMS

bare-metal restore
disk quota
file ownership
File Server Resource Manager
  (FSRM)
hard quota
manual backup
NTFS quota

quota template
scheduled backup
Shadow Copies of Shared Folders
soft quota
thresholds
Volume Shadow Copies Service
  (VSS)
VSS copy backup

VSS full backup
wbadmin
Windows PowerShell
Windows Recovery
  Environment (WinRE)

Contoso, Ltd., is a manufacturing firm that maintains offices across the United States. Each Contoso office supports a number of file servers that are used to store critical design, accounting, and marketing files to support Contoso's operations. Employees in each office work multiple shifts during peak production periods, and IT staff is not always available to immediately assist when files are accidentally deleted. Additionally, Contoso management is concerned that staff are storing non-work-related files on Contoso file servers. Finally, IT staff need to develop a plan to back up and restore critical files in the event of a hardware failure or other disaster recovery scenario. Contoso, Ltd., has already deployed Windows Server 2008 file servers to provide file and print services to Contoso staff; they will now use the features of Windows Server 2008 to manage and maintain file services on an ongoing basis.

In this final lesson, we will discuss concepts and tasks relating to the maintenance of files and folders on a Windows Server 2008 computer. We will begin with a discussion of Shadow Copies of Shared Folders, a Windows feature that allows users to perform self-service restores of previous versions of files and folders in case of accidental deletion or unwanted modifications. We will then turn to the File Server Resource Manager (FSRM), an optional role service that is part of the File Server role that allows administrators to configure advanced file server functionality such as disk quotas, file screens, and e-mail notifications of user quota activities. We will conclude with a description of the Windows Server Backup feature, a new feature in Windows Server 2008 that performs file and volume-level backups using Volume Shadow Copies.

■ Configuring Shadow Copies of Shared Folders

Shadow Copies of Shared Folders is a Windows Server 2008 mechanism that automatically retains copies of files on a server volume in multiple versions from specific points in time. When users accidentally overwrite or delete files, they can access the shadow copies to restore earlier versions. This feature is designed to prevent administrators from having to load backup media to restore individual files for users. Shadow Copies is a file-based fault tolerance mechanism that does not provide protection against disk failures, but it does protect against accidental file deletions that inconvenience users and administrators on a regular basis.

CERTIFICATION READY?
Configure Shadow Copies
4.3

Shadow Copies of Shared Folders creates point-in-time copies of files that are stored on file shares on Windows Server 2003 or Windows Server 2008 file servers. Using Shadow Copies of Shared Folders allows users to access previous versions of files without requiring adminis-trator intervention, which can reduce administrator burden in the following scenarios:

- Recovering files that were accidentally deleted
- Recovering files that were accidentally overwritten
- Comparing previous versions of a file to the current version

Shadow Copies of Shared Folders uses the *Volume Shadow Copies Service (VSS)*. Shadow Copies of Shared Folders functionality is enabled at the volume level, which means that it will be enabled or disabled for all shared folders on the C:\ drive, the D:\ drive, etc. Shadow Copies of Shared Folders works by periodically taking a snapshot of the contents of all shared folders on a particular volume, and storing those snapshots to allow users and administra-tors to refer back to them later for any of the purposes described above. The client software required to use Shadow Copies of Shared Folders is built into Windows XP Service Pack 2 and later, Windows Vista, and Windows Server 2008; the necessary software for previous operating systems can be downloaded from the Microsoft Web site.

TAKE NOTE*

Shadow copies are read-only; you cannot modify the contents of a shadow copy.

Before configuring Shadow Copies of Shared Folders, you must formulate a plan for where shadow copies will be stored and how much space will be allocated to storing those shadow copies. You must allocate a minimum of 300MB of space to store shadow copies. The default value for shadow copy storage is 10% of the source volume; that is, the volume that is being copied, with a minimum allocation of 300MB and a maximum allocation of 3GB. You can configure Shadow Copies of Shared Folders to store snapshots on the same volume as the files being copied, or else you can store the shadow copies on a separate volume. When esti-mating storage requirements for Shadow Copies of Shared Folders, keep in mind that files that change frequently will have higher snapshot storage requirements than files that do not change often. For example, 500 files that are modified once a month will require less snap-shot storage than 50 files that are changed multiple times a day. It is important to allocate sufficient disk space to support your Shadow Copies of Shared Folders deployment, since when this storage limit is reached, older versions of shadow copies will be deleted without any means of restoring them. Additionally, if you need to move your shadow copies storage from one volume to another, you will need to delete any shadow copies that were stored on the original volume and must "start from scratch" on the new volume.

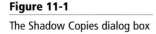
Your next planning decision is determining the schedule that Shadow Copies of Shared Folders will use in taking its snapshots. Once you have enabled Shadow Copies of Shared Folders for a particular volume, the default schedule will create a snapshot twice per day, seven days per week, at 7:00 A.M. and 12:00 P.M. Before modifying this default schedule, keep the following things in mind:

- A maximum of 64 shadow copies can be stored on a particular volume. When this limit is reached, the oldest snapshot will be deleted to make room for the most recent snapshot. Using the default schedule (and assuming that you have allocated sufficient disk space for your snapshots), taking two snapshots a day will enable 32 days of availability for snapshots. If you increase the frequency of snapshots, to four or eight times per day for example, this will decrease the number of days of history available, shortening it to 16 days in the case of four snapshots per day and 8 days in the case of eight snapshots per day.

- Microsoft recommends that you do not configure Shadow Copies of Shared Folders to take more than one snapshot per hour.

CONFIGURE SHADOW COPIES OF SHARED FOLDERS

GET READY. This exercise assumes that you have created one or more file shares on a Windows Server 2008 computer, and that you are logged on with administrative privileges.

1. Click **Start**, and then click **All Programs→Accessories→Windows Explorer**. The Windows Explorer window appears.

2. In the Folders list, expand the **Computer** container, right-click a volume and, from the context menu, select **Configure Shadow Copies**. The Shadow Copies dialog box appears, as shown in Figure 11-1.

Figure 11-1

The Shadow Copies dialog box

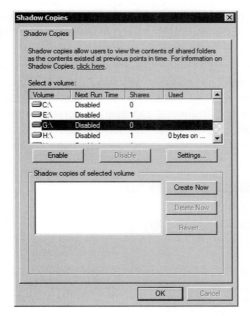

3. In the Select a Volume box, choose the volume for which you want to enable Shadow Copies. By default, when you enable Shadow Copies for a volume, the system uses the following settings:

- The system stores the shadow copies on the selected volume.
- The system reserves 300 megabytes of disk space for the shadow copies.
- The system creates shadow copies at 7:00 A.M. and 12:00 P.M. every weekday.

4. To modify the default parameters, click **Settings**. The Settings dialog box appears, as shown in Figure 11-2.

Figure 11-2

The Settings dialog box

5. In the Storage Area box, specify the volume where you want to store the shadow copies. For a server operating with a high I/O load, such as a file server, Microsoft recommends that, for best performance, you create the Shadow Copies storage area on another volume, one that does not have Shadow Copies enabled.

6. Specify the Maximum Size for the storage area, or choose the **No limit** option. If the storage area should become filled, the system begins deleting the oldest shadow copies, so if there are a lot of large files stored on the volume, increasing the size of the storage area can be beneficial. However, no matter how much space you allocate to the storage area, Windows Server 2008 supports a maximum of 64 shadow copies for each volume, after which the system begins deleting the oldest copies.

7. Click **Schedule**. The Schedule dialog box appears, as shown in Figure 11-3. Using the controls provided, you can modify the existing Shadow Copies tasks, delete them, or create new ones, based on the needs of your users. Scheduling shadow copies to occur too frequently can degrade server performance and cause copies to be aged out too quickly, while scheduling them to occur too infrequently can cause users to lose work because the most recent copy is too old.

Figure 11-3

The Schedule dialog box

8. Click **OK** twice to close the Schedule and Settings dialog boxes.

9. Click **Enable**. The system enables the Shadow Copies feature for the selected volume and creates the first copy in the designated storage area.

10. Close any open windows.

CLOSE. You can log off of the Windows Server 2008 computer, or else stay logged on for subsequent exercises.

After you complete this procedure, users can restore previous versions of files on the selected volumes by right-clicking on the file and selecting Restore previous versions, as shown in Figure 11-4. Once you have selected this option, you will be taken to the Previous Versions tab of the file in question, as shown in Figure 11-5.

Figure 11-4

Accessing restore previous versions functionality

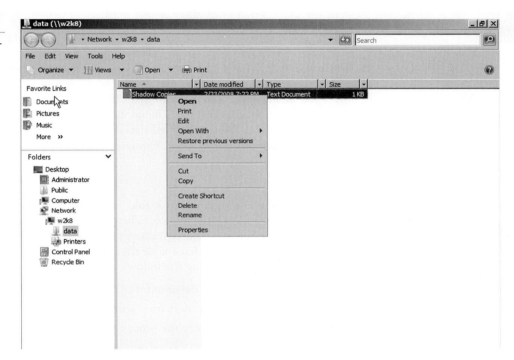

Figure 11-5

Viewing the Previous Versions tab

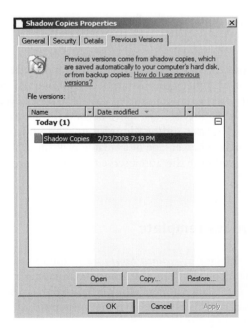

From the Previous Versions tab, you have one of three options for any snapshots listed:

- Open—This allows you to open a read-only copy of the file, useful for comparing it against the current version of the file.
- Copy—This allows you to create a copy of the file in an alternate location.
- Restore—This will restore the snapshot to the original file location. *This option will overwrite the existing version!*

If you have inadvertently deleted a file, you can access it from the Previous Versions tab of the file's parent folder. For example, if you accidentally delete the FY2008.xlsx file located in the \\w2k8\data share, right-click the ~\data share and select Restore previous versions from there.

■ Configuring Disk Quotas

THE BOTTOM LINE

In Windows Server 2008, a **disk quota** is simply a limit that is placed on the disk space a user is permitted to consume in a particular volume or folder. Quotas are based on the notion of **file ownership**. Windows automatically makes a user the owner of all files that he or she creates on a server volume. The quota system tracks all of the files owned by each user and adds their sizes. When the total size of a given user's files reaches the quota specified by the server administrator, the system takes action, also specified by the administrator.

CERTIFICATION READY?
Manage Disk Quotas
4.5

When you install the File Services server role, you have the option to install the **File Server Resource Manager (FSRM)** role service. When you select this role service, Windows Server 2008 installs the File Server Resource Manager console, first introduced in Windows Server 2003 R2, which provides tools that enable file server administrators to monitor and regulate their server storage, by performing the following tasks:

- Establish quotas that limit the amount of storage space allotted to each user.
- Create screens that prevent users from storing specific types of files on server drives.
- Create templates that simplify the process of applying quotas and screens.
- Automatically send e-mail messages to users and/or administrators when quotas are exceeded or nearly exceeded.
- Generate reports providing details of users' storage activities.

REF

For more information on deploying the File Services role, refer to Lesson 6.

Using FSRM, the actions the system takes when a user approaches or reaches a quota are highly configurable. For example, administrators can configure quotas to be hard or soft. A **hard quota** prohibits users from consuming any disk space beyond the allotted amount, while a **soft quota** allows the user storage space beyond the allotted amount and just sends an e-mail notification to the user and/or administrator. Administrators can also specify the **thresholds**, which dictate the percentage of available disk space at which the system should send notifications, and configure the quota server to generate event log entries and reports in response to quota thresholds.

Creating a Disk Quota Template

For enterprise networks, creating **quota templates** is the recommended method for managing quota assignments on a large scale. A quota template is a collection of settings that defines a number of configuration items for disk quotas; because it is a template, this collection of settings can be used to create numerous quota assignments, all containing consistent configuration settings.

A quota template is a collection of settings that define the following:

- Whether a quota should be hard or soft
- What thresholds FSRM should apply to the quota
- What actions FSRM should take when a user reaches a threshold

The File Server Resource Manager console includes several predefined templates, which you can use to create your own template. To create a quota template, use the following procedure.

 CREATE A DISK QUOTA TEMPLATE

GET READY. Log on to Windows Server 2008 using an account with local or domain administrative privileges. When the logon process is completed, close the Initial Configuration Tasks window and any other windows that appear.

1. Open Server Manager, right-click the **File Services** role, and select **Add Role Services**.

2. Place a checkmark next to **File Server Resource Manager**, and then click **Next**.

3. On the Configure Storage Usage Monitoring screen, place a checkmark next to the volume(s) for which you want to enable storage monitoring.

4. Click **Next** twice and then **Install**, and then click **Close** when the installation has completed.

5. Click **Start**, and then click **Administrative Tools→File Server Resource Manager**. The File Server Resource Manager console appears, as shown in Figure 11-6.

Figure 11-6

The File Server Resource Manager console

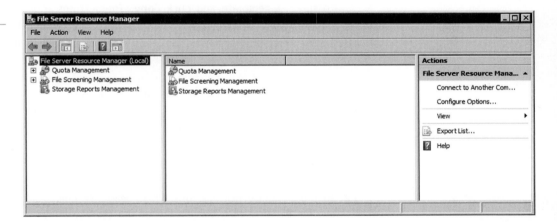

6. Expand the **Quota Management** node, right-click the **Quota Templates** node and, from the Action menu, select **Create Quota Template**. The Create Quota Template dialog box appears, as shown in Figure 11-7.

Figure 11-7

The Create Quota Template
dialog box

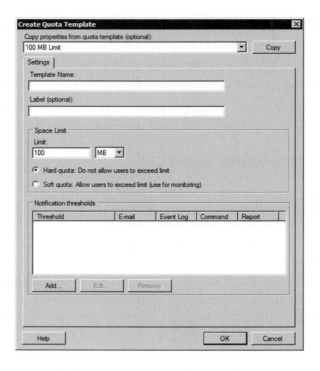

7. If you want to create a new quota template based on the settings in one of the existing templates, click the **Copy properties from quota template** dropdown list to select a template and click **Copy**. The settings from the template appear in the dialog box, so that you can modify them as needed.

8. In the Template Name text box, key the name you will use to identify the template.

9. Optionally, in the Label text box, you can key a term that will be associated with all of the quotas you create using the template.

10. In the Space Limit box, specify the amount of storage space you want to allot to each individual user and specify whether you want to create a hard quota or a soft quota.

11. In the Notification Thresholds box, click **Add**. The Add Threshold dialog box appears.

12. In the Generate Notifications When Usage Reaches (%) text box, specify a threshold in the form of a percentage of the storage quota.

13. Use the controls on the following tabs to specify the actions you want taken when a user reaches the specified threshold:

   • E-mail Message—Select the appropriate checkbox to specify whether you want the system to send an e-mail message to an administrator, to the user, or both, as shown in Figure 11-8. For administrators, you can specify the e-mail addresses of one or more persons separated by semicolons. For the user, you can modify the text of the default e-mail message.

Figure 11-8

The E-mail Message tab on the Add Threshold dialog box

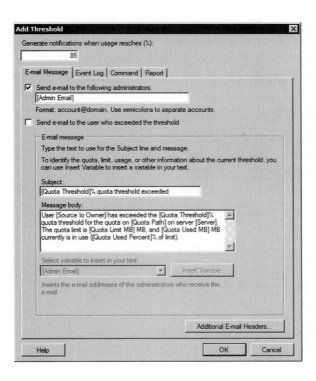

TAKE NOTE*

The Windows Server 2008 computer must be running the Simple Mail Transfer Protocol (SMTP) service to be able to send e-mail messages. To install SMTP, you must use Server Manager to add the SMTP Server feature.

- Event Log—Select the **Send warning to event log** checkbox to create a log entry when a user reaches the threshold, as shown in Figure 11-9. You can modify the wording of the log entry in the text box provided.

Figure 11-9

The Event Log tab on the Add Threshold dialog box

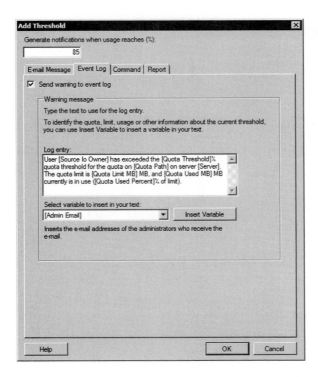

• Command—Select the **Run this command or script** checkbox to specify a program or script file that the system should execute when a user reaches the threshold, as shown in Figure 11-10. You can also specify command arguments, a working directory, and the type of account the system should use to run the program or script.

Figure 11-10

The Command tab on the Add Threshold dialog box

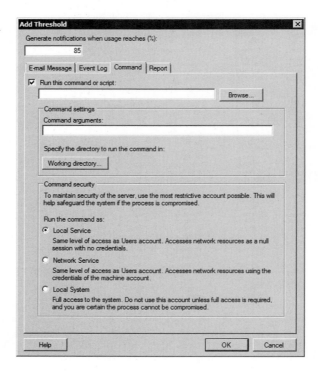

• Report—Select the **Generate reports** checkbox, and then select the checkboxes for the reports you want the system to generate, as shown in Figure 11-11. You can also specify that the system e-mail the selected reports to an administrator or to the user who exceeded the threshold.

Figure 11-11

The Report tab on the Add Threshold dialog box

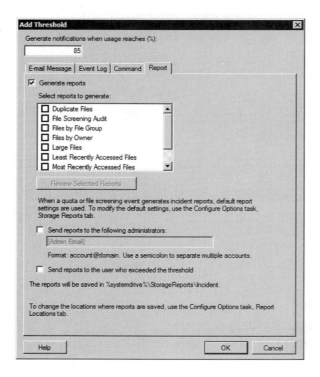

14. Click **OK** to close the dialog box and add the new threshold to the Notification Thresholds list on the Create Quota Template dialog box.

15. Repeat steps 7 through 10 to create additional thresholds, if desired. When you have created all of the thresholds you need, click **OK** to create the quota template.

STOP. You can close the File Server Resource Manager console, or else leave it open for a subsequent exercise.

Using quota templates simplifies the quota management process, in much the same way as assigning permissions to groups, rather than users. If you use a template to create quotas, and you want to change the properties of all of your quotas at once, you can simply modify the template, and the system applies the changes to all of the associated quotas automatically.

Creating a Disk Quota

After you have created your quota templates, you can create the quotas themselves. To create a quota, use the following procedure.

 CREATE A DISK QUOTA

GET READY. Log on to Windows Server 2008 using an account with local or domain administrative privileges. When the logon process is completed, close the Initial Configuration Tasks window and any other windows that appear.

1. Click **Start**, and then click **Administrative Tools→File Server Resource Manager**. The File Server Resource Manager console appears.

2. Expand the **Quota Management** node, right-click the **Quotas** folder and, from the context menu, select **Create Quota**. The Create Quota dialog box appears, as shown in Figure 11-12.

Figure 11-12

The Create Quota dialog box

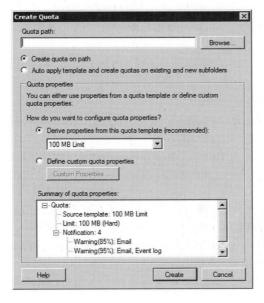

3. In the Quota Path text box, key or browse to the name of the volume or folder for which you want to create a quota.

4. Select one of the following application options:

   • Create quota on path—Creates a single quota for the specified volume or folder.

- Auto apply template and create quotas on existing and new subfolders—Causes FSRM to automatically create a quota, based on a template, for each subfolder in the designated path, and for every new subfolder created in that path.

5. Select one of the following properties options:
   - Derive properties from this quota template—Configures the quota using the settings of the template you select from the drop-down list.
   - Define custom quota properties—Enables you to specify custom settings for the quota. Clicking the **Custom Properties** button opens a Quota Properties dialog box for the selected volume or folder, which contains the same controls as the Create Quota Template dialog box discussed in the previous section.

6. Click **Create**. The new quota appears in the console's details pane.

STOP. You can close the File Server Resource Manager console, or leave it open for subsequent exercises.

Quotas are also available on NTFS volumes without installing the File Server Resource Manager role service, but these *NTFS quotas* are limited to controlling storage on entire volumes on a per-user basis. When you create FSRM quotas for volumes or folders, however, they apply to all users. NTFS quotas are also limited to creating event log entries only, while FSRM quotas can also send e-mail notifications, execute commands, and generate reports, as well as log events.

■ Generating Storage Reports

THE BOTTOM LINE

Reporting is one of the keys to efficient storage management. File Server Resource Manager is capable of generating a variety of reports that enable administrators to examine the state of their file server volumes and identify transgressors or company storage policies.

The reports that FSRM can create are as follows:

- Duplicate Files—Creates a list of files that are the same size and have the same last modified date.
- File Screening Audit—Creates a list of the audit events generated by file screening violations for specific users during a specific time period.
- Files By File Group—Creates a list of files sorted by selected file groups in the File Server Resource Manager console.
- Files By Owner—Creates a list of files sorted by selected users that own them.
- Large Files—Creates a list of files conforming to a specified file spec that are a specified size or larger.
- Least Recently Accessed Files—Creates a list of files conforming to a specified file spec that have not been accessed for a specified number of days.
- Most Recently Accessed Files—Creates a list of files conforming to a specified file spec that have been accessed within a specified number of days.
- Quota Usage—Creates a list of quotas that exceed a specified percentage of the storage limit.

➔ GENERATE A SCHEDULED STORAGE REPORT

GET READY. Log on to Windows Server 2008 using an account with domain administrative privileges. When the logon process is completed, close the Initial Configuration Tasks window and any other windows that appear.

1. Click **Start**, and then click **Administrative Tools→File Server Resource Manager**. The File Server Resource Manager console appears.

2. Right-click the **Storage Reports Management** node and, from the context menu, select **Schedule a New Report Task**. The Storage Reports Task Properties dialog box appears, as shown in Figure 11-13.

Figure 11-13

The Storage Reports Task Properties dialog box

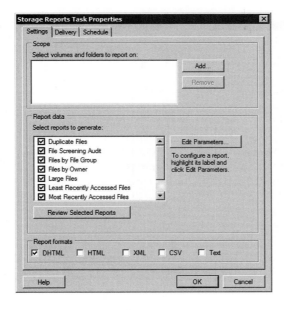

3. On the Settings tab, click **Add** and, in the Browse For Folder dialog box that appears, select the volume or folder on which you want a report. Repeat this step to select multiple volumes or folders, if desired.

4. In the Report Data box, select the reports that you want to generate. When you select a report and click **Edit Parameters**, a Report Parameters dialog box appears, in which you can configure the parameters for that specific report.

5. In the Report Formats box, select the checkboxes for the formats you want FSRM to use when creating the reports.

6. If you want FSRM to send the reports to administrators via e-mail, click the **Delivery** tab, as shown in Figure 11-14, select the **Send reports to the following administrators** checkbox, and key one or more e-mail addresses (separated by semicolons) in the text box.

Figure 11-14

The Delivery tab of the Storage Reports Task Properties dialog box

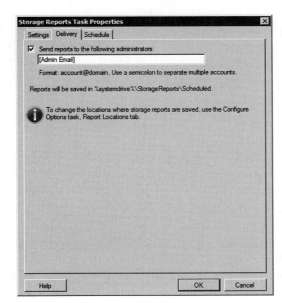

7. Click the **Schedule** tab and then click **Create Schedule**. A Schedule dialog box appears.

8. Click **New**, and use the Schedule Task, Start Time, and Schedule Task Daily controls to specify when you want FSRM to create the reports, as shown in Figure 11-15. You can also click **Advanced** for more detailed scheduling options.

Figure 11-15

The Schedule dialog box

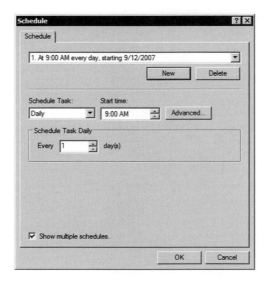

9. Click **OK** to close the Schedule dialog box and click **OK** again to close the Storage Reports Task Properties dialog box.

STOP. You can log off of the Windows Server 2008 computer, or remain logged on for subsequent exercises.

The report is now added to the Windows Server 2008 list of scheduled tasks. The server will generate it at the specified time.

■ Backing Up Windows Server 2008

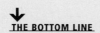

THE BOTTOM LINE

One of the most essential duties of an administrator is ensuring that data and operating system information is backed up in case of a failure. Procedures that include the frequency of backups in addition to the type of information that needs to be backed up should be planned and implemented in every organization. Windows Server 2008 introduces a new technology for performing backups, called *Windows Server Backup*. Similar to Shadow Copies of Shared Folders, Windows Server Backup uses the Volume Shadow Copies Service (VSS) to perform snapshots of the items being protected by backup.

CERTIFICATION READY?
Configure backup and restore

4.4

Depending on the number of servers in your organization, your plan may vary. For example, if you have only one file server in your environment that stores data for numerous departments, then you must back up this computer frequently in case of a failure. In another scenario that includes multiple file servers and several infrastructure servers that store data and delivering applications, the data stored on each server is backed up separately.

To back up Active Directory, you must install the Windows Server Backup feature from the Server Manager console. If you wish to perform backups from the command line, you will also need to install *Windows PowerShell*, which is a new command-line and task-based scripting technology that is included with Windows Server 2008, although PowerShell cannot be installed on Server Core in Windows Server 2008. Windows Server Backup supports the

use of CD and DVD drives as backup destinations, but does not support magnetic tapes as backup media. Additionally, you cannot perform backups to dynamic volumes.

Unlike previous versions of Windows, the new Windows Server Backup tool does not allow you to back up individual files or directories; you must back up the entire volume that hosts the files that you want to protect. This means that you must configure a backup destination that is at least as large as the volume or volumes that you wish to back up.

Windows Server 2008 supports two types of backup:

- *Manual backup.* This backup can be initiated by using Server Backup or the Wbadmin. exe command-line tool when a backup is needed. You must be a member of the Administrators group or the Backup Operators group to launch a manual backup.
- *Scheduled backup.* Members of the local Administrators group can schedule backups using the Windows Server Backup utility or the Wbadmin.exe command-line tool. Scheduled backups will reformat the target drive that hosts the backup files, and thus can be performed only on a local physical drive that does not host any critical volumes.

 PERFORM A MANUAL WINDOWS SERVER 2008 BACKUP

GET READY. To perform this backup, you must have a second hard drive volume available that is at least 1MB larger than the volume(s) of the server that you are backing up; you must also be logged onto the server with administrative privileges.

PART A—Install the Windows Server Backup Feature

1. If the Server Manager MMC does not appear automatically when you log onto the server, click the **Start** button and click **Server Manager**.
2. In the left-hand pane, click **Features**. In the right-hand pane, click **Add features**. The Select Features screen appears.
3. Place a checkmark next to **Windows Powershell**. Click the plus sign next to **Windows Server Backup Features**. Place a checkmark next to **Windows Server Backup** and **Command-line Tools**.
4. Click **Next,** and then click **Install**. When the installation completes, click **Close**.
5. On the Start menu, click **Administrative Tools** and select **Windows Server Backup**. The Windows Server Backup window is displayed.
6. In the right pane, select **Backup Once**. The Backup Options window is displayed, as shown in Figure 11-16.

Figure 11-16

Configuring one-time backup options

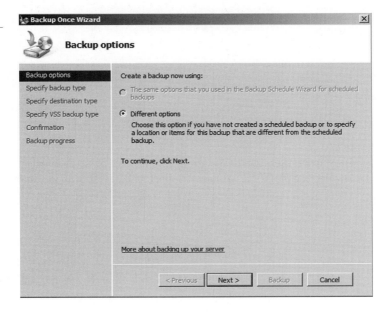

7. Because you have not configured scheduled backups, the only available option is the Different Options radio button. Click **Next** to continue. The Select Backup Configuration window is displayed, as shown in Figure 11-17.

Figure 11-17

Specifying the backup type

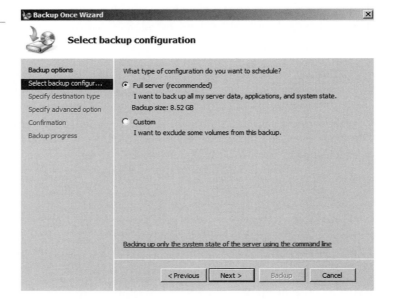

8. If you are backing up to a local device, select **Custom** and click **Next**. The Select Backup Items window is displayed, as shown in Figure 11-18.

Figure 11-18

Selecting volumes to be backed up

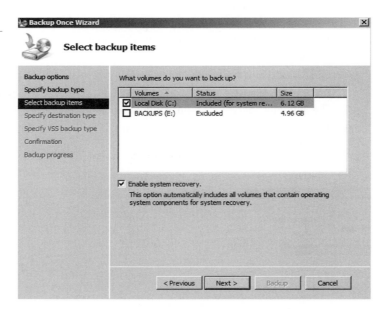

9. Ensure that the destination volume has been deselected and click **Next**. The Specify Destination Type window is displayed, as shown in Figure 11-19.

Figure 11-19

Specifying the destination type

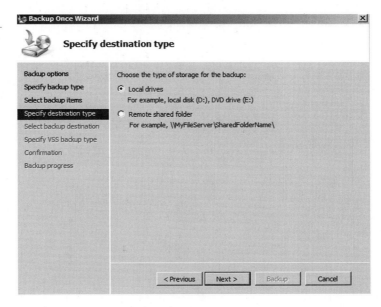

10. Select a local drive or a remote shared folder to store this backup and click **Next**. The Select Backup Destination window is displayed, as shown in Figure 11-20.

Figure 11-20

Selecting the backup destination

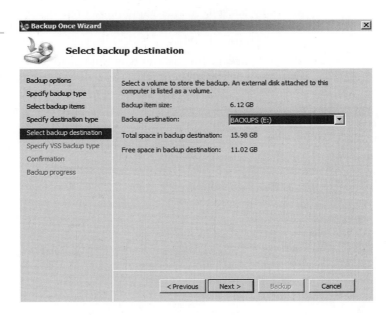

11. In the Backup destination drop-down box, select the appropriate backup destination and click **Next**. The Specify Advanced Option window is displayed, as shown in Figure 11-21.

Figure 11-21

Specifying the VSS backup type

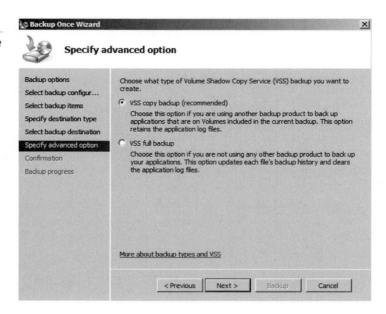

12. Select one of the following backup types and click **Next**. The Confirmation window is displayed, as shown in Figure 11-22.

a. **VSS copy backup.** This backup type will retain the Application log files on the local server. Select this backup type if you will be using a third-party backup tool in addition to Windows Server Backup.

b. **VSS full backup.** This backup type will update each file's backup history and will clear the Application log files.

Figure 11-22

Confirming backup selections

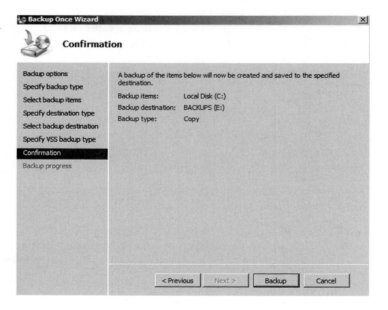

13. To begin the backup process, click **Backup**. The Backup Progress window is displayed, as shown in Figure 11-23.

Figure 11-23

Viewing an in-progress backup

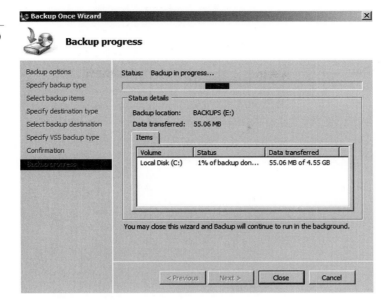

14. When the backup is complete, click **Close**.

PAUSE. Leave the Windows Server Backup window open for the next exercise.

You have just configured a one-time backup of the critical volumes on a Windows Server 2008 server. In the next exercise, you will configure a backup schedule to provide regular backup protection for a Windows Server 2008 computer.

 CONFIGURE SCHEDULED WINDOWS SERVER 2008 BACKUPS

GET READY. To perform this exercise you must be logged into the server as a member of the Administrators group. To perform this backup, you must have a second hard drive volume available that is at least 1 MB larger than the critical volumes of the server that you are backing up. These steps assume that you are backing up to a local volume. You must also have the Window Server Backup feature installed on the Windows Server 2008 computer; this can be installed from the Server Manager console if you have not done so already.

1. Log on to the server as a member of the local Administrators group. On the Start menu, click **Administrative Tools** and select **Windows Server Backup**. The Windows Server Backup window is displayed.

2. In the right pane, select **Backup Schedule**. The Getting Started window is displayed.

3. Click **Next**. The Select backup configuration window is displayed.

4. If you are backing up to a local device, select **Custom** and click **Next**. The Select Backup Items window is displayed.

5. Verify that the destination volume has not been selected and click **Next**. The Specify Backup Time window is displayed, as shown in Figure 11-24.

Figure 11-24

Specifying a backup time

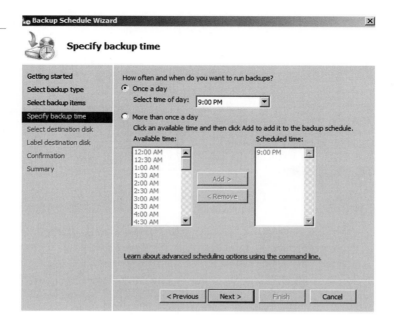

6. Select the time that you want the backups to take place and click **Next**. The Select Destination Disk window is displayed.
7. If your backup destination disk does not appear automatically, click **Show All Available Disks**, place a checkmark next to the destination, and click **OK**.
8. Place a checkmark next to the desired destination disk and click **Next**. A Windows Server Backup warning is displayed, as shown in Figure 11-25.

Figure 11-25

Confirming the backup destination

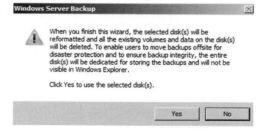

9. Read the warning and click **Yes** to continue. The Label Destination Disk window is displayed.
10. Click **Next** to continue. The Confirmation window is displayed.
11. Click **Finish** to schedule the backup. The destination disk will be formatted automatically. Click **Close** to return to the Windows Server Backup window.

PAUSE. Close the Windows Server Backup MMC snap-in.

You have now configured scheduled backups of a Windows Server 2008 computer. To modify or delete the scheduled job, use the Task Scheduler. To access the Task Scheduler, click All Programs, click Accessories, and then click the System Tools menu. In the next exercise, we will discuss performing a restore of a Windows Server 2008 computer.

■ Restoring Windows Server 2008

THE BOTTOM LINE

Hand in hand with knowledge of the backup process in Windows Server 2008 is the importance of being able to perform restores when required. Whether you need to restore an individual file or folder that a user has inadvertently deleted, or if you need to restore all of the data stored on an entire volume due to a hardware failure on a server, restores of Windows Server 2008 can be performed using the Windows Server Backup MMC snap-in, as well as the *wbadmin* command-line utility. You can also perform a *bare-metal restore* of a server that has experienced a catastrophic hardware failure by using the *Windows Recovery Environment (WinRE)*, a special boot mode that provides a centralized platform for operating system recovery. Unlike traditional restores in which data files are restored onto an existing operating system, a bare-metal restore allows you to restore operating system and data files onto a server that does not have a pre-existing operating system.

When restoring data in Windows Server 2008, you can choose to restore data from a local server, or from a remote server. You can choose to perform two types of restores:

- Files and folders—This restore allows you browse to individual files and folders to restore, in cases where you need to restore only a limited amount of information.
- Volumes—This restore will recover an entire volume. This option cannot be selected from the Windows Server Backup utility if the selected volume contains operating system components.

When restoring individual files and folders, there are additional choices to make when performing a restore:

- Recovery destination—You can restore files and folders to their original location, or to another location on the local server or a remote server.
- Overwrite options—When the restore operation finds files and folders in the recovery location, the restore can do one of three things:
  a. Create copies—so that you have both the existing and the restored version of the restored file/folder.
  b. Overwrite—any existing files with files that are being restored.
  c. Do not recover—so that any existing files/folders will not be overwritten.
- Security settings—Allows you to restore the NTFS permissions on the files and folders, or to allow the restored information to inherit the security of the restoration location.

In the following exercise, you will restore an individual folder from the backup that you preformed in the previous section.

RESTORE WINDOWS SERVER 2008

GET READY. These steps assume that you have performed a backup of the C:\ volume as described in the previous exercise, and that you are logged onto the Windows Server 2008 computer with administrative credentials.

1. Log on to the server as a member of the local Administrators group. On the Start menu, click **Administrative Tools** and select **Windows Server Backup**. The Windows Server Backup window is displayed.
2. In the right pane, select **Recover**. The Getting Started window is displayed.
3. Select the **This server** radio button, and then click **Next**. The Select Backup Date screen appears.

4. Select the date and time of the backup that you want to restore from, and then click **Next**. The Select Recovery Type screen appears, as shown in Figure 11-26.

Figure 11-26

Selecting the recovery type

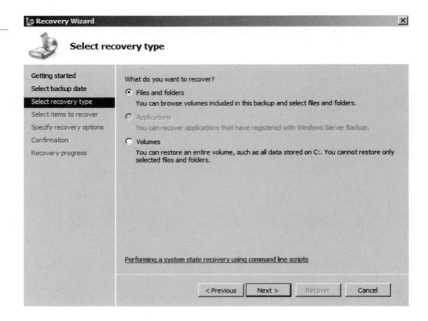

5. Select the **Files and folders** radio button and then click **Next**. The Select items to recover screen appears.

6. Browse to the file or folder that you wish to recover, and then click **Next**. The Specify Recovery Options screen appears, as shown in Figure 11-27.

Figure 11-27

Configuring recovery options

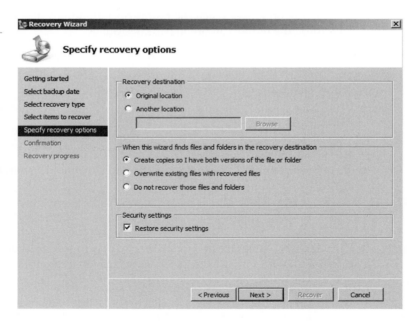

7. Make your desired restore options selections and then click **Next**. Click **Recover** to begin the file restore process. Click **Close** when the restore operation has completed.

CLOSE. Log off of the Windows Server 2008 computer.

In the previous exercise, you performed a restore of a Windows Server 2008 computer.

SUMMARY SKILL MATRIX

IN THIS LESSON YOU LEARNED:

- Shadow Copies of Shared Folders is based on the Volume Shadow Copy Service (VSS), and allows users to access previous versions of files in the event that they are accidentally deleted or overwritten.

- Shadow Copies of Shared Folders is enabled at a volume level, and affects all shared folders on a particular volume.

- The Restore Previous Versions functionality allows users to access and restore their own Shared Copies of Shared Folders snapshots without requiring administrative intervention.

- A disk quota is a limit on the disk space a user is permitted to consume in a particular volume or folder.

- Disk quotas are based on file ownership. The quota system tracks all of the files owned by each user and adds their sizes.

- When the total size of a given user's files reaches the quota specified by the server administrator, the system takes action.

- Windows Server 2008 introduces the Windows Server Backup feature, which uses VSS to back up servers at the volume level.

■ Knowledge Assessment

Matching

Match the following definitions with the appropriate term.

- **a.** disk quota
- **b.** File Server Resource Manager (FSRM)
- **c.** manual backup
- **d.** NTFS quota
- **e.** Shadow Copies of Shared Folders
- **f.** threshold
- **g.** Volume Shadow Copies Service (VSS)
- **h.** wbadmin
- **i.** Windows PowerShell
- **j.** Windows Recovery Environment (WinRE)

_____ 1. Administrators can specify these to dictate the percentage of available disk space at which actions associated with disk quotas will take effect.

_____ 2. This is a new command-line and task-based scripting technology that is included with Windows Server 2008.

_____ 3. This is a limit that is placed on the disk space a user is permitted to consume in a particular volume or folder.

_____ 4. This is a special Windows Server 2008 boot mode that provides a centralized platform for performing operating system recovery.

_____ 5. These are available on NTFS volumes on servers that the File Server Resource Manager role service is not installed on.

_____ **6.** This is the service that both Shadow Copies of Shared Folders and Windows Server Backup are based on.

_____ **7.** This can be initiated on an ad hoc basis by using Windows Server Backup or wbadmin.exe.

_____ **8.** This File Services role service provides tools that enable file server administrators to monitor and regulate their server storage.

_____ **9.** This feature automatically retains copies of files on a server volume in multiple versions from specific points in time.

_____ **10.** This is the command-line utility used to perform backup and restore operations in Windows Server 2008.

Multiple Choice

Select all answers that apply for the following questions.

1. This type of backup will completely reformat the target drive that hosts the backup files.
   - **a.** VSS full backup
   - **b.** normal backup
   - **c.** manual backup
   - **d.** scheduled backup

2. This type of disk quota allows the user to access storage space beyond the allotted amount and simply sends an e-mail notification when the quota has been exceeded.
   - **a.** hard quota
   - **b.** soft quota
   - **c.** manual quota
   - **d.** automatic quota

3. This type of restore can be used to recover an entire server after it has experienced a hardware failure or other disaster recovery scenario.
   - **a.** bare-metal restore
   - **b.** manual restore
   - **c.** volume restore
   - **d.** critical restore

4. This backup type will retain the Application log files on the local server after the backup is completed.
   - **a.** VSS full backup
   - **b.** manual backup
   - **c.** copy backup
   - **d.** scheduled backup

5. This quota type prohibits users from consuming any disk space beyond what has been defined within the quota.
   - **a.** hard quota
   - **b.** soft quota
   - **c.** manual quota
   - **d.** NTFS quota

6. This is the only type of quota available on servers that do not have the File Server Resource Manager role service installed.
   - **a.** hard quota
   - **b.** soft quota
   - **c.** manual quota
   - **d.** NTFS quota

7. All Windows disk quotas are based on the following to determine the amount of space being used by a particular user.
   - **a.** Volume Shadow Copies
   - **b.** snapshots
   - **c.** file ownership
   - **d.** volume size

8. This backup type will update the server's backup history and will clear the Application log files on the server.
   - **a.** VSS full backup
   - **b.** manual backup
   - **c.** copy backup
   - **d.** scheduled backup

9. This collection of disk quota settings can be used to create numerous quota assignments all containing consistent configuration settings.
   - **a.** hard quota
   - **b.** soft quota
   - **c.** quota template
   - **d.** NTFS quota

10. This backup technology was introduced by Windows Server 2008 and relies on the Volume Shadow Copy Service (VSS).
   a. Windows Server Backup
   b. VSS full backup
   c. Shared Copies of Shadowed Folders
   d. snapshot backups

■ Case Scenarios

Scenario 11-1: Managing File Storage on a Windows Server 2008 Network

You are the network administrator for Trey Research, a medical research firm with offices in Newark, New Jersey; Troy, Michigan; and Palo Alto, California. You have deployed multiple Windows Server 2008 file servers across your organization to allow researchers to store and access critical research files for the various projects they are working on. However, it has come to your attention that numerous administrative staff are saving non-work-related files to the same file servers, such as photos, movie files, and MP3 files. Trey Research management has tasked you with ensuring that storage on company file servers is not overtaxed with these files; however, work-related files should still be permitted. Which Windows Server 2008 file technologies can you use to solve this problem?

Appendix A
Windows Server 2008 Network Infrastructure Configuration: Exam 70-642

Matrix Skill	Skill Number	Lesson Number
Configure IPv4 & IPv6 addressing	1.1	1
Configure Dynamic Host Configuration Protocol (DHCP)	1.2	3
Configure routing	1.3	5
Configure IPsec	1.4	9
Configure a Domain Name System (DNS) server	2.1	4
Configure DNS zones	2.2	4
Configure DNS records	2.3	4
Configure DNS replication	2.4	4
Configure name resolution for client	2.5	4
Configure remote access	3.1	5
Configure Network Access Protection (NAP)	3.2	10
Configure network authentication	3.3	9
Configure wireless access	3.4	5
Configure firewall settings	3.5	9
Configure a file server	4.1	6
Configure Distributed File System (DFS)	4.2	6
Configure shadow copy services	4.3	11
Configure backup and restore	4.4	11
Manage disk quotas	4.5	11
Configure and monitor print services	4.6	7
Configure Windows Server Update Services (WSUS) server settings	5.1	8
Capture performance data	5.2	8
Monitor event logs	5.3	8
Gather network data	5.4	8

Lab Setup Guide

■ Getting Started

The *Windows Server 2008 Network Infrastructure Configuration* title of the Microsoft Official Academic Course (MOAC) series includes two books: a textbook and a lab manual. The exercises in the lab manual are designed for classroom use under the supervision of an instructor or a lab aide. In an academic setting, the computer classroom might be used by a variety of classes each day, so you must plan your setup procedure accordingly. For example, consider automating the classroom setup procedure and using removable fixed disks in the classroom. Use the automated setup procedure to rapidly configure the classroom environment and remove the fixed disks after teaching this class each day.

■ Classroom Setup

This course should be taught in a classroom containing networked computers where students can develop their skills through hands-on experience with Microsoft Windows Server 2008. The exercises in the lab manual require the computers to be installed and configured in a specific manner. Failure to adhere to the setup instructions in this document can produce unanticipated results when the students perform the exercises.

TAKE NOTE*

You can either use multiple physical machines for each student, or you can install the server and client as virtual machines on a single physical machine using Microsoft Virtual PC or a similar virtual machine environment. If you use Virtual PC, your physical machine must comply with the minimum requirements for Windows Server 2008. Virtual PC also requires 1.6GHz processor speed or faster and 640MB RAM (1GB recommended) over and above the RAM required by the hosting operating system for each virtual guest that will be running on the host computer.

Windows Server 2008 Requirements

A physical computer running Windows Server 2008 requires the following hardware and software.

HARDWARE REQUIREMENTS

All hardware must be on the Microsoft Windows Server 2008 Windows Catalog.
- One 1GHz processor (2GHz or greater recommended)
- 512MB RAM (2GB or greater recommended)
- 10GB hard disk minimum (40GB or greater recommended)
- One DVD-ROM drive
- One mouse
- One Super VGA display adapter and monitor
- One Ethernet network interface adapter

SOFTWARE REQUIREMENTS

The software listed below is required for the course.

- Microsoft Windows Server 2008 (Evaluation edition available as a free download from Microsoft's Web site at *http://technet.microsoft.com*)

In order to perform several optional labs, the software listed below is required:

- Microsoft Windows Vista Ultimate (evaluation edition available as a free download from Microsoft's Web site at *http://technet.microsoft.com*)

Classroom Configuration and Network Considerations

Each student's server is configured as a Windows Server 2008 stand-alone server in a workgroup configuration. The instructor's computer is configured as a Windows Server 2008 domain controller for the purposes of the first Lab exercise, using the following configuration:

- Active Directory domain name: lucernepublishing.com
- Computer name: INSTRUCTOR01
- Fully qualified domain name (FQDN): instructor01.lucernepublishing.com

For several optional exercises, each student will require two additional server computers—one running the Windows Server 2008 Server Core installation and one running Windows Vista, Enterprise Edition.

> **TAKE NOTE** *
>
> To maintain consistency with the order of the textbook that this lab manual accompanies, Lab 1 will address configuring TCP/IP addressing on one or more already-installed Windows Server 2008 computers. Lab 2 will then require you to remove the 2008 installations that were used in Lab 1 in order to perform actual installations of the Windows Server 2008 operating system. Depending on the pre-existing skill set of your students, instructors may wish to reverse the order of Labs 1 and 2 to reduce the setup/teardown required between the two labs. Sidebars in Lab 1 indicate any necessary changes if the instructor chooses to reverse the order of Labs 1 and 2.

A Note on the Use of Virtualization

The lab exercises were written using Windows Server 2008 and Windows Vista installed as virtual guests in Microsoft Virtual Server 2005 R2 and the exercises were tested with virtual guests in Microsoft Virtual PC. Depending on your needs, you can install multiple guests using Virtual Server, Virtual PC, or VMWare. Keep in mind that running multiple virtual "guests" on a single physical "host" can greatly increase the hardware requirements needed by the physical host; be sure to test these configurations before attempting to use virtual guests to teach in an actual classroom environment in order to ensure that performance is acceptable.

Additionally, you may wish to use advanced virtualization features such as snapshots, undo disks, and differencing disks to decrease the amount of time needed to deploy multiple virtual servers, as well as the time required to roll back the changes made in each individual lab. The use of these advanced virtualization features is beyond the scope of this document; consult the documentation for your virtualization software of choice to determine if this would prove valuable in your environment.

Installing Windows Server 2008

If your computer has an existing 32-bit operating system installed, start the computer as usual and insert the Windows Server 2008 Installation disk. The Microsoft Windows 2008 window opens automatically. In the left pane of the window, select Install Windows Server 2008. If the Microsoft Windows 2008 window does not open automatically, double-click the CD-ROM drive in Windows Explorer to launch the auto-play feature.

If your computer does not have an operating system installed, you will need to boot your computer from the Windows Server 2008 Installation disk. When you boot from the disk, the Windows Server 2008 Setup program starts automatically.

After Windows Server 2008 Setup is launched, follow the steps below to continue the installation.

> **TAKE NOTE** *
>
> The steps below assume that you are performing a new installation; the steps to upgrade to Windows Server 2008 from an existing operating system will differ slightly.

 INSTALL WINDOWS SERVER 2008

TAKE NOTE *

Depending on how your school's network is set up, you might need to use different values for settings, such as IP addresses, to match your actual networking environment.

GET READY. You will now install the Windows Server 2008 operating system. These steps require the Windows Server 2008 installation media, as well as a valid product key if appropriate to your lab environment.

1. Insert the Windows Server 2008 installation media and power on the physical or virtual server.

2. You will see the initial installation screen. Here you are prompted to configure the following three items:
   - Language to install: for example, English or German
   - Time and currency format: for example, English (United States) or French (Switzerland)
   - Keyboard/input layout: for example, US or United Kingdom

3. Click **Next**, followed by **Install Now**.

4. Depending on the type of media you are using to install the software, you might be prompted to enter the Windows product key. If prompted, enter a legitimate Windows product key and click **Next**.

5. Next you will be prompted to install either the full version of Windows Server 2008 or Server Core. Select a full install or a Server Core install as appropriate for the particular image that you are building. Click **Next** to continue.

6. On the subsequent screen, you will be prompted to accept the Windows Server 2008 license terms. Read the licensing terms and then place a checkmark next to **I accept the license terms.** Click **Next** to continue the installation.

7. You will be prompted to select an upgrade installation or a clean install. If you are installing Windows onto brand new hardware, you will notice that the Upgrade option is grayed out and only the Custom option is available. Select the **Custom** installation option.

8. On the subsequent screen, you will be prompted to select the hard drive partition on which to install Windows. Select the appropriate partition and click **Next**. At this point, the installation process will begin. The remainder of the installation is largely automated. To improve the security of a Windows Server 2008 installation, you will be prompted to establish a complex password on the final reboot.

PAUSE. In this exercise, you performed the initial installation of the Windows Server 2008 operating system on a newly formatted computer.

> **TAKE NOTE** *
>
> After Windows Server 2008 Setup restarts, the computer might try to boot from the Windows Server 2008 DVD. If this happens, you will be prompted to press a key to boot from the DVD; if you do not press a key, Windows Server 2008 should start normally. However, if the Windows Server 2008 Setup routing restarts automatically, simply remove the installation media and then restart the computer.

COMPLETE POST-INSTALLATION TASKS ON THE SERVER

GET READY. After the installation is complete and the computer has restarted, you should see the Welcome To Windows dialog box. In this exercise, you will install the Virtual Machine Additions onto the Virtual PC instance in question. (If you are using separate physical machines rather than VM instances, skip this section.)

1. Press (Ctrl) + (Alt) + (Delete) and enter the username and password you specified earlier to log on *(Administrator/MSPress#1)*. The Initial Configuration Tasks dialog box is displayed. Leave this page displayed, because students will use this interface during the first lab exercise.

2. If you are using Virtual PC, install Virtual Machine Additions. To do so, select **Install Or Update Virtual Machine Additions** from the Actions menu of the Virtual PC menu, and then follow the prompts. After the installation, you will be prompted to restart Windows Server 2008. After restarting, repeat step 1 of this section to log on.

PAUSE. In this exercise, you installed the Virtual Machine Additions onto one or more Virtual PC or Microsoft Virtual Server instances of the Windows Server 2008 operating system. In the next exercise, you will install and configure the Active Directory Domain Services role on the instructor computer in order to demonstrate Active Directory integration during several lab exercises.

> **TAKE NOTE***
>
> At some point, the operating system will prompt you to activate the server. When that happens, follow the steps to activate the server.

Installing Active Directory on the Instructor's Computer

 INSTALL ACTIVE DIRECTORY ON THE INSTRUCTOR'S COMPUTER

GET READY. In this exercise you will configure a single-forest Active Directory domain named *lucernepublishing.com*. This exercise assumes that the server in question has been configured with a static IP address.

1. Press (Ctrl) + (Alt) + (Delete) on the instructor's computer and log on as the default administrator of the local computer. Your username will be *Administrator*. The password will be *MSPress#1* or the password that you configured when the server was built. The Initial Configuration Tasks screen will be displayed automatically.

2. Configure the following items prior to installing Active Directory:

   - Time zone and current time
   - Network configuration: Static IP address, subnet mask, default gateway
   - Enable automatic updates and feedback
   - Computer name: INSTRUCTOR01

3. Reboot the computer when instructed. After it reboots, log on using administrative credentials.

4. Close the Initial Configuration Tasks screen.

5. If the Server Manager screen does not appear automatically, click the **Start** button, and then click **Server Manager**.

6. Expand the Server Manager window to full screen if necessary.

7. In the left pane of Server Manager, double-click **Roles**.

8. Click **Add Role**. Click **Next** to bypass the initial Welcome screen. The Select Server Roles screen is displayed.

9. Place a checkmark next to **Active Directory Domain Services**. Click **Next**. The Active Directory Domain Services screen is displayed.

10. Read the introductory information to Active Directory Domain Services and click **Next**. The Confirm Installation Selections screen is displayed.

11. Read the confirmation information to prepare for the installation. Click **Install** to install the AD Domain Services role. The Installation Results screen is displayed.

12. Click **Close this wizard** and launch the **Active Directory Domain Services Installation Wizard (dcpromo.exe)**. The Welcome to the Active Directory Domain Services Installation Wizard screen is displayed.

13. Click **Next** twice to continue. The Choose a Deployment Configuration screen is displayed.

14. Click the **Create a new domain in a new forest** radio button, then click **Next.** The Name the Forest Root domain screen is displayed.

15. Key **lucernepublishing.com** as the name of the new domain and click Next. The Domain NetBIOS Name screen appears.

16. Key **LP** and click **Next**. The Set Forest Functional Level screen is displayed.

17. Select **Windows Server 2008** and click **Next**. The Additional Domain Controller Options screen is displayed.

18. Verify that the DNS Server checkbox is selected, and then click **Next**. A warning message is displayed concerning DNS delegations. Read the warning message and click **Yes** to continue. The Location for Database, Log Files, and SYSVOL screen is displayed.

19. Accept the default selections and click **Next** to continue. The Directory Services Restore Mode Administrator Password screen is displayed.

20. Enter **MSPress#1** into the Password and Confirm Password text boxes and click **Next** to continue. The Summary screen is displayed.

21. Review your installation choices and click **Next** to continue. The Active Directory Domain Services Installation Wizard screen is displayed, indicating that the Active Directory DS service is being installed. The Completing the Active Directory Domain Services Installation Wizard screen is displayed.

22. Click **Finish**. When prompted, click **Restart Now** to restart the newly configured domain controller.

PAUSE. In this exercise, you configured the instructor's computer as a domain controller in the lucernepublishing.com domain. In the next exercise, you will configure a DHCP server to allow the lab computers to obtain IP addresses automatically. If your lab network uses DHCP through another mechanism, such as a hardware-based router, you can skip this section.

⊕ INSTALL AND CONFIGURE THE DHCP SERVER

GET READY. In this exercise you will install and configure a DHCP server on the INSTRUCTOR01 computer.

1. Press (Ctrl) + (Alt) + (Delete) on the instructor's computer and log on as the default administrator of the local computer. Your username will be *Administrator*. The password will be *MSPress#1* or the password that you configured when the server was built. The Server Manager screen will be displayed automatically.

2. Expand the Server Manager window to full screen if necessary.

3. In the left pane of Server Manager, double-click **Roles**.

4. Click **Add Roles**. Click **Next** to dismiss the initial Welcome screen. The Select Server Roles screen is displayed.

5. Place a checkmark next to **DHCP Server**. Click **Next**. The Introduction to DHCP Server screen is displayed.

6. Read the information about the DHCP Server role and click **Next**. The Specify IPv4 DNS Server Settings screen is displayed.

7. Leave all text boxes as is and click **Next**. The Specify IPv4 WINS Server Settings screen is displayed.

8. Leave the default radio button selected and click **Next**. The Add or Edit DHCP Scopes screen is displayed.

9. Click **Add** to create a DHCP scope for your network. The Add Scope screen is displayed.

10. Enter the following information, customized as appropriate for your classroom setup:

   - Scope Name: **70-642 Lab**
   - Starting IP address: **192.168.1.100**
   - Ending IP address: **192.168.1.254**
   - Subnet mask: **255.255.255.0**
   - Default gateway: **192.168.1.1**
   - Subnet type: **Wired**

11. Verify that there is a checkmark next to **Activate this scope**, and then click **OK**.

12. Click **Next**. The Configure DHCPv6 Stateless Mode screen is displayed.

13. Leave the default radio button selected and click **Next**. The Specify IPv6 DNS Server Settings screen is displayed.

14. Leave all text boxes blank and click **Next**. The Authorize DHCP Server screen is displayed.

15. Leave the default radio button selected and click **Next**. The Confirm Installation Selections screen is displayed.

16. Click **Install**. When the installation is completed, click **Close**.

STOP. You have now completed all the necessary steps to set up the instructor's computer and all the student computers to use the *Windows Server 2008 Network Infrastructure Configuration* Lab Manual. This includes installing Windows Server 2008 on all student computers, as well as configuring the instructor's computer as a DHCP server and as a domain controller in the lucernepublishing.com domain.

Additional Setup Considerations for Individual Labs

In Lab 5, performing exercises involving the Routing & Remote Access service will require each computer to be configured with a second network interface card (NIC) to simulate network routing within the lab environment. This can either be accomplished by installing a second NIC within the physical machines, or by configuring Virtual Networking within the virtualization product. To assist students in completing this lab, prepare a diagram of the network in which they will be working, similar to the one shown in Figure 1.

Lab 7 involves creating and configuring printers on a Windows Server 2008 computer. The lab instructions involve setting up a "dummy" HP LaserJet 4 printer; however, if your lab environment has a physical printer available that students can work with, you may modify the

Figure 1

Sample network diagram for Lab 5

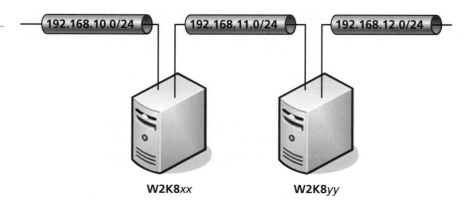

exercise instructions accordingly. The Lab Challenge Exercise in Lab 7 requires the creation of a test Organizational Unit (OU) and user accounts for students to test deploying printers through Group Policy. A Group Policy Object (GPO) should be linked to the OU containing the test user accounts that students can use to deploy printer connections.

Lab 8 involves making the following out-of-band downloaded executables available to students:

- Microsoft Network Monitor 3.1
- Microsoft Report Viewer Redistributable 2005
- Windows Server Update Services 3.0 SP1

TAKE NOTE*

If your lab environment does not allow Internet access, you will need an upstream WSUS server available during Lab 8 for students to point their WSUS server to. You will also need to provide configuration specifics on the name or IP address of this server for your students. The Lab 8 instructions assume that the student-created WSUS server has Internet access available.

TAKE NOTE*

If your lab environment requires proxy server configuration in order to access the Internet, you will need to provide this configuration information to your students prior to Project 8.4, Configuring Windows Server Update Services. The Lab 8 instructions assume that the lab environment does not require proxy server configuration.

In Lab 11, performing exercises using Windows Server Backup will require each computer to be configured with a secondary hard drive that is of equal or greater capacity to the system drive configured on each machine.

You have now completed the necessary steps for setup of the labs for the *Windows Server 2008 Network Infrastructure Configuration* Lab Manual. This includes installing Windows Server 2008 as well as configuring the instructor's computer as a DHCP server and as a domain controller in the lucernepublishing.com domain.

Glossary

802.1X enforcement NAP enforcement method that uses 802.1X-aware network access points, such as network switches or wireless assess points, to restrict network access of noncompliant resources

A

Accounting Remote Access component that maintains information about successful and failed connections to a remote access server

Active Directory-integrated zone a DNS zone that stores its data within the Active Directory database

address (a) resource record a DNS resource record that maps an individual host name to an IP address

Address Resolution Protocol (ARP) used to map a known IP address to an unknown MAC address

Administrative Events a built-in custom view in the Windows Server 2008 Event Viewer that collects Critical, Error, and Warning events from all logs on the server

Always Call Back To: the Callback Option that always calls the user back at a pre-configured number

Application Layer the top-most layer of the OSI model, where DHCP and other network applications function

Application Logs records events associated with software that is installed on the server

Applications and Services provides collections of Event Viewer entries associated with server hardware, Internet Explorer, and other Windows-based applications and components

authentication the process of confirming a user's identity

Authentication Exemption a connection security rule used to specify one or more computers that do not need to be authenticated in order to pass traffic

Authentication Header (AH) an IPSec protocol that provides authentication, integrity, and anti-replay for the entire packet

authentication methods a security algorithm and type used for IPSec authentication and key exchange

Authentication Server (AS) an 802.1X component that verifies the supplicant's authentication credentials

authenticator an 802.1X component that requests authentication credentials from supplicants

authoritative a DNS server that hosts a primary or secondary zone for a particular DNS domain

authoritative answer a response from a DNS server that hosts a primary or secondary zone for the DNS domain being queried

authorize the process of enabling an Active Directory DHCP server to provide DHCP services to clients

Autoenrollment PKI feature supported by Windows Server 2003 and later, which allows users and computers to automatically enroll for certificates based on one or more certificate templates

Automatic Private IP Addressing (APIPA) a service in Windows XP, Windows Server 2003, Windows Vista, and Windows Server 2008 that can automatically configure client IP addresses in the absence of a DHCP server; APIPA addresses do not contain a default gateway and can only be used to communicate on the local subnet

automatic restores restores performed by a DHCP server whenever database corruption is detected

automatic updates enables you to obtain critical software updates by automatically interacting with the Windows Update Web site

available address pool the list of TCP/IP addresses within a DHCP scope that can be distributed to DHCP clients

B

Background Intelligent Transfer Service (BITS) Windows service that optimizes network downloads by using idle network bandwidth

background zone loading a new feature in Active Directory–integrated DNS in Windows Server 2008 that allows DNS data to be available more quickly when a server is first booted up

Bandwidth Allocation Protocol (BAP) remote access functionality that

automatically adds and drops connections based on client usage

bare-metal restore a restore in which the computer system is restored from "bare metal"; i.e., without any requirements as to previously installed software or operating system

basic disks disks that use partition tables that are recognized by older operating systems such as MS-DOS and Windows 95/98

Basic Encryption (MPPE 40-bit) low (40-bit) encryption used for VPN connections

bits binary sequences of 0s and 1s used to encode traffic onto physical network media

boot volume the volume containing the operating system files

broadcast address reserved IP address used to transmit data to all hosts located on a particular network

C

cache.dns a file containing the root DNS servers

caching-only server a DNS server that hosts no zones

Callback Options a Remote Access setting that will disconnect a connecting client and re-initiate the connection from the server side

canonical name (CNAME) resource record creates an alias to an existing A or AAAA record

Capture Filter a feature of Network Monitor that will capture only the specific network traffic that you specify

Certificate Practice Statement (CPS) an AD CS component that provides a detailed explanation of how a particular Certification Authority manages certificates and keys

Certificate Revocation List (CRL) a PKI component that identifies certificates that have been revoked or terminated, and the corresponding user, computer, or service

Certificate templates a PKI component used by a CA to simplify the administration and issuance of digital certificates

Certification Authority (CA) an entity, such as a Windows Server 2008 server running the AD CS server role, that issues and manages digital certificates for use in a PKI

Certification Authority Web Enrollment a PKI feature that allows users to manually request certificates using a Web interface

certutil a command-line utility for managing Active Directory Certificate Services

Challenge Handshake Authentication Protocol (CHAP) a generic authentication method that offers encryption of authentication data through the MD5 hashing scheme

checkpoint file indicates the last information that was successfully written to a JET database

checksum a mathematical value that is used to provide an integrity check for a network packet

CIDR notation the most common means of expressing a CIDR network address, such as 192.168.1.0/24 or 192.168.1.128/25

cipher suite a collection of cryptographic algorithms used to encrypt data

Class Options DHCP options applied based on type, either vendor classes or user classes

classful addressing a means of segregating TCP/IP networks into Class A, Class B, and Class C networks based on the network address taking up the 1st, 1st and 2nd, or 1st three octets of the IP address

Classless Inter-Domain Routing (CIDR) a means of more granularly segregating TCP/IP networks based on the number of bytes used by the network address versus the host address

client failback a DFS feature that allows clients to be referred to alternate servers if one server is not available, and then be referred back to the most appropriate server when it comes back online

Client Options DHCP options that apply to a single DHCP client; these will override a server option or scope option if one has been configured

collector-initiated a subscription in which the destination computer polls the source computers to pull the relevant information

compact to optimize a DHCP database to reclaim unused space created by deleted records

conditional forwarder a DNS configuration option that refers queries to remote forwarders based on the domain name contained within the query

Configuration information specific configuration data used to determine how a server is configured and whether

changes to that configuration are affecting its performance

connection security rules a Windows Firewall component that requires two peer computers to mutually authenticate before they can pass information between them

content synchronization service a server-side component on your organization's intranet that retrieves the latest critical updates from the Windows Update Web site

cookie text files sent by a server to a Web browser, used for authenticating, tracking, and maintaining specific information about users

cost the deciding factor used by routers when two different routes exist to the same destination; given multiple routes to the same destination network, the router will choose the route with the lowest cost

country code top-level domain names that map to individual countries, such as .uk, .pl, .it

custom filters contains views of all the printers hosted by the print servers listed in the console

Custom view a new feature in the Windows Server 2008 Event Viewer that allows you to create custom views of events that are recorded

D

data collector set a configuration item that allows you to organize a set of performance counters, event traces, and system configuration data into a single "object" that you can reuse on one or more Windows Server 2008 servers

Data collector set templates templates used to create pre-configured data collector sets

data modification an attack in which a network packet that is in transit over a network can be altered to send counterfeit data

Data-Link Layer Layer 2 of the OSI model

default gateway allows a host to communicate with devices that reside on a remote network

Default route a routing table entry that indicates the route that will be used if no other defined routes match a particular destination

demand-dial routing a routing connection that is only initiated when traffic needs to be passed through it

Denial of service attacks (DoS) a type of attack that prevents the normal use of computers or network resources

DFS namespace a DFS component that presents a single unified view of files and folders that are physically stored across multiple computers

DFS namespace server the server responsible for maintaining the list of DFS shared folders and the physical servers that they correspond to

DHCP client a computer that receives its IP address information from a DHCP server

DHCP enforcement a NAP enforcement method that relies on DHCP to enforce client compliance

DHCP lease defines the duration for which a DHCP-assigned IP address is valid

DHCP Relay Agent a host that forwards DHCP requests to a DHCP server on a remote server, eliminating the need to deploy a DHCP server on each subnet

DHCP Server a server that assigns IP address information automatically to DHCP clients

DHCPACK sent by a DHCP server to acknowledge the client's acceptance of a DHCP lease

DHCPDECLINE sent by a DHCP client to a DHCP server to indicate that it is not accepting a DHCP lease that was sent by a DHCPOFFER message

DHCPDISCOVER a broadcast-based DHCP messasge used by clients to locate available DHCP servers

DHCPINFORM a DHCP message used to detect rogue DHCP servers

DHCPNACK sent by a DHCP server to deny a client's DHCPREQUEST message

DHCPOFFER a broadcast-based DHCP message used by DHCP servers to offer IP address information to a requesting client

DHCPRELEASE sent by a DHCP client to relinquish an IP address and cancel te remaining lease

DHCPREQUEST used by a DHCP client to signal acceptance of a DHCP lease that was sent by a DHCPOFFER message

dial-in properties properties of an individual user account that will allow or deny a remote access connection

dial-on-demand routing see "demand-dial routing"

Dial-Up Networking (DUN) creates a physical connection to a remote network by using a dial-up device such as a POTS modem or a demand-dial ISDN modem

digital certificate a PKI component that contains identifying information about a particular user, computer, or service

directly attached network routes routes to destination networks for which the router in question is directly attached

Discretionary Access Control List (DACL) enables you to specify which users and groups may modify the DNS zones and records

disk quota a limit that is placed on the disk space a user is permitted to consume in a particular volume or folder

Display Filter a feature of Network Monitor that will display only the specific network traffic that you specify

Distributed File System (DFS) a Windows Server 2008 role that allows for a unified file namespace across multiple physical servers, as well as file replication between servers

DNS namespace a hierarchical, tree-structured list of DNS host names and domain names

DNS query the process of requesting DNS information from a Windows server

DNS resolver the DNS client software that submits DNS name resolution queries to DNS servers

DNS round robin a load balancing mechanism used by DNS servers to share and distribute network resource loads

DNS server cache a list of recently resolved DNS queries maintained in RAM by a DNS server to speed subsequent queries for the same information

DNS servers Windows servers that host the DNS server role to provide name resolution to clients

dnscmd a command-line tool used to manage DNS servers, domains, zones, and resource records

DomainDNSZones a DNS replication scope that copies DNS data to all DCs in a domain that are configured as DNS servers

dotted-decimal notation the most common means of expressing an IPv4 address, such as 192.168.1.154

dynamic disks disks that enable more advanced configuration options, but that are not recognized by operating systems prior to Windows 2000

Dynamic Host Configuration Protocol (DHCP) a service used to automate the distribution of TCP/IP addresses and associated configuration information, such as the subnet mask, default gateway and preferred DNS servers.

dynamic rekeying determination of new keying material through a new Diffie-Hellman exchange that takes place on a regular basis

E

EAP-Logoff an 802.1X packet sent from a supplicant to an authenticator, instructing the supplicant to place the port back in an unauthenticated state

EAP-Request an 802.1X packet sent from an authenticator to a supplicant, requesting their EAP information

EAP-Response an 802.1X packet sent from a supplicant to an authenticator, supplying EAP information

Encapsulating Security Payload (ESP) an IPSec protocol that provides confidentiality (in addition to authentication, integrity, and anti-replay) for the IP payload

Enforcement Client a NAP component that enables a particular NAP enforcement mechanism

enforcement method a NAP component that enables administrators to impose consistent client status

enforcement point a server that houses the NAP Enforcement Server component

Enforcement Server (ES) a NAP component that imposes a particular enforcement method

Enhanced Metafile Format (EMF) a default print format used by Windows 2000, Windows XP and Windows Server 2003

enterprise CA a CA that is integrated with Active Directory to allow additional funcitonality

event trace data data is collected over time to provide a real-time view into the behavior and performance of the server operating systems and any applications that it is running

Everyone a special identity group that includes all users of a Windows computer, including anonymous users

exceptions a Windows Firewall configuration item that allows specifically defined traffic to traverse the firewall

exclusion range a portion of an IP address range that will not be distributed to DHCP clients by a DHCP server

extended partition a partition that can host data, but not the computer operating system

Extensible Authentication Protocol (EAP) an 802.1X authentication framework

Extensible Authentication Protocol-Message Digest 5 Challenge Handshake Authentication Protocol (EAP-MD5 CHAP) a version of CHAP that is ported to the EAP framework.

F

File ownership property of a Windows file or folder that indicates which user or group is the owner of the item

File Server Resource Manager (FSRM) an optional role service in the File Service role that enables quotas, file screens, quota templates, and e-mail notifications

file-backed zone see "standard zone"

filter action defines how IPSec should secure network traffic

ForestDNSZones a DNS replication scope that copies DNS data to all DCs in a forest that are configured as a DNS server

forward lookup zone a zone that responds to client requests to map known host names to IP addresses

Forwarded events records events that were forwarded to the Event Viewer on this server

forwarder a DNS configuration option that refers queries that cannot be resolved by the local DNS server to another DNS server on the same network or on a remote network

forwarding-only server a DNS server that will not perform any recursion after forwarders fail; if it cannot resolve a query by using its configured forwarders, it will return a negative response to the query

frames data at Layer 2 of the OSI model (the Data Link Layer) is organized into frames for processing by higher levels of the OSI model

full mesh topology a replication model in which each member server replicates data with every other member server

full zone transfer (AXFR) copying the entire contents of a DNS zone during a zone transfer

fully qualified domain name (FQDN) a DNS name comprised of the host name with the domain name appended to it, such as server1.contoso.com, where server1 is the host name and contoso.com is the domain name

G

gateway NIC that is used to transmit data to a remote network

GUID Partition Table (GPT) a partition style used by dynamic disks

H

hard quota a disk quota that prevents users from saving information if they exceed the defined quota amount

hardware-based router a router running on a dedicated hardware appliance that is only used for performing network routing

hash one-way cryptographic algorithm that takes an input message of arbitrary length and produces a fixed-length digest

hash-based message authentication code (HMAC) see "Integrity Check Value (ICV)"

header information encapsulating the data contained inside of a network packet

health certificate a NAP component used to maintain information about the health compliance (or lack thereof) of a NAP client

health policy server a NAP component that receives health information from NAP enforcement points.

Health Registration Authority (HRA) a NAP component that can obtain health certificates from client computers when the IPSec enforcement method is in use

Health Requirement Server a NAP component that provides current health state information to NPS health policy servers

host a computer, printer, or other physical device configured with a network interface card

host (A) record maps an FQDN to an IPv4 address

host (AAAA) record maps an FQDN to an IPv6 address

host address the portion of an IP address that is unique to an individual device

Host routes a routing table entry that defines a route to a particular destination host rather than a destination network

HOSTS files text files used to provide name resolution for early TCP/IP networks

hub a network device that operates at the Physical Layer (Layer 1) of the OSI model

hub/spoke topology a replication model in which a small number of central servers maintain connections with remote servers, but remote servers to not replicate directly with one another

I

identity spoofing an attack in which an attacker can falsify or "spoof" the identity of either the sending or receiving computer

IGMP Router & Proxy used for multicast forwarding

in-addr.arpa domain a DNS zone used for reverse lookup queries of IPv4 DNS records

incremental zone transfer (IXFR) copying only the contents of a DNS zone that have changed since the last zone transfer to cut down on network traffic

Initial Configuration Tasks a post-installation startup screen that provides a unified administrative interface to configure common items when a server has been newly installed

Integrity Check Value (ICV) a cryptographic checksum that protects each TCP/IP packet protected by IPSec

interface a network interface card

intermediate CA a CA that is subordinate to a root CA within a hierarchical PKI infrastucture

Internet Connection Sharing (ICS) a feature that allows multiple users to share an Internet connection that is directly attached to a single computer

Internet Engineering Task Force (IEFT) an industry standards body that helps define Requests for Comments (RFCs) to define protocols such as FTP and LDAP

Internet Key Exchange (IKE) a standard that defines a mechanism to establish Security Associations

Internet Printing Protocol (IPP) protocol that allows users to send print jobs to printers via an IIS server

Internet Protocol Security (IPSec) enforcement a NAP enforcement method that relies on IPSec to enforce client compliance

Internet Security Association and Key Management Protocol (ISAKMP) a protocol that is used to dynamically negotiate a mutual set of security requirements between two hosts that are attempting to communicate with each other

Internet Service Providers (ISPs) commercial or not-for-profit entities that provide customers with a means of accessing the Internet

IP address a means of identifying a unique host on a TCP/IP network

IP filter a subset of network traffic based on IP address

IP filter list the concatenation of one or more IP filters, which define a range of network traffic

IP version 4 (IPv4) the version of TCP/IP that has been most widely implemented on modern networks

IP version 6 (IPv6) a newer implementation of TCP/IP that includes a much larger address space and numerous security improvements over IPv4

ip6.arpa domain the DNS zone used for reverse lookup queries of IPv6 DNS records

IPSec a suite of protocols used to provide security for TCP/IP hosts at the Internet layer

IPSec policy a shared set of IPSec configuration information that allows multiple computers to communicate

IPSec Policy Agent used to retrieve information about IPSec policies and to pass this information to other IPSec components

ISAKMP SA an IPSec security association used to protect IPSec security negotiations

Isolation a connection security rule used to restrict inbound and outbound connections

iterative query a DNS query sent to a DNS server in which the querying host requests it to return the best answer it can provide using its own information, and without seeking further assistance from other DNS servers

J

Joint Engine Technology (JET) a database format used by the DHCP database

K

key archival the process by which private keys in an Active Directory environment are maintained by the CA for retrieval by a recovery agent

Key Management Service (KMS) a license key that allows you to manage the licensing process using an internal licensing server installed on your own network

key recovery agents user accounts that are configured with a Key Recovery Agent certificate that allows them to recover private keys on behalf of users/computers/services whose private keys have been lost or corrupted

keyed hash a hash that includes the secret key in its calculation

L

Layer 3 devices see "router"

leaf objects host names representing a single physical device such as a computer or printer

limited broadcast address a reserved IP address (255.255.255.255) used as the broadcast address for all networks and routers

LM Authentication the weakest form of NTLM authentication, which has been in use since the earliest days of Windows networking

local print devices a print device that is directly attached to a physical computer

locally-attached print device a print device that is directly attached to a physical computer, such as through a parallel port or USB port

loopback address a reserved IP address (127.0.0.1) used for troubleshooting and testing

M

mail exchanger (MX) record a DNS record that allows e-mail applications to locate e-mail servers

main mode negotiation used to determine encryption key material and security protection for use in protecting subsequent communications

main mode SA see "ISAKMP SA"

Manage Documents a printer permission that allows users to manage all users' documents

Manage Printers a printer permission that allows users to manage user documents as well as manage the configuration of printers

man-in-the-middle attack an attack in which someone between the two communicating computers is actively monitoring, capturing, and controlling the data

manual backup a one-time backup performed using Windows Server Backup, which can be performed by members of the Administrators or Backup Operators group

MBR (Master Boot Record) a partition style used by basic disks

Media Access Control (MAC) address a hard-coded hexadecimal address configured for each Network Interface Card (NIC)

member a single server within a DFS replication group

metric a column in a routing table that indicates the cost of using one route instead of another

mirrored volume a logical unit of disk space comprised of two physical disks, in which the data has been copied exactly from the first disk to the second for fault tolerance

modem bank a collection of multiple physical modems to enable multiple simultaneous dial-up networking connections

modem-pooling equiment see "modem bank"

mount point a logical unit of disk space that will appear as a folder within an existing volume

MS-CHAPv1 an authentication method that relies on one-way authentication to encrypt authentication and connection data

MS-CHAPv2 an authentication method that relies on mutual authentication to encrypt authentication and connection data

multilink a remote access functionality that aggregates multiple dial-up connections to increase the available bandwidth

multinets multiple logical subnets contained within a single network

Multiple Activation Key (MAK) an activation key used for a one-time activation with Microsoft's hosted activation service

Multiple master replication a replication model that can accept data writes from multiple servers, not just a single primary server

multi-port repeater see "hub"

mutual authentication a process used to establish trust between the communicating systems, after which only trusted systems can communicate with each other

N

name resolution the process of mapping an IP address to a human-readable "friendly" name, such as www.lucernepublishing.com

namespace a virtual view of shared folders on different servers as provided by the Distributed File System service

namespace server the DFS server that stores the configuration of a particular DFS namespace

NAP administration server a NAP component that manages NAP server-side components

NAP Agent a NAP component that maintains information about the health of the NAP client computer

NetBIOS the primary method of name resolution on Windows networks prior to the move to DNS within Active Directory

netmask a column in a routing table that indicates the subnet mask of the destination network

network access control a standard for allowing or disallowing network access based on administrator-specified criterion

network access server a server that provides a single point of access for users to access a remote network, such as a RADIUS server or Network Policy Server

network address the portion of an IP address that is shared by all hosts on the same subnet

network address translation (NAT) allows one or more private IP addresses to be mapped to one or more public IP addresses to allow hosts with private IP addresses to communicate on the Internet or another public network

Network and Sharing Center the Control Panel location that allows you to manage and monitor all aspects of Windows Server 2008 networking

network destination a column in a routing table that indicates the remote network that a particular route should be used to reach

Network Device Enrollment Service (NDES) an AD CS service that allows devices, such as hardware-based routers and other network devices and appliances, to enroll for certificates within a Windows Server 2008 PKI

network discovery a network service that locates and queries network resources and shares for information

network interface print device a print device that is connected directly to a Local Area Network (LAN)

Network Layer Layer 3 of the OSI model

network location a configuration setting that allows you to configure one or more network connections to receive unified security settings: you may define different security settings for "home" network locations versus "public" network locations

Network Policy Server (NPS) the Windows Server 2008 implementation of RADIUS

network protocols provide the logical "language" to allow computers to communicate across a physical network medium

network type the type of connection affected by an IPSec policy

network-attached print device a print device that is connected directly to a TCP/IP network

No callback the Callback Option that disables callback functionality

No Encryption a VPN connectivity that does not use any encryption

NPS Network Policy a Remote Access component that maintains information about which users can and cannot access a remote access server

NPS service a NAP component that combines Statement of Health Responses into a single System Statement of Health Response

nslookup a command-line tool used to perform DNS queries

NT LAN Manager (NTLM) a Windows authentication protocol used to authenticate legacy clients and clients configured in a workgroup

NTFS quotas disk quotas that control storage on entire volumes on a per-user basis, for use without the File Server Resource Manager (FSRM) role

NTLM Authentication a user authentication based on the NT LAN Manager authentication protocol

NTLMv2 Authentication the strongest form of NTLM authentication

O

Oakley Key Determination Protocol a protocol used to generate secret key material

octet a portion of an IP address that is 4 bytes in length

online responder an AD CS service that responds to requests from clients concerning the revocation status of a particular certificate, sending back a digitally signed response indicating the certificate's current status

Open Shortest Path First (OSPF) a routing protocol in which individual routers maintained a database of all reachable networks that it was aware of, and shared this database with neighboring routers

Open Systems Interconnection (OSI) model a model for network communications, consisting of seven layers from Physical to Application

P

packet sniffer computer software or computer hardware that can intercept and monitor network traffic in real-time

packet sniffing a network attack that monitors and reads network packets as they traverse a wired or wireless network

Packets data at Layer 3 of the OSI model (the Network Layer) is organized into packets for transmission to local or remote networks

parity additional information added to a RAID-5 volume to provide fault tolerance in the event of a single disk failure

partition see "volume"

partition structure the logical partition structure of one or more physical hard disks

Password Authentication Protocol (PAP) a generic authentication method that does not encrypt authentication data

payload the data contents of a network packet

perfmon a CLI command used to launch the Performance Monitor MMC snap-in

Performance counters specific processes or events that you want to track within the Reliability and Performance Monitor

Performance Log Users a security group that has all the rights of the Performance Monitor Users group, plus the ability to create and modify data collector sets

Performance Monitor a view that provides a visual display of performance counters within Reliability & Performance data

Performance Monitor Users a security group that allows users to view real-time and historical performance and reliability data

persistent policies policies that override Active Directory–based or local IPSec policies, and enhance security during computer startup

Physical Layer Layer 1 of the OSI model, where bits of data interface with the physical network media

pointer (PTR) resource record a DNS resource record that maps a known IP address to a host name

Point-to-Point Tunneling Protocol (PPTP) a legacy VPN protocol that is supported by older operating systems as well as Windows Server 2008

PowerShell a new command-line and task-based scripting technology that is included with Windows Server 2008

primary member the first server installed within a DFS replication group, used to "seed" replication to other members

primary name server a DNS server that hosts a primary zone for one or more DNS domains

primary partition a partition that can host the computer's operating system

Print a printer permission that allows users to print and manage their own documents

print device printer hardware that produces hard copy documents on paper or other print media

Print server a device that receives print jobs from clients and sends them to print devices that are either locally attached or connected to the network

printer the software interface through which a computer communicates with a print device

printer driver a piece of software that converts the print jobs generated by applications into an appropriate string of commands for a specific print device

printer pool a single logical printer connected to multiple physical printers to increase the output of the logical printer

private key a component of public key cryptography that is only known to each individual certificate holder

promiscuous mode a version of Network Monitor that can capture 100 percent of the network traffic available to the network interface

PTR Reousrce Record maps an IP address to an FQDN

public key a component of public key cryptography that is known to the public at large

public key cryptography an encryption method that uses a two-part key: a public key and a private key

Q

quick mode messages ISAKMP messages that are encrypted using the ISAKMP SA

quick mode negotiation the portion of IPSec negotiation in which Security Associations are negotiated, and where the computers negotiate the primary protocols (AH and/or ESP), the hash algorithm, and the encryption algorithm to use for data transfer

quick mode SA an IPSec security association used to protect data sent between the IPSec peers

quota template a collection of settings that defines a number of configuration items for disk quotas

R

RAID-5 volume a logical unit of disk space comprised of three or more physical disks, in which data has been interleaved with additional parity for a balance between performance and fault tolerance

Reconciliation the process of verifying the contents of the DHCP database against the DHCP Registry values

recovery agents configured within a CA to allow one or more users (typically administrators) in an Active Directory environment to recover private keys for users, computers, or services if their keys are lost

Recursion the process of "Tree-walking" used by DNS servers when performing iterative queries

recursive query a DNS query sent to a DNS server in which the querying host asks the DNS server to provide a definitive answer to the query

referral a response from a DFS namespace server that directs clients to the appropriate physical server

Reliability and Performance Monitor a tool located within the Administrative Tools folder that combines features that had previously been spread across a number of tools: Performance Logs and Alerts, Server Performance Advisor, and System Monitor

Reliability Monitor a view within Reliability & Performance Monitor that provides information about system events that can affect a server's stability

Remediation servers a NAP component that allows out-of-compliance clients to regain compliance, by downloading necessary updates/software/etc.

Remote Differential Compression (RDC) a replication protocol used by DFS in Windows Server 2008

Remote network routes routes to destination networks that the router in question is not directly attached to

repair mode an installation option that provides an environment designed to allow you to diagnose and correct a damaged Windows installation

replay a network attack in which network traffic is captured by a packet sniffer and then re-inserted onto the network at a later time to access information or resources

replication group a collection of DFS servers that replicate data between each other

replication scope the number of servers to which DNS information is copied and updated

Requests for Comments (RFC) documents released by the IETF to define protocols such as FTP and LDAP

reservations configures a consistent IP address for a DHCP-enabled host

resource record an element of data that allows DNS servers to resolve client queries

resource record set a list of resource records that matches a particular DNS query

Resource View the default view within Reliability & Performance Monitor

Reverse Address Resolution Protocol (RARP) used to map a known MAC address to an unknown IP address

reverse lookup zone a zone that responds to client requests to map known IP addresses to host names

revocation configuration a PKI configuration item that allows Online Responders to respond to client requests for certificate revocation status

rogue DHCP server a DHCP server that has not been authorized within Active Directory

root CA a Certification Authority that is authoritative for all Certificate Services within a given network

root hints using the top-level Internet DNS servers to resolve a query

router a Layer 3 network device that transmits data between local and remote networks

Router Information Protocol version 2 (RIPv2) a routing protocol supported by the Routing & Remote Access service in Windows Server 2008

router-to-router VPN a secure connection maintained between two router endpoints, to create a secure VPN tunnel between disparate organizations

routes provide destination routers to allow routers to transmit traffic to remote networks

routing the process of transferring data across a network from one LAN to another

routing protocols used in lieu of static routes in more complex network environments to simplify the administration of network routing

S

scavenging the process of removing dynamic DNS records as they become out-of-date

scheduled backup a recurring backup performed using Windows Server Backup that will reformat the destination drive prior to performing the backup

Scope Options DHCP options that apply to a single DHCP scope; these will override a DHCP server option if one has been configured

scopes in DHCP, the portion of the TCP/IP address space that is allocated for a particular group of computers, typically on a single subnet

secondary name server a DNS server that hosts a secondary zone for one or more DNS domains

secondary zone database files the database files used by DNS servers that host secondary DNS zones

second-level domains DNS domains that are registered to individuals or organzations, such as microsoft, hp, dell, etc.

secure dynamic updates allows DNS records to be updated only by the client that first registered the record

security association (SA) a common set of security requirements shared between two hosts

Security logs records events associated with successful or failed access to secured resources on the server

Security Parameters Index (SPI) information stored as a field in the IPSec headers that indicates which SA the destination should use

self-enrollment a feature that enables users to request their own PKI certificates, typically through a Web browser

Server Core an installation option in Windows Server 2008 that provides a minimal installation footprint designed to run only key infrastructure services

Server Options DHCP options that apply to all scopes configured on a DHCP server

Server service a Windows service that allows computers to share files with other network users and computers

Server-to-server a connection security rule that secures traffic between two servers or two groups of servers

Set by Caller the Callback Option that allows the user to specify the callback number at the time the connection is made

Setup log records events associated with server installation, adding and removing server roles, installing applications, etc.

Shadow Copies of Shared Folders a Windows Server 2008 mechanism that automatically retains copies of files on a server volume in multiple versions from specific points in time

shared secret key a cyrptography method in which secret key information is known by both parties

Shiva Password Authentication Protocol (SPAP) a weakly encrypted authentication protocol that offers interoperability with Shiva remote networking products

Simple Certificate Enrollment Protocol (SCEP) a protocol used by the Network Device Enrollment Service

simple volume a logical unit of disk space comprised of space contained on a single physical disk

Single master replication a replication model that can only accept data writes from a single primary server

smart card Small physical devices, usually the size of a credit card or keychain fob, that have a digital certificate installed on them

smart card reader a physical device attached to a workstation that allows users to use a smart card to authenticate to an Active Directory domain, access a Web site, or authenticate to other secured resources

soft quota a disk quota that notifies administrators when a user exceeds the quota limit, but does not prevent the user from saving information in excess of the defined quota

software-based router a router running on a computer running an operating system such as Windows Server 2008 that can also be used for other functions

source computer initiated a subscription in which each source computer must be configured to push the relevant information to the server that has been configured as the repository

spanned volume a logical unit of disk space comprised of space contained on multiple physical disks

standalone CA a CA that is not integrated with an Active Directory environment

standard zone a DNS zone that stores its data in a text file on the DNS server

stateful firewall a firewall that can track and maintain information based on the status of a connection

Statement of Health (SOH) a NAP component that indicates the status of a particular System Health Agent

Statement of Health Response (SoHR) a NAP component generated by an SHV in response to client Statements of Health

static IP address an IP address that has been manually configured by an administrator

Static routes configuration information that manually informs a network router of the destination of network packets destined for remote networks

striped volume a logical unit of disk space comprised of space that has been interleaved across multiple physical disks for improved read performance

Strong Encryption a 56-bit encryption used for VPN connections

Strongest Encryption a 128-bit encryption used for VPN connections

stub zone a DNS zone that contains sufficient information to locate authoritative name servers for a DNS domain

subdomains lower-level domains within a second-level domains, such as sales. lucernepublishing.com

subnet a logical grouping of computers within a TCP/IP network, used to reduce network traffic and streamline administration

subnet mask used to define which portion of an IP address is the network address and which portion is the host address

subnetting the process of subdividing TCP/IP networks into smaller units called "subnets"

superscope an administrative grouping of multiple contiguous DHCP scopes

supplicant an 802.1X device that is seeking access to the network, such as a laptop attempting to access a wireless access point

switch a Layer 2 network device that examines the source and destination MAC address of the network data to determine where the data should be sent

System Health Agent (SHA) a NAP component that maintains information and reporting on one or more elements of the health of a NAP client

System Health Validator (SHV) a NAP component that returns Statement of Health Responses based on client Statements of Health

System log records information associated with operating system events such as server restarts, issues with services, etc.

System Statement of Health (SSOH) a collection of Statements of Health for all SHAs configured on a client computer

System Statement of Health Response (SSOHR) a NAP component that combines individual Statement of Health Responses before returning them to the NAP enforcement client

system volume the volume containing the files necessary to boot a computer

T

T1 represents half of the DHCP lease time

T2 represents 87.5% of the DHCP lease time

targets the physical servers that host data represented within a DFS namespace

Terminal Services Gateway (TS Gateway) enforcement NAP enforcement method that restricts connection attempts by TS Gateway clients

threshold the percentage of a disk quota at which users and administrators can be notified and/or an event logged to the Windows Event Viewer on the server

Time to Live (TTL) the amount of time for which a DNS record is valid before it must be re-verified

top-level domain the top-most domains in the DNS namespace hierarchy, such as .com, .org, or .biz

topology the physical or logical layout of a network

Transmission Control Protocol/Internet Protocol (TCP/IP) the most common network protocol in use today; the network protocol used on the Internet

transport mode an IPSec mode used to provide end-to-end security

Trivial File Transfer Protocol (TFTP) a lightweight version of FTP that uses UDP traffic rather than tCP

tunnel mode an IPSec mode used to provide site-to-site communications that cross the Internet (or other public networks)

tunnel setting the IP address of an IPSec tunnel endpoint

tunnelling protocol a protocol used by VPN software to transmit trafic securely over a non-secure network such as the Internet

U

Unauthenticated access a configuration setting that allows remote access users to connect to a remote access server without providing credentials

User Datagram Protocol (UDP) a connectionless, non-acknowledgement-based TCP/IP protocol used for low-overhead communication

V

Verify Caller ID a Remote Access security setting that will confirm that a remote access connection originates from a specified calling location

Virtual Private Network (VPN) creates a secured logical connection to a remote network over a non-secure network such as the Internet

volume a logical unit of disk space comprised of space contained on one or more physical disks

Volume Activation a process used to manage software activation for multiple installations of Windows within an enterprise network

Volume Activation Management Tool (VMAT) a software tool used to activate software that uses Multiple Activation Keys

Volume Shadow Copies Service (VSS) a Windows service utilized by the Shadow Copies of Shared Folders feature, as well as Windows Server Backup

VPN client software that initiates a secured VPN connection to a public-facing remote access server capable of creating VPN connections

VPN enforcement method a NAP enforcement method that restricts the level of network access that a remote access client can obtain, based on the health information that the client presents when the VPN connection is made

VSS copy backup a Windows Server Backup backup type that will not clear the Application Log on the computer that is being backed up

VSS full backup a Windows Server Backup backup type that will clear the Application Log on the computer that is being backed up

W

wbadmin a command-line tool used to perform Windows Server Backup operations

web enrollment an AD CS feature that allows users to connect to a Windows Server 2008 CA through a Web browser to request certificates and obtain an up-to-date Certificate Revocation List

Windows Event Collector Service allows you to configure a single server as a repository of Event Viewer information for multiple computers

Windows Firewall a software-based firewall that is built into the Windows Server 2008 operating system

Windows Logs the traditional view of the Windows Event Viewer

Windows powerShell see 'Powershell'

Windows Recovery Environment (WinRE) a special Windows boot mode that provides a centralized platform for operating system recovery

Windows Server Backup a Windows Server 2008 feature that allows you to perform one-time and recurring scheduled backups of a Windows server

Windows Server Update Services (WSUS) a Windows service that allows you to centralize the management of critical software updates on a Windows network

Windows Update Catalog a Web site that lists hardware and software designed for use with Windows Vista, Windows XP, Microsoft Windows 2000 Server products, and products in the Windows Server 2003 and Windows Server 2008 family

WINS a Windows networking service that automates the process of NetBIOS name resolution on an enterprise network

WINS server a Windows server providing the WINS server service for automated management and centralization of NetBIOS name resolution

Wireless Networking a Windows Server 2008 feature that installs and configures wireless connections and wireless LAN profiles

WS-Management protocol a protocol used by the Windows Event Collector Service to manage subscriptions and forwarded events

X

XML Printer Specification (XPS) a new, XML-based print format used by Windows Vista and Windows Server 2008

Z

zone a collection of host name-to-IP address mappings stored on a DNS server

zone transfer the process of copying DNS zone data from a server hosting a primary zone to a server hosting a secondary zone